Legal Reasoning Case Files

Legal Reasoning Case Files

Kris Franklin

PROFESSOR OF LAW AND
DIRECTOR OF ACADEMIC INITIATIVES,
NEW YORK LAW SCHOOL

CAROLINA ACADEMIC PRESS
Durham, North Carolina

Library of Congress Cataloging-in-Publication Data

Names: Franklin, Kris, 1967– author.
Title: Legal reasoning case files / by Kris Franklin.
Description: Durham, North Carolina : Carolina Academic
    Press, LLC, [2019] | Includes bibliographical references and index.
Identifiers: LCCN 2018059294 | ISBN 9781531006488 (alk. paper)
Subjects: LCSH: Law—United States—Problems, exercises, etc. |
    Law—United States—Case studies. | Law—United States—
    Methodology.
Classification: LCC KF386 .F67 2019 | DDC 349.73—dc23
LC record available at https://lccn.loc.gov/2018059294

e-ISBN 978-1-5310-0649-5

Carolina Academic Press, LLC
700 Kent Street
Durham, North Carolina 27701
Telephone (919) 489-7486
Fax (919) 493-5668
www.cap-press.com

Printed in the United States of America
2020 Printing

For Sarah, always…

Contents

Acknowledgments

This book could not have been completed without the contributions of so many colleagues, students, family and friends.

Thank you first to New York Law School for research support and encouragement. Endless appreciation to the NYLS administrators and faculty who took a risk in asking me to develop a course based on these kinds of materials. And thank you to all of the colleagues who commented on early drafts and the many NYLS adjunct faculty who helped make them teachable. I am grateful for all of their many contributions, but especially indebted to the responses of Vicki Eastus, Rebecca Flanagan, Linda Feldman, Kim Hawkins, Martha Hochberger, Russell McClain and Louis Schulze. Particular kudos to Jennifer Carr's sharp copyediting pencil throughout the manuscript.

Several of these chapters could not have been completed without the extraordinarily able research assistance of Myra Guevara. Some materials included in this text were adapted from drafts created by Wesley Brandt, Ryan Callinan, Dana Mallon, Nicole Masri, Kelsey Miller, Chris Murphy, and Luke Shemeth, all of whom I appreciate and admire.

I am fortunate that Carolina Academic Press is ever eager to innovate and create a home for new kinds of academic textbooks. Many thanks in particular to Carol McGeehan both for skilled publishing work and enjoyable conversation.

Finally, it is simply not possible to give enough thanks to my family. Sarah Chinn inspires my work—constantly—and edits it joyfully. Gabriel and Lia support the time and effort with unflagging cheer. And Kelly, Ron and Pat make me laugh and keep me going.

Introduction

Becoming a skilled attorney is hard.

There is a massive amount of new and technical material to learn, and there are many advanced skills to master. These skills include all of the legal ones, naturally, plus the wide array of general proficiencies that any successful professional might need and that most law students have not yet fully acquired. And in addition to gaining so much new knowledge and expertise, there is the necessity of gaining enough practical experience to hone the good judgment lawyers need to help clients resolve their problems. All of this simply takes time and a great deal of practice.

Unfortunately, both time and opportunities for frequent practice are usually in short supply in law school. Under pressure to cover so much material, most law school classes spend little if any time reviewing, consolidating, or practicing to deploy the material studied. Even the more experience-oriented courses in the law school curriculum have a great deal to cover in a short span of time. Writing classes must teach new genres and techniques, while clinics are often driven by the exigent needs of their actual clients.

But educators know that the best way to learn new things is to repeatedly rehearse and to connect new concepts and skills to what has already been learned. Legal reasoning, judgment, and firm comprehension of complex legal rules all take time to percolate. It takes—as the cliché goes—a minute to learn yet a lifetime to master. So where can law students refine and consolidate their learning as they prepare to become smart, capable attorneys? There is room, and need, in the law school curriculum for students to practice and reinforce the fundamentals of legal thinking. This text provides the foundation for that hands-on learning.

This Text Hones Legal Reasoning

Much has been written about what it means to "think like a lawyer." Does it mean thinking carefully? Of course, but that can't possibly be enough. Critically? Definitely, but law cannot claim to be the only profession that demands critical thinking. Unemotionally? No. Rationality is important in law, but then so are empathy and humanity. Using laws? Yes of course, but not entirely: no attorney can ever know all of the law even within a very narrow specialty, and non-lawyers are plenty capable of reading and understanding many legal materials.

So what is it, then, that is uniquely "lawyerly" about what we do?

I believe that what most distinguishes lawyers' thinking is our consistent underlying legal method. Lawyers: (1) understand **legal rules** in a deeply meaningful and contextualized way, and we then (2) carefully **apply** those rules to specific **facts** to reach conclusions or build arguments, having (3) thoughtfully considered all possible interpretations and **counter-arguments**. Moreover we (4) meticulously **explain and support** every step in our analysis so that others can follow and evaluate our reasoning. We follow these steps over and over again, and we become more adept at them as we grow in our field.

If you truly understand how legal reasoning operates you may recognize these steps as in some ways a distillation of the IRAC[1] method of analysis you have probably been taught at some point in your law school career (or CRAC[2] or CReAC[3] if you lead with a conclusion rather than an identification of the issue in question). This makes perfect sense, because the centerpiece of IRAC or any of its acronym analogues is the interaction between legal rules and their application to given facts. That in part explains why the R and the A are consistent across the many ways of describing/ distilling legal analysis. It would even be fair to say that having this "legal analysis = rules applied to facts" formula become second nature to you is *the* primary objective of the first year of law school. Once it becomes an automatic part of your thinking and writing you may find that you can deviate from the rigidity that IRAC sometimes suggests. That's perfectly fine—good writing can take many forms when you have the "grammar" of legal thinking down pat.

This text provides an opportunity for you to refine your core legal reasoning skills through a series of short but realistic exercises. Some of the work expected here may seem simple and straightforward (while other parts will probably appear quite challenging). Don't be fooled, though—experienced attorneys know that there is *always* a way to make their work clearer, more thoughtful, more subtle, or more effectively presented. In fact, never being fully satisfied with our own efforts and seeking always to find a way to work more strategically may *itself* be a hallmark of the way lawyers think. As you work your way through this course and this text, please always aim to strengthen your analytical skills while continuing to follow the basic steps fundamental to all lawyerly reasoning.

How the Text Is Structured

You will work through a series of legal problems

This text consists of case file exercises grounded in basic subjects taught in nearly every law school in the country. The problems here are meant to seem realistic. Ideally, you will also find them compelling.

If you are past your first semester of law school, much of the legal doctrine at issue in these problems should be familiar to you. That is by design. First, repetition and review are good. Repetition breeds retention. (Who among us has not completed a class and come across its material later, only to discover to our dismay how much of it we have forgotten?) Repetition also reinforces what you already know while adding nuance to your understanding. And finally, repetition of common legal principles means that you should be able to spend less time absorbing the law itself, and consequently place more emphasis in these exercises on how you read, write, and think about the law.

---

1. Issue, Rule, Application, Conclusion.

2. Conclusion, Rule, Application, Conclusion. Practicing lawyers frequently begin legal arguments from the premise they want the court to reach, which is why this may be the most common form of analysis they use. But law students are often encouraged not to do so for a couple of reasons. Professors may want students to fully state the legal question at hand, which the Issue approach requires. Equally importantly, much of "thinking like a lawyer" involves seeing a question from multiple perspectives, and law professors may be concerned that beginning with a particular conclusion can lead to overly one-sided analysis.

3. Conclusion, Rule, rule Explanation, Application, Conclusion. The explanation of the rule is particularly important when it is not a standard and universally agreed-upon part of black letter law.

The problems apply unambiguous legal rules

One of the most exciting things about the law is that it cannot possibly be comprehensive enough to cover every possible circumstance in human experience. And law professors just *love* doubt and ambiguity—we like to create exams, exercises, and assignments that exploit uncertainty, and then we expect law students to consider all possible angles to approach every issue. If at its most central core legal analysis can be reduced to applying legal rules to facts, then there are really only a few ways for law professors to introduce the ambiguity we want our students to explore:

1. We can take advantage of a lack of clarity in the applicable legal rules themselves (by introducing alternative and inconsistent rules either over time or in differing jurisdictions, or by situating the issue in an area that the rules arguably might or might not apply to)
2. We can create facts that could go either way
3. We can do both at the same time

From what you have seen so far in law school, is it a big surprise that we tend to spend a lot of time having fun with that third option? For good reason, type 3 questions are sometimes the most challenging and central ones on law school essay exams. They require students to grapple in complicated ways with the most vexing questions of what the law means, why it is the way it is, how it should (or should not) be extended, and to whom it applies. Put that way, it is a pretty efficient way to see how deeply students really grasp what they have learned.

Similarly, legal writing or lawyering skills classes tend to situate their most important assignments in areas where the applicable rule of law is not fully established. Often that means, for example, that an assigned memorandum or brief will have students work on a topic to which no single black-letter rule unequivocally applies. This forces students to learn rule synthesis: that is, how to construct a "rule" (sometimes a sub-rule or potential exception to a more general rule) out of inferences drawn from multiple sources and then providing a persuasive explanation showing why it is, or ought to be, understood as a correct statement of law. Learning to synthesize rules is an incredibly important skill for lawyers to develop. And it is one that can take the course of a career to fully cultivate. Working on such projects is demanding, and takes a great deal of time.

But it is certainly *not* true that every legal question is a novel one. Established legal rules exist, and it is frequently true that the questions lawyers encounter fall squarely within well-settled black-letter law. Attention to preparing law students to handle *ambiguity* in law—the hallmark of so many profound legal questions—is a centerpiece of many law school classes and examinations. Thus the traditional law school curriculum may not provide enough opportunity for you to get better at the more routine process of understanding legal rules, applying them to facts (while considering alternatives) and carefully explaining your logic.[4] This text is intended to help fill in that gap. The exercises here will give you repeated opportunities to carefully apply established legal rules (ones that you probably encounter in foundational law classes) while you continue to develop the necessary legal analytical skills that your classes, and the practice of law, will require.

---

4. Hopefully this list of steps already sounds familiar: it is simply a rephrased version of the fundamental steps of legal reasoning articulated in the section "Legal reasoning is legal method" above. This will certainly not be the last time that those steps are repeated in this text. They are crucial in all legal analysis. Thus they worth repeating, restating, and reinforcing until they become automatic. Unconsciously always following this process to address legal questions is in effect what people *mean* when they say "thinking like a lawyer."

The problems ask you to do things that new attorneys typically do

Most people learn better by doing things rather than by simply being told about them. And the only way to gain experience in something is, well, to do it. Therefore one important goal of the problems in this book is to give you projects to work on that look and feel like the kinds of things beginning lawyers are often asked to produce.

In courses that teach vital legal research and writing skills, law students are often introduced to some of the most common and formal tasks given to junior lawyers, i.e., drafting legal memos or briefs. These are important tools in practice, and they are also excellent educational assignments. But they are not the only, or in many instances primary, kinds of writing that most lawyers do. Furthermore, they tend to be complex and time-consuming to produce, which limits the number of projects any student can reasonably work on in any single class.[5]

The problems here, then, are shorter and somewhat different in focus from those usually encountered in an introductory legal writing course. These assignments ask you to take the same principles of legal reasoning that you might use in those kinds of writing projects, but to apply them to shorter and sometimes more unceremonious types of legal writing like affidavits, professional letters, emails, or informal memos. You should find that your central analytical steps remain constant even while you adapt your tone or approach to the specific genre of writing that you are engaged in.

The problems rely on the kinds of materials and documents lawyers actually use

The case files in this text consist of exactly the kinds of records and other materials that you would be likely to encounter in practice. They are entirely fictional, but are made to look and work exactly like ones you might see in real life. In a sense, reviewing and preparing documents is what most lawyers *do*, or at least it is what we spend a lot of our time doing. Other than what we gather from personal conversations with our clients or witnesses, virtually all of the facts of every lawyer's case are gleaned from documents that we gather and examine. It simply makes sense as you learn law to gather information the same way that you will once you enter practice.

The exercises connect what lawyers do to what law students learn

Despite the fact that most law schools spend a lot of time orienting new law students by explaining that law school is probably quite different from other types of educational endeavors, it still feels a lot like *school*. You mostly read, attend lectures, and ultimately you take tests on what you have studied. Notwithstanding oft-repeated warnings that the legal educational experience is very different, this familiar structure can make the day-to-day experience of taking law classes feel a lot like college. As a result, beginning law students typically struggle to relate the work that they do in casebook classes, legal writing and simulation or clinical courses, and internships or summer jobs.

But once you face law school examinations it becomes apparent how important it will be to effectively use what you learn in all law classes. Law school essay exams test you not just on your knowledge of what you have studied, but also your mastery of how you might *use* a course's material in practice. Essentially, most tests in law school replicate the experience of a new client walking into an actual law office—it just so happens, of course, that the client presents a myriad of problems that conveniently overlap with topics studied in that course. In fact, this is at least part of what law professors mean when we try to explain why law school is different. Law practice requires actively

---

5. This also explains why the case file assignments in this text do not ask you to do outside research. Any responsible attorney handling these problems in real life would probably devote time to finding out more about both the applicable law and the facts of the cases than are included here. But in an effort to make your workload manageable, this text tries to provide enough material for effective analysis without the added responsibilities of conducting your own legal research or fact development.

using the law to address problems presented by our clients, and law school exams try as best they can to require the same skills.

The exercises help you transfer what you learn in each of your law classes to all of the others

Law professors frequently tell students that the analytical skills they develop in one area will be transferable to all of them. But in saying so we sometimes leave out one key point; the core legal reasoning skills are indeed transferrable, *but they require thoughtful adaptation to the differing demands of each kind of work that you will do.*

This text is intended to help you improve your ability to transfer skills. One way we do that is by moving among different subjects. Each chapter sets its problem within in a different topic drawn from a core law school subject. This helps you refresh your understanding of the specific material covered, of course, but is intended also to encourage you to develop a richer understanding of the subject matter itself. Many law students presume that any differences they see among the classes they take must be due to the individual approaches of their professors. Some probably are, but focusing on that obscures the fact there are genuine variances in how legal disciplines operate. When you understand those distinctions you can go about learning and using the law more skillfully within each subject.

For your purposes though, perhaps the most important way we help you transfer your growing lawyering skills is by alternating between typical lawyer-like law practice assignments and typical law-student-like tests that rely upon the same body of legal rules. First you will learn (or review) the law in question while working through a document case file, and preparing the assigned practice document. Next, you will switch up by seeing how the same rules can be used in a more academic context. Thus, at the conclusion of each chapter you will be given a new set of facts. You can use the same legal rules presented in the case file to analyze the new problem. Or to put it more directly in terms that probably matter to you, you will be given a new question that looks an awful lot like a single-topic essay examination. Can you take what you have learned in working through the case file assignment and immediately apply it to this new problem?

Each chapter includes and analyzes a sample student response to the "exam" question. Review it carefully so that you can get a better idea of what law professors are usually looking for. (You would be well advised to write out your own response to the question before reading the sample answers given. Remember: practice may not always make perfect but it leads you a lot further along the way. And we learn from our own experience far more deeply than from just reading about other peoples' experiences!) Your professor may decide to assign additional essay or quiz assignments based on the case file materials to further support your understanding of the legal rules or to give you additional opportunities to practice applying them.

The exercises connect to skills you will need to pass the bar

One of the significant shifts law graduates encounter when they begin to prepare for the bar exam is that the law school world of glorious uncertainty has suddenly been set aside. The bar exam tests candidates on areas of well-settled law, and it uses questions for which there should be only one clearly right answer. But even on the bar exam, identifying the correct legal rule is no guarantee of giving the correct response or of garnering full credit. That's because in addition to testing rules of law, the bar exam is still also testing legal analysis. Improving those analytical skills while you are in law school will give you an enormous leg up when you go to take the bar exam.

And while the materials in this book are not intended to precisely replicate the ones you will encounter on the bar exam, they do significantly echo them. The case file assignments might look similar to those you might come across on the Multistate Performance Test (MPT) or an analogous performance test developed specifically for your state. There, too, you will be expected to review a series of documents to gather the facts of the case, apply fundamental legal rules to the assigned problem, and draft whatever practice-style document the particular question demands. Similarly, the exam-like assignments in this book resemble the short one- to two-issue questions that are more typical of the Multistate Essay Examination (MEE) than the more intricate and ambiguous issue-spotter questions usually found in law school.

If you think about it, even though these are not bar materials per se, and the class you are taking is probably not geared explicitly toward bar preparation, it nonetheless makes sense to preview some bar-adjacent work earlier on in your law studies. Neither law school nor the bar exam are intended to fully complete your professional training, but they are each supposed to be vital steps in that direction. Law school is meant to prepare you to begin and learn from the practice of law, and the bar exam is supposed to be an assessment of your readiness to begin professional practice. Thus the more we can use practice-like and bar-like exercises in your legal education the more prepared you will be for what is to come.

Commentary in the text draws from current learning science

There is actually rather a lot of research about what it takes for students to learn in law school.[6] As a quick summary of what we know about complex skills mastery, it would probably be accurate to say simply that the more active the learning is, the better. The more intentional it is (meaning, the more concretely you articulate to yourself what you are doing and why), the better. And the more opportunities you have to practice and get feedback, and then to incorporate that feedback into subsequent work, the better. That's precisely what this text and the course you are using it for are intended to provide.

The comments and structure of this text are carefully grounded in what we know to be the best practices for law school learning. Your objective is probably to become an excellent lawyer rather than a scholar of adult learning theory, so I have tried to avoid education jargon wherever possible. But knowing how to learn and improve in law school is an important part of producing stronger work, which will sometimes require making the theory underlying what we are doing explicit.

The assignments are straightforward, but that does not mean they are easy

In law, straightforward does not equate to simple. Expert legal reasoning is richly layered, and small details can mean the difference between whether something is spectacularly persuasive or fails to effectively serve its intended purpose. That is precisely why it is worth improving your legal reasoning with practice.

Moreover, different lawyers can and will approach problems differently. There is room in each of the problems and exercises included within this text for variations in approach. No one solution can ever be the only right one. But this does not mean that all approaches will be equivalently successful, which is part of what makes legal work so challenging.

---

6. For an excellent summation of some of the best practices in learning law, see Louis N. Schulze, Jr., *Using Science to Build Better Learners: One School's Successful Efforts to Raise its Bar Passage Rates in an Era of Decline*, 12 F.I.U. L. Rev. ___ (forthcoming 2017). For an empirical analysis of the long-reaching effects of practice and feedback in law school coursework see Daniel Schwarcz & Dion Farganis, *The Effect of Individualized Feedback on Law School Performance*, 67 J. Legal Ed. 1 (2017).

Skills You Will Strengthen

One advantage of a course intended to reinforce your analytical and critical reasoning skills is that it can consolidate the skills you acquire from all other law school classes. Most of what you will do as you proceed through this text should not be entirely new to you. At its best, your work with these materials should serve to pull together what you have learned and are continuing to learn in all of your law school classes.

It may help to consider the discrete skills of legal reasoning in the form of a list:

- ✓ Understand the problem to be solved
- ✓ Utilize legal and non-legal documents
- ✓ Extract material facts
- ✓ Use legal authority
    - · filter sources of law for weight and relevance
    - · read cases critically
    - · comprehend and make use of statutes
- ✓ State rules of law accurately and precisely
- ✓ Apply rules to facts
- ✓ Methodically explain every step in your analysis
- ✓ Evaluate counterarguments
- ✓ Articulate policy considerations
- ✓ Present analysis effectively, with thoughtful attention to the intended audience
- ✓ Demonstrate sound and reliable legal judgment

Just as will be true when you actually start to practice law, every problem in this text will draw upon *all* of these skills. But that does not mean that each skill is equally accentuated with every task, and it would be overwhelming to try to tackle each and every one of these skills equally with every project. Therefore different chapters will focus more attention on different aspects of these analytical skills, though naturally the most central—thoughtfully applying correct rules of law to facts—will always receive attention. If you put together what you learn over the course of several of these assignments, you should improve your analytical skills considerably.

The skills we are especially focusing on in the unit will be listed at the beginning of each chapter. There will also be commentary and side notes as we proceed through the case files. In part these notes are intended to draw your attention to the sophisticated ways that lawyers think, read, and question the material they encounter. Ideally, these notes may help you to identify explicitly the skills you may be drawing from without even being aware of them. That's important, because the more conscious you are about your own thought processes the more likely you are to sharpen them. The notes and comments therefore anticipate that you will bring increasingly greater sophistication to your work with the materials as the text progresses.

Learning From Your Own Work

Your legal education is your own. It helps very much to approach law school as not the end of school, but as the beginning of a professional career. One in which you will aim over the course of a lifetime to continually become more proficient.

Everything researchers have discovered about learning and skills acquisition shows the most effective learners are those who are self-directed. Students who look critically at all of their work and aim to decide for themselves what was successful in it, and how to make it better, are apt to show the most progress over the duration of a course or a curriculum. Or to put it differently, no matter where you start or what kinds of assistance you get from your teachers or other resources, you will be most likely to end up an excellent student and lawyer if you are proactive in reviewing your own work and in carefully evaluating every choice made along the way.

As you work through each case file you should aim to become a better reader of the cases and materials, more efficient in crafting your responses, and more creative in organizing your thoughts. Use each problem as an opportunity to read your own writing the way your audience (or your professor!) would receive it, and see if you can anticipate what would be needed to improve it. Try to consider what is common (and therefore fundamental) about all of the most successful answers to both the case file assignment and the essay question, and what changes with each different assignment. This will help you decide what is core to legal reasoning and what is specific to each of the types of document or text you have worked on.

We are going to give you a good workout. Embrace it and watch your analytical muscles strengthen.

Legal Reasoning Case Files

Chapter 1

Torts

Assignment: *Prepare a Pre-litigation Demand Letter*

Based on the materials in the file, please draft a demand letter to defendant Certified Lumber asking for reimbursement prior to your firm filing suit on your client's behalf. Target length is fewer than 1000 words exclusive of salutations, titles, or other standard non-substantive introductory material.

Analytical Skills to Focus On

- ✓ Extracting material facts (inextricably tied to knowing the law)
- ✓ Reading cases effectively
- ✓ Applying rules to facts
- ✓ Flexibly transferring skills
- ✓ Learning by self-evaluating and setting mastery goals

Case File

As will be true for each of the chapters in this text, the materials in the case file are first given to you in one complete set so that you will have them all together. You should read them all carefully on your own before diving into the commentary and questions that follow. As you read through the materials ask yourself:

1. What narrative can you construct about the facts at issue? Which facts are generally agreed upon and what (if anything) is contested?

2. What rule or legal principle is implicated? Is it one you are familiar with? If so, is the rule expressed in the same way that you have previously encountered, or are there differences? In what way do the nuances of the language here change or add to your understanding of how the law operates?

3. What does each document in the case file add to your understanding of the problem?

4. How authoritative is each document as a source of fact or law?

5. What materials are *not* here that you would want to review to better understand your case? How will those omissions affect your work on the assignment? Are there ways to work around what you do not know?

To aid in your comprehension of the case file there are occasional side comments embedded in shaded boxes within the materials. This commentary is intended to contextualize the material and should not be considered part of the actual document.

A project checklist is included at the end of the chapter. Use it to review and edit your drafts as you strive for maximal effectiveness.

· ·

Chapter 1 Case File

Your exercise packet contains the following:

- File notes from the senior lawyer who conducted the client intake interview
- Medical bills documenting accident-related expenses
- State and federal regulations pertaining to proper means of securing cargo on commercial motor vehicles
- Relevant sections of the RESTATEMENT 3D OF TORTS
- Relevant cases to use in your analysis

Thinking about Torts

Torts is almost always taught as a first-year subject, and usually in the first semester. Why might that be? It is certainly true that a large volume of litigation is made up of tort claims and it is an important subject for future lawyers to understand, but that alone may not fully explain why it is so frequently an introductory subject. What does?

Consider that torts are built from elements. All torts problems therefore require articulating the elements and applying each one to the facts at hand to determine whether it may arguably be satisfied. Chances are, studying an intentional tort like battery, or starting with negligence, were one of the first places you learned to do elemental analysis in law school. That was probably intended at least in part to teach you how to approach legal questions methodically, and to always thoughtfully analyze each and every element of any rule made up of them.

But the answer may also lie in the fact that torts rules are comparatively simple. Torts *questions*, on the other hand, are not. Torts raise important conceptual questions about law itself: What is the extent of our responsibility to one another? What kinds of behavioral incentives do we want to build into the law, and why? If your Torts class felt a bit like a philosophy course (many do), it is because it is so often true that applying the elements of a tort to the facts still does not produce a definitive answer to whether there is, or should be, liability. That often makes tort questions especially good ones for thinking conceptually, and for examining the role of good policy in rule interpretation and application.

· ·

Arch & Associates

**114 Montesque Ave.
St. Paul, MN 55102**

File notes

Name: Edmund Tanger
Date: February 2, 20_____
Reason for consult: Personal Injury, auto accident, truck cargo not properly secured

Intake Information

Client seeks compensation for personal injuries sustained when he was struck in the right leg by a 12-foot beam that fell off the back of a flatbed truck owned by defendant Certified Lumber, Inc., and operated by driver Marcus Perlin. The incident occurred on May 22 of last year as Client was on Wythe Avenue, about a quarter of a block from its intersection with Division Road in Hennepin County.

Client was walking on the northbound/southbound sidewalk when he heard a noise behind him. He turned, and then both heard and saw the defendant's truck hit the curb as it attempted to complete a right turn from Division Road onto Wythe Avenue. Client stated that shortly thereafter a beam fell from the truck, rolled onto the ground, and struck his right leg. Client states the incident happened too quickly for him to move out of the way.

Marcus Perlin, one of Certified Lumber's field managers, was driving and had supervised the loading of its cargo. At the time of the accident his truck was carrying two packages or "units" of cargo, each containing 40 to 45 steel beams used for commercial construction. Each beam was approximately 3" x 8" x 12' in size. The units were placed on the flatbed side by side. According to Client, from what he could see after the accident it appeared that two of the truck's tie-down straps had been wrapped around the units.

The incident occurred within minutes after Perlin left the Kent Avenue lot where the cargo was initially loaded onto the truck bed. Client believes Perlin was traveling at approximately 10–15 mph (speed limit on this street is 25 mph). Client was crossing the street diagonally toward the truck. Client cannot precisely recall all of the details of the accident itself. He does, however, remember the events immediately before and afterward.

Client recalls sitting on the curb of Wythe Avenue and seeing approximately 20 beams lying in the street three to four feet away from the curb. He also saw a flatbed truck with Certified Lumber logos

---

It is very important for lawyers to document their work. Most attorneys add notes to client files each time they interact with a client, a witness, their opposing counsel, or the court. Efficiency is important in a busy law practice and these kinds of notes are generally only for the attorney's own purposes, so they may take the form of quick shorthand. But they should also be thorough, and clear enough that if needed another lawyer in the office could review the file and get up to speed on the case.

As you read this attorney's notes you should ask yourself whether he seems to have included all of the information needed to proceed on the case, and whether he has satisfied his competing objectives of productivity and clarity.

Note that the intake attorney is short-handing when he references a defendant: no lawsuit has been filed yet. He is also referencing only one defendant, Certified Lumber. This may also be slightly inaccurate. When/if the suit is filed you may want to name both the company and the driver as co-defendants. But the company probably has the money and carries the insurance, so it stands to reason that it is probably the target of an initial demand for compensation.

What do the speed limit and presence of multiple pedestrians suggest to you about the kind of roadway the truck was on?

stopped, with one wheel up on the curb. Client noted that in the truck's cargo area there were two straps separated by approximately six feet. The straps were "hanging, just hanging there, almost like— it wasn't hooked up, so because all the beams fell out . . . The straps were hanging loose . . ."

Client suffered a broken tibia and extensive bruising. He was unable to perform his duties as a municipal bus driver during his recovery, and was therefore out of work for 10 weeks. Afterward, he required intensive physical therapy for a period of three months. Client states that he earns an annual salary of $42,000, payable biweekly as $1615.38 before taxes. Copies of medical bills and a summary of physical therapy billing are included in file (NOTE: will need to secure copies of individual billing statements at later date). Additionally, he reports nightmares stemming from the traumatic events. (Seek $80-120K pain and suffering?)

Preliminary investigation

Several witnesses to the accident assisted Client after his injury. One called emergency services but left the scene before providing her name or contact information. Two others stayed to help Client into the ambulance. These witnesses gave statements to police investigators stating that they had seen the beams coming loose off the truck even before the truck drove onto the curb, but that driving on the curb had sent the beams tumbling into the street. (NOTE: copies of police accident reports requested but not yet received from Records Office.)

> The existence and credibility of these witnesses will probably be very important if this case goes to trial. So far, your law office seems not to have spoken with them. Is it crucial to try to speak with the witnesses before completing the demand letter? Why or why not?

While waiting for the ambulance with client, both witnesses also told Client orally that in their opinions, the cargo on the truck had been loosely or improperly secured even before the truck went over the curb. Witnesses' names were given as Mabel Hampton and Joan Nestle. Hampton is listed online as residing at 73 Alder Street, (612) 533-0012. A brief call confirmed she was willing to talk with an investigator from our office and seems to have no hesitation about giving testimony on Client's behalf. Nestle does not appear in the phone registry or in a quick online search, so will require further effort to locate.

Phone call to John Boos, whom we frequently use for expert testimony in cargo injury cases, confirms that in his opinion two ties would not be sufficient for two units of beams over 10 feet in length. He believes that standard practice would require at least three tie-downs made of synthetic webbing or steel chain sufficient to hold the working load, and that four ties would not be considered overkill. (NOTE: will need to determine working load and whether Defendants exceeded the limits. But it seems that the beams slipped out from inadequate placement of securing devices rather than actually breaking the restraints, so this may not matter.)

Work plan

1. Gather original copies of all pertinent bills and reports.
2. Send initial demand letter to Certified Lumber.
3. If demand does not spur productive settlement negotiations proceed to serve and file Summons and Complaint. (Statute of Limitations = six years, so we are not yet pressed for time.)

> It is perhaps uncommon that this lawyer chose to write out an enumerated plan for the next steps in the case. But it is certainly good practice. It keeps the lawyer organized and clearheaded while he is probably juggling many other important matters. It would also be invaluable if an emergency suddenly required some other attorney to attend to the case.

Lawyers need to be able to comprehend and rely on documents produced in a variety of professional settings. From this hospital bill and the PT bill that follows, what information will you actually use in your demand letter? At this early stage in the case is there anything a good lawyer should be looking at in these bills other than whatever information will be central to the demand?

Doc✚or's Hospital

2126 Grosvenor Avenue Minneapolis, MN 55403

Edmund Tanger
114 Humboldt St.
Minneapolis, MN 55401

May 22, 20__

Important Message

Thank you for choosing Doctor's Hospital as your healthcare provider. We have billed your insurance carrier listed below for services provided. We will keep you informed on the status of your account balance. If your insurance carrier does not release payment in a timely manner, we may ask you for assistance in resolving the payment delay. You may want to check with your primary physician now to assure there is a proper referral (if required) for these services to prevent a payment delay.

Account Summary

Patient Name: **Edmund Tanger**

Total Charges	$ 5,441.00
Amount Pending Insurance	$ 5,441.00
Amount You Now Owe	Pending Insurance

Insurance Information

Please verify that this information is correct.

Insurer: BCBS

ID#: BHA304981874

Patient Services Provided

Description	Total
ER/RM	1,225.00
X-RAY	900.00
PHARMACY	205.00
PROFESSIONAL	1577.00
FEES LAB	315.00
TRANSPORT	1,219.00
TOTAL CHARGES	$ 5,441.00

Contact Us

- Account information changes, balance verification, credit card payments and payment arrangements can be made through our automated phone system 24 hours a day.

- To speak with a Customer Service Specialist, contact us Monday through Friday, 8:00 am to 8:00 pm at (614) 789-6084.

Doc+or's Hospital

```
                    DOCTOR'S HOSPITAL           PAGE :     2
                    2621 GROSVENOR AVE.
                    MINNEAPOLIS, MD 55403

TANGER, EDMUND              NEW ADMISSION               TIME: 10:47am
DATE:   05-22-20__
UNIT, ROOM #:  ER 38-A
MED REC #: 23905v                      INS: BCBS
BIRTHDATE & AGE: 10/25/19__ [42]
SEX: MALE                                  SS#: 341-59-7878
RACE: n/a


          ------------------- ADMISSION INFORMATION -------------------
DIAG 1: TIBIAL PLATEAU FRACTURE      DIAG 7:
DIAG 2: MEDIAL COLLATERAL LIGAMENT   DIAG 8: MTBI (GCS-42)
          INFLAMMATION
DIAG 3: PATELLAR CONTUSION R         DIAG 9:
DIAG 4: PATELLAR SUBLUXATION         DIAG 10:
DIAG 5: MENISCAL TEAR                DIAG 11:
DIAG 6: EPIDERMAL ABRASIONS          DIAG 12:


NEXT OF KIN: EMILY TANGER            RELATION: SISTER
Street Address:  184 WOODLEY STREET
City, State, Zip:  MINNEAPOLIS, MN 55401


Cell Phone:          (612) 673-8389
Business Phone:          (   )

EMERGENCY CONTACT: EMILY TANGER      RELATION: SISTER
Street Address:  184 WOODLEY STREET
City, State, Zip:

Cell Phone:          (612) 673-8389
Business Phone:          (   )
----------------------------------------------------------------
HEALTH CARE PROXY:

          ------------------- DISCHARGE INFORMATION -------------------
DISCHARGE CONDITION   :  -- SATISF -- UNIMP -- EXP -- AUT

DISCHARGE DISPOSITION : HOME __  NAME _____
DISCHARGE DIAG        :


BCBS #: BHA304981874


MD. SIGNATURE_____ MD.
```

Premier Physical Therapy™

447 Clark Street
Minneapolis MN 55102
www.PremierPT.com

Billing Summary

Patient No. 5531   Edmund Tanger

Date	CPT #s*	Charge	Status
8-9	91001 97110 97140 97530	$205.00	Paid
8-11	97110 97140 97530	$125.00	Paid
8-16	97110 97140 97530	$125.00	Paid
8-18	97110 97140 97530	$125.00	Paid
8-22	97110 97140 97530	$125.00	Paid
8-25	97110 97140 97530	$125.00	Paid
8-30	97110 97140 97530	$125.00	Paid
9-1	97110 97140 97530	$125.00	Paid
9-6	97110 97140 97530	$125.00	Paid
9-8	97110 97140 97530	$125.00	Paid
9-13	97110 97140 97530	$125.00	Paid
9-15	97750 97110 97140 97530	$155.00	Paid
9-20	97110 97140 97530	$125.00	Paid
9-22	97110 97140 97530	$125.00	Paid
9-27	97110 97140 97530	$125.00	Paid
9-30	97110 97140 97530	$125.00	Paid
10-4	97110 97140 97530	$125.00	Paid
10-6	97750 97110 97140 97530	$155.00	Paid
10-11	97110 97140 97530	$125.00	Paid
10-13	97110 97140 97530	$125.00	Paid
10-18	97110 97140 97530	$125.00	Paid
10-20	97110 97140 97530	$125.00	Paid
10-26	97110 97140 97530	$125.00	Paid
	Current balance	$00.00	

*Current Procedural Terminology coding per AMA

Note that this is a Minnesota state statute. What kinds of roadways do you think it applies to? Are there any streets or roads it may not cover? How will the answers to those questions affect the significance of this document for your case?

M.S.A. § 169.81

169.81. Height and length limitations
Effective: July 1, 2015

Subdivision 1. Height. (a) Except as provided in paragraph (b), no vehicle unladen or with load shall exceed a height of 13 feet six inches.

(b) A double-deck bus may not exceed a height of 14 feet three inches. Any carrier operating a double-deck bus exceeding 13 feet six inches shall obtain from the commissioner, with respect to highways under the commissioner's jurisdiction, and from local authorities, with respect to highways under their jurisdiction, an annual permit to operate the bus upon any highway under the jurisdiction of the party granting the permit. Annual permits shall be issued in accordance with applicable provisions of section 169.86. The fee for an annual permit issued by the commissioner is as provided in section 169.86, subdivision 5.

Subd. 2. Length of single vehicle; exceptions. (a) Statewide, no single vehicle may exceed 45 feet in overall length, including load and front and rear bumpers, except mobile cranes, which may not exceed 48 feet in overall length.

(b) Statewide, no semitrailer may exceed 48 feet in overall length, including bumper and load, but excluding non-cargo-carrying equipment, such as refrigeration units or air compressors, necessary for safe and efficient operation and located on the end of the semitrailer adjacent to the truck-tractor. However, statewide, a single semitrailer may exceed 48 feet, but not 53 feet, if the distance from the kingpin to the centerline of the rear axle group of the semitrailer does not exceed 43 feet.

(c) Statewide, no single trailer may have an overall length exceeding 45 feet, including the tow bar assembly but exclusive of rear bumpers that do not increase the overall length by more than six inches.

(d) For determining compliance with this subdivision, the length of the semitrailer or trailer must be determined separately from the overall length of the combination of vehicles.

(e) No semitrailer or trailer used in a three-vehicle combination may have an overall length in excess of 28- ½ feet, exclusive of:

> (1) non-cargo-carrying accessory equipment, including refrigeration units or air compressors and upper coupler plates, necessary for safe and efficient operation, located on the end of the semitrailer or trailer adjacent to the truck or truck-tractor;

* * *

Subd. 4. Projecting loads. The load upon any vehicle operated alone, or the load upon the front vehicle of a combination of vehicles, shall not extend more than three feet beyond the front wheels of such vehicle or the front bumper of such vehicle if it is equipped with such a bumper.

Subd. 5. Manner of loading. No vehicle shall be driven or moved on any highway unless such vehicle is so constructed, loaded, or the load securely covered as to prevent any of its load from dropping, sifting, leaking, blowing, or otherwise escaping therefrom, except that sand may be dropped for the purpose of securing traction, or water or other substances may be sprinkled on a roadway in cleaning or maintaining such roadway. This subdivision shall not apply to motor vehicles operated by a farmer or the farmer's agent when transporting produce such as small grains, shelled corn, soybeans, or other farm produce of a size and density not likely to cause injury to persons or damage to property on escaping in small amounts from a vehicle. Violation of this subdivision by a vehicle that is carrying farm produce and that is not exempted by the preceding sentence is a petty misdemeanor.

Subd. 5a. Firewood load. No vehicle that has a cargo area without a rear wall may be driven or moved on a trunk highway with a load of cut firewood of less than three feet in length unless the rear of the cargo area is covered with a material of sufficient strength to prevent any part of the load from escaping from the rear. No person shall transport firewood in any vehicle in an unsafe manner. Violation of this subdivision is a petty misdemeanor except that a peace officer may issue a citation that amounts to a warning (1) for a first offense, and (2) if, in the judgment of the citing peace officer at the site, the load of firewood is made safe for transport.

Subd. 5b. Securing load; exceptions. (a) The driver of a vehicle transporting sand, gravel, aggregate, dirt, lime rock, silica, or similar material shall ensure that the cargo compartment of the vehicle is securely covered if:

(1) the vertical distance from the top of an exterior wall of the cargo compartment to the load, when measured downward along the inside surface of the wall, is less than six inches; or

(2) the horizontal distance from the top of an exterior wall of the cargo compartment to the load is less than two feet.

> (b) The driver shall not operate a vehicle to transport sand, gravel, aggregate, dirt, lime rock, silica, or similar material in or on any part of the vehicle other than in the cargo container. The driver shall clean the vehicle of loose sand, gravel, aggregate, dirt, lime rock, silica, or similar material before the vehicle is moved on a road, street, or highway following loading or unloading.

> (c) A driver of a vehicle used to transport garbage, rubbish, trash, debris, or similar material is not required to cover the transported material as long as (1) the vehicle is being operated at a speed less than 30 miles per hour, (2) the vehicle is not being operated on an interstate highway, and (3) no part of the load escapes from the vehicle. A driver shall immediately retrieve material that escapes from the vehicle, when safe to do so.

Note that these are federal regulations. (Remember: regulations are promulgated by duly constituted agencies and carry the force of law.) Since these regulations are from the federal government, what kinds of roadways do you think that means they apply to? Are any roadways likely *not* subject to this statute? How will the answers affect the significance of this document for your case?

Federal Motor Safety Carrier Administration Regulations

Part 393

PARTS AND ACCESSORIES NECESSARY FOR SAFE OPERATION

§ 393.110: What else do I have to do to determine the minimum number of tiedowns?

(a) When tiedowns are used as part of a cargo securement system, the minimum number of tiedowns required to secure an article or group of articles against movement depends on the length of the article(s) being secured, and the requirements of paragraphs (b) and (c) of this section. These requirements are in addition to the rules under § 393.106.

(b) When an article is not blocked or positioned to prevent movement in the forward direction by a headerboard, bulkhead, other cargo that is positioned to prevent movement, or other appropriate blocking devices, it must be secured by at least:

    (1) One tiedown for articles 5 feet (1.52 meters) or less in length, and 1,100 pounds (500 kg) or less in weight;

    (2) Two tiedowns if the article is:

        (i) 5 feet (1.52 meters) or less in length and more than 1,100 pounds (500 kg) in weight; or

        (ii) Longer than 5 feet (1.52 meters) but less than or equal to 10 feet (3.04 meters) in length, irrespective of the weight.

    (3) Two tiedowns if the article is longer than 10 feet (3.04 meters), and one additional tiedown for every 10 feet (3.04 meters) of article length, or fraction thereof, beyond the first 10 feet (3.04 meters) of length.

(c) If an individual article is blocked, braced, or immobilized to prevent movement in the forward direction by a headerboard, bulkhead, other articles which are adequately secured or by an appropriate blocking or immobilization method, it must be secured by at least one tiedown for every 3.04 meters (10 feet) of article length, or fraction thereof.

(d) *Special rule for special purpose vehicles.* The rules in this section do not apply to a vehicle transporting one or more articles of cargo such as, but not limited to, machinery or fabricated structural items (e.g., steel or concrete beams, crane booms, girders, and trusses, etc.) which, because of their design, size, shape, or weight, must be fastened by special methods. However, any article of cargo carried on that vehicle must be securely and adequately fastened to the vehicle.

Citation: [67 FR 61225, Sept. 27, 2002, as amended at 71 FR 35833, June 22, 2006]

Restatement (Third) of Torts

Chapter 3. The Negligence Doctrine and Negligence Liability

§ 3 Negligence

A person acts negligently if the person does not exercise reasonable care under all the circumstances. Primary factors to consider in ascertaining whether the person's conduct lacks reasonable care are the foreseeable likelihood that the person's conduct will result in harm, the foreseeable severity of any harm that may ensue, and the burden of precautions to eliminate or reduce the risk of harm.

§ 13 Custom

(a) An actor's compliance with the custom of the community, or of others in like circumstances, is evidence that the actor's conduct is not negligent but does not preclude a finding of negligence.

(b) An actor's departure from the custom of the community, or of others in like circumstances, in a way that increases risk is evidence of the actor's negligence but does not require a finding of negligence.

§ 14 Statutory Violations as Negligence Per Se

An actor is negligent if, without excuse, the actor violates a statute that is designed to protect against the type of accident the actor's conduct causes, and if the accident victim is within the class of persons the statute is designed to protect.

§ 15 Excused Violations

An actor's violation of a statute is excused and not negligence if:

(a) the violation is reasonable in light of the actor's childhood, physical disability, or physical incapacitation;

(b) the actor exercises reasonable care in attempting to comply with the statute;

(c) the actor neither knows nor should know of the factual circumstances that render the statute applicable;

(d) the actor's violation of the statute is due to the confusing way in which the requirements of the statute are presented to the public; or

(e) the actor's compliance with the statute would involve a greater risk of physical harm to the actor or to others than noncompliance.

§ 16 Statutory Compliance

(a) An actor's compliance with a pertinent statute, while evidence of nonnegligence, does not preclude a finding that the actor is negligent under § 3 for failing to adopt precautions in addition to those mandated by the statute.

(b) If an actor's adoption of a precaution would require the actor to violate a statute, the actor cannot be found negligent for failing to adopt that precaution.

285 Minn. 477
Supreme Court of Minnesota.
Armin SCHMIDT et al., Appellants,
v.
Ronald H. BENINGA et al., Respondents.
No. 41591.

|

Jan. 5, 1970.

Syllabus by the Court

1. Where reasonable men may differ as to what constitutes ordinary care upon the evidence presented, questions of negligence are questions of fact for the jury; and it is only in the clearest of cases where the facts are undisputed and it is plain that all reasonable men can draw only one conclusion that the question of negligence becomes one of law.

2. A motion for a directed verdict presents only a question of law. It admits for the purpose of the motion the credibility of the evidence for the adverse party and every inference which may fairly be drawn from the evidence.

3. Where several persons are engaged in the same work, in which the negligent or unskillful performance of his part by one may cause danger to the others, and in which each must necessarily depend for his safety upon the good faith, skill, and prudence of each of the others in doing his part of the work, it is the duty of each to the others engaged on the work to exercise the care and skill ordinarily employed by prudent men in similar circumstances, and he is liable for any injury occurring to any one of the others by reason of a neglect to use such care and skill.

> These numbered paragraphs may helpful to you, but they are offered as a summary. Are they part of the court's opinion? Can you cite them, or should you only use them for reference?

4. The observance of a custom or failure to observe it does not necessarily amount to due care or the lack of it, but such evidence is admissible as tending to show what a reasonable person would do under the same or similar circumstances.

5. If an act is one which the party ought, in the exercise of ordinary care, to have anticipated was liable to result in injury to others, then he is liable for any injury resulting from it, although he could not have anticipated the particular injury which did happen.

6. Based upon the record here, it is held that the trial court was not justified in directing a verdict for the defendants.

Attorneys and Law Firms

Robins, Davis & Lyons and Dale I. Larson and Jeffrey S. Halpern, Minneapolis, for appellants.

Cummins, Cummins & Gislason, St. Paul, for respondents.

Heard before KNUTSON, C.J., and NELSON, MURPHY, PETERSON, and GRAFF, JJ.

OPINION

GRAFF, Justice.˙
• Acting as Justice of the Supreme Court by appointment pursuant to Minn.Const. art. 6, s 2, and Minn. St. 2.724, subd. 2.

This is an appeal from an order denying plaintiffs' motion for a new trial.

The sole question on this appeal is whether it was error for the trial court to direct a verdict for defendants at the close of plaintiffs' case.

The facts giving rise to the accident in this case are unusual. There is relatively little dispute concerning them, but the parties disagree as to what conclusions are to be drawn from such facts. The Farmers Grain Company operates a grain elevator in Marietta, Minnesota. Grain and other commodities were brought to the elevator by farmers in the locality. These products were brought to the elevator in 'straight jobs'-trucks with dual wheels and front axles and with boxes ranging in size from 12 to 18 feet. Some of the grain brought to the elevator was moved out by railroad, some was ground for feed, and some was moved out by larger tractor-trailers. The elevator is laid out in an east-west direction, with the entrance at the east and the exit at the west side. The elevator was built before large-sized tractor-trailers were used for transportation.

The floor of the elevator is flat and level. It contained a scale 36 feet long and approximately 9 feet wide. The east end of the scale was 2 1/2 or 3 feet from a ramp and the west end of the scale was approximately 20 or 21 feet from the west door of the elevator. Trucks would approach the scale from the east by proceeding up a 30-foot incline which slopes approximately 20 degrees and terminates 2 1/2 or 3 feet east of the scale. A tractor-trailer whose length was in excess of the length of the scale could not be weighed in a single step. To weigh the units whose length was in excess of the scale, a two-step or a split-weighing procedure was employed. This procedure was in use for some period of time and was generally understood by the elevator employees and the drivers of tractor-trailer units whose length exceeded that of the scale. The procedure was to drive the empty tractor-trailer so that first only the tractor would be on the scale. This left the trailer wheels partially resting on the east, sloped scale approach. A wooden block was then placed behind the outside front tire of the rear tandem on the right side of the trailer. This was done to eliminate any 'drag' of the trailer during weighing and the trailer would be held in position by the block. After the block was in place, the trailer brakes were generally applied. After the tractor was weighed, the block would be removed and the entire unit would be driven ahead so only the trailer was on the scale. The trailer would then be weighed. It would then be loaded with grain or some other commodity and the weighing procedure would be followed in reverse. That is, the loaded trailer would first be weighed and then the tractor-trailer was backed up to the east and down the slope until the tractor was alone on the scale. The trailer would then be blocked as before and the tractor weighed. When a tractor-trailer was being weighed, there was not enough room on the left side between the elevator wall and the tractor-trailer to walk. There is no issue concerning the accuracy of this weighing procedure. The block of wood used to block the trailer was approximately 14 inches long, 8 inches wide, and 6 inches high.

After the entire loading and weighing procedure was completed, the driver, after receiving a signal by voice or hand from an employee of the elevator, would release the trailer brakes and proceed slowly forward a short distance to take the trailer weight off the block. The driver would then stop the unit and the elevator employee would take out the block. The driver would watch in his right rear-view mirror for a second signal or wait until he heard a voice signal from the elevator employee. Upon receiving such a signal, he would drive his tractor-trailer away from the elevator.

An accident occurred on the afternoon of October 13, 1964, and as a result plaintiff Armin Schmidt lost his right leg. It was a clear day, there was no precipitation, and the surface upon which Schmidt was standing at the time of the accident was dry. Schmidt had worked at the elevator as a truckdriver and general laborer for approximately 2 1/2 years. At the time of the accident, Schmidt was 42 years old and a graduate of the local high school. His principal work before being employed at the elevator was farming, driving a school bus, and selling fertilizer. As a laborer at the elevator for 2 1/2 years, he was constantly involved and totally familiar with the split-weighing procedure used at the elevator for larger units. Until this accident the procedure had never caused any difficulty or injury. Schmidt testified with respect to the procedure for the removal of the block: 'We felt there was no hazard there at all'; '(w)e considered it safe the way we was doing it'; 'I never heard any complaints from anybody, from any drivers or anybody else.' Schmidt was fully satisfied that it was a safe procedure and in discussions had with his coworkers and his employer all were satisfied that it was a safe procedure that involved no risk or danger.

Plaintiff Employers Mutual of Wausau has a subrogation right arising out of its payments to Schmidt as the workmen's compensation insurance carrier for Schmidt's employer, Farmers Grain Company.

Defendant Ronald Beninga was the driver of the tractor-trailer at the time of the accident. Beninga was 21 years old at the time of the accident. He began working for defendant Curtis E. Johnson as a driver of a tractor-trailer truck about the middle of September 1964. Defendant Johnson was doing business as Marietta Truck Lines and he is a defendant in this capacity as well as in his individual capacity. Johnson and Beninga are brothers-in-law.

> Do you know what a "subrogation right" is? If not, you need to look it up. Good students have usually learned to discern general meaning from context, but law requires greater precision than that.
>
> If you are unsure of the meaning of a non-legal term, look it up in an ordinary dictionary. If you do not know a legal term, look it up in a law dictionary. And if you see a term with a plain English meaning that seems to have a specific legal connotation, be sure you know what that is, or again, look it up in a law dictionary.

The particular tractor-trailer driven by Beninga on the day of the accident had been loaded and weighed at the elevator at least 60 to 70 times per year. It did not differ in any material manner from the other tractor-trailer units that came to the elevator for loading and weighing. The tractor driven by Beninga was a GMC Diesel of the snub-nose type where the driver sits above the engine. It had a wheel base of approximately 15 feet and its length would be increased by the amount of overhang in front and in back. The trailer used by Beninga was a grain type trailer about 8 feet wide and approximately 37 feet long with tandem rear wheels. The overall length of this combined tractor-trailer exceeded the 36-foot scale at the elevator. When fully loaded, as it was at the time of the accident, the tractor-trailer weighed about 73,000 pounds. Beninga had frequently driven this particular tractor-trailer. His compensation was a flat fee for every trip, depending on the distance. Beninga testified that the tractor-trailer was in good working order and was adequately equipped at the time of the accident. He had considerable experience in driving trucks, had a chauffeur's license, and was legally licensed to drive a tractor-trailer.

Beninga was familiar with the availability and use of the two outside rear-view mirrors mounted on the sides of the tractor. He was experienced in backing up different types of trucks and trailers and using rear-view mirrors during these operations. For several weeks prior to the accident, he had driven this tractor-trailer to the elevator to pick up or deliver loads almost every day. It was a busy season for hauling and he was doing as much hauling as he could. He was fully acquainted with the physical facts and the general operation of the elevator and was also thoroughly familiar with the two-step or split-weighing procedure employed at the elevator in weighing tractor-trailer units which were longer than the scale. He admitted he was completely acquainted with the use of the wooden block and the procedure for removing the block during both stages of the split-weighing procedure. Beninga testified that when he was ready to proceed off the ramp after the final weighing was completed, he would be directed ahead usually by means of a hand signal and sometimes by a verbal signal from the elevator employee.

Shortly before the accident Schmidt had returned to the elevator after delivering a load of feed in the county. When he came to the elevator, the tractor-trailer driven by Beninga was either being loaded or was practically filled. Beninga was in the office getting his weight or scale ticket and Schmidt was waiting for him to come out, so he could pull the block out and Beninga could leave. Schmidt saw Beninga come out of the office and walk around the front of the tractor to get in. Beninga released the brakes on the trailer

and by means of the right rear-view mirror saw Schmidt down by the block. Schmidt was waiting on a platform a step down from and adjacent to the approach and bent over slightly to grab hold of the block with both hands. The amount of the block behind the tire was about 8 inches. Schmidt put his hands on the part of the block that was not behind the tire and said, 'All right.' Beninga admits receiving a signal from Schmidt at this point. Beninga stated that this signal meant that Schmidt was ready to pull the block out and that Beninga should pull ahead slowly and continue moving, which he says he did. Beninga was aware of the fact that the block had to be removed before he could proceed. The tractor-trailer started to move forward. Schmidt began to pull the block and removed about 4 or 5 inches of the block. At that point the block was apparently propelled outward by the outside rear tandem tire and struck Schmidt between the ankle and knee of the right leg. No one saw the block come out and hit Schmidt. The distance between the two outside tandem wheels was approximately 12 to 13 inches measured at the height of the block and approximately 18 to 20 inches at ground level. The distance between the back end of the block and the nearest portion of the next tire was 5 or 6 inches.

Beninga testified that he was aware that the only way he could know that the block was removed was to watch in his right rear-view mirror. Beninga states after looking in his right rear-view mirror and seeing Schmidt by the block, he never looked in his right rear-view mirror again until after the accident.

The deposition of Beninga was taken on June 15, 1967, and the trial of this case commenced on October 16, 1967. As a part of his cross-examination at the trial, some of the questions and answers in the deposition were read to Beninga and he admitted that such questions were asked of him and he gave such answers. These answers were to the effect that he was aware of the customary procedure employed in weighing as was described at the trial. As to the signal he stated as follows:

'Well, the guy with the block would have signaled me with an arm signal to move ahead and then stop, and he would remove the block and wave me ahead, to go on ahead.'

As to the second stop, the questions and answers were as follows:

'Q And you actually saw Mr. Schmidt come into that rear view mirror range and get down there and get hold of that block, is that right?

'A Yes, sir.

'Q And then as he was holding onto this he what, waved with one hand, signaling you to go ahead?

'A Yes, sir.

'Q And that was the only signal he gave you, is that correct?

'A As I remember it.

'Q Did he give you any verbal signal or was this only a hand wave?

'A I do not recall.

'Q That hand wave meant to you to pull ahead slightly and stop, is that correct?

'A Yes, sir.

'Q In other words, you were supposed to pull far enough ahead to take the pressure off that block so he could pull it out?

'A Yes, sir.'

Counsel for defendants on redirect examination asked Beninga concerning questions asked and answers given in a subsequent part of the deposition. Here Beninga said it was not the procedure to receive a second signal to drive ahead. In answer to a question as to how he knew when to drive completely ahead he stated, 'It's just-after you receive your signal and you move and make your stop or pause, you just continue on out.'

In cross-examination, Schmidt was asked whether he was concerned that his hands may have slipped and caused the accident. Schmidt testified that 'I feel my hands never did slip' and that he was not concerned with that possibility. Counsel for the defense then offered for impeachment purposes a four-page statement given by Schmidt on October 29, 1964, to an agent of the workmen's compensation insurance carrier for the elevator. This statement was taken when Schmidt was at General Hospital in Minneapolis and after his leg was amputated on October 21, 1964. The statement was received in evidence over objection. In this statement Schmidt stated, 'I don't know why the rear wheels caught the block-maybe my hand slipped

or maybe the truck went too fast-everything happened so fast it's hard to tell exactly what happened.'

Plaintiffs contend that the evidence demonstrates that Beninga was negligent at the time and place in question. Plaintiffs assert that the evidence shows a failure to exercise reasonable care in the operation of the tractor-trailer. Plaintiffs further assert that Beninga failed to follow the customary procedure, which he knew or should have known that Schmidt would rely upon. Defendants' sole contention is that the evidence fails to show that any of the acts or omissions of Beninga involved a reasonably foreseeable risk of injury to Schmidt or anyone else. Plaintiffs claim that the evidence clearly meets the test of 'foreseeability.'

[1][2] 1. We have made it clear under what circumstances it is proper to direct a verdict. In Brittain v. City of Minneapolis, 250 Minn. 376, 389, 84 N.W.2d 646, 655, we stated the rule as follows:

'Ordinarily, it is only where there is an entire absence of evidence tending to establish negligence that a court can enter upon the province of the jury and direct a verdict for the defendant. LeVasseur v. Minneapolis St. Ry. Co., 221 Minn. 205, 21 N.W.2d 522. Where reasonable men may differ as to what constitutes ordinary care and proximate causal connection upon the evidence presented, questions of negligence and proximate cause, as well as contributory negligence, are questions of fact for the jury; and it is only in the clearest of cases where the facts are undisputed and it is plain that all reasonable men can draw only one conclusion that the question of negligence becomes one of law. Schrader v. Kriesel, 232 Minn. 238, 45 N.W.2d 395; Sanders v. Gilbertson, 224 Minn. 546, 29 N.W.2d 357.'

2. In Swedeen v. Swedeen, 270 Minn. 491, 496, 134 N.W.2d 871, 875, we said:

'In considering the claim that the trial court erred in directing a verdict for defendant, we are governed by those decisions which hold that a motion for a directed verdict should be granted only in those unequivocal cases where, in the light of the evidence as a whole, it would clearly be the duty of the trial court to set aside a contrary verdict as being manifestly against the evidence or contrary to the law in the case. Hanrahan v. Safway Steel Scaffold Co., 233

Minn. 171, 46 N.W.2d 243; Van Tassel v. Patterson, 235 Minn. 152, 50 N.W.2d 113; Crea v. Wuellner, 235 Minn. 408, 51 N.W.2d 283. It is for the jury, not the court, to determine weight to be given to testimony and to decide what it proves. Cameron v. Evans, 241 Minn. 200, 62 N.W.2d 793; Zuber v. Northern Pacific Ry. Co., 246 Minn. 157, 74 N.W.2d 641; Storbakken v. Soderberg, 246 Minn. 434, 75 N.W.2d 496. A verdict should be directed only when it is plain that all reasonable men can draw but one conclusion. Where varying inferences may be drawn from the testimony, the case should be submitted to the jury. Sviggum v. Phillips, 217 Minn. 586, 15 N.W.2d 109; Olson v. Evert, 224 Minn. 528, 28 N.W.2d 753; Audette v. Lindahl, 231 Minn. 239, 42 N.W.2d 717.'

The credibility of the evidence and every inference which may fairly be drawn therefrom must be viewed in a light most favorable to plaintiffs upon defendants' motion for a directed verdict. See, Wm. Mueller & Sons v. Chanhassen Redi Mix, 273 Minn. 214, 140 N.W.2d 326; Downey v. Frey, 269 Minn. 66, 130 N.W.2d 349; Lovejoy v. Minneapolis-Moline Power Imp. Co., 248 Minn. 319, 79 N.W.2d 688.

> Be sure that you fully understand the procedural posture of every case you read. Do you see why the court here is referring to what the jury "could have found"? The answer is given at the very beginning of the opinion: the trial court granted defendants' motion for a directed verdict. If the facts presented at trial could lead a reasonable jury to only one conclusion—finding for defendants—then the court's ruling was correct. If there is even a tiny chance that a trier of fact could lawfully have reached a different conclusion, then the trial court was wrong.

[3][4] 3. The jury could have found that the elevator employees, including Schmidt, were working together with Beninga in so far as unloading, loading, and weighing at the elevator were concerned. If so, there would be a duty of each to the other to exercise the care and skill ordinarily employed by prudent men in similar circumstances, and there would be liability for any injury by reason of a neglect of such care or skill. The principle is stated in 13B Dunnell, Dig. (3 ed.) s 6975, as follows:

'Where several persons are engaged in the same work, in which the negligent or unskillful performance of his part by one may cause danger to the others, and in which each must necessarily depend for his safety upon the good faith, skill, and prudence of each of the others in doing his part of the work, it is the duty of each to the others engaged on the work to exercise the care and skill ordinarily employed by prudent men in similar circumstances, and he is liable for any injury occurring to any one of the others by reason of a neglect to use such care and skill.'

The jury could have found that Beninga did not maintain a proper lookout. Beninga saw Schmidt at the block in his right rear-view mirror and knew that Schmidt was waiting to pull out the block. Beninga admits that he received a hand or oral signal. Beninga was fully aware that the only way he would know whether the block was removed before he proceeded was to watch in his right rear-view mirror. Beninga stated that the only way he would know whether the block was out while he was in the tractor-trailer was to look to the rear. Beninga knew that the block was there; he knew the block had to be removed before he drove off the scales; and yet he did not bother to look. The jury in considering these facts could also take into account that it was a busy season for hauling, that Beninga was doing as much hauling as he could, and that he was paid a flat fee for every trip. The unequivocal duty of a driver of a vehicle to maintain a proper lookout is well settled whether the vehicle is on or off the highway. See, LaBelle v. Swanson, 248 Minn. 35, 78 N.W.2d 358; Schneider v. Texas Co., 244 Minn. 131, 69 N.W.2d 329; Swanson v. J. L. Shiely Co., 234 Minn. 548, 48 N.W.2d 848; 13B Dunnell, Dig. (3 ed.) s 6997a. In LaBelle v. Swanson, Supra, we held that the duty of a driver to maintain a proper lookout for workmen extends to workmen of whom the driver is not aware and with whom he is not working. We stated in that case: 'A motorist's observation for the purpose of discovering hazards, which the ordinarily prudent man would reasonably anticipate, presupposes that, in the exercise of ordinary care, the observation will be taken at a time and place when it will be effective.' 248 Minn. 39, 78 N.W.2d 362. The jury could have found that a reasonably prudent person would have looked in the right rear-view mirror at an effective time and place to ascertain that the block was removed before the driver drove off the scale.

Depending upon the circumstances in a particular case, the rate of speed, the failure to stop, and the failure to pause or slow down may constitute the lack of reasonable care. Reasonable care is that degree of care which a reasonably prudent person would exercise under the same or similar circumstances. Ahlstrom v. Minneapolis, St. P. & S.S.M.R. Co., 244 Minn. 1, 9, 68 N.W.2d 873, 879. The jury could have found that the exercise of reasonable care required that Beninga in driving the tractor-trailer should have stopped, or at the very least paused sufficiently after the pressure on the block was released. Beninga knew that he should pause or halt to give Schmidt sufficient time to remove the block. Beninga admits he did neither. The evidence as to the speed of the tractor-trailer after the first signal was given is meager. Beninga states he drove slowly after receiving the first signal. In the written statement Schmidt gave on October 29, 1964,[1] he stated '(M)aybe the truck went too fast.' The crux of the speed issue was whether Beninga was going slowly enough to permit Schmidt to extricate the block, and the jury could have found that the speed of the tractor-trailer after receiving the first signal was not slow enough to permit removal of the block.

[1] Schmidt's testimony that he was not concerned with the possibility that his hands may have slipped was impeached by the statement. The only foundation for its admission into evidence related to the possibility of Schmidt's hands slipping, yet the entire statement was received over objection.

4. The customary procedure for weighing large tractor-trailer units at the elevator was gone into thoroughly at the trial. The only dispute as to the customary procedure was what the driver should do after receiving the initial signal. When the evidence is viewed in the light most favorable to plaintiffs, the customary procedure was that after receiving the first signal, the driver was to relieve the pressure on the block and then stop, and then, upon receiving a second signal, was to drive off the scale. Beninga admitted that this was the customary procedure at the time his deposition was taken, and at the trial he admitted that he had so testified in his deposition. Such testimony during the trial is not merely impeaching testimony, it is the admission of a party and as such was substantive evidence which alone would be sufficient to sustain plaintiffs' burden of proof on the question of the custom. See, In Re Estate of Olson, 227 Minn. 289, 301, 35 N.W.2d 439, 447; Leifson v. Henning, 210 Minn. 311, 313, 298 N.W. 41, 42; Guile v. Greenberg, 192 Minn. 548, 556, 257 N.W. 649, 652.

[5][6] The evidence shows that the customary procedure existed at the elevator and was known and followed by employees of the elevator and drivers, including Beninga. Beninga failed to follow the customary procedure in this instance, without any notice to Schmidt. The evidence indicates that as long as the customary procedure was followed, no difficulties had been encountered with the removal of the block. The observance of a custom or failure to observe it does not necessarily amount to due care or the lack of it, but such evidence is admissible as tending to show what a reasonably prudent person would do under the same or similar circumstances. See, Hartmon v. National Heater Co., 240 Minn. 264, 277, 60 N.W.2d 804, 812; Kelly v. Southern Minn. Ry. Co., 28 Minn. 98, 9 N.W. 588; 13B Dunnell, Dig. (3 ed.) s 7049. Under the evidence the jury could have found that Beninga, by not following the customary procedure at the elevator, did not act as a reasonably prudent person would do under the same or similar circumstances. At the same time it must be recognized that the doing of a negligent act is not excused by the fact that it is customary. See, Scattergood v. Keil, 233 Minn. 340, 343, 45 N.W.2d 650, 653.

5. Defendants' principal contention on this appeal is that Beninga could not be found to be negligent on the evidence because there was no reasonably ground to anticipate that the acts or omissions of Beninga would or might result in any injury to anybody.

[7] The principles relating to 'foreseeability' were laid down by Mr. Justice Mitchell in Christianson v. Chicago, St. P.M. & O. Ry. Co., 67 Minn. 94, 97, 69 N.W. 640, 641, as follows:

'What a man may reasonably anticipate is important, and may be decisive, in determining whether an act is negligent, but is not at all decisive in determining whether that act is the proximate cause of an injury which ensues. If a person had no reasonable ground to anticipate that a particular act would or might result in any injury to anybody, then, of course, the act would not be negligent at all; but, if the act itself is negligent, then the person guilty of it is equally liable for all its natural and proximate consequences, whether he could have foreseen them or not. Otherwise expressed, the law is that if the act is one which the party ought, in the exercise of ordinary care, to have anticipated was liable to result in injury to others, then he is liable for any injury proximately resulting from it, although he could not have anticipated the particular injury which did happen.'

In Dellwo v. Pearson, 259 Minn. 452, 456, 107 N.W.2d 859, 862, 97 A.L.R.2d 866, 870, we affirmed the rule of the Christianson case relating to proximate cause and stated that 'negligence is tested by foresight but proximate cause is determined by hindsight.' We have consistently followed the Christianson rule. See, Peterson v. Truelson, 249 Minn. 530, 538, 83 N.W.2d 236, 241. There are many decisions relating to foreseeability and probability of injury as a test of liability for negligence. The cases relating to 'unforeseeable' accidents are generally collected in 13B Dunnell, Dig. (3 ed.) s 7008, while the principles of negligence applicable generally to other accidents are collected in Id. s 6969, et seq. The parties here are in general agreement about what the rule is but differ in the conclusion to be drawn by the application of the rule to the facts.

6. At the close of plaintiffs' case, defendants made a motion for a directed verdict on the issues of Beninga's negligence, Schmidt's contributory negligence, and Schmidt's assumption of risk. The arguments on the motion were directed only to the issue of Beninga's negligence. The trial court made it clear that it was directing a verdict solely on the issue of Beninga's negligence and that it was not done on the issues of Schmidt's contributory negligence or assumption of risk. Earlier herein we called attention to Brittain v. City of Minneapolis, Supra. That case states the rules when a verdict should or should not be directed: When reasonable men may differ as to what constitutes ordinary care upon the evidence, the question of negligence is one of fact for the jury; in the clearest of cases where the facts are undisputed and it is plain that all reasonable man can draw only one conclusion, the question of negligence is one of law.

Whenever a person is placed in such a position with regard to another that it is obvious that if he does not use due care in his own conduct he will cause injury to that person, the duty at once arises to exercise care commensurate with the situation in which he thus finds himself to avoid such injury. See, Depue v. Flatau, 100 Minn. 299 111 N.W. 1, 8 L.R.A.,N.S., 485. Beninga was completely familiar with the use of the block and aware of the small distance from the back end of the block to the nearest portion of the rear tire. Beninga saw Schmidt's position at the block through his right rear-view mirror just before the first signal was given. Beninga was an experienced driver and he knew that if the block was not completely removed, the right rear tire would collide with the block. Considering the relative weights of the tractor trailer and the block and that the tractor trailer was moving, it seems reasonable if anything was to move as a result of the collision it would be the block. Beninga testified that if the block was not removed, 'I do not believe you'd pull over it.' Experienced drivers are generally aware that the end of an object impinged by the edge of a moving inflated tire on a motor vehicle will be propelled outward with some force. It is reasonably foreseeable that one may be injured in removing a block between the rear outside tires if the tractor trailer is driven at such a speed that there is not time to get the block out. The exact manner in which Schmidt would be injured under such circumstances need not be perceived. See, Dellwo v. Pearson, Supra and Christianson v. Chicago, St. P.M. & O. Ry. Co., Supra. The foregoing is deemed to be sufficient to demonstrate that reasonable men may differ as to what constitutes care upon the evidence and that the question of negligence in this case is one of fact for the jury.

For the reasons heretofore stated, a new trial must be granted.

Reversed and a new trial granted.

489 N.W.2d 281
Court of Appeals of Minnesota.

John ZORGDRAGER, Appellant,

v.

STATE WIDE SALES, INC., Defendant and
Third-Party Plaintiff, Respondent,

v.

LONG PRAIRIE PACKING COMPANY,
Third-Party Defendant, Respondent.
No. C5-92-520.

|

Sept. 15, 1992.

282 *Syllabus by the Court*

1. The violation of an Occupational Safety and Health Administration regulation constitutes negligence per se, provided certain criteria are met.

2. The trial court did not abuse discretion in denying a new trial on the basis of surprise.

3. The evidence supports the jury's finding that State Wide Sales was not negligent.

Attorneys and Law Firms

Susan E. Broin, Todd Young Law Firm, St. Paul, for John Zorgdrager, appellant.

Leon R. Erstad, Minneapolis, for State Wide Sales, Inc., defendant and third-party plaintiff, respondent.

Thomas E. Marshall, Mahoney, Dougherty & Mahoney, Minneapolis, for Long Prairie Packing Co., third-party defendant, respondent.

Considered and decided by DAVIES, P.J., and PARKER and PETERSON, JJ.

OPINION

PARKER, Judge.

John Zorgdrager filed suit against State Wide Sales, Inc., and its employee, Gary Allen, after he was injured when the forklift he was driving fell off State Wide's truck. State Wide filed a third-party complaint against Long Prairie Packing Co., Zorgdrager's employer, claiming Long Prairie was responsible for the employee's injuries because of improper supervision and failure to provide a safe workplace.

Following trial, the jury, by special verdict, found Long Prairie 70 percent negligent, Zorgdrager 30 percent negligent, and State Wide not negligent. This appeal followed.

Zorgdrager challenges the trial court's jury instruction on Occupational Safety and Health Administration (OSHA) regulations and the trial court's order denying his motion for a new trial on the basis of surprise. He also contends that the evidence requires reversal of the jury's special verdict finding State Wide not negligent. We affirm.

FACTS

On December 21, 1989, Gary Allen, a truck driver for State Wide, delivered material to Long Prairie Packing Co. Allen backed into the unloading area, put the truck's transmission in neutral, and set the emergency brake. Because it was very cold, he kept the truck's engine running in order to maintain heat in the cab.

When backing into the loading area, Allen noticed signs warning truck drivers to chock their wheels before unloading the truck. He looked for wheel chocks to place under the rear tires of the truck to prevent it from rolling forward and located only one chock in the loading dock area. The top of that chock had been worn off, but Allen placed it under the rear left outside tire before notifying Long Prairie of his delivery.

John Zorgdrager, a Long Prairie employee, was directed to unload this truck. He drove a forklift, with the fork tines a few feet in the air, down an incline leading to the bed of the truck. Two witnesses testified at trial that Zorgdrager was driving the forklift faster than necessary. Just as he drove onto the truck it moved forward from the dock, creating a gap, and he and the forklift fell to the ground. Zorgdrager sustained a fracture to his arm due to the fall and complains that this injury has adversely affected his earning capacity since.

Michael Manning, Zorgdrager's expert witness, testified that it is standard industry practice for truck drivers to turn off the truck's engine, put the truck in gear, set its emergency brake, and place chocks under both rear tires before unloading. Failure to follow these

So this case seems to be dealing with methods for safely loading cargo onto trucks! That would excite you a great deal if you were conducting your own legal research and came across this one. But look carefully and conceptually at the rule of law and how it applies to the facts. It is not necessarily true that the most facially similar cases will end up being the most legally analogizable ones.

procedures is, he testified, a violation of standard industry practice and custom. Manning expressed the opinion that if Allen had followed standard industry practice, this accident would not have occurred.

Manning further testified that OSHA regulations require employers to ensure that chocks are placed under the two rear tires and the emergency brake set before a truck is unloaded. However, OSHA regulations do not require a truck driver to turn off the engine and put the truck in gear. Even though employers rely on truck drivers to chock the tires and set the emergency brake, OSHA makes employers responsible for taking these precautions. OSHA regulations also require employers to train their employees in the proper use of a forklift.

Ivan Russell, State Wide's safety expert, testified that Zorgdrager caused State Wide's truck to move away from the loading dock by driving the forklift too fast down the incline leading to the truck. Russell also testified that the wheel chock moved away from the truck because the leading edge and top of the chock were worn or broken off. Therefore, in Russell's opinion, the defective wheel chock and Zorgdrager's excessive speed caused the accident.

ISSUES

1. Did the trial court err in instructing the jury that violation of an OSHA regulation constitutes negligence per se?

2. Did the trial court err in denying Zorgdrager's motion for a new trial on the basis of surprise?

3. Does the evidence support the jury's finding that State Wide was not negligent?

DISCUSSION

I

"On appeal, this court need not defer to the trial court's conclusion when reviewing questions of law." *County of Lake v. Courtney,* 451 N.W.2d 338, 340 (Minn.App.1990), *pet. for rev. denied* (Minn. Apr. 13, 1990). However,

> the trial court is allowed considerable latitude in the language used in [jury] instructions, and a new trial will not be granted when they fairly and correctly state the applicable law. Errors in jury instructions are fundamental if they destroy the substantial correctness of the charge as

a whole, cause a miscarriage of justice, or result in substantial prejudice.

State Bank of Hamburg v. Stoeckmann, 417 N.W.2d 113, 116 (Minn. App.1987) (citation omitted), *pet. for rev. denied* (Minn. Feb. 17, 1988).

During trial, Zorgdrager moved the trial court to instruct the jury that the violation of an OSHA regulation is evidence of negligence, rather than negligence per se. Instead, the trial court ruled that the violation of an OSHA regulation constitutes negligence per se, provided certain criteria are met. The trial court found these criteria satisfied in this case and therefore instructed the jury that the violation of an OSHA regulatory duty is negligence unless justification or excuse is established. Zorgdrager argues that this instruction was erroneous and prejudiced his case.

[1] Zorgdrager cites *Behlke v. Conwed Corp.,* 474 N.W.2d 351, 359 (Minn.App.1991), *pet. for rev. denied* (Minn. Oct. 11, 1991), for the proposition that the violation of "[a]n OSHA regulation does not establish negligence per se." However, this remark was dictum, not a holding of the case. Furthermore, Zorgdrager took the sentence out of context.

> It is well settled that breach of a statute gives rise to negligence per se if the persons harmed by that violation are within the intended protection of the statute and the harm suffered is of the type the legislation was intended to prevent.

Pacific Indem. Co. v. Thompson-Yaeger, Inc., 260 N.W.2d 548, 558 (Minn.1977); *see also Mervin v. Magney Constr. Co.,* 416 N.W.2d 121, 124 n. 1 (Minn.1987); *Johnson v. Farmers & Merchants State Bank,* 320 N.W.2d 892, 897 (Minn.1982). Minnesota has adopted federal OSHA regulations by statute. *See* Minn. Stat. § 182.65, subd. 2(f) (1990).

[2] [3] The trial court in this case correctly ruled that the violation of an OSHA regulation constitutes negligence per se, provided the *Pacific Indemnity* criteria are met. The trial court found that these criteria were satisfied and, accordingly, instructed the jury that violation of a regulatory duty is negligence. The trial court fairly and correctly stated the applicable law.

[4] Inasmuch as we hold the instruction not to have been erroneous, we need not address any purported prejudicial effect. Despite appellant's argument, we perceive no reason why the jury would have problems with determining comparable fault applying negligence per se relative to common law negligence. Juries in Minnesota

commonly determine comparative fault by applying different standards to different parties.

II

[5] In *Nachtsheim v. Wartnick,* 411 N.W.2d 882, 889 (Minn.App.1987), *pet. for rev. denied* (Minn. Oct. 28, 1987), this court stated:

> Whether to grant a new trial for surprise is largely within the discretion of the trial court and its decision will rarely be reversed on appeal.

Furthermore, it is within the trial judge's discretion to admit expert testimony, and his "decision will not be reversed unless there is a clear abuse of [that] discretion." *McPherson v. Buege,* 360 N.W.2d 344, 348 (Minn. App.1984).

Zorgdrager argues that the trial judge abused discretion in denying a new trial on the basis of "surprise" testimony by one of State Wide's expert witnesses. He maintains that State Wide failed to disclose that Ivan Russell would testify that, in his opinion, the wheel chock supplied to Allen by Long Prairie was defective and contributed to the occurrence of the accident. Zorgdrager complains that this evidence prejudiced his case because it shifted the blame for his injuries to Long Prairie and away from State Wide and the truck driver, Allen.

[6] At trial, Zorgdrager's expert witness testified that OSHA regulations require *both* rear tires of a truck to be chocked before a truck is unloaded. One major issue was whether Allen's failure to chock both tires caused the accident. One of State Wide's defenses was that Allen found only one chock in the loading dock area and the top of that chock was worn off. From the pleadings and through discovery, it should have been clear to Zorgdrager that the condition of the chock could be an issue at trial.

Photographs of the defective chock were first provided by the employer, Long Prairie, to State Wide at the same time they were provided to Zorgdrager, one day before trial. It is difficult, under these circumstances, to see how the disputed opinion could have surprised any but the unwary.

We note further that Zorgdrager did not serve expert witness interrogatories or seek to depose State Wide's expert. Because Mr. Russell's identity was disclosed well in advance of trial, Zorgdrager had an opportunity to discover what his testimony would entail. The trial court did not err in denying Zorgdrager's motion for a new trial on the basis of surprise.

III

[7] In *Karnes v. Milo Beauty & Barber Supply,* 441 N.W.2d 565, 567 (Minn.App.1989), *pet. for rev. denied* (Minn. Aug. 15, 1989), this court stated:

> On review, answers to special verdict questions will not be set aside unless they are perverse and palpably contrary to the evidence or where the evidence is so clear to leave no room for differences among reasonable people. The evidence must be reviewed in the light most favorable to the jury verdict.

(Citation omitted.) "The test is whether the answer can be reconciled in any reasonable manner consistent with the evidence and its fair inferences." *Gillespie v. Klun,* 406 N.W.2d 547, 557 (Minn.App.1987), *pet. for rev. denied* (Minn. July 9, 1987). If the jury's special verdict finding can be reconciled on any theory, the verdict will not be disturbed. *Travelers Ins. Co. v. Horseshoe Lake Farms, Inc.,* 456 N.W.2d 453, 459 (Minn.App.1990).

Zorgdrager contends that the jury's special verdict answer finding State Wide not to have been negligent is contrary to the evidence and must be set aside. He also argues that the trial court should have granted his motion for JNOV because the evidence shows Allen to have been negligent in violating industry safety standards by failing to chock both tires, failing to turn off the truck's engine, and failing to put the truck's transmission in gear.

[8] There was evidence from which the jury found that Long Prairie violated OSHA regulations by failing to ensure that chocks were placed behind both rear tires of the truck before it was unloaded. This opinion evidence, together with eyewitness evidence of Zorgdrager's contributory negligence, would have allowed the jury reasonably to conclude, as it did, that State Wide and Allen were not negligent and that the causative negligence was that of plaintiff and his employer.

DECISION

The trial court correctly instructed the jury that violations of OSHA regulations constitute negligence per se, provided certain criteria are met. The trial court did not err in denying Zorgdrager's motion for a new trial on the basis of surprise. The trial court did not err in refusing to set aside the jury's special verdict answer that State Wide was not negligent, or in denying Zorgdrager's motion for JNOV.

Affirmed.

547 N.W.2d 693

Supreme Court of Minnesota.

Frank BILLS, Respondent,

v.

WILLOW RUN I APARTMENTS, a Partnership, under the law of the State of Minnesota, et al., petitioners, Appellants.

No. C4-94-2358.

|

May 16, 1996.

Syllabus by the Court

A landlord or owner is not negligent per se for a violation of the Uniform Building Code unless: (1) the landlord or owner knew or should have known of the Code violation; (2) the landlord or owner failed to take reasonable steps to remedy the violation; (3) the injury suffered was the kind the Code was meant to prevent; and (4) the violation was the proximate cause of the injury or damage.

Attorneys and Law Firms

Kay Nord Hunt, Lemmen, Nelson, Cole & Stageberg, Minneapolis, Emilro R. Givliani, Lee L. Labore & Assocs., Hopkins, for appellants.

Michael Zender, Willmar, for respondent.

Louise Ann Dovre, Rider, Bennett, Egan & Arundel, Minneapolis, amici curiae, for Minnesota Defense Lawyers Assoc.

Paul A. Sortland, Minneapolis, amici curiae, for Minnesota Trial Lawyers Assoc.

Heard, considered and decided by the court en banc.

OPINION

TOM L JANOVICH, Justice.

On February 6, 1993, Frank Bills was injured when he fell on an exterior landing outside of his apartment building, Willow Run in Willmar, Minnesota. At the height of a sleet storm, while leaving the building at approximately 6:45 a.m. on his way to work, Bills stepped out of the door onto the landing and slipped on ice that had accumulated as a result of the storm. The exit was well-lit and Bills was aware of the sleet storm that had begun the night before. Bills testified he "took one step out, and [he] went straight up and ended up landing on [his] back." He now claims he suffers continual pain from this accident; his injuries causing reduced mobility in his back.

Bills sued Willow Run alleging that the landing, its handrails and risers were in violation of the Uniform Building Code (UBC). It is Bills' contention that Willow Run's violation of the UBC was the proximate cause of his injuries and that such a violation is negligence per se.

Willow Run filed two motions for summary judgment and the trial court denied both motions. The case went to a jury trial in September of 1994. Bills called a building inspector to testify. The inspector had inspected the landing at Bills' request after the accident. The inspector determined that the landing was six and three-quarters inches below the threshold of the doorway and that the 1970 UBC, in effect at the time the building was constructed, required a 2–inch threshold. The inspector also testified that the handrails on the landing were 91 inches apart and the UBC required them to be no more than 88 inches apart. On cross-examination the inspector conceded that the two-riser stairs did not require handrails under the UBC. He also testified that the issuance of a certificate of occupancy would lead a reasonable building owner to believe that the building met all of the UBC requirements.

At the close of Bills' case in chief, the trial court granted Willow Run's motion for a directed verdict on the grounds that Bills had failed to show Willow Run had either actual or constructive knowledge of the alleged defective condition and UBC violation, and the trial court believed the accident probably would have happened regardless of the violation given the inclement weather conditions. Bills moved for a new trial based on trial court error, contending the trial court improperly concluded that he had not produced sufficient evidence of negligence to justify submission of the case to a jury, and that the trial court improperly concluded a violation of the UBC was not negligence per se. The motion for a new trial was denied.

Bills appealed and the court of appeals reversed. The court of appeals found that a violation of the UBC was negligence per se and "resulted in hidden or unanticipated dangers." *Bills v. Willow Run I Apartments,* 534 N.W.2d 286, 290 (Minn.App.1995). The court of appeals found sufficient evidence to present a question of fact to the jury as to the proximate cause of Bills' injuries.

So this is a landlord liability case. At first glance that doesn't seem very relevant to securing cargo on trucks. How will you use this case?

We now reverse, finding that common law landlord/tenant standards of liability apply. Thus, without notice of the violation and an opportunity to remedy, the landlord or owner is not negligent per se. We disagree with the court of appeals' decision that a UBC violation impliedly creates hidden or unanticipated dangers, thus somehow imputing knowledge to the landlord and owner.

In *Alderman's Inc. v. Shanks,* 536 N.W.2d 4 (Minn.1995), we held "that breach of a statute gives rise to negligence per se if the *persons harmed by that violation are within the intended protection of the statute,* and the *harm suffered is of the type the legislation was intended to prevent." Id.* at 8 (original emphasis) (quoting *Pacific Indemnity Co. v. Thompson–Yaeger, Inc.,* 260 N.W.2d 548 (Minn.1977)). However, in the case of a landlord, violation of the UBC without notice will not create negligence per se. In *Johnson v. O'Brien,* 258 Minn. 502, 105 N.W.2d 244 (1960), we held that the liability of a landlord extends to those dangerous conditions of which he had knowledge and those dangerous conditions "of which he had reasonable grounds to suspect." *Id.,* 105 N.W.2d at 246. If there is no knowledge or suspicion of any dangerous conditions, there is no negligence per se.

[1] Bills argued that Willow Run was negligent per se because the landing on which he fell met neither the Willmar Building Code nor the UBC. He argues that Willow Run had an obligation to know that the violation existed and could not simply rely on one inspector as proof that the landing was safe. It is his contention that Willow Run, as owner of the complex, should have known that the landing did not meet UBC height requirements and it should not be able to claim ignorance of the law. This argument is flawed.

Willow Run reasonably relied on the inspection reports of a state building inspector. Under Bills' theory, every landlord or owner would be required to re-inspect his/her building after the certified building inspector issued an occupancy permit and inspection report. Failure to do so could leave the landlord or owner liable under a negligence per se claim, if an inspector failed to identify a UBC violation and a tenant was injured.

Bills had knowledge of the threshold differential because he had lived there for seven months and had used the entry "countless times." He was also aware that it was still sleeting when he left for work the morning of the fall. Bills concedes that he slipped on the ice. He claims, however, that his injuries were directly caused by the violations of the UBC. It is his contention that, had the handrails and landing met Code, he would not have fallen, but would have been able to right himself after he slipped. Bills can only speculate that he may have been able to catch himself; he may also still have fallen and injured himself because the ice was the major factor in his fall, not the landing differential.

The North Carolina Supreme Court set a standard in similar cases in its opinion in *Lamm v. Bissette Realty, Inc.,* 327 N.C. 412, 395 S.E.2d 112, 114 (1990):

[T]he owner of a building may not be found negligent *per se* for a violation of the Code unless: (1) the owner knew or should have known of the Code violation; (2) the owner failed to take reasonable steps to remedy the violation; and (3) the violation proximately caused injury or damage.

We find this standard to have merit. It links the negligence per se and common law landlord/tenant standards into one that defines a fair and just result. This standard also marries well with section 104 of the 1994 version of the UBC. Section 104 sets out the rules of notice and remedy, and the consequences of failure to remedy once notice has been given.[1]

1 Section 104 of the 1994 Uniform Building Code has several sections that cover everything from the inspector's authority to testing procedures to ensure code compliance. In section 104.2.5 Occupancy violations, the Code states:

> whenever any building or structure * * * regulated by this code is being used contrary to the provisions of this code, the building official may order such use discontinued and the structure, or portion thereof, vacated by notice served on any person causing such use to be continued. Such person shall discontinue the use * * * after receipt of such notice to make the structure * * * comply with the requirements of this code.

1 U.B.C. § 104.2.5 (1994)(emphasis added).

[2] A landlord or owner is not negligent per se for a violation of the UBC unless: (1) the landlord or owner knew or should have known of the Code violation; (2) the landlord or owner failed to take reasonable steps to remedy the violation; (3) the injury suffered was the kind the Code was meant to prevent; and (4) the violation was the proximate cause of the injury or damage.

Ah—there's a statute in the preceding paragraph and a discussion of the rules of negligence per se here. Perhaps now it is becoming clearer how you can use this case....

We address briefly the reason the trial court granted the motion for a directed verdict. Bills argues that the trial court should have allowed the case to go to the jury. In *Usher v. Allstate Insurance Co.,* 300 Minn. 52, 218 N.W.2d 201 (1974), we held that the "trial court's authority to direct a verdict is to be exercised cautiously and sparingly. Caution is especially required where the motion is made upon the ground of failure of proof at the close of plaintiff's case in chief * * *." *Id.* 218 N.W.2d at 205 (citations omitted).

While the trial court's speculation may not have been correct that the fall would, even without the UBC violation, have occurred given the inclement weather, the decision itself was still sound. It was based upon the fact that Bills did not present any evidence that Willow Run knew of the Code violation. Bills did not show that the Code was designed to prevent persons from slipping on icy surfaces; and Bills brought forth no evidence that Willow Run's violation of the building code was the proximate cause of the accident.

We now reverse the court of appeals and remand to the trial court for reinstatement of the directed verdict.

Reversed and remanded.

615 N.W.2d 397
Court of Appeals of Minnesota.

Janice FUNCHESS, Trustee for the Heirs of J.W. HAYNES, decedent, Appellant,

v.

CECIL NEWMAN CORPORATION, et al., Respondents.

No. C8-00-90.

Aug. 8, 2000.

Review Granted Oct. 17, 2000.

> Uh-oh, this case has been overruled (on factual grounds not directly altering the substance of the law that could be applied to your case). Does it help you in any way? Ask yourself: why would we include it in this case file? Can you cite it? If so, what, if any, qualifiers should you include?

Reversed and remanded; motion denied.

Anderson, J., filed dissenting opinion.

Attorneys and Law Firms

John O. Murrin, III, Christopher A. LaNave, Murrin Law Firm, Edina, for appellant.

William F. Mohrman, Mohrman & Kaardal, P.A., Minneapolis, for respondents.

Considered and decided by AMUNDSON, Presiding Judge, CRIPPEN, Judge, and ANDERSON, Judge.

OPINION

AMUNDSON, Judge.

After third parties entered an apartment and killed a tenant, the tenant's wrongful death trustee sued the landlord, alleging the landlord's negligence contributed to the tenant's death. The landlord moved for summary judgment, and the district court granted the motion. Tenant's trustee appeals, alleging that (a) a Minneapolis housing ordinance required the landlord to repair the door to the apartment; (b) regardless of the duty imposed by the Minneapolis Housing ordinance, the landlord had an independent duty to make sure that the apartment was secure; and (c) the lease required the landlord to repair the door.

FACTS

On May 12, 1995, J.W. Haynes was murdered in his apartment. Intruders gained access to the apartment building without using force and subsequently entered the apartment he shared with his girlfriend and their son. Haynes' mother, appellant Janice Funchess, commenced a wrongful-death action against respondent Cecil Newman Corporation (Newman), owner of Haynes' apartment building. Funchess alleged that the assailants were able to gain entrance to the building through a security door that had a broken lock. The district court granted summary judgment, finding that Newman owed no duty to Haynes. This appeal followed.

ISSUES

I. Was respondent obligated to protect decedent from the criminal acts of third parties?

II. Did respondent owe the decedent a statutory duty of care to maintain door locks in working condition? If so, were sufficient questions of material fact raised, rendering the district court's grant of summary judgment erroneous?

III. Is the intervening cause of a criminal act sufficiently foreseeable, so as to maintain the chain of causation?

IV. Did respondent have a contractual duty to maintain the door locks in working condition?

V. Should appellant's motion to strike portions of respondent's brief be granted?

ANALYSIS

[1] [2] Summary judgment may be granted when there is no genuine issue of material fact and either party is entitled to judgment as a matter of law. Minn. R. Civ. P. 56.03. To prevail on a negligence claim, a plaintiff must show: (1) the existence of a duty; (2) breach of that duty; (3) that the breach proximately caused the injury; and (4) injury in fact. *Hudson v. Snyder Body, Inc.,* 326 N.W.2d 149, 157 (Minn.1982). The existence of a legal duty may be imposed by either the common law or a statute, *Steffey v. Soo Line R.R.,* 498 N.W.2d 304, 307 (Minn. App.1993), *review denied* (Minn. May 28, 1993), and is a question of law for the court to determine. *Larson v. Larson,* 373 N.W.2d 287, 289 (Minn.1985). But the determination of whether a duty has been breached is generally within the province of the jury. *Smith v. Carriere,* 316 N.W.2d 574, 575 (Minn.1982).

I. Common Law Duty and Special Relationship Exception

This appeal centers on what duty, if any, Newman owed Haynes. The district court granted summary judgment because it determined that Newman had no duty to protect Haynes. Specifically, the court concluded that no special relationship existed between Newman and Haynes that would give rise to a duty to protect.

Holding a landlord liable for the intentional criminal acts of a third party is a modern development, representing a change from the common law. *See Errico v. Southland Corp.*, 509 N.W.2d 585, 587 (Minn. App.1993) (generally, a person "has no duty to control the conduct of a third person in order to prevent that person from causing injury to another"), *review denied* (Minn. Jan. 27, 1994); *see also Donaldson v. Young Women's Christian Ass'n*, 539 N.W.2d 789, 792 (Minn.1995) (a person generally has no duty to act for the protection of another, even if he or she realizes or should realize that action is necessary).

[3] [4] [5] A landlord-tenant relationship, standing alone, is not sufficient to give rise to the duty to protect. *See Spitzak v. Hylands, Ltd.*, 500 N.W.2d 154, 156–57 (Minn.App.1993) (failing to find landlord liable where apartment complex neither exposed tenants to greater risks, nor presented a unique opportunity for criminals and criminal activity), *review denied* (Minn. July 15, 1993).[1] But a party may owe such a duty where a special relationship exists between that party and another that gives the other the right to protection. *Errico*, 509 N.W.2d at 587. When a special relationship exists, a party has the duty to take reasonable precautions against foreseeable criminal acts of third parties. *Id.* The rationale running through special relationships is that one party relinquishes part of its autonomy, or the ability to control the environment, in favor of another, usually dominant, party. *See id.* (special relationships exist when one entrusts her safety to another and the other accepts that entrustment). The imposition of liability on the dominant party not only redresses the imbalance of power, but places the precautionary burden more directly on such party. *Id.*

1 Liability can be imposed on landlords for the criminal acts of third parties in certain situations. [citations omitted]

Historically, this principle did not apply to a typical landlord-tenant relationship. In pre-industrial-age leases, tenants did not usually relinquish their autonomy or their ability to control their surroundings. A typical tenant had full control over the land, including its own actions on the land. Thus, these relationships were properly excluded from the special relationships. Changes in society have caused modern leases to differ materially from those in the past. The hotel-and-guest relationship was one of the first to be considered special. Courts extended the special relationship to hotels because the reasons for the rule were acutely present; guests had no autonomy or ability to control

their surroundings. Likewise, tenants in apartment buildings, whose leases are often of short duration, cannot be expected to secure common areas of the building by individually making the necessary expenditures, for example, to install and maintain locks on outside entrances. *See Tedder v. Raskin*, 728 S.W.2d 343, 348 (Tenn.App.1987) (landlord may be liable for injuries to tenants from third-party crimes on the premises because landlord is in far superior position to take necessary steps to secure premises).

[6] When Haynes signed the lease, he relinquished to Newman exclusive control over building security, the building's security devices, and the areas outside his apartment unit. These factors are sufficient to create the existence of a special relationship as the logical extrapolation of the existing common law governing the special-relationship between innkeeper and guest. *See generally Boone v. Martinez*, 567 N.W.2d 508, 510 (Minn.1997) (discussing innkeeper liability in the context of a tavern's duty to maintain safety and order for protection of its patrons). Because the special relationship exception applies, Newman had the duty to use reasonable care to prevent foreseeable criminal acts of third parties. Newman may have breached this duty if it took no action to remedy the defective lock, a genuine issue of a material fact.

[7] [8] But even if Newman had no duty to protect Haynes by providing reasonable security measures, it did have a duty to maintain the security measures already undertaken for the protection of its tenants. Specifically, by providing a secured back door to the building, Newman assumed the duty to maintain the locking mechanism on that door. *See Cracraft v. City of St. Louis Park*, 279 N.W.2d 801, 806 (Minn.1979) (finding municipality's duty of care with regard to fire code violations when municipality assumes to act for the protection of others, as distinguished from acting merely for itself when it inspects property for fire-code violations); *see also State by Humphrey v. Philip Morris, Inc.*, 551 N.W.2d 490, 493 (Minn.1996) ("[O]ne who assumes to act, even though gratuitously, may thereby become subject to the duty of acting carefully, if he acts at all.").

[9] [10] Where a person or entity voluntarily assumes a duty, then that duty must be exercised with reasonable care and the failure to so act may result in liability. *Nickelson v. Mall of Am. Co.*, 593 N.W.2d 723, 726 (Minn.App.1999). We conclude that Newman had a duty to maintain the security locking mechanism on

the apartment building's back door. The parties dispute whether, in fact, the locking mechanism was working properly at the time of Haynes' murder. This, of course, is another unresolved genuine issue of material fact. Not recognizing this, the district court again erred in granting summary judgment to Newman.

II. Statutory Duty

[11] [12] Funchess also argues that Newman's duty arose by statute. The difference between a statutorily imposed duty and a duty arising under common law is that the duty imposed by statute is fixed. *Zerby v. Warren,* 297 Minn. 134, 139, 210 N.W.2d 58, 62 (1973). If an ordinance imposes a duty and one neglects to perform that duty, then he or she is "liable to those for whose protection the statute was enacted for any damages resulting proximately from such * * * neglect." *Henderson v. Bjork Monument Co.,* 222 Minn. 241, 245, 24 N.W.2d 42, 45 (1946) (citation omitted). A breach of this nature generally constitutes conclusive evidence of negligence, or negligence per se. *Zerby,* 297 Minn. at 139, 210 N.W.2d at 62. Minneapolis, Minn., Code of Ordinances § 244.675 (1998), requires that all doorways leading to the exterior or entry of a multiple dwelling, such as the apartment building in question, "be secured by a locking device * * * that will engage and lock automatically when the door is in the closed position within the frame provided." The ordinance also mandates that "[a]ll locking devices required by this section shall be kept in a professional state of maintenance and repair." *Id.*

The parties dispute whether the locking mechanism on the back door was broken. Funchess presented the affidavit of Angela Bennett, who stated that on the day of the murder, she was able to enter the apartment through the back door without using a key, although nothing was propping the door open and no one opened the door for her. Newman, on the other hand, introduced an affidavit from Randy Gott, stating that tenants often thwarted the locking mechanism on the back door by propping the door open. Additionally, Gott's affidavit asserted it was not uncommon for people to be buzzed into the building by other tenants.

[13] [14] Considering the ordinance-imposed duty to maintain the locking mechanism on the back door, the district court's grant of summary judgment was premature. Determinations regarding breach and causation—that is, whether the lock in this case was actually broken—generally present questions of fact properly determined by a jury. *See Smith,* 316 N.W.2d at 575 (breach); *Lubbers v. Anderson,* 539 N.W.2d 398, 402 (Minn.1995) (causation). When reasonable minds could reach only one conclusion, the existence of proximate cause is, of course, a question of law. *Lubbers,* 539 N.W.2d at 402. But there must also be a showing that the defendant's conduct "was a substantial factor in bringing about the injury." *Flom v. Flom,* 291 N.W.2d 914, 917 (Minn.1980).

[15] Here, Newman owed a duty to Haynes to keep the back-door lock working properly. Assuming, for purposes of this appeal, that Newman breached this duty by allowing the back-door lock to remain in a state of disrepair, it cannot be said that Newman would have no reason to anticipate that breach of this duty would result in injury to its tenants. The parties disagree whether the alleged breach of this duty was a substantial factor in bringing about Haynes' death, or whether Haynes himself was responsible by allowing his assailants access into the building. More than one conclusion as to the causes of Haynes' death can be reached, and because reasonable minds could differ on the issue of causation, summary judgment in favor of Newman should not have been granted.

III. Intervening Cause

[16] A theoretical problem results when the actual harm is caused by a force other than that initiated by the negligent actor. These forces may supersede the original actor's liability. *See Pearson v. Henkemeyer,* 503 N.W.2d 504, 507 (Minn.App.1993) (generally, a third party's criminal act "breaks the causation chain" unless the criminal act "is reasonably foreseeable"), *review denied* (Minn. Sept. 30, 1993). An intervening cause is one that comes about after the negligent act. It must come between the negligent act of the actor and the resulting harm, shifting the responsibility for the harm to the intervening act. If the actual harm is caused by an intervening act, the negligent actor is absolved from liability. *See* Restatement (Second) of Torts § 448 (1965).

[17] [18] [19] But where the occurrence of the intervening act is reasonably foreseeable, the chain of causation will not be broken. *Id.* In this case, the assault is entirely foreseeable under the totality of the circumstances. A lock is intended to prevent crimes against people and property within the area it secures. If the lock is ineffective, a crime is a foreseeable result. This is especially the case where, as here, the building is located in an area notorious for criminal activity. When a landlord beaches his duty to maintain a lock, the landlord

may be held liable for the foreseeable result—in this case, a violent assault resulting in death.

IV. Lease As Contract

[20] [21] [22] A lease is one form of contract. *Minneapolis Pub. Hous. Auth. v. Lor,* 591 N.W.2d 700, 704 (Minn.1999). As such, the parties can insert almost any provision they choose. Here, the lease required the landlord to "maintain the common areas and facilities in safe condition * * * [and] make necessary repairs with reasonable promptness." Where contract language is unambiguous, we will give it its plain and ordinary meaning. *Bob Useldinger & Sons, Inc. v. Hangsleben,* 505 N.W.2d 323, 328 (Minn.1993). A reasonable construction of the lease requires Newman to maintain the locks on the building doors in working condition and to repair them promptly if they are not locking properly. A question of fact exists as to whether Newman breached its contractual duty to keep the back-door lock in working condition. Thus, the district court's grant of summary judgment to Newman was premature.

V. Motion to Strike

Appellant requests that this court strike portions of respondent's brief that rely on alleged hearsay statements given by Newman's security guard. *See Walker v. Wayne County, Iowa,* 850 F.2d 433, 434 (8th Cir.1988) (in a summary judgment proceeding, only evidence admissible or usable at trial should be considered). But we need not consider the security guard's reports of alleged comments made by residents of the apartment in determining whether sufficient facts are in dispute to render summary judgment improper. Because we find the objected-to portions of Newman's brief irrelevant to our decision, we deny appellant's motion to strike.

DECISION

Newman owed the decedent a common-law duty, a statutory duty, and a contractual duty to maintain the security locking mechanism on the back door of the apartment building in working condition. These duties were not abrogated by the foreseeable criminal acts of a third party. Because genuine issues of material fact exists with regard to the security door's condition and causation, we reverse the district court's grant of summary judgment and remand for further proceedings.

Reversed and remanded; motion denied. G. BARRY

ANDERSON, Judge (dissenting).

I respectfully dissent.

I believe the majority opinion in this case represents an extension of a very narrow exception that Minnesota courts have applied to negligence claims.

Historically, Minnesota courts have rejected negligence actions against a property owner for injuries to a tenant caused by the criminal activities of another, usually finding that the property owner had no duty to protect the tenant. *Spitzak v. Hylands,* 500 N.W.2d 154 (Minn.App.1993); *H.B. v. Whittemore,* 552 N.W.2d 705, 709, 710 (Minn.1996) (no special relationship existed to impose a duty on a trailer-park manager to protect children from another resident even though the manager knew the resident had a prior conviction for child molestation).

> Dissents are opinions that cannot garner the support of a majority of judges. They are not law. So why would judges ever write them, and why would lawyers or law students ever read them? Often we don't. But judges take the time to write and publish their dissents when they strongly believe that the majority is incorrectly understanding the rule or incorrectly applying it to the facts of the case. Sometimes they succeed in persuading higher courts that they are right, or convincing legislators to redraft the applicable law to clarify the source of the dispute.
>
> Cases in law school textbooks tend to be edited pretty heavily, so if you encounter both a majority and dissenting opinion they are both probably included for a reason. Read each carefully, both to pull out their differing legal theories and to try to determine just why the casebook authors thought it was important that you read both.

The exception expanded by the majority here provides that a duty may exist "if there is a special relationship between the parties and * * * the risk of harm is foreseeable." *N.W. v. Anderson,* 478 N.W.2d 542, 544 (Minn.App.1991). That case warned, however, that the supreme court has developed "a rather rigid standard" and specifically went on to note that the standard applied only when "specific threats are made against specific victims." *Id.* at 544.

There is no evidence in this case that the relationship between the decedent and the respondents was in any way special. At the end of the day this relationship was nothing more than an ordinary and routine landlord/tenant business transaction. If a special relationship exists here, under these facts, it is difficult to determine when a special relationship in any other ordinary landlord/tenant business transaction would not exist. Indeed, the principles enunciated here represent a worrisome expansion of landlord liability.

As to the alleged violation of the Minneapolis housing ordinance, because the issue was not raised at the district court it was waived and thus it need not be addressed by this court. *Thiele v. Stich,* 425 N.W.2d 580 (Minn.1988). But even if the principle in *Thiele* is not applied here and the merits of the claim are reached, the Minnesota Supreme Court has made clear in *Bills v. Willow Run I Apartments,* 547 N.W.2d 693, 695 (Minn.1996), that the principles of negligence per se do not apply unless the owner knew of the code violation and, among other things, failed to take reasonable steps to remedy the violation. There is little, if any, evidence in the record establishing either notice to the landlord or failure to cure by the landlord.

Ultimately, every crime is, to a greater or lesser extent, "foreseeable." The Minnesota Supreme Court has, succinctly and thoroughly, addressed the difficulty of foreseeability in the context of criminal acts of third parties by noting:

The question whether a private party must provide protection for another is not solved merely by recourse to "foreseeability". Everyone can foresee the commission of crime virtually anywhere and at any time. If foreseeability itself gave rise to a duty to provide "police" protection for others, every residential curtilage, every shop, every store, every manufacturing plant would have to be patrolled by private arms of the owner. And since hijacking and attack upon occupants of motor vehicles are also foreseeable, it would be the duty of every motorist to provide armed protection for his passengers and the property of others. Of course, none of this is at all palatable. * * *

How can one know what measures will protect against the thug, the narcotic addict, the degenerate, the psychopath, the psychotic?

Pietila v. Congdon, 362 N.W.2d 328 (Minn.1985) (claim that private-property owner is liable in negligence for injuries suffered by a guest as a result of criminal attack [murder]).

Under the facts of this case, there is no foreseeability, and thus no negligence, on the part of the landlord.

Finally, I would sustain the judgment of the district court simply because the plaintiff, under any legal theory, cannot establish causation. There isn't a shred of evidence anywhere in the record demonstrating how the murderers entered the building and appellant addresses this issue only by way of an affidavit in which it is noted that the murderers "must have" entered the building through the back door. There is no particular reason to believe this as there are no eye witnesses to the entrance of the murderers onto the property, no documentary or visual entrance that the murderers entered through the back door and, indeed, there isn't even any sign of forcible entry into the decedent's apartment. Even assuming the highly dubious existence of a duty and a breach of duty, plaintiffs must still demonstrate a causal connection between the breach and injury and this they have not done. The district court should be affirmed on the basis of causation alone.

I would affirm the grant of summary judgment rendered by the district court.

Understand the Problem

What is the purpose of a demand letter?

Put simply, a demand letter is a written request in which one lawyer asks another attorney or party to do something (or sometimes to refrain from doing something, though more often that kind of request is referred to as a "cease-and-desist" letter).

The kind of pre-litigation demand letter this assignment asks for is usually intended to lay out the basis for a client's claims, in the hope of opening settlement negotiations prior to proceeding to the more costly step of litigation. In some instances demand letters are legal prerequisites to filing a complaint, in which case the statute may set out specific requirements for the letter (not the case here). In circumstances like yours where a demand letter is not mandatory before commencing a lawsuit, what goes into the letter will be up to you.

According to law professor Richard K. Neumann Jr., for a demand letter to be persuasive it should do three things:

(1) State your client's position on the facts and the law;

(2) Tell the other side what you expect them to do; and

(3) Give them incentives to comply with your demand.[1]

Sometimes in law practice attorneys might focus only on the facts of a case in a demand letter and would leave out most of the applicable rules of law. They may do so because they assume the legal basis for their claim is already fully understood by opposing counsel, because they want to hold back on fully articulating their legal theories, or because they do not actually expect to achieve resolution before litigation and instead view the letter's purpose as solely about persuading the other side of the strength of their case. That is *not* your objective in this assignment—you should aim to articulate the legal basis for your claim by summarizing both the legal rules and their application to the facts in order to show your client has a strong case.

In addition to being persuasive, your letter should also be clear, readable, and as brief as possible. If it absolutely has to be longer than a couple of pages, consider breaking it up into sections to make it more easily skimmed and accessible to your reader.

What will convince the other side to settle?

Let's begin with some obvious starting points. The accident here seems to have been purely un-intentional, so your case will almost certainly sound solely on negligence. Depending on jurisdiction we might express the elements of negligence slightly differently, but you have probably learned that a plaintiff has to show:

1. a **Duty** of care

2. which was **Breached**

3. **Causing** (Actually and Proximately)

4. **Harm** [damages] to the plaintiff

At trial your client will have the burden of proving each of these elements by a preponderance of the evidence. This means that even at this early stage in the case an attorney should be thinking about how to gather sufficient evidence for every element: e.g., to demonstrate damages relating to medical expenses you will need to produce originals of the hospital bills, and perhaps subpoena as a witness a representative from the hospital's accounting department to authenticate them.

---

1. Legal Reasoning And Legal Writing: Structure, Strategy And Style 85 (5th ed. 2005).

Yet even though a good lawyer should already be anticipating what will be necessary for all elements of the negligence claim, this does not necessarily mean that each of them is equally important now in the demand letter. For example, the hospital bill you have seems to be a consolidated summary of charges intended primarily to show the patient the total amount owed. For trial you may eventually need original billing statements from every hospital department broken down into specific individual charges. But do you really have to have that kind of detail now? Probably not, because your primary objective is just to show you've got a good chance of winning a case if you brought one, and to state how much compensation your client is seeking to recover. Including a simple statement about how much compensation you seek may be enough to cover this element for the purpose of this demand letter.[2]

To figure out which elements you should emphasize in your demand letter, it will be helpful to spend some time thinking like the defense attorney.

If you received such a letter, would damages be your first concern? Doubtful. You would probably expect that at some point you would force opposing counsel to substantiate the amount in question, and that you would aim where possible either to exclude or challenge the evidence of damages that were offered. But for now, you are likely focused on other questions. You would take for granted that if this accident actually happened the way the plaintiff describes then some harm probably occurred (solid three-inch by eight-inch steel beams dropping onto a person's leg = ouch). In a similar vein, are you really going to pin your hope for a successful defense on the possibility that the plaintiff won't be able to show causation? (Steel beams falling from any height onto a human leg makes injury pretty direct and foreseeable).

Chances are, then, opposing counsel's attention is most immediately focused on wondering whether you will be able to show that the defendant owed any duty to the client, and whether this particular accident was the result of a breach of any duty that may have existed. Both of these elements may end up genuinely contested as this case develops. But as any tort law expert knows (and by expert here we mean you, a law student who is soon to be a lawyer) an easy way to sidestep contentious debate of these issues would be to show negligence per se. Short of that, showing that defendant violated industry norms or customs in securing cargo might go a long way toward establishing negligent behavior.[3]

> Can you quickly explain why? Remember that a determination that conduct was negligent per se essentially takes breach of duty off the table and allows plaintiffs to proceed directly to causation and harm. Breach of custom is not so sweeping or absolute, but it is valuable evidence that conduct may be considered negligent.

What all of this means is that your demand letter should at the very least contain information sufficient to establish your ability to make out all elements of a negligence claim against Certified Lumber. You should probably devote the most attention, however, to your contention that the defendants did in fact breach a duty of care owed to Tanger. Assuming you believe it is warranted,

---

2. Which is not to suggest that there might not be strategic advantages to providing more detail. If the goal is a quick and easy settlement, it may well make sense to be more specific about how you arrive at the sum you are demanding. Or to suggest that you have a strong case by subtly emphasizing the kinds of evidence you will be able to produce. But these important tactical considerations do not alter the underlying fact that to satisfy the elements of a negligence claim all you must do for the moment is in some way articulate that your client has experienced harm that should be compensated.

3. Another means of sidestepping proof of breach in this case might be invoking *res ipsa loquitur*. Indeed it is quite arguable that this is the sort of accident which only occurs when cargo in negligently secured, that the defendant had exclusive control over the truck' cargo, and that no actions by the plaintiff or any other person contributed to the injury-causing circumstances. So maybe this is a theory you would choose to avail yourself of as this case proceeds. But invoking *res ipsa* doctrine at this point in the case has some strategic perils. The doctrine developed in cases where it was challenging to identify precisely what had happened, and most lawyers and law students learned in that context. As a result, relying on *res ipsa* now may suggest to opposing counsel that you do not believe that you will be able prove a breach of duty. That implication is hardly consistent with inducing a quick settlement. Moreover, demand letters are not expected to recite all possible avenues to press your claims and there is no waiver of issues that are not introduced. You are therefore advised either to mention *res ipsa* only tangentially in your demand letter or to omit it altogether.

you should explain why the defendants' conduct was negligent per se, or alternatively, why it violated industry customs in a way that would make it easy to find that defendants breached their duties.

Extract Material Facts

Remember: which facts are material will depend on what the law is

Material facts are those relevant to determining the legal question at issue. But that can pretty quickly lead lawyers to some fairly circular reasoning. Facts[4] are only "material" if they matter with respect to the applicable law. So then what law applies? Rules that help decide the issues pertaining to the facts at hand. Starting to get pretty inextricable, isn't it? In the end, what is material may be in the eye of the beholder. But if we cannot definitively determine which facts are material until we know exactly which legal rules apply, where and how do we ever start?

Circular or not, as lawyers working on a case we simply *have* to start somewhere. First on the agenda is usually trying to get down the story of what happened or what may be at issue in the problem presented by your client. One benefit of legal education is that you gain enough general knowledge of legal rules to at least have a rough sense what law might apply, so that you can begin to formulate a working sense of which parts of the story will matter legally. Start there, but do not make the mistake of presuming that you are ever finished digesting the facts your case may turn upon. As long as you treat your internal version of what matters as provisional, and continue to review and revise it in light of the specific applicable law as you uncover it, you are probably doing all that you can.

For this case file you know you will eventually have to prove that Certified Lumber's employees were somehow negligent in securing the steel beams the truck was transporting, and that this poor tethering of the cargo actually and proximately caused Tanger's verified injuries.[5] We have also concluded that proving breach of duty may be the most important and challenging part of our case, and we know that part of the job will be easier if we can show a violation of a pertinent statute, ordinance, or industry custom.

What all this suggests is that facts pertaining to how the accident occurred, and to the usual or required practices for securing commercial cargo in transit, are pretty likely to be material to the most important arguments in this case.

How did this accident happen?

We should start by noting what information we have so far, what witnesses will be available to talk to as the case progresses, and what we can ascertain about their credibility. People who might provide useful information in this case include our client Edmund Tanger; the driver Marcus Perlin (who might not be willing to talk to us, and in any case cannot be contacted by us directly if he is represented by counsel); Mabel Hampton and Joan Nestle, the witnesses we know about so far; and

---

4. "Facts" should probably be in quotations here because we are using the term to mean both those realities that can be unquestionably established, and those events or interpretations which may be argued by a party but with which the opposing party might not agree. In other words, it is worth noting explicitly that for purposes of legal analysis, the "facts" in the equation may be either **alleged** or already **determined**. Perhaps the legal profession should come up with some other term to distinguish what parties are *arguing* is true from what has been fully settled. Given the gorgeous complexity of the English language it seems a safe bet that we will not do so any time soon.

5. If the case goes to trial and you name both Marcus Perlin and Certified Lumber as defendants you may further allege that Perlin was negligent in driving onto the curb and jostling the cargo. Since the demand you are drafting at the moment is going just to the lumber company, can you see why it might be unwise to raise that issue now? It opens the possibility of the two defendants arguing with one another over whose alleged negligence actually caused the injury, which makes a quick settlement with one of the parties less likely.

Jon Boos, whom we will probably use as an expert witness (though because he does this profession-ally we should be aware that he may charge for any examination of the case beyond an initial cursory consultation).

Is the story we are hearing from these folks consistent? Do we have any reason to doubt what any of them have to tell us? So far probably not, though of course we should continue to work to verify their versions of events and locate additional evidence if possible. In the meantime while we continue investigating, we likely have a clear enough sense of what we expect to be able to prove that we can at least tentatively construct an image of what took place. That is probably sufficient for the purpose of writing a quick demand letter even if we continue to investigate prior to and after filing a formal Complaint.

Assuming what the client reported is accurate, it seems that large steel beams being transported by Certified Lumber/Perlin's truck came loose as Perlin was driving, perhaps up onto the curb. The street the truck was on appears to have been a small municipal road rather than a more major thoroughfare (inferred from the 25-mph speed limit). From what we know so far the truck seems to have been moving fairly slowly, and well under the established speed limit. When the beams fell they struck our client, who was walking nearby.

> Your thoughts in reading the file notes should have gone something like: "Be-cause the speed limit is 25 and there were pedestrians it may be a local street. At the very least it probably wasn't a highway or major thorough-fare. That means it probably wasn't an interstate highway, so may be governed by state law."
>
> Of course you'll need to confirm that, but using out-of-law-school knowledge to draw reasonable inferences is a useful way to enrich your analysis.

What we don't know for sure could matter as well, though. Was Tanger in the street or was he on the sidewalk when he was hit by the beams? He reports that before the accident he had been "crossing the street diagonal-ly." Does that sound like the best practice to you? Is it even legal? Good lawyers read into the facts and try to picture them so they can imagine not just what took place, but what *might* have taken place. That's how we anticipate problems in our cases to avoid unpleasant last-minute surprises in our opponent's evidence.

But this is why it is important to remember that determining which facts are material is recursive: we need to remember what the rules are to decide whether any of this is legally significant.

Take a moment to imagine the worst-case scenario that seems possible from what we know: what if your client was jaywalking when the accident occurred and jaywalking was a violation of Minnesota law? Then in addi-tion to having been subject to a ticket or other law enforcement sanction (which as far as we know did not happen) your client would probably have been behaving negligently. Yikes—now you can picture opposing counsel raising contributory negligence as a defense! And perhaps claiming con-tributory negligence per se for good measure! But wait a minute before you panic. Both the rules of negligence generally, and the rules of negli-gence per se, require that the unlawful conduct was the cause of the injury. Was that the case here? If not, then perhaps our client's means of crossing the street is not in fact material to the harm that he suffered.

> This kind of thinking shows what it real-ly means to understand a rule of law. You need to do more than simply be able to state the rule accurately and precisely (although that's a baseline requirement). You have to grasp the concept deeply to be able to quickly sort through when it does and does not apply. Were you able to think this point through for our problem before read-ing this prompt? If not, keep working on deepening your comprehension.

What do we know about how cargo is supposed to be secured?

Our case file provides at least three sources of information on how truck cargo should to be secured: the expert witness, the Minnesota stat-ute, and the federal regulations. Read all three carefully to decide whether they are consistent. Remember that differences are not automatically in-consistencies, and ask yourself what a reasonable loader of steel beams would do in light of the information provided by each of these sources.

> For an example of a "difference" that does not lead to an "inconsistency," imagine that one state required that cargo be tied down with "webbing at least 3" in width" while another was si-lent about the type of material re-quired. Tying cargo with 4-inch web-bing would comply with both rules.

Next, ask what each source contributes to your case and how authoritative it is. For example, Mr. Boos' observations seem helpful to your case, but how and in what way? For starters, even though his opinion is just that, an individual judgment, and so will not make out a negligence per se argument, it *can* certainly help to establish a general breach of a duty of care. It may well be valuable evidence for that element. But is there any stronger way to use this testimony?

Your last step will be to look at the language of the statutes and regulations that you are working with. You know that if the way the cargo was loaded does not follow the practices required by applicable statutes, your case will be easier to win because in effect the first two elements will be off the table (and you believe that substantiating causation and damages will be straightforward). But look carefully. For there to be negligence per se you will need to establish two things: that the cargo in question was not loaded according to the guidelines *and* that the guidelines in question were legally binding on the defendants. If you can meet both of these requirements then the rules will be enormously helpful to you.

If you cannot, does that necessarily mean that the rules are useless in building your case? Lawyers think creatively. We cannot ignore the law and only rarely can change it, but within the rules and facts we have arrayed we try to find ways to use every possible piece of support for our cases.

[By the way, one important point to observe for your legal studies is that thus far we are discussing the potential statutes and regulations regarding how cargo should be secured for trucking in our consideration of the "facts" in this case file. These are indeed rules of law, so why would we not talk

> Law students sometimes struggle to discern whether they are dealing with matters of law or fact, and it is worth recognizing that this example shows us that to make that determination we should look *conceptually* at what is genuinely at issue.

about them as the "rules" here? Hopefully the answer is self-evident—they may have been rules that applied to the truck company's loading of cargo, but for the purpose of negligence per se the existence (and arguable relevance) of these guidelines serves as a **fact** to which the tort **law** of custom and/or negligence per se may or may not apply. Here, for determining negligent conduct, we are wondering precisely what were the governing guidelines pertaining to cargo transport, so for our analysis they function as factual evidence.]

State Rules of Law Accurately and Precisely

What legal authority do you have?

The first thing an experienced attorney might do with the case file here is to skim through the materials to locate sources of law and then immediately categorize and prioritize them. You will recall that the *Restatement of Torts 3d* is a secondary source, and a national one at that. By definition, this means it is not a definitive resource for finding Minnesota law. Yet seasoned attorneys might nevertheless scan that material first before moving on to the state cases. Why? Because secondary sources are often the best place to gain a review or summary of common black-letter law.

Most seasoned attorneys are not embarrassed to need some brush-up on topics that they know they once studied, but may not recall in detail. Going through related sections of a Restatement before getting into the specific state case law will familiarize a reader with the broad outlines of the rules so she or he knows what to look for when reading the cases. It may sometimes help a careful reader to note where a particular jurisdiction deviates from more common legal principles, which could be important to understanding the precise rules in that state. In addition, the *Restatement of Torts* is cited frequently by advocates and judges and is considered a rather important resource in tort law. It cannot possibly hurt to know how it defines the elements of negligence and negligence per se or how it explains the role of custom in proving breach.

Once you have absorbed the general doctrine it will be time to move on to the case law. Here, too, an experienced attorney would probably be fairly methodical: skimming first to see what kinds of courts decided the cases (for our problem all are from state courts within Minnesota, so unless overruled, probably all binding authority for your case), next to see how the cases are organized (chronologically), what topics they address (one covers custom as proof of negligent conduct, while three seem more helpful for understanding negligence per se), and finally whether they remain good law (last case appears to have been overruled, which should raise red flags). The next step, then, will be to focus on getting what you need from the case law.

Read cases effectively

Anyone who has begun law school has probably spent some time thinking about how to read cases. Digesting courts' decisions into case briefs or similar notes is how most students prepare for most law classes most of the time. So does that mean that you have fully mastered that skill? Maybe, but perhaps there is still more you can do to develop further expertise.

At the outset, note that for this project you are reading cases for a different purpose than when you read to prepare for many law classes. You represent a particular client, and you have a specific objective. You want to understand exactly how negligence per se and custom work in Minnesota negligence claims in the hope that they will strengthen your case. So read and take notes with those particular goals in mind.

Researcher Leah M. Christensen compared the way that novices (beginning law students) and experts (practicing lawyers and judges) read legal opinions, and she found some striking differences.[6] While reading through cases experienced attorneys read more deliberately and less by default. They spent far more time than law students did in connecting what they read to their prior knowledge and understanding of the law, considering the purpose of their reading, and bringing in real-world experience to contextualize what happened in the case. They often had specific questions or hypotheses they were testing as they read, and they were more willing to challenge or disagree with the text even if it was binding authority. Finally, and perhaps most freeing for some law students, they read flexibly—skipping or skimming parts that were less closely related to their purpose, and switching the order in which they read to suit their own needs (i.e., early on in their reading many flipped ahead to learn the outcome of the case if that was not made clear at the outset of the opinion, then they returned to reading the decision in sequence).

What all this means is that to read cases like an expert lawyer you must do so actively and with a clear purpose in mind. When you are confused about a point you should work to resolve your confusion before you move on. And not incidentally, you should ask whether the confusion is your own, or whether it points instead to some lack of clarity or inconsistency within the text itself. (And if it is yours, clarify before continuing; if it is the court's, pinpoint exactly what is confused, and try to consider possible reasons for the lack of clarity.) You should read critically, which means that you are permitted—no, *urged*—to "talk back to" the text. Always read to discern not just what the case is saying, but also what it is *not* saying that it could.

In subsequent chapters you will not receive quite this much direction (yet you may nonetheless be disappointed to find that the points still do not tell you exactly what to draw from the case law to complete your assignment), but for this case file your supervisor would expect you to see that:

✓ A clear-cut goal is to find the specific rules of negligence per se and custom evidence in tort that are used in Minnesota so you can use them in your demand letter.

✓ This means that the details of procedural posture and evidentiary standards may not matter to you as much as they did to the actual lawyers and parties in some of these cases.

---

6. Leah M. Christensen, *The Paradox of Legal Expertise: A Study of Experts and Novices Reading the Law*, 2008 B.Y.U. Educ. & L.J. 53 (2008).

✓ The first case, *Schmidt v. Beninga*, addresses only evidence of community custom, while the next three focus on negligence per se. Accordingly, those three should probably be read and examined together while the first one can be considered independently.

✓ Several of these cases have facts quite similar to yours in that they deal with accidents relating to commercial trucking. Two others have to do with a landlord's liability for harmful incidents that allegedly resulted from improper maintenance. It is always tempting to presume that the cases with the most directly comparable facts will be the most helpful to you. But that's not really how legal analysis works. Instead, we are either looking for clear statements of abstracted legal principles (rules) or facts that are analogous because they pose the same legal questions, not just because they are alike.

> Grouping the cases this way is essential because it helps you determine how to use the rules. When a rule of law is derived from multiple sources you must "synthesize" it—meaning craft a rule statement that is consistent and harmonious with all sources (and sometimes is subtly crated to lean toward your favored interpretation). If the rule is definitively established you simply need to state and cite it. When drawing from one source it's more certain that your rule will be one of the latter. From multiple sources you'll need to decide whether synthesis is required, which will depend on how similarly the cases describe and deploy the rule.

✓ The overruled *Funchess* case is most likely not one you are going to want to cite to opposing counsel. Much of it pertains to issues that are not vital to your case, like intervening cause or the unique duties that owed when an alleged tortfeasor and the plaintiff have a "special relationship." So as was hinted in the call-out box near the beginning of the case, you should ask yourself why this case was even included in the file.[7]

Explain the rules that support your position

As we have already observed, legal analysis at its most basic = rules of law applied to facts. Thus you will always in some fashion have to articulate the rules of law that you are using.

For this project you should expect that your letter to Certified Lumber will almost certainly be sent immediately to their counsel. Perhaps for that audience you need not didactically explain the basic elements of negligence, which could come across as patronizing. But at the very least you will need to show why you believe they can be met. And if you expect to argue that either the company or its driver breached a duty owed to the plaintiff by violating a statute, regulation, or common shipping practice, you should expect to be more explicit about the principles of law on which you rely.

Describing legal rules precisely from an advocate's position is as much an art as a science. Attorneys-at-law are court officers who are bound by the oaths and ethics of our profession to portray the law accurately. This is unquestionably your first obligation. But then there is your commitment to advocate for your client. Lawyers seek to find strategic advantage wherever they can, so is it any surprise that we usually try to state the law truthfully but also favorably? In other words, where there is room for reasonable interpretation, most attorneys would tilt their descriptions of legal rules

---

7. Or ask alternatively, why you were not also given the subsequent opinion. And therein lies some hint of the answer: perhaps it was not crucial for you to read the overruling case because the Court of Appeals decision was provided less as an authority for you to rely on and more of a resource to aid in your understanding.

Either question—why this case or why not that one—is a terrific one to ponder. In actual practice you will naturally be researching and identifying your own authorities, but for educational purposes you are frequently given selected cases and statutes to read. In their haste to comprehend assigned reading material law students often overlook the most obvious question to consider: Why was it assigned? Does it change or set out important legal doctrine? Is it simply one of many examples of similar decision? Does it show a progression in legal thought, or valuable counterpoint when juxtaposed with other assigned material? The more thoughtfully you ask and try to answer these kinds of questions the more effectively (and as an added bonus, efficiently) you will read for all of your classes. And of course, the more thoroughly prepared you will be when you begin to practice law.

toward their client's position. Not too much: even aside from important ethical problems in skewed interpretation, there are strategic concerns of losing credibility if your positions are obviously open to very credible alternative views. The sweet spot is usually interpreting favorably just enough to subtly tilt how the law is framed in the direction of your client's interests.

Ask yourself whether those tactical considerations apply in this case. Will both you and opposing counsel describe the Minnesota rules of negligence per se in exactly the same way? Where the rules are so clearly settled that all parties would concur in every detail then there is little strategic work left to do. All of the action will then be in the ways counsel argue that they do or do not apply to facts. Which circumstances are more apt for this case file, and for what questions?

One last point for now about stating rules of law: remember that legal language is both functional and technical. In short, the legal profession is one of communication, and phrasing that helps clarify meaning for an intended audience is always helpful. But meticulous accuracy matters as well. Lawyers cannot rephrase rules just to make better prose, and there are times when particular words or phrases have such exact meaning or connotations that no substitute could convey the precise meaning needed.

Apply Rules to Facts

Careful elucidation of exactly how the rules governing a situation apply to specific facts is the most important part of legal reasoning. Why is it, then, that this is often the part that law students are inclined to shortchange or omit? So much so that if anything can be said to be the greatest determiner of law school grades, it is probably the quality of explanations provided in legal analysis. All things being equal, most of the time most law students work incredibly hard and learn what they have to, no matter how complicated. Frequently, therefore, the subtle differences of who understands and explains it most effectively can make the difference between acceptable and outstanding work.

To truly understand why this is the case, it is helpful to remember just why it is that explanations matter so much in law. Our legal system is adversarial: legal work is always conducted in the shadow of actual or potential conflict.[8]

Thus unlike other disciplines in which it might be presumed that an audience wants to follow along a particular line of thinking as it is being conveyed, readers and listeners of legal arguments are presumed to be trying to disagree with them wherever possible. Explanations fill in the gaps that a law-trained reader can be unwilling to supply.

Lawyers need not (indeed, should not) take on a defensive tone, but we do tend to write defensively in the form of methodically outlining every step in our thinking so as not to be accused of skipping steps or making assumptions. We also write protectively when we try to anticipate possible objections to our interpretations of law or characterization of facts, and proceed either to respond directly to potential counter-arguments or to box them out of significance in the way that we position our cases.

All of which is to say that no matter how well you have learned the material you are studying in law school, or how thoughtfully you have mastered the reasoning skills that beginning law students are introduced to, crafting thorough and effective explanations of how legal rules apply to facts is

---

8. To be sure, only a comparatively small minority of licensed attorneys practice primarily as litigators or appellate practitioners. Many of the rest work to provide in-house legal advice, help put together deals, or do other kinds of non-adversarial work. But it is still fair to say that lawyers work within the *possibility* of conflict, even if our goal is simply to prevent it from arising. Thus one way to be recognized as an accomplished transactional lawyer is by anticipating the kinds of conflict that can subsequently arise from a deal and working in advance either to head them off, or at the very least to position your client as favorably as possible in any future skirmish.

probably something you can get even better at. And the good news is that if you do, you are likely to see a boost in your academic performance and your professional effectiveness.

One way to tighten up your explanations is to imagine the spaces where you might pounce on ambiguity or incompleteness if you were opposing counsel. Another is to pause when you edit to ask yourself "Why?" about every single sentence, clause, or phrase that you have written. If what springs to mind in answer to that question is something like "well because…." then you may be telling yourself to find some way to work the substance of your intuitive "because" clause more directly into your draft.

Present Analysis Effectively, with Thoughtful Attention to Your Intended Audience

Keep in mind that you have a specific objective for your letter and that it will likely have multiple readers. In addition to your own client, these will include the opposing party, the attorney who will ultimately advise that party, and anyone else the party is likely to show the letter to (perhaps their insurance company). The letter should convincingly explain the reasons why these people should do what you ask, and should tell them what will happen if the party does not comply with your requests.

Be insistent about your position without being overly aggressive. Sometimes lawyers write demand letters in an acerbic tone in the hope that this will successfully intimidate the other side and therefore lead to productive settlement talks. But most people find such belligerence off-putting. And it can backfire by making those on the other side far more eager to fight back rather than to engage in amicable negotiation.

Because at least some of your audience consists of laypeople your letter should be comprehensible to a general audience. You anticipate counsel being brought in, though, so your letter should also make clear to an attorney who reads it why you believe your client to have a legitimate claim. If possible, it should anticipate and respond to likely counterarguments so as to demonstrate the probable success of your case. This means that you will need to be clear about the legal rules you believe apply, provide at least enough support to suggest that your interpretation is correct, and explain why that law should lead to your client's success should you proceed to litigation.

For the sake of brevity and readability you might find yourself taking some shortcuts in the way yo explain and support your legal positions that would not be appropriate in more formal briefs or legal memos. For example, you might find that you provide somewhat less explanation of case law than would be expected in a court document. As long as your letter includes the fundamentals—that is, that it somehow shows why the rules at issue applied to facts can make out a viable claim—it will be an acceptable adaptation to this particular form of professional writing.

Now, Transfer What You've Done to a Law School Setting

Legal analysis is similar in every setting

If you are willing to be just a little bit flexible, then everything you learn about law and lawyer's work in one setting can probably be used in another.

Suppose you learned CRAC as an organizational framework in your legal research and writing class, but your criminal law professor wants you to use IRAC on your midterm. No problem, you've got this! "The treehouse can be considered a dwelling under the burglary statute because it was adapted for residential use overnight" (which is a conclusion) becomes something more like "to determine the degree of burglary charge a court must decide whether the treehouse was sufficiently adapted for overnight residential use so it can be considered a dwelling" (which is an issue statement). Not really that hard to translate, right?

Indeed, if you are flexible about small changes you may even see that some things that seem entirely opposite may not be quite as contradictory as they first appear. Take a fairly common scenario frustrating many a beginning law student: one professor demands that students use IRAC to analyze exam questions, and another equally effusively insists that she really doesn't want to see those tedious IRACs when she grades. Should you write differently when you take their tests? Well, in small details, sure. But each exam will require legal analysis, so somehow you will have to apply rules to facts for both of them. Professor IRAC is trying to ensure that you follow the steps of sound legal reasoning for each of the important issues in the exam. Professor NoIRAC wants to help you avoid the clumsy inefficiency (and sometimes bad writing) that can flow from too formulaic an adherence to IRACing every possible point in a multi-issue essay. And both of them want you to carefully consider all sides of every debatable issue even though that is not explicit in the CRAC/IRAC shorthand. Assuming you do all of that for all of the issues contained in a given question while employing the correct rules of law and fully developing your reasoning, do you really believe that both professors will not be equally pleased with your efforts?

I hope this example helps illustrate just how important flexible thinking actually is as a professional objective. It is especially difficult to be malleable as a novice because you do not yet know what is important, which is why beginners tend to follow expert advice fairly literally. In some ways, thorough mastery of a particular skill is required to figure out what can be adjusted in different circumstances, and what is absolutely non-negotiable. Yet for advanced skills like legal reasoning you can really only gain the genuine conceptual expertise that will permit you to be suitably flexible through repeated practice. To move from being a novice legal thinker to an expert one as quickly as possible you should flexibly apply the core steps of legal reasoning by practicing them in different settings.

So now that you have practiced reasoning through a negligence per se and custom problem in a demand letter, let's switch to putting essentially the same issues into the form of a law school essay exam.

Sample exam question

Essay – 40 minutes

Last September Karl Forrest attended a family member's funeral. Following the viewing at Bechtel Funeral Home ("Bechtel"), a funeral director instructed Forrest that if he intended to participate in the funeral procession to the church he should go to his vehicle and wait for further instructions in the parking lot. Forrest went to his car, where he was told by a Bechtel employee to line up with the other vehicles, keep his headlights illuminated, follow the car in front of him, and to stay in line. The Bechtel employee a placed a sticker marked "funeral" on the passenger side of Forrest's windshield. The procession then left the funeral home's parking lot.

As the procession approached the intersection with 8th Avenue, (a major intersection with heavy traffic) the front of the grouping proceeded through a green light. The light changed before the entire procession made its way through the intersection. Plaintiff Patricia Chin was driving along 8th Avenue and stopped by a red light on the corner of 8th Avenue and Walnut Street. When her light turned green Chin began to drive across the Walnut Street intersection. Midway through the intersection, the rear of her van was struck by Forrest's car.

Forrest had been following the cars in front of him in the funeral procession. He did not look up at the light prior to entering the intersection, and he did not see Chin's vehicle until the moment of impact. When asked in a deposition why he entered the intersection without checking the color of the traffic signal, Forrest said that he was under the impression that it was ok to ignore any red lights because he was travelling in a funeral procession.

Chin sued both Forrest and Bechtel for the injuries she sustained in the accident. Bechtel moves to have the case against it dismissed, arguing that the company had violated no legal duty owed to Chin. Chin counters that funeral homes have a statutory and customary duty to protect the public when conducting funeral processions.

Papers submitted by the parties in support and opposition to Bechtel's motion bring the following to the Court's attention:

1. State regulations for funeral home licensure address only matters of hygiene, required equipment, employee safety and obligations of financial disclosure to the bereaved and are silent about the conduct of funeral processions.

2. City ordinance § 43.2 indicates that "[i]f a procession of any kind takes longer than five minutes to pass a given point it may be interrupted as needed for the passage of any traffic which may be waiting." The section of the city's code says nothing about traffic signals, and the code has no other sections pertaining to automobile processions.

3. A witness for the funeral home provided a sworn affidavit attesting that the instructions given to Forrest were the usual ones commonly given in the funeral industry, and that funeral home employees are generally not expected to instruct funeral procession participants regarding their legal responsibilities either to obey or to ignore traffic signals.

4. The same witness further observed that in his experience, motorists "usually" pulled over to permit funeral processions to pass in their entirety, regardless of traffic signals.

5. § 124.55 of the State's motor vehicle regulations prohibits automobiles from entering into an intersection "unless all traffic signals indicate that the driver has permission to enter and the driver has ascertained the intersection is unobstructed and safe to enter."

Should the Court allow the case to proceed against Bechtel Funeral Home or should it dismiss that part of Chin's case?

Preparing to attack the exam question

There is plenty you could do before you ever went in to take this exam. You can anticipate that you will be asked a negligence question, that the primary concerns will have to do with breach and duty, and that there will arguably be some question of whether the elements of negligence per se or custom will be applicable. Why? Because law professors tend to test what they teach, and this is what you have covered.

But you can do more than just review the law and anticipate topics—you can actually prepare yourself to spot issues. One thing that *has* to exist for a negligence per se claim is some arguably applicable law or ordinance. Look for one. If you don't see one, you probably do not have that claim. Prepare also to look for actions suggesting that people are following community norms, whether they are ones that are explicit or simply commonly understood. There's your custom argument.

Law school examinations are difficult and stressful, and you will usually be pressed for time. So why wait until you are actually in the room taking the test to do this kind of thinking? Notice how much you can actually anticipate and plan to look for before you ever set foot in the exam room.

You can prepare even better, though, if you look carefully at the elements of each claim. Think about what you might do if you were a law professor seeking to truly test your students' comprehension of negligence per se. You might want to challenge them by giving them some sort of statute, regulation, or ordinance to suggest the possibility of negligence per se, but making that rule arguably not related to the kind of harm suffered by the plaintiff. With that kind of design the students who do not know the negligence per se rules will miss the issue entirely, the average law student will spot the issue but may gloss over the fact that it is suggested but ends up not solving the problem, and only the most sophisticated may see that they should consider but ultimately reject the doctrine.

Sample answer with commentary

Below is an example of what might be a reasonably high-scoring student response. The sample is far from perfect, but it is typical of what a strong law student might be able to complete in the short time given for the problem. Some of the inevitable mechanical mistakes that appear in tightly timed exam writing have been omitted, but otherwise this is intended to illustrate both the answer that a good student might give, and a professor's response to it.

Student Answer

To have a prima facie case against Bechtel, Chin would need to provide evidence for all elements of negligence (duty, breach, cause of action/proximate cause, and injury). Chin will not be able to show that Bechtel owed her any legal duty, so the Court should dismiss the case against the funeral home.

> This is a pretty efficient opening paragraph. The parenthetical clause quickly demonstrates knowledge of the basic negligence elements, and the student is then able to focus immediately on the ones that matter. She takes a clear position that the case against the funeral home will fail. This can help make the discussion to follow more focused, but it does run the risk of leading to one-sided analysis.

A party is negligent per se (automatically satisfying the breach of duty elements of a negligence tort) when there is a law or ordinance mandating specific conduct. Chin's best and likely only statutory argument would be City Ordinance §43.2. This section says nothing about traffic signals, however, and the code includes no other mention of automobile proceedings. Chin's best argument would be that the language "may be interrupted as needed for the passage of any traffic which may be waiting" applies to her situation. A court should find, however, that the key phrase "may be interrupted" refers only to some other person or party who would be doing the interrupting. The ordinance would not apply in Chin's case because there was no such person interrupting the procession and allowing traffic through.

> The included definition of negligence per se is not incorrect, but it is incomplete. It omits elements requiring that the statute at issue be designed to prevent automobile accidents, and that Chin must be within the category of persons the rule is intended to protect.

Chin might argue that the traffic light itself might be understood as the thing interrupting the procession. A court would likely reject that interpretation. If that were actually intended to be the meaning of the statute then the legislature would likely have made that clear in the drafting. Instead there is no mention of funeral processions even though §124.55 regulates how drivers should approach intersections, and the drafters of the statute would almost certainly have been aware of the existence of funeral processions, so could have included rules pertaining to them if they had wanted. Thus the best interpretation of the statute's purpose is that it was intended to create the statutory duty for all drivers whether traveling in processional groups or not. Karl Forrest violated the relevant statute and may be liable to Chin, but Bechtel did not.

> This paragraph makes a real effort to explain its conclusions and to show how they are supported by the facts (facts in this instance being statutory language). Particularly impressive is that the analysis is justified by the absence of language that could have been present, yet is not. That kind of "reasoning from the negative" requires imagination and good judgment. It is a pretty advanced and important skill.

Bechtel also did not violate any customary duty. Community customs may be used to help determine if a party has breached any legal duty. Here, the sworn affidavit attested that funeral home employees ordinarily do not instruct procession participants about their legal responsibility to obey or to ignore traffic signals. Furthermore, the witness observed it was usual for motorists to pull over and wait for funeral processions to pass before moving on (with no indication whether traffic lights were ordinarily observed). Both of these points suggest there was in fact no established community practice Bechtel failed to follow. If anything, Chin's accident came as a result of her own breach of a customary duty that she as a motorist should owe to funeral procession participants.

> The closing wraps up the analysis by giving the reader a direct answer to the call of the test question. Note that this particular sentence/paragraph might also have worked if it had been used as an introductory thesis statement.

There is insufficient evidence to show there is a statutory or customary duty flowing from Bechtel to Chin, so she cannot make out a negligence case against the funeral home.

Learn From Your Work

In law school, you alone are in charge of your learning and your success. Your professors, school administrators, and maybe your classmates, will only guide you. Students who believe that they are responsible for what and how they learn will not only do better in law school but will also set themselves up for a lifetime of professional learning, which is an essential component of good lawyering. In additional to becoming expert at the law, then, it will help you a great deal to become expert at learning itself. Throughout this text we will point out some of the characteristics of optimal learning that you may already engage in, or might want to consider.[9]

One place to start thinking about your own learning is in looking carefully at your own objectives. Everyone knows that it is important to set goals for yourself, right?

In general yes, but some kinds of goals are more helpful than others. Most of us intuitively set "performance goals" for ourselves: "I want to get an A on this assignment" or "I will be satisfied with myself if I can place in the top half of my class." The problem is that these motivators tend not to maximize outcomes. People who do not reach their own personal targets may become discouraged, while those who do attain them may be satisfied and complacent rather than aiming still higher. Carol Dweck's research[10] shows that students who instead set "mastery goals" for themselves tend to perform better than those who don't.

Mastery goals are less focused on specific outcomes and more concerned with processes: "I am going to keep reading these cases until I can explain to my roommate exactly when a violation of custom can be used by plaintiffs to establish negligent conduct." Mastery goals should be achievable in a fairly short time: e.g., "by the end of this study session" rather than "by the end of this month." They should be specific and testable, which is why the given example has the student explaining an idea out loud to another person (ideally one who does not already grasp the concept). It is too easy to presume incorrectly that a goal has been met if it is entirely internal: "I've read for a long time and the cases make sense to me, so I *think* I understand how custom works in negligence." (Note: this is also why you are so strongly encouraged to actually *write out* your answers to essay questions before reviewing model answers; writing out your answer is a testable goal.)

Finally, mastery goals should stretch your limits somewhat, but not unreasonably. A goal of writing a letter so powerful that it will immediately cause defendants' counsel to capitulate to your every demand will probably not be achievable because you cannot control defendants' reactions. A goal of improving the explanation in your demand letter for why § 393.110 creates a statutory duty that Certified Lumber violated in Tanger's case is probably achievable, and might in the end help persuade a defendant to give in.

---

9. For additional information and resources, see Michael Hunter Schwartz, Expert Learning for Law Students (2d ed. 2008).

10. Carol S. Dweck, *Self-Theories: Their Role in Motivation, Personality, and Development*, 1 Essays in Soc. Psych. 1 (2000).

Torts Project Checklist

Read your own drafts while looking carefully for each point raised below. If the points are included, please make sure that they are presented and explained to the best of your ability. If they are not, then consider whether your analysis can be made more complete.

1. Where does your analysis establish the basic elements of negligence?

2. Do you identify for the reader which elements are most at issue in your particular problem (and let's be honest, given the nature of the legal questions we are wrestling with that's pretty likely to be duty and/or breach)?

3. If you are arguing defendants violated some statute or ordinance and are thus negligent per se, where does your analysis explain:

    a. Which binding rules of law were allegedly violated;

    b. What specific actions or inaction broke the rule in question;

    c. That the statute was designed to prevent the kind of harm allegedly suffered by the plaintiff;

    d. How we know that this is the kind of harm intended to be prevented by the rule;

    e. Why we can conclude that the plaintiff is the kind of person the statute was meant to protect?

4. If you are counter-arguing that defendants complied with a pertinent statute or ordinance, which may be evidence that their conduct was not negligent, where does your analysis explain:

    a. Which binding rules of law were followed;

    b. How we know that defendants' conduct conformed to the rule in question;

    c. That compliance with applicable statutes does not automatically relieve defendants of negligence liability;

    d. Why the rule-following conduct should be viewed in this particular instance as evidence of defendants' lack of negligence?

5. If you are arguing that defendants violated some community or industry custom, which may be evidence that their conduct was negligent, where does your analysis explain:

    a. Which customs or norms were violated;

    b. How we know that these are commonly observed customs;

    c. What specific actions or inaction broke the norms in question;

    d. That failure to follow community or industry standards in ways that increase risk of injury may be evidence of negligent behavior?

6. If you are counter-arguing that defendants followed some community or industry custom, which may be evidence that their conduct was not negligent, where does your analysis explain:

    a. Which customs or norms were followed;

    b. How we know that these are commonly observed customs;

    c. How, specifically, defendants' actions or inactions conformed to the custom;

    d. That acting consistent with community or industry customs may be evidence that defendants were not negligent (but is not dispositive)?

7. Is the evidence of defendants' conduct or inaction presented in a way that gives a clear picture of what plaintiff thinks happened?

8. Are alternative interpretations of key events refuted either directly or indirectly?

9. Does the organization of the analysis fit the reasoning? Does it follow the traditional logic of applying rules of law to facts?

10. Is the discussion clearly presented, and would it make sense to the reader?

11. Was the analysis proofread, with technical errors and awkwardness eliminated?

Chapter 2

Contracts

Assignment: *Prepare an Informal Bench Memorandum for a Judge*

Based on the materials in the file, please draft an informal memo explaining whether the court should grant respondent's motion to dismiss the case against him. Target length is fewer than 1200 words exclusive of salutations, titles, or other standard non-substantive introductory material.

Analytical Skills to Focus On

✓ Using legal and non-legal documents
✓ Comprehending legal rules (especially what kinds of facts can implicate them)
✓ Using policy
✓ Developing professional judgment

Case File

The materials in the case file are compiled in one complete set so that you will have them all together. You should read them carefully several times before diving into the commentary and questions that follow. As you read through the materials ask yourself the same basic questions that practicing attorneys must always consider in new cases:

1. What happened here, and what stories will each side tell about the key facts? Which facts are generally agreed upon and what (if anything) is contested?

2. What rules or legal principles apply?

3. What do the documents in the case file add to the problem?

4. How authoritative is each document?

5. What materials are *not* here that you would want to review to better understand the case? Are there ways to work around what you do not know?

A project checklist is included at the end of the chapter. Use it to review and edit your drafts as you strive for maximal effectiveness.

Chapter 2 Case File

Your exercise packet contains the following:
- Memo from the Arizona state court judge you work for
- The Complaint filed in *Relich v. Leigh*
- A copy of the Disclosure Statement completed by Maurice Leigh, attached to the complaint
- Relevant sections of the RESTATEMENT 2D OF CONTRACTS
- Relevant cases to use in your analysis

Thinking about Contracts

Contracts classes often confound beginning law students. Many students report that they do not feel as if they understand the material until the very end of the course. If that's true there is probably a good reason—analyzing contract questions requires a big-picture understanding of how the topics within the subject fit together. To address a contracts issue you always need to know where you are within a standardized methodical process. Essentially, Contracts operates as a flow chart.

Contracts courses might begin with any number of topics. Some start with offer/acceptance, some with consideration, some with calculating damages, and other variations abound. There are good reasons why a contracts professors might choose to focus on any of these at the outset, and thinking about the reasons for your professor's choices will help you understand the emphasis of your particular class. But in the end, it doesn't matter where your class opens; once you understand contract law you should see that you always attack a contracts question by asking: (1) Was a contract properly formed? (2) If so, were its terms breached? (3) Does the defendant have any defenses? (4) How should we determine the appropriate compensation for the (alleged) breach? (5) If there was no binding agreement between the parties, are there any equitable remedies available to make either or both whole?

This is so because legal issues pertaining to contract law tend to come up primarily when there is conflict. Contracts issues typically arise when one party thinks the other has breached a legally binding deal and wants compensation. The defending party probably doesn't want to pay. So what to do? Well, if there was no enforceable contract there might not be any way for the other party to collect. Thus the first and probably best option for the defense is to argue that there was no contract in the first place, assuming there is any viable way to make that claim. If that argument does not result in precluding any liability for breach, then defendant's next goal will be to eliminate or minimize whatever damages may be owed. A lawyer or law student who can picture this real-life progression will have a much easier time understanding how the larger pieces of contract law end up fitting together.

MEMORANDUM

To: Judicial clerk
From: Judge Carol Meyer
Re: *Relich v. Leigh*
Date: January 14, 20___

Last week, what was supposed to be a brief scheduling conference in the contract rescission case *Ida Relich v. Maurice Leigh* [Case No. 011013] became complicated when the parties began arguing the merits. I couldn't blame them, really—this one is pretty wild. Plaintiff sued to rescind the sale of the residence she had purchased after finding out that it is known as a "haunted house," and apparently was the site of a fairly grisly double murder early in the last century.

Defendant's counsel insists 16 A.R.S. Rules of Civil Procedure 12(b)(6) entitles her client Maurice Leigh to have the case dismissed for failure to state a claim upon which relief may be granted, and is consequently entitled to keep the proceeds of the sale of his former home. Petitioner's counsel asserts that the facts as alleged in the complaint, if true, are sufficient to warrant relief from the sale of the property in question.

After both lawyers squabbled about the substance of the case I decided that it would make sense to look into whether there was any possible way that this claim had any merit before it went any further. I am therefore treating defendant's counsel's request to dismiss the case as an oral motion currently pending

> So in this case we are dealing with a pre-trial motion to dismiss. Will that matter to the analysis? We do not know yet. But as soon as it is established that the case is pre-trial it is immediately apparent that there are not yet settled facts— only allegations of the parties. Furthermore, we know from the type of motion to dismiss that we will proceed as if all of the facts alleged by plaintiff are true.

before the Court. For the sake of expediency, and to avoid having either party incur additional unnecessary attorney's fees while we looked into this one, I indicated that I would first try to resolve the matter without written briefs from the parties. With your assistance I believe it will be possible to consider the question of whether relief from this sale can be granted by reviewing our case law and the facts alleged in the complaint.

> It would be much more typical for the judge to adjourn the case to have the attorneys formally submit written motions and responses. But most courts have crowded dockets, so it is not uncommon for judges to try to get to the heart of the matter as quickly as they can.

A little background that you may or may not remember from your review of Property in preparation for the Arizona bar: Arizona is one of the few states left without a statute mandating specific disclosures by sellers in residential real estate transactions. In theory that should mean information exchanged about property is purely up to the parties to negotiate. But in reality, in just about all transactions one or both realtors insist that the contract for sale include a completed disclosure on the SPDS form created by the Arizona Association of Realtors. So the disclosure winds up being legally required by contract, which is exactly what happened here.

Please review the Complaint and its attached Disclosure Statement, together with some cases and Restatement sections on point that I had Debbie pull while she was at the library on the Hudson matter. Draft an informal memo advising me whether to dismiss the case or to proceed. This is not one of your old law school assignments and I don't need to you to get bogged down in formalities. I am simply looking for a quick, straightforward, and most of all **readable** discussion of your conclusions, together with a **complete explanation of your reasoning** and the authority supporting it.

IN THE SUPERIOR COURT OF THE STATE OF ARIZONA
IN AND FOR THE COUNTY OF MARICOPA

```
-----------------------------------------------------------------x
Ida Relich                                      )
                              Plaintiff,         )
                    - v. -                        )        Case Number 011013
Maurice Leigh,                                    )        COMPLAINT
                              Defendant.          )
-----------------------------------------------------------------x
```

Plaintiff Ida Relich, by her attorney Thomasa Tirado, comes now before this court and says:

1. On or about October 18, 20___, Defendant entered into a Contract of Sale with Plaintiff for the residential property located at 305 Oakmont Avenue (hereinafter "Property").

> A Complaint is supposed to set out the factual and legal bases for each of the complaining party's claims. Most lawyers find drafting complaints to be a demanding art. They must be specific enough to meet statutory requirements and to survive expected motions to dismiss. Nonetheless, attorneys sometimes aim to draft complaints that are as loose and general as they can get away with. In part this is to avoid contradicting facts that may emerge later, but it is also to avoid giving more information to the other side than is strictly required. As you read through this Complaint, see if you agree with the way that Ms. Tirado balanced those competing interests.

2. The sale of the subject Property was predicated upon the representations made by Defendant seller in the Disclosure Statement attached to this Complaint as Exhibit A.

3. Defendant's Disclosure Statement omits important and material information about the Property.

4. The omitted information affects the value of the Property.

> When you review the elements of the contracts defenses at issue in this case, come back to review these points and ask yourself what each numbered paragraph contributes and why the attorney framed them the way she did.

5. The omitted information would, if known, have affected Plaintiff's decision-making process regarding the purchase of the Property.

6. The Property is widely reputed to be possessed by poltergeists.

7. Defendant and his visitors have reportedly seen these poltergeists on numerous occasions, and the presence of poltergeists has been reported upon in the local press.

8. Defendant himself gave an interview with local news station KNXV approximately two years before listing the house for sale, in which he reported having seen the specter of an elderly woman hovering near the rear entrance to the Property, and of a younger man "walking" near its kitchen.

> Proximity and juxtaposition suggest meaning to readers (whether they register it consciously or not). Consider the attorney's reasons for placing this point immediately after the one that precedes it.

9. Plaintiff is relocating to Arizona from Texas, and had no reason to be familiar with the local lore regarding the Property.

10. Upon learning of the reputation of the Property's haunting, Plaintiff undertook to research its history and discovered at the local library a newspaper report describing a grisly multiple homicide that took place in the Property in 1932. The murder victims included an elderly woman and her younger nephew. Plaintiff has reason to believe that the haunted reputation of the Property stems from this established event.

> This use of an evocative word like "grisly" stands out in the otherwise detached tone of this document. Why do you think the attorney included the term?

-1-

11. Defendant was under a duty to disclose what he knew regarding the Property's reputation.

12. Defendant was aware of the Property's reputation for paranormal activity.

13. Defendant may have known, and/or should have known, about the homicides previously committed on the Property.

14. If defendant was unaware of the homicides in the Property's past, then this history would constitute a mistake by both parties.

15. The mistake referenced in paragraph 14, if there was one, is basic to the agreement reached between the Plaintiff and Defendant.

Do you see how this story is designed to allude to the elderly woman and the younger man from paragraph 8 without having to explicitly contend that they are the ghosts of the murder victims?

PRAYER FOR RELIEF

WHEREFORE, Plaintiff respectfully requests the Court issue an order:

1. Rescinding the sale between the parties of the Property, located at 305 Oakmont Avenue, AND

2. Awarding consequential damages in the amount of $28,052.00, OR

3. In the alternative, awarding restitution for the diminished value of the property.

4. Together with awarding such other relief as may be just and proper.

DATED this 17th day of December, 20_____.

THE CULPEPPER LAW FIRM, LLC

By /s/ *Thomasa Tirado*

2203 30th Street, Suite 200
Phoenix, Arizona, 85014
Attorneys for Plaintiff

> **What is this form, and who seems to have filled it out?**

RESIDENTIAL SELLER DISCLOSURE ADVISORY

Document updated:
October 2017

ARIZONA REALTORS
REAL SOLUTIONS. REALTOR. SUCCESS.

WHEN IN DOUBT – DISCLOSE!

Arizona law <u>requires</u> the seller to disclose material (important) facts about the property, even if you are not asked by the buyer or a real estate agent. These disclosure obligations remain even if you and the buyer agree that no Seller's Property Disclosure Statement ("SPDS") will be provided.

The SPDS is designed to assist you, the seller, in making these legally required disclosures and to avoid inadvertent nondisclosures of material facts. To satisfy your disclosure obligations and protect yourself against alleged nondisclosure, you should complete the SPDS by answering all questions as truthfully and as thoroughly as possible. Attach copies of any available invoices, warranties, inspection reports, and leases, to insure that you are disclosing accurate information. Use the blank lines to explain your answers. If you do not have the personal knowledge to answer a question, it is important not to guess – use the blank lines to explain the situation.

 If the buyer asks you about an aspect of the property, you have a duty to disclose the information, even if you do not consider the information material.* You also have a legal duty to disclose facts when disclosure is necessary to prevent a previous statement from being misleading or misrepresented: for example, if something changes.

If you do not make the legally required disclosures, you may be subject to civil liability. Under certain circumstances, nondisclosure of a fact is the same as saying that the fact does not exist. Therefore, nondisclosure may be given the same legal effect as fraud.

If you are using the Arizona Association of REALTORS® ("AAR") Residential Resale Real Estate Purchase Contract, the seller is required to deliver "a completed AAR Residential SPDS form to the Buyer within three (3) days after Contract acceptance." If the Seller does not provide the SPDS as the Contract requires, the Seller is potentially in breach of the Contract, thereby enabling the Buyer to cancel the transaction and receive the earnest money deposit.

* By law, sellers are not obligated to disclose that the property is or has been: (1) a site of a natural death, suicide, homicide, or any other crime classified as a felony; (2) owned or occupied by a person exposed to HIV, or diagnosed as having AIDS or any other disease not known to be transmitted through common occupancy of real estate; or (3) located in the vicinity of a sex offender. However, the law does not protect a seller who makes an intentional misrepresentation. For example, if you are asked whether there has been a death on the property and you know that there was such a death, you should not answer "no" or "I don't know." Instead you should either answer truthfully or respond that you are not legally required to answer the question.

RESIDENTIAL SELLER'S PROPERTY
DISCLOSURE STATEMENT (SPDS) *(To be completed by Seller)*

Document updated:
October 2017

ARIZONA REALTORS
REAL ESTATE ONE REALTOR SUCCESS.

The pre-printed portion of this form has been drafted by the Arizona Association of REALTORS®. Any change in the pre-printed language of this form must be made in a prominent manner. No representations are made as to the legal validity, adequacy and/or effects of any provision, including tax consequences thereof. If you desire legal, tax or other professional advice, please consult your attorney, tax advisor or professional consultant.

MESSAGE TO THE SELLER:

Sellers are obligated by law to disclose all known material (important) facts about the Property to the Buyer. The SPDS is designed to assist you in making these disclosures. If you know something important about the Property that is not addressed on the SPDS, add that information to the form. Prospective Buyers may rely on the information you provide.

INSTRUCTIONS: (1) Complete this form yourself. (2) Answer all questions truthfully and as fully as possible. (3) Attach all available supporting documentation. (4) Use explanation lines as necessary. (5) If you do not have the personal knowledge to answer a question, use the explanation lines to explain. *By signing on page 7, you acknowledge that the failure to disclose known material information about the Property may result in liability.*

MESSAGE TO THE BUYER:

Although Sellers are obligated to disclose all known material (important) facts about the Property, there are likely facts about the Property that the Sellers do not know. Therefore, it is important that you take an active role in obtaining information about the Property.

INSTRUCTIONS: (1) Review this form and any attachments carefully. (2) Verify all important information. (3) Ask about any incomplete or inadequate responses. (4) Inquire about any concerns not addressed on the SPDS. (5) Review all other applicable documents, such as CC&R's, association bylaws, surveys, rules, and the title report or commitment. (6) Obtain professional inspections of the Property. (7) Investigate the surrounding area.

THE FOLLOWING ARE REPRESENTATIONS OF THE SELLER(S) AND ARE NOT VERIFIED BY THE BROKER(S) OR AGENT(S).

PROPERTY AND OWNERSHIP

1. As used herein, "Property" shall mean the real property and all fixtures and improvements thereon and appurtenances incidental thereto,
2. plus fixtures and personal property described in the Contract.
3. PROPERTY ADDRESS: __305 Oakmont Ave.__ (STREET ADDRESS)   __Pheonix__ (CITY)   __AZ__ (STATE)   __85011__ (ZIP)

4. Does the Property include any leased land? ☐ Yes ☒ No
5. Explain: _____
6. Is the Property located in an unincorporated area of the county? ☐ Yes ☒ No If yes, and five or fewer parcels of land other than subdivided land
7. are being transferred, the Seller must furnish the Buyer with a written Affidavit of Disclosure in the form required by law.
8. LEGAL OWNER(S) OF PROPERTY: __Maurice Leigh__ Date Purchased: __6-17-208__

9. The Property is currently: ☒ Owner-occupied ☐ Leased ☐ Estate ☐ Foreclosure ☐ Vacant If vacant, how long?_____
10. If a rental property, how long? _____ Expiration date of current lease: _____ (Attach a copy of the lease if available.)
11. If any refundable deposits or prepaid rents are being held, by whom and how much? Explain: _____
12. _____

13. Is the legal owner(s) of the Property a foreign person pursuant to the Foreign Investment in Real Property Tax Act (FIRPTA)?
14. ☐ Yes ☒ No If yes, consult a tax advisor; mandatory withholding may apply.
15. Is the Property located in a community defined by the fair housing laws as housing for older persons? ☐ Yes ☒ No
16. Explain: _____
17. Approximate year built: __1906__. If Property was built prior to 1978, Seller must furnish the Buyer with a lead-based paint disclosure form.

18. | **NOTICE TO BUYER: If the Property is in a subdivision, a subdivision public report, which contains a variety of**
19. | **information about the subdivision at the time the subdivision was approved, may be available by contacting the Arizona**
20. | **Department of Real Estate or the homebuilder. The public report information may be outdated. www.azre.gov.**

>>

Residential Seller's Property Disclosure Statement (SPDS)
Updated: October 2017 • Copyright © 2017 Arizona Association of REALTORS®.
All rights reserved.

Initials> __7R__
BUYER | BUYER

Page 1 of 7

Residential Seller's Property Disclosure Statement (SPDS) >>

	YES	NO	
21.	☐	☒	Have you entered into any agreement to transfer your interest in the Property in any way, including rental renewals
22.			or options to purchase? Explain: _____
23.	☐	☒	Are you aware if there are any association(s) governing the Property?
24.			If yes, provide contact(s) information: Name: _____ Phone #: _____
25.			Name: _____ Phone #: _____
26.			If yes, are there any fees? How much? $_____ How often? _____
27.			How much? $_____ How often? _____
28.	☐	☒	Are you aware of any association fees payable upon transfer of the Property? Explain: _____
29.			_____
30.	☐	☒	Are you aware of any proposed or existing association assessment(s)? Explain: _____
31.			_____
32.	☐	☒	Are you aware of any pending or anticipated disputes or litigation regarding the Property or the association(s)?
33.			Explain: _____
34.	☐	☒	Are you aware of any of the following recorded against the Property? (Check all that apply):
35.			☐ Judgment liens ☐ Tax liens ☐ Other non-consensual liens
36.			Explain: _____
37.	☐	☒	Are you aware of any assessments affecting the Property? (Check all that apply):
38.			☐ Paving ☐ Sewer ☐ Water ☐ Electric ☐ Other
39.			Explain: _____
40.	☐	☒	Are you aware of any title issues affecting the Property? (Check all that apply):
41.			☐ Recorded easements ☐ Use restrictions ☐ Lot line disputes ☐ Encroachments
42.			☐ Unrecorded easements ☐ Use permits ☐ Other _____
43.			Explain: _____
44.	☐	☒	Are you aware if the Property is located within the boundaries of a Community Facilities District (CFD)?
45.			If yes, provide the name of the CFD: _____
46.			_____
47.	☐	☒	Are you aware of any public or private use paths or roadways on or across the Property?
48.			Explain: _____
49.	☐	☒	Are you aware of any problems with legal or physical access to the Property? Explain: _____
50.			The road/street access to the Property is maintained by the ☐ County ☐ City ☐ Homeowners' Association ☐ Privately
51.	☐	☒	If privately maintained, is there a recorded road maintenance agreement? Explain: _____
52.	☐	☒	Are you aware of any violation(s) of any of the following? (Check all that apply):
53.			☐ Zoning ☐ Building Codes ☐ Utility Service ☐ Sanitary health regulations
54.			☐ Covenants, Conditions, Restrictions (CC&R's) ☐ Other _____ (Attach a copy of notice(s) of violation if available.)
55.			Explain: _____
56.			_____
57.	☐	☒	Are you aware of any homeowner's insurance claims having been filed against the Property?
58.			Explain: _____

59. 60. 61.	**NOTICE TO BUYER:** Your claims history, your credit report, the Property's claims history and other factors may affect the insurability of the Property and at what cost. Under Arizona law, your insurance company may cancel your homeowner's insurance within 60 days after the effective date. Contact your insurance company.

BUILDING AND SAFETY INFORMATION

	YES	NO	
62.	YES	NO	**ROOF / STRUCTURAL:**
63.			NOTICE TO BUYER: Contact a professional to verify the condition of the roof.
64.	☒	☐	Are you aware of any past or present roof leaks? Explain: _Small leak in bedroom #2_
65.			_in Spring 2011. Fully repaired_
66.	☐	☒	Are you aware of any other past or present roof problems? Explain: _____
67.			_____

>>

Residential Seller's Property Disclosure Statement (SPDS)
Updated: October 2017 • Copyright © 2017 Arizona Association of REALTORS®.
All rights reserved.

Initials> [TR] BUYER | BUYER

Residential Seller's Property Disclosure Statement (SPDS) >>

	YES	NO	
68.	X	☐	Are you aware of any roof repairs? Explain: _as noted in 64 above_
69.			
70.	☐	X	Is there a roof warranty? (Attach a copy of warranty if available.)
71.	☐	X	If yes, is the roof warranty transferable? Cost to transfer _____
72.	☐	X	Are you aware of any interior wall/ceiling/door/window/floor problems? Explain: _____
73.			
74.	☐	X	Are you aware of any cracks or settling involving the foundation, exterior walls or slab? Explain: _____
75.			
76.	☐	X	Are you aware of any chimney or fireplace problems, if applicable? Explain: _____
77.			
78.	☐	X	Are you aware of any damage to any structure on the Property by any of the following? (Check all that apply):
79.			☐ Flood ☐ Fire ☐ Wind ☐ Expansive soil(s) ☐ Water ☐ Hail ☐ Other _____
80.			Explain: _____

81. **WOOD INFESTATION:**
82.   Are you aware of any of the following:

	YES	NO	
83.	☐	X	Past presence of termites or other wood destroying organisms on the Property?
84.	☐	X	Current presence of termites or other wood destroying organisms on the Property?
85.	☐	X	Past or present damage to the Property by termites or other wood destroying organisms?
86.			Explain: _____
87.			
88.	X	☐	Are you aware of past or present treatment(s) of the Property for termites or other wood destroying organisms?
89.			If yes, date last treatment was performed: _Prophylactic termite treatment in spring 2005_
90.			Name of treatment provider(s): _Aphis_ _+ annual checkup since_
91.	X	☐	Is there a treatment warranty? (Attach a copy of warranty if available.)
92.	X	☐	If yes, is the treatment warranty transferrable?

93.   **NOTICE TO BUYER: Contact Office of Pest Management for past termite reports or**
94.   **treatment history. www.sb.state.az.us**

95. **HEATING & COOLING:**
96.   Heating: Type(s) _electric_
97.   Approximate Age(s) _9 years_
98.   Cooling: Type(s) _retrofit a/c mini-split system - whole house_
99.   Approximate Age(s) _12 years_

	YES	NO	
100.	☐	X	Are you aware of any past or present problems with the heating or cooling system(s)?
101.			Explain: _____

102. **PLUMBING:**

	YES	NO	
103.	X	☐	Are you aware of the type of water pipes, such as galvanized, copper, PVC, CPVC or polybutylene?
104.			If yes, identify: _Copper_
105.	☐	X	Are you aware of any past or present plumbing problems? Explain: _____
106.			
107.	☐	X	Are you aware of any water pressure problems? Explain: _____
108.			Type of water heater(s): ☐ Gas ☐ Electric ☐ Solar Approx. age(s): _____
109.	☐	X	Are you aware of any past or present water heater problems? Explain: _____
110.			
111.	X	☐	Is there a landscape watering system? If yes, type: ☐ automatic timer ☐ manual ☐ both
112.	☐	X	If yes, are you aware of any past or present problems with the landscape watering system?
113.			Explain: _____
114.	☐	X	Are there any water treatment systems? (Check all that apply):
115.			☐ water filtration ☐ reverse osmosis ☐ water softener ☐ Other _____
116.			Is water treatment system(s) ☐ owned ☐ leased (Attach a copy of lease if available.)
117.	☐	X	Are you aware of any past or present problems with the water treatment system(s)?
118.			Explain: _____

>>

Initials > | _JR_ |
BUYER | BUYER

Residential Seller's Property Disclosure Statement (SPDS) >>

	YES	NO	
119.			**SWIMMING POOL/SPA/HOT TUB/SAUNA/WATER FEATURE:**
120.	☐	☒	Does the Property contain any of the following? (Check all that apply):
121.			☐ Swimming pool ☐ Spa ☐ Hot tub ☐ Sauna ☐ Water feature
122.	☐	☐ *N/A*	If yes, are either of the following heated? ☐ Swimming pool ☐ Spa If yes, type of heat: _____
123.	☐	☐	Are you aware of any past or present problems relating to the swimming pool, spa, hot tub, sauna or water feature?
124.			Explain: _____
125.			**ELECTRICAL AND OTHER RELATED SYSTEMS:**
126.	☐	☒	Are you aware of any past or present problems with the electrical system? Explain: _____
127.			_____
128.	☐	☒	Is there a security system? If yes, is it (Check all that apply):
129.			☐ Leased (Attach a copy of lease if available.) ☐ Owned ☐ Monitored ☐ Other _____
130.	☐	☒	Are you aware of any past or present problems with the security system? Explain: _____
131.			_____
132.	☒	☐	Does the Property contain any of the following systems or detectors?(Check all that apply):
133.			☒ Smoke/fire detection ☐ Fire suppression (sprinklers) ☐ Carbon monoxide detector
134.			If yes, are you aware of any past or present problems with the above systems? Explain: _____
135.			_____
136.			**MISCELLANEOUS:**
137.	☒	☐	Are you aware of any animals/pets that have resided in the Property? If yes, what kind: _____
138.			_____ Siamese cat 1999 – 2006
139.	☐	☒	Are you aware of or have you observed any of the following on the Property? (Check all that apply):
140.			☐ Scorpions ☐ Rabid animals ☐ Bee swarms ☐ Rodents ☐ Reptiles ☐ Bed Bugs ☐ Other: _____
141.			Explain: _____
142.	☐	☒	Has the Property been serviced or treated for pests, reptiles, insects, birds or animals? If yes, how often: _____
143.			Name of service provider(s): _____ Date of last service: _____
144.	☐	☒	Are you aware of any work done on the Property, such as building, plumbing, electrical or other improvements or
145.			alterations or room conversions? **(If no, skip to line 156.)**
146.			Explain: _____
147.			_____
148.			_____
149.			_____
150.	☐	☒	Were permits for the work required? Explain: _____
151.	☐	☒	If yes, were permits for the work obtained? Explain: _____
152.	☐	☒	Was the work performed by a person licensed to perform the work? Explain: _____
153.	☐	☒	Was approval for the work required by any association governing the property? Explain: _____
154.			If yes, was approval granted by the association? Explain: _____
155.	☐	☒	Was the work completed? Explain: _____
156.	☐	☒	Are there any security bars or other obstructions to door or window openings? Explain: _____
157.	☐	☒	Are you aware of any past or present problems with any built-in appliances? Explain: _____
158.			
159.	☐	☒	Are there any leased propane tanks, equipment or other systems on the Property? (Attach a copy of lease if available.)
160.			Explain: _____
161.			_____

>>

Residential Seller's Property Disclosure Statement (SPDS)
Updated: October 2017 • Copyright © 2017 Arizona Association of REALTORS®.
All rights reserved.

Initials > | *TR* |
 BUYER | BUYER

Page 4 of 7

Residential Seller's Property Disclosure Statement (SPDS) >>

UTILITIES

162. **DOES THE PROPERTY CURRENTLY RECEIVE THE FOLLOWING SERVICES?**

YES   NO   **PROVIDER**

163.   ☒   ☐   Electricity: ....   A2 E
164.   ☒   ☐   Fuel: ☒ Natural gas ☐ Propane ☐ Oil ....
165.   ☒   ☐   Cable / Satellite: ....   Comcast
166.   ☒   ☐   Internet:...   Fios
167.   ☐   ☒   Telephone: ....
168.   ☐   ☒   Garbage Collection: ....
169.   ☒   ☐   Fire:...   City of Pheonix
170.   ☐   ☒   Irrigation:...
171.   ☐   ☒   Water Source:
172.   ☐   ☐   ☐ Public ☐ Private water co. ☐ Hauled water ......
173.   ☒ Private well ☐ Shared well If water source is a private or shared well, complete and attach
174.   Domestic Water Well/Water Use Addendum.

175. | **NOTICE TO BUYER:** If the Property is served by a well, private water company or a municipal water provider,
176. | the Arizona Department of Water Resources may not have made a water supply determination.
177. | For more information about water supply, or any of the above services, contact the provider.

178.   ☐   ☒   Are you aware of any past or present drinking water problems? Explain: _____
179.   _____
180.   ☐   ☐   U.S. Postal Service delivery is available at: ☒ Property ☐ Cluster Mailbox ☐ Post Office ☐ Other _____
181.   ☐   ☒   Are there any alternate power systems serving the Property? **(If no, skip to line 190.)**
182.   If yes, indicate type (Check all that apply):
183.   ☐ Solar ☐ Wind ☐ Generator ☐ Other _____
184.   Are you aware of any past or present problems with the alternate power system(s)? Explain: _____
185.   _____
186.   ☐   ☒   Are any alternate power systems serving the Property leased? Explain: _____
187.   _____
188.   If yes, provide name and phone number of the leasing company (Attach copy of lease if available): _____
189.   _____

190. | **NOTICE TO BUYER:** If the Property is served by a solar system, Buyer is advised to read all pertinent
191. | documents and review the cost, insurability, operation, and value of the system, among other items.

ENVIRONMENTAL INFORMATION

YES   NO

192.   ☐   ☒   Are you aware of any past or present issues or problems with any of the following on the Property? (Check all that apply):
193.   ☐ Soil settlement/expansion ☐ Drainage/grade ☐ Erosion ☐ Fissures ☐ Dampness/moisture ☐ Other
194.   Explain: _____
195.   ☐   ☒   Are you aware of any past or present issues or problems in close proximity to the Property related to any of
196.   the following? (Check all that apply):
197.   ☐ Soil settlement/expansion ☐ Drainage/grade ☐ Erosion ☐ Fissures ☐ Other _____
198.   Explain: _____

199. | **NOTICE TO BUYER:** The Arizona Department of Real Estate provides earth fissure maps to any member
200. | of the public in printed or electronic format upon request and on its website at www.azre.gov.

201.   ☐   ☒   Are you aware if the Property is subject to any present or proposed effects of any of the following? (Check all that apply):
202.   ☐ Airport noise ☐ Traffic noise ☐ Rail line noise ☐ Neighborhood noise ☐ Landfill ☐ Toxic waste disposal
203.   ☐ Odors ☐ Nuisances ☐ Sand/gravel operations ☐ Other _____
204.   Explain: _____
205.   ☐   ☒   Are you aware if any portion of the Property has ever been used as a "Clandestine drug laboratory" (manufacture of,
206.   or storage of, chemicals or equipment used in manufacturing methamphetamine, ecstasy or LSD)?
                                                                                                            >>

Residential Seller's Property Disclosure Statement (SPDS) >>

	YES	NO	
207.	X	☐	Are you aware if the Property is located in the vicinity of a public or private airport?
208.			Explain: ___10 miles away, but in a few flight paths___

209. 210. 211. 212. 213.	**NOTICE TO SELLER AND BUYER:** Pursuant to Arizona law a Seller shall provide a written disclosure to the Buyer if the Property is located in territory in the vicinity of a military airport or ancillary military facility as delineated on a map prepared by the State Land Department. The Department of Real Estate also is obligated to record a document at the County Recorder's Office disclosing if the Property is under restricted air space and to maintain the State Land Department Military Airport Map on its website at www.azre.gov.

214.	☐	X	Is the Property located in the vicinity of a military airport or ancillary military facility?
215.			Explain: _____
216.	☐	X	Are you aware of the presence of any of the following on the Property, past or present? (Check all that apply):
217.			☐ Asbestos ☐ Radon gas ☐ Lead-based paint ☐ Pesticides ☐ Underground storage tanks ☐ Fuel/chemical storage
218.			Explain: _____
219.	☐	X	Are you aware if the Property is located within or subject to any of the following ordinances? (Check all that apply):
220.			☐ Superfund / WQARF / CERCLA ☐ Wetlands area ☐ Natural Area Open Spaces
221.	☐	X	Are you aware of any open mine shafts/tunnels or abandoned wells on the Property?
222.			If yes, describe location: _____
223.	☐	X	Are you aware if any portion of the Property is in a flood plain/way? Explain: _____
224.			_____

225. 226. 227. 228. 229. 230. 231. 232. 233. 234. 235. 236. 237. 238.	**NOTICE TO BUYER:** Your mortgage lender [may] [will] require you to purchase flood insurance in connection with your purchase of this property. The National Flood Insurance Program provides for the availability of flood insurance and establishes flood insurance policy premiums based on the risk of flooding in the area where properties are located. Recent changes to federal law (The Biggert-Waters Flood Insurance Reform Act of 2012 and the Homeowner Flood Insurance Affordability Act of 2014, in particular) will result in changes to flood insurance premiums that are likely to be higher, and in the future may be substantially higher, than premiums paid for flood insurance prior to or at the time of sale of the property. As a result, purchasers of property should not rely on the premiums paid for flood insurance on this property previously as an indication of the premiums that will apply after completion of the purchase. In considering purchase of this property you should consult with one or more carriers of flood insurance for a better understanding of flood insurance coverage, current and anticipated future flood insurance premiums, whether the prior owner's policy may be assumed by a subsequent purchaser of the property, and other matters related to the purchase of flood insurance for the property. You may also wish to contact the Federal Emergency Management Agency (FEMA) for more information about flood insurance as it relates to this property.

239.	☐	X	Are you aware of any portion of the Property ever having been flooded? Explain: _____
240.			_____
241.	☐	X	Are you aware of any water damage or water leaks of any kind on the Property? Explain: _____
242.			_____
243.	☐	X	Are you aware of any past or present mold growth on the Property? If yes, explain: _____
244.			_____

SEWER/WASTEWATER TREATMENT

	YES	NO	
245.	X	☐	Is the entire Property connected to a sewer?
246.	X N/A	☐	If no, is a portion of the Property connected to a sewer? Explain: _____
247.			_____
248.	X	☐	If the entire Property or a portion of the Property is connected to a sewer, has a professional verified the sewer connection?
249.			If yes, how and when: _____

250.	**NOTICE TO BUYER:** Contact a professional to conduct a sewer verification test.

251.	Type of sewer: X Public ☐ Private ☐ Planned and approved sewer system, but not connected
252.	Name of Provider: ___AZ Waste Management___

>>

Initials> | 7 R |
| BUYER | BUYER |

Residential Seller's Property Disclosure Statement (SPDS) >>

	YES	NO	
253.	☐	☒	Are you aware of any past or present problems with the sewer? Explain: _____
254.	☐	☒	Is the Property served by an On-Site Wastewater Treatment Facility? **(If no, skip to line 267.)**
255.			If yes, the Facility is: ☐ Conventional septic system ☐ Alternative system; type: _____
256.	☐	☒	If the Facility is an alternative system, is it currently being serviced under a maintenance contract?
257.			If yes, name of contractor: _____ Phone #: _____
258.			Approximate year Facility installed: _____ (Attach copy of permit if available.)
259.	☐	☒	Are you aware of any repairs or alterations made to this Facility since original installation?
260.			Explain: _____
261.			_____
262.			Approximate date of last Facility inspection and/or pumping of septic tank: _____
263.	☐	☒	Are you aware of any past or present problems with the Facility? Explain: _____
264.			_____
265.			**NOTICE TO SELLER AND BUYER: The Arizona Department of Environmental Quality requires a Pre-Transfer
266.			Inspection of On-Site Wastewater Treatment Facilities on re-sale properties.**

OTHER CONDITIONS AND FACTORS

267. What other material (important) information are you aware of concerning the Property that might affect the Buyer's decision-making
268. process, the value of the Property, or its use? Explain: _____
269. _____

ADDITIONAL EXPLANATIONS

270. _____
271. _____
272. _____
273. _____
274. _____
275. _____
276. _____
277. _____
278. _____
279. _____

280. **SELLER CERTIFICATION:** Seller certifies that the information contained herein is true and complete to the best of Seller's
281. knowledge as of the date signed. Seller agrees that any changes in the information contained herein will be disclosed in writing by Seller
282. to Buyer prior to Close of Escrow, including any information that may be revealed by subsequent inspections. Seller acknowledges
283. receipt of Residential Seller Disclosure Advisory titled *When in Doubt — Disclose.*

284. _____   9-13-20_____
     ^ SELLER'S SIGNATURE   MO/DA/YR   ^ SELLER'S SIGNATURE   MO/DA/YR

285. **Reviewed and updated: Initials:** _____ / _____   10-10-20___
                                          SELLER   SELLER   MO/DA/YR

286. **BUYER'S ACKNOWLEDGMENT:** Buyer acknowledges that the information contained herein is based only on the Seller's actual
287. knowledge and is not a warranty of any kind. Buyer acknowledges Buyer's obligation to investigate any material (important) facts in
288. regard to the Property. Buyer is encouraged to obtain Property inspections by professional independent third parties and to
289. consider obtaining a home warranty protection plan.

290. **NOTICE:** Buyer acknowledges that by law, Sellers, Lessors and Brokers are not obligated to disclose that the Property is or has been: (1) the site
291. of a natural death, suicide, homicide, or any other crime classified as a felony; (2) owned or occupied by a person exposed to HIV, diagnosed as
292. having AIDS or any other disease not known to be transmitted through common occupancy of real estate; or (3) located in the vicinity of a sex offender.

293. **By signing below, Buyer acknowledges receipt only of this SPDS. If Buyer disapproves of any items provided herein, Buyer
294. shall deliver to Seller written notice of the items disapproved as provided in the Contract.**

295. _____   10/10/20___
     ^ BUYER'S SIGNATURE   MO/DA/YR   ^ BUYER'S SIGNATURE   MO/DA/YR

Restatement (Second) of Contracts
Chapter 6. Mistake

§ 151 Mistake Defined

A mistake is a belief that is not in accord with the facts.

§ 152 When Mistake of Both Parties Makes a Contract Voidable

(1) Where a mistake of both parties at the time a contract was made as to a basic assumption on which the contract was made has a material effect on the agreed exchange of performances, the contract is voidable by the adversely affected party unless he bears the risk of the mistake under the rule stated in § 154.

> Law students frequently struggle to differentiate mistake from misrepresentation claims. In part this may be because the same core facts can give rise to both defenses. But the elements of the two are quite different, so naturally the facts needed to support the defenses are quite distinct. Pay careful attention here to how a mistake is defined, and compare with the definition of a misrepresentation in § 159 below. Do you see the difference in emphasis?

(2) In determining whether the mistake has a material effect on the agreed exchange of performances, account is taken of any relief by way of reformation, restitution, or otherwise.

§ 153 When Mistake of One Party Makes a Contract Voidable

Where a mistake of one party at the time a contract was made as to a basic assumption on which he made the contract has a material effect on the agreed exchange of performances that is adverse to him, the contract is voidable by him if he does not bear the risk of the mistake under the rule stated in § 154, and

   (a) the effect of the mistake is such that enforcement of the contract would be unconscionable, or

   (b) the other party had reason to know of the mistake or his fault caused the mistake.

§ 154 When a Party Bears the Risk of a Mistake

A party bears the risk of a mistake when

   (a) the risk is allocated to him by agreement of the parties, or

   (b) he is aware, at the time the contract is made, that he has only limited knowledge with respect to the facts to which the mistake relates but treats his limited knowledge as sufficient, or

   (c) the risk is allocated to him by the court on the ground that it is reasonable in the circumstances to do so.

§ 155 When Mistake of Both Parties as to Written Expression Justifies Reformation

Where a writing that evidences or embodies an agreement in whole or in part fails to express the agreement because of a mistake of both parties as to the contents or effect of the writing, the court may at the request of a party reform the writing to express the agreement, except to the extent that rights of third parties such as good faith purchasers for value will be unfairly affected.

§ 157 Effect of Fault of Party Seeking Relief

A mistaken party's fault in failing to know or discover the facts before making the contract does not bar him from avoidance or reformation under the rules stated in this Chapter, unless his fault amounts to a failure to act in good faith and in accordance with reasonable standards of fair dealing.

§ 158 Relief Including Restitution

Note: The current position of the American Law Institute concerning every form of restitution in a contractual context is set forth in Restatement Third, Restitution and Unjust Enrichment (R3RUE), formally adopted in 2010 and published in 2011. On the topic of this section, see especially R3RUE § 34.

(1) In any case governed by the rules stated in this Chapter, either party may have a claim for relief including restitution under the rules stated in §§ 240 and 376.

(2) In any case governed by the rules stated in this Chapter, if those rules together with the rules stated in Chapter 16 will not avoid injustice, the court may grant relief on such terms as justice requires including protection of the parties' reliance interests.

Restatement (Second) of Contracts

Chapter 7. Misrepresentation, Duress and Undue Influence

Topic 1. Misrepresentation

§ 159 Misrepresentation Defined

A misrepresentation is an assertion that is not in accord with the facts.

§ 160 When Action is Equivalent to an Assertion (Concealment)

Action intended or known to be likely to prevent another from learning a fact is equivalent to an assertion that the fact does not exist.

§ 162 When a Misrepresentation Is Fraudulent or Material

(1) A misrepresentation is fraudulent if the maker intends his assertion to induce a party to manifest his assent and the maker

(a) knows or believes that the assertion is not in accord with the facts, or

(b) does not have the confidence that he states or implies in the truth of the assertion, or

(c) knows that he does not have the basis that he states or implies for the assertion.

(2) A misrepresentation is material if it would be likely to induce a reasonable person to manifest his assent, or if the maker knows that it would be likely to induce the recipient to do so.

§ 163 When a Misrepresentation Prevents Formation of a Contract

If a misrepresentation as to the character or essential terms of a proposed contract induces conduct that appears to be a manifestation of assent by one who neither knows nor has reasonable opportunity to know of the character or essential terms of the proposed contract, his conduct is not effective as a manifestation of assent.

§ 164 When a Misrepresentation Makes a Contract Voidable

(1) If a party's manifestation of assent is induced by either a fraudulent or a material misrepresentation by the other party upon which the recipient is justified in relying, the contract is voidable by the recipient.

(2) If a party's manifestation of assent is induced by either a fraudulent or a material misrepresentation by one who is not a party to the transaction upon which the recipient is justified in relying, the contract is voidable by the recipient, unless the other party to the transaction in good faith and without reason to know of the misrepresentation either gives value or relies materially on the transaction.

§ 165 Cure by Change of Circumstances

If a contract is voidable because of a misrepresentation and, before notice of an intention to avoid the contract, the facts come into accord with the assertion, the contract is no longer voidable unless the recipient has been harmed by relying on the misrepresentation.

§ 166 When a Misrepresentation as to a Writing Justifies Reformation

If a party's manifestation of assent is induced by the other party's fraudulent misrepresentation as to the contents or effect of a writing evidencing or embodying in whole or in part an agreement, the court at the request of the recipient may reform the writing to express the terms of the agreement as asserted,

(a) if the recipient was justified in relying on the misrepresentation, and

(b) except to the extent that rights of third parties such as good faith purchasers for value will be unfairly affected.

§ 167 When a Misrepresentation Is an Inducing Cause

A misrepresentation induces a party's manifestation of assent if it substantially contributes to his decision to manifest his assent.

151 Ariz. 81
Court of Appeals of Arizona,
Division 1, Department B.

Warren G. HILL and Gloria R. Hill,
husband and wife, Plaintiffs-Appellants and
Cross-Appellees,

v.

Ora G. JONES and Barbara R. Jones,
husband and wife, Defendants-Appellees and
Cross-Appellants.

1 CA-CIV 7889.

|

Mar. 11, 1986.

|

Reconsideration Denied April 23, 1986.

|

Review Denied Oct. 1, 1986.

Attorneys and Law Firms

Knollmiller, Herrick, Brown & Arenofsky by
Thomas N. Swift, Tempe, for Warren and Gloria
Hill.

Johnson & Shelley by Bryn R. Johnson, Mesa, for
Ora and Barbara Jones.

OPINION

MEYERSON, Judge.

Must the seller of a residence disclose to the buyer
facts pertaining to past termite infestation? This is the
primary question presented in this appeal. Plaintiffs
Warren G. Hill and Gloria R. Hill (buyers) filed suit to
rescind an agreement to purchase a residence. Buyers
alleged that Ora G. Jones and Barbara R. Jones (sellers) had made misrepresentations concerning termite
damage in the residence and had failed to disclose to
them the existence of the damage and history of termite infestation in the residence. The trial court dismissed the claim for misrepresentation based upon a
so-called integration clause in the parties' agreement.

Sellers then sought summary judgment on the "concealment" claim arguing that they had no duty to
disclose information pertaining to termite infestation
and that even if they did, the record failed to show all
of the elements necessary for fraudulent concealment.
The trial court granted summary judgment, finding
that there was "no genuinely disputed issue of material fact and that the law favors the ... defendants." The

trial court awarded sellers $1,000.00 in attorney's fees.
Buyers have appealed from the judgment and sellers
have cross-appealed from the trial court's ruling on
attorney's fees.

I. FACTS

In 1982, buyers entered into an agreement to purchase
sellers' residence for $72,000. The agreement was en-
tered after buyers made several visits to the home. The
purchase agreement provided that sellers were to pay
for and place in escrow a termite inspection report
stating that the property was free from evidence of
termite infestation. Escrow was scheduled to close two
months later.

One of the central features of the house is a parquet
teak floor covering the sunken living room, the dining
room, the entryway and portions of the halls. On a
subsequent visit to the house, and when sellers were
present, buyers noticed a small "ripple" in the wood
floor on the step leading up to the dining room from
the sunken living room. Mr. Hill asked if the ripple
could be termite damage. Mrs. Jones answered that it
was water damage. A few years previously, a broken
water heater in the house had in fact caused water
damage in the area of the dining room and steps
which necessitated that some repairs be made to the
floor. No further discussion on the subject, however,
took place between the parties at that time or after-
wards.

Mr. Hill, through his job as maintenance supervisor at
a school district, had seen similar "ripples" in wood
which had turned out to be termite damage. Mr. Hill
was not totally satisfied with Mrs. Jones's explanation,
but he felt that the termite inspection report would
reveal whether the ripple was due to termites or some
other cause.

The termite inspection report stated that there was no
visible evidence of infestation. The report failed to
note the existence of physical damage or evidence of
previous treatment. The realtor notified the parties
that the property had passed the termite inspection.
Apparently, neither party actually saw the report prior
to close of escrow.

After moving into the house, buyers found a pam-
phlet left in one of the drawers entitled "Termites, the
Silent Saboteurs." They learned from a neighbor that
the house had some termite infestation in the past.
Shortly after the close of escrow, Mrs. Hill noticed
that the wood on the steps leading down to the

sunken living room was crumbling. She called an exterminator who confirmed the existence of termite damage to the floor and steps and to wood columns in the house. The estimated cost of repairing the wood floor alone was approximately $5,000.

Through discovery after their lawsuit was filed, buyers learned the following. When sellers purchased the residence in 1974, they received two termite guarantees that had been given to the previous owner by Truly Nolen, as well as a diagram showing termite treatment at the residence that had taken place in 1963. The guarantees provided for semi-annual inspections and annual termite booster treatments. The accompanying diagram stated that the existing damage had not been repaired. The second guarantee, dated 1965, reinstated the earlier contract for inspection and treatment. Mr. Jones admitted that he read the guarantees when he received them. Sellers renewed the guarantees when they purchased the residence in 1974. They also paid the annual fee each year until they sold the home.

On two occasions during sellers' ownership of the house but while they were at their other residence in Minnesota, a neighbor noticed "streamers" evidencing live termites in the wood tile floor near the entryway. On both occasions, Truly Nolen gave a booster treatment for termites. On the second incident, Truly Nolen drilled through one of the wood tiles to treat for termites. The neighbor showed Mr. Jones the area where the damage and treatment had occurred. Sellers had also seen termites on the back fence and had replaced and treated portions of the fence.

Sellers did not mention any of this information to buyers prior to close of escrow. They did not mention the past termite infestation and treatment to the realtor or to the termite inspector. There was evidence of holes on the patio that had been drilled years previously to treat for termites. The inspector returned to the residence to determine why he had not found evidence of prior treatment and termite damage. He indicated that he had not seen the holes in the patio because of boxes stacked there. It is unclear whether the boxes had been placed there by buyers or sellers. He had not found the damage inside the house because a large plant, which buyers had purchased from sellers, covered the area. After investigating the second time, the inspector found the damage and evidence of past treatment. He acknowledged that this information should have appeared in the report. He complained,

however, that he should have been told of any history of termite infestation and treatment before he performed his inspection and that it was customary for the inspector to be given such information.

Other evidence presented to the trial court was that during their numerous visits to the residence before close of escrow, buyers had unrestricted access to view and inspect the entire house. Both Mr. and Mrs. Hill had seen termite damage and were therefore familiar with what it might look like. Mr. Hill had seen termite damage on the fence at this property. Mrs. Hill had noticed the holes on the patio but claimed not to realize at the time what they were for. Buyers asked no questions about termites except when they asked if the "ripple" on the stairs was termite damage. Mrs. Hill admitted she was not "trying" to find problems with the house because she really wanted it.

II. CONTRACT INTEGRATION CLAUSE

[1] We first turn to the trial court's ruling that the agreement of the parties did not give buyers the right to rely on the statement made by Mrs. Jones that the "ripple" in the floor was water damage. We find this ruling to be in error. The contract provision upon which the trial court based its ruling reads as follows:

> That the Purchaser has investigated the said premises, and the Broker and the Seller are hereby released from all responsibility regarding the valuation thereof, and neither Purchaser, Seller, nor Broker shall be bound by any understanding, agreement, promise, representation or stipulation expressed or implied, not specified herein.

In *Lufty v. R.D. Roper & Sons Motor Co.*, 57 Ariz. 495, 506, 115 P.2d 161, 166 (1941), the Arizona Supreme Court considered a similar clause in an agreement and concluded that "any provision in a contract making it possible for a party thereto to free himself from the consequences of his own fraud in procuring its execution is invalid and necessarily constitutes no defense." The court went on to hold that "parol evidence is always admissible to show fraud, and this is true, even though it has the effect of varying the terms of a writing between the parties." 57 Ariz. at 506–507, 115 P.2d at 166; *Barnes v. Lopez*, 25 Ariz.App. 477, 480, 544 P.2d 694, 697 (1976). In this case, the claimed misrepresentation occurred after the parties executed the contract.[1] Assuming, for the purposes of this decision, that the integration clause would extend to statements made subsequent to the execution of the contract, the clause could not shield sellers from liability should buyers be able to prove fraud.

1 Buyers' fraud theory is apparently based on the premise that they were not bound under the contract until a satisfactory termite inspection report was submitted.

III. DUTY TO DISCLOSE

[2] The principal legal question presented in this appeal is whether a seller has a duty to disclose to the buyer the existence of termite damage in a residential dwelling known to the seller, but not to the buyer, which materially affects the value of the property. For the reasons stated herein, we hold that such a duty exists.

This is not the place to trace the history of the doctrine of *caveat emptor*. Suffice it to say that its vitality has waned during the latter half of the 20th century. *E.g., Richards v. Powercraft Homes, Inc.,* 139 Ariz. 242, 678 P.2d 427 (1984) (implied warranty of workmanship and habitability extends to subsequent buyers of homes); *see generally Quashnock v. Frost,* 299 Pa.Super. 9, 445 A.2d 121 (1982); *Ollerman v. O'Rourke Co.,* 94 Wis.2d 17, 288 N.W.2d 95 (1980). The modern view is that a vendor has an affirmative duty to disclose material facts where:

1. Disclosure is necessary to prevent a previous assertion from being a misrepresentation or from being fraudulent or material;

2. Disclosure would correct a mistake of the other party as to a basic assumption on which that party is making the contract and if nondisclosure amounts to a failure to act in good faith and in accordance with reasonable standards of fair dealing;

3. Disclosure would correct a mistake of the other party as to the contents or effect of a writing, evidencing or embodying an agreement in whole or in part;

4. The other person is entitled to know the fact because of a relationship of trust and confidence between them.

Restatement (Second) of Contracts § 161 (1981) (*Restatement*); *see Restatement (Second) of Torts* § 551 (1977).

Arizona courts have long recognized that under certain circumstances there may be a "duty to speak." *Van Buren v. Pima Community College Dist. Bd.,* 113 Ariz. 85, 87, 546 P.2d 821, 823 (1976); *Batty v. Arizona State Dental Bd.,* 57 Ariz. 239, 254, 112 P.2d 870, 877 (1941). As the supreme court noted in the context of a confidential relationship, "[s]uppression of a material fact which a party is bound in good faith to disclose is equivalent to a false representation." *Leigh v. Loyd,* 74 Ariz. 84, 87, 244 P.2d 356, 358 (1952); *National Housing Indus. Inc. v. E.L. Jones Dev. Co.,* 118 Ariz. 374, 379, 576 P.2d 1374, 1379 (1978).

> As you read this you should be considering whether this is a mistake case, a misrepresentation case, or a separate defense of concealment.

Thus, the important question we must answer is whether under the facts of this case, buyers should have been permitted to present to the jury their claim that sellers were under a duty to disclose their (sellers') knowledge of termite infestation in the residence. This broader question involves two inquiries. First, must a seller of residential property advise the buyer of material facts within his knowledge pertaining to the value of the property? Second, may termite damage and the existence of past infestation constitute such material facts?

The doctrine imposing a duty to disclose is akin to the well-established contractual rules pertaining to relief from contracts based upon mistake. Although the law of contracts supports the finality of transactions, over the years courts have recognized that under certain limited circumstances it is unjust to strictly enforce the policy favoring finality. Thus, for example, even a unilateral mistake of one party to a transaction may justify rescission. *Restatement* § 153.

There is also a judicial policy promoting honesty and fair dealing in business relationships. This policy is expressed in the law of fraudulent and negligent misrepresentations. Where a misrepresentation is fraudulent or where a negligent misrepresentation is one of material fact, the policy of finality rightly gives way to the policy of promoting honest dealings between the parties. *See Restatement* § 164(1).

Under certain circumstances nondisclosure of a fact known to one party may be equivalent to the assertion that the fact does not exist. For example "[w]hen one conveys a false impression by the disclosure of some facts and the concealment of others, such concealment is in

> This paragraph seems to definitively establish exactly which contract defense the case is addressing. If you weren't certain of that before, it will help to go back and re-read the earlier parts of the opinion in light of what you now know to be at issue.

effect a false representation that what is disclosed is the whole truth." *State v. Coddington,* 135 Ariz. 480, 481, 662 P.2d 155, 156 (App.1983). Thus, nondisclosure may be equated with and given the same legal effect as fraud and misrepresentation. One category of cases where this has been done involves the area of nondisclosure of material facts affecting the value of property, known to the seller but not reasonably capable of being known to the buyer.

[3] Courts have formulated this "duty to disclose" in slightly different ways. For example, the Florida Supreme Court recently declared that "where the seller of a home knows of facts materially affecting the value of the property which are not readily observable and are not known to the buyer, the seller is under a duty to disclose them to the buyer." *Johnson v. Davis,* 480 So.2d 625, 629 (Fla.1985) (defective roof in three-year old home). In California, the rule has been stated this way:

> [W]here the seller knows of facts materially affecting the value or desirability of the property which are known or accessible only to him and also knows that such facts are not known to, or within the reach of the diligent attention and observation of the buyer, the seller is under a duty to disclose them to the buyer.

Lingsch v. Savage, 213 Cal.App.2d 729, 735, 29 Cal. Rptr. 201, 204 (1963); *contra Ray v. Montgomery,* 399 So.2d 230 (Ala.1980); *see generally* W. Prosser & W. Keeton, *The Law of Torts* § 106 (5th ed.1984).[2] We find that the Florida formulation of the disclosure rule properly balances the legitimate interests of the parties in a transaction for the sale of a private residence and accordingly adopt it for such cases.

2 There are variations on this same theme. For example, Pennsylvania has limited the obligation of disclosure to cases of dangerous defects. *Glanski v. Ervine*, 269 Pa.Super. 182, 191, 409 A.2d 425, 430 (1979).

[4] As can be seen, the rule requiring disclosure is invoked in the case of material facts.[3] Thus, we are led to the second inquiry-whether the existence of termite damage in a residential dwelling is the type of material fact which gives rise to the duty to disclose. The existence of termite damage and past termite infestation has been considered by other courts to be sufficiently material to warrant disclosure. *See generally* Annot., 22 A.L.R.3d 972 (1968).

3 Arizona has recognized that a duty to disclose may arise where the buyer makes an inquiry of the seller, regardless of whether or not the fact is material. *Universal Inv. Co. v. Sahara Motor Inn, Inc.*, 127 Ariz. 213, 215, 619 P.2d 485, 487 (1980). The inquiry by buyers whether the ripple was termite damage imposed a duty upon sellers to disclose what information they knew concerning the existence of termite infestation in the residence.

In *Lynn v. Taylor,* 7 Kan.App.2d 369, 642 P.2d 131 (1982), the purchaser of a termite-damaged residence brought suit against the seller and realtor for fraud and against the termite inspector for negligence. An initial termite report found evidence of prior termite infestation and recommended treatment. A second report indicated that the house was termite free. The first report was not given to the buyer. The seller contended that because treatment would not have repaired the existing damage, the first report was not material. The buyer testified that he would not have purchased the house had he known of the first report. Under these circumstances, the court concluded that the facts contained in the first report were material. *See Hunt v. Walker,* 483 S.W.2d 732 (Tenn.App.1971) (severe damage to the residence by past termite infestation); *Mercer v. Woodard,* 166 Ga.App. 119, 123, 303 S.E.2d 475, 481–82 (1983) (duty of disclosure extends to fact of past termite damage).

[5] Although sellers have attempted to draw a distinction between live termites[4] and past infestation, the concept of materiality is an elastic one which is not limited by the termites' health. "A matter is material if it is one to which a reasonable person would attach importance in determining his choice of action in the transaction in question." *Lynn v. Taylor,* 7 Kan.App.2d at 371, 642 P.2d at 134–35. For example, termite damage substantially affecting the structural soundness of the residence may be material even if there is no evidence of present infestation. Unless reasonable minds could not differ, materiality is a factual matter which must be determined by the trier of fact. The termite damage in this case may or may not be material. Accordingly, we conclude that buyers should be allowed to present their case to a jury.

4 Sellers acknowledge that a duty of disclosure would exist if live termites were present. *Obde v. Schlemeyer*, 56 Wash.2d 449, 353 P.2d 672 (1960).

Sellers argue that even assuming the existence of a duty to disclose, summary judgment was proper because the record shows that their "silence . . . did not induce or influence" the buyers. This is so, sellers contend, because Mr. Hill stated in his deposition that he intended to rely on the termite inspection report. But this argument begs the question. If sellers were fully aware of the extent of termite damage and if such information had been disclosed to buyers, a jury could accept Mr. Hill's testimony that had he known of the termite damage he would not have purchased the house.

[6] Sellers further contend that buyers were put on notice of the possible existence of termite infestation and were therefore "chargeable with the knowledge which [an] inquiry, if made, would have revealed." *Godfrey v. Navratil,* 3 Ariz.App. 47, 51, 411 P.2d 470 (1966) (quoting *Luke v. Smith,* 13 Ariz. 155, 162, 108 P. 494, 496 (1910)). It is also true that "a party may ... reasonably expect the other to take normal steps to inform himself and to draw his own conclusions." *Restatement* § 161 comment d. Under the facts of this case, the question of buyers' knowledge of the termite problem (or their diligence in attempting to inform themselves about the termite problem) should be left to the jury.[5]

5 Sellers also contend that they had no knowledge of any existing termite damage in the house. An extended discussion of the facts on this point is unnecessary. Simply stated, the facts are in conflict on this issue.

By virtue of our holding, sellers' cross-appeal is moot. Reversed and remanded.

CONTRERAS, P.J., and YALE McFATE, J. (Retired), concur.

Note: The Honorable Yale McFate, a retired judge of the Court of Appeals, was authorized to participate in the disposition of this matter by the Chief Justice of the Arizona Supreme Court pursuant to Ariz. Const. art. VI, § 20.

180 Ariz. 486
Court of Appeals of Arizona,
Division 2, Department B.
Willie G. WAGNER, dba Wagner's Auto Body &
Sales, Plaintiff/Counterdefendant/Appellee/
Cross-Appellant,

v.

John RAO and Cathy RAO, husband and wife,
Defendants/Counterclaimants/Appellants/
Cross-Appellees.
No. 2 CA-CV 94-0129.

|

Oct. 31, 1994.

Attorneys and Law Firms

Kenneth W. Schutt, Jr., P.C. by Kenneth W. Schutt, Jr. and Michael A. Cordier, Scottsdale, for plaintiff/counterdefendant/appellee/cross-appellant.

Palmer Law Offices by Adam P. Palmer, Phoenix, for defendants/counterclaimants/appellants/cross-appellees.

OPINION

ESPINOSA, Presiding Judge.

This appeal is taken from the trial court's granting of summary judgment in favor of appellee Willie G. Wagner, dba Wagner's Auto Body & Sales, in his breach of contract action and from its dismissal of appellants John and Cathy Rao's counterclaim alleging fraud. The issue presented is whether an "as is" provision and an integration clause in a contract for the sale of a "classic car" precluded the Raos' fraud claim as a defense to its enforcement.[1] Essentially, we must determine whether Rao, by signing the contract, gave up any right to rely on Wagner's prior representations about the condition of the car.

1   Although the Raos failed to directly challenge the contract in their response to the motion for summary judgment, their counterclaim seeking rescission and their arguments both below and on appeal essentially set forth an affirmative challenge to the validity of the contract. We see no reason to engage in separate contract and tort analyses under the facts and arguments raised. See *generally* 2 Dan B. Dobbs, *Law of Remedies* § 9.1 at 545–46 (1993).

Standard of Review

[1][2] Summary judgment is proper where the facts produced in support of the claim or defense have so little probative value that reasonable people could not agree with the conclusion advanced by the proponent of the claim or defense and there are no genuine issues of material fact. *Orme School v. Reeves,* 166 Ariz. 301, 802 P.2d 1000 (1990). In reviewing a grant of summary judgment, we view the evidence in a light favorable to the opposing party. "The evidence of the non-movant is to be believed, and all justifiable inferences are to be drawn in his favor." *Id.* at 309–10, 802 P.2d at 1008–09 (quoting *Anderson v. Liberty Lobby,* 477 U.S. 242, 255, 106 S.Ct. 2505, 2513, 91 L.Ed.2d 202, 216 (1986)).

Factual and Procedural Background

In March 1992, Wagner took a 1967 Mercedes 300SE convertible to Las Vegas, Nevada to be sold at the Kruse Classic Car Auction. It was displayed at the auction for three days, but did not sell because the bidding did not meet Wagner's reserve price. John Rao was at the auction attempting to sell a car of his own. According to Rao, after he saw the Mercedes on display, Wagner approached him and they discussed Rao's purchasing the car. Wagner told him that the car was a "ground up restoration," a term understood by car restorers to mean that the vehicle had been restored to near "show room" condition. This representation was also made in a cardboard advertisement in the window of the Mercedes. Wagner and Rao could not agree on a sale price and Rao returned to his home in Arizona.

That evening, Wagner telephoned Rao and they again discussed Rao's purchasing the vehicle. Rao agreed to buy the Mercedes for $16,000 cash plus either a forty-foot enclosed aluminum trailer or an additional $17,500 in cash. Since Rao had not inspected the Mercedes, he requested that it be delivered during the day. The car was not delivered until 8:00 p.m. the following day and Rao was unable to inspect it due to the late hour. He nevertheless signed a "Used Vehicle Order" without reading the entire document and tendered a check payable to Wagner for $16,000, allegedly because the driver wished to return to Kansas that night.

The vehicle order, a preprinted, double-sided, one-page document, in addition to certain handwritten terms, provided prominently on the front page that the vehicle was being "*SOLD AS IS* ... without any guarantee, express or implied." On the back page, it stated that "[a]ll promises, statements, understandings or agreements of any kind pertaining to this contract not specified herein are hereby expressly waived."

Rao signed the order in two places, after the "as is" provision and directly below a paragraph that stated, "I have read the face and back of this order, and agree to this purchase contract."

A few days after signing the contract, Rao inspected the car and discovered rust on the entire undercarriage. He also found that the windshield wiper motor had been disconnected and that when it was connected, the wipers operated continuously. Around this time, Rao received an offer from a third party to buy his trailer for $19,000. Rao then took the Mercedes to be inspected by two auto body shops, which identified a number of other latent defects. On April 9, Rao sold the trailer to the third party. Rao later informed Wagner that he had misrepresented the condition and quality of the car and demanded that Wagner return his money in full. Wagner refused and demanded delivery of the trailer.

A couple of months later, Wagner sued the Raos for breach of contract. They answered and counterclaimed, alleging fraudulent misrepresentation and concealment. Wagner moved for summary judgment, arguing that Rao had breached the contract by failing to deliver the trailer. Wagner also sought summary judgment on the Raos' counterclaim, contending that Rao had waived his right to assert any warranties, promises or representations not expressly set forth in the contract. The Raos did not directly oppose the breach of contract claim, but instead challenged summary judgment on the basis of their counterclaim, contending that the contract did not limit their tort remedies and that fact issues existed. The trial court granted summary judgment and dismissed the Raos' tort claims, finding "there was no 'battle of the forms,' the parties were on 'equal footing' during the negotiation process, and the waiver was knowingly bargained for." Because we find that the Raos' factually supported allegations of misrepresentation require a different analysis, and that consequently, there are genuine issues of material fact, we reverse.

"As Is" Clause

[3][4] As a general rule, the words "as is" in a contract do not deprive a buyer of the right to prove fraud or misrepresentation inducing execution of the contract. *See CNC Service Center, Inc. v. CNC Service Center, Inc.,* 731 F.Supp. 293 (N.D.Ill.1990); *Reilly v. Mosley,* 165 Ga.App. 479, 301 S.E.2d 649 (1983); *St. Croix Printing Equipment, Inc. v. Rockwell International Corp.,* 428

N.W.2d 877 (Minn.App.1988); *Leavitt v. Stanley,* 132 N.H. 727, 571 A.2d 269 (1990). *See also* Elizabeth T. Tsai, Annotation, *Liability for Representations and Express Warranties in Connection with Sale of Used Motor Vehicle,* 36 A.L.R.3d 125 at § 16[b] (1971). The principle expressed in the rule is that when fraud enters into a transaction to the extent of inducing execution of a written document, the instrument never becomes a valid contract, and the party seeking to rescind the contract is not bound by its terms. *City Dodge, Inc. v. Gardner,* 232 Ga. 766, 208 S.E.2d 794 (1974); *see Sarwark Motor Sales, Inc. v. Husband,* 5 Ariz.App. 304, 426 P.2d 404 (1967). This rule acknowledges the reality of contractual transactions and recognizes that affirmative representations of fact often go to the heart of the bargain. *See* A.R.S. §§ 47-2313 and 47-2316(A) (Arizona Uniform Commercial Code provisions governing creation and exclusion of express warranties).

In a setting similar to the case at hand, this court declined to enforce a contractual exclusion of warranties when there was a material misrepresentation preceding a sale. In *Sarwark,* a car dealer had advertised a used car as, among other things, having "[v]ery low mileage." 5 Ariz.App. at 306, 426 P.2d at 406. After responding to the ad, the purchaser signed a contract expressly negating any warranty as to mileage and stating that the purchase was "As Is-No Guarantee." Subsequently, the buyer learned that the mileage shown on the odometer was not the true mileage, and he sought to rescind the contract on the ground of fraud. In defense, the dealer argued that the contract negated any warranty as to model, mileage, or condition. Following a jury verdict in favor of the buyer, we affirmed, holding that the jury was justified in finding that he was entitled to rely on the dealer's representation notwithstanding the "as is" clause.

[5] The situation in this case is virtually indistinguishable from *Sarwark. See also Reilly.* We therefore find that Rao's claim of fraud was not precluded by the "as is" language in the contract. However, we must also consider the effect of the integration clause on Rao's claim.

Integration Clause

[6] Although parties may contractually disclaim potential tort liability by a clear expression of intent to do so, *Salt River Project Agricultural Improvement & Power Dist. v. Westinghouse Electric Corp.,* 143 Ariz. 368, 694 P.2d 198 (1984), our courts have carved out an exception for cases involving fraud. *See Lufty v.*

R.D. Roper & Sons Motor Co., 57 Ariz. 495, 115 P.2d 161 (1941); *Hill v. Jones,* 151 Ariz. 81, 725 P.2d 1115 (App.1986). In *Lufty,* the Arizona Supreme Court considered the effect of an integration clause in a contract for the purchase of a Cord sedan that was similar to the clause used here. There, the seller represented to the buyer that the car was a 1937 model when in fact it was a 1936 model. In finding the integration clause unenforceable, the court concluded that "any provision in a contract making it possible for a party thereto to free himself from the consequences of his own fraud in procuring its execution is invalid and necessarily constitutes no defense." 57 Ariz. at 506, 115 P.2d at 166.

In *Hill,* the issue was whether a home seller had a duty to disclose to the buyer the existence of termite damage, which was known to the seller but not to the buyer and which materially affected the value of the residence. The trial court dismissed the buyers' claim for misrepresentation based upon an integration clause in the contract disclaiming any representations not specified therein. Relying on *Lufty,* Division One of this court reversed, holding that "the clause could not shield sellers from liability should buyers be able to prove fraud." *Hill,* 151 Ariz. at 83, 725 P.2d at 1117.

This court followed *Hill* in *Formento v. Encanto Business Park,* 154 Ariz. 495, 744 P.2d 22 (App.1987). In that case, the trial court had precluded evidence of Encanto's alleged negligent misrepresentations and express warranties, made both before and after the execution of the parties' agreement, which contained an integration clause and an express disclaimer of representations. We reversed, holding that the parol evidence rule does not bar evidence of fraud in the inducement of a contract and that a seller should not be permitted to hide behind an integration clause to avoid the consequences of a misrepresentation.

"Although the law of contracts supports the finality of transactions, ... courts have recognized that under certain limited circumstances it is unjust to strictly enforce the policy favoring finality....

There is also a judicial policy promoting honesty and fair dealing in business relationships. The policy is expressed in the law of fraudulent and negligent misrepresentations. Where a misrepresentation is fraudulent or where a negligent misrepresentation is one of material fact, the policy of finality rightly gives way to the policy of promoting honest dealings between the parties."

Id. at 499, 744 P.2d at 26 (quoting *Hill,* 151 Ariz. at 84, 725 P.2d at 1118); *see also City Dodge, Inc.;* Restatement (Second) of Contracts § 164(1) (1981).

[7] Here, it is undisputed that Wagner advertised and affirmatively represented the Mercedes as a "ground up restoration" during negotiations with Rao. We conclude that the question of whether Rao waived any right to rely on those representations cannot be determined on the basis of the existence of the "as is" provision or the integration clause in the contract. Accordingly, Rao is entitled to a trial on the merits and to present evidence on whether Wagner's representations were false or fraudulent and whether Rao relied on the representations in entering the contract. *Formento.* Of course, Wagner is entitled to introduce evidence to the contrary, including any relating to the reasonableness of Rao's reliance and his motivation in renouncing the contract.

Disposition

The trial court's grant of summary judgment for Wagner and dismissal of the Raos' fraud claim are reversed. The case is remanded for further proceedings and the award of Wagner's attorney's fees is vacated as premature. In light of our disposition, we do not address Wagner's cross-appeal.

DRUKE, C.J., and HATHAWAY, J., concur.

Sales of residential property might be different from other kinds of commercial transactions. The stakes are likely to be higher, because for most people these transactions are largest they will make in a lifetime. And courts may be especially conscious of information asymmetry between sellers who have lived in a home and buyers who have only toured it once or twice.

A case dealing with the sale of a classic car and an "as is" clause seems significantly different from the matters at issue in Relich v. Leigh. Why do you think the judge's research assistant chose this as one of the few cases you should review?

150 Ariz. 94

Supreme Court of Arizona, In Banc.

Roy C. RENNER, Lawrence B. Colton, and Kofa Farms, Inc., an Arizona corporation, Plaintiffs-Appellees,

v.

Kenneth E. KEHL and Octavia L. Kehl, husband and wife, Lane Moyle and Jannette G. Moyle, husband and wife, dba K & M Farms, an Arizona partnership, Defendants-Appellants.

No. CV–86–0111–PR.

|

June 25, 1986.

Attorneys and Law Firms

Engler, Engler & Weil by John A. Weil, Yuma, for plaintiffs-appellees.

Ronald F. Jones, Yuma, for defendants-appellants.

Opinion

GORDON, Vice Chief Justice.

This Petition for Review was granted in order to determine the measure of damages available to the plaintiff upon rescission of a land contract. We have jurisdiction pursuant to Ariz. Const. art. 6 § 5(3) and Rule 23, Ariz.R.Civ.App.P., 17A A.R.S.

In 1981 the petitioners, defendants below, acquired from the State of Arizona agricultural development leases covering 2,262 acres of unimproved desert land near Yuma. The petitioners made no attempt to develop the property themselves, but instead decided to sell their interest in the land. The respondents, plaintiffs below, were residents of the state of Washington interested in the large scale commercial cultivation of jojoba. The respondents and their agent, who was familiar with commercial jojoba development, were shown the petitioners' property and became interested in purchasing it. The property appeared to be ideal for the respondents' purposes; the soil and climate were good and both parties were of the opinion that sufficient water was available beneath the land to sustain jojoba production. The respondents made it clear that they were interested in the property only for jojoba production and required adequate water supplies.

The respondents decided to buy the leases and on June 5, 1981, executed a Real Estate Purchase Contract to that effect. Respondents agreed to pay $222,200 for the leases, and paid petitioners $80,200 as a down payment, the remainder to be paid in annual installments. In November of 1981 respondents began development of the property for jojoba production. As part of the development process the respondents had five test wells drilled, none of which produced water of sufficient quantity or quality for commercial jojoba cultivation. After spending approximately $229,000 developing the land respondents determined that the aquifer underlying the property was inadequate for commercial development of jojoba. At this point the project was abandoned and the respondents sued to rescind the purchase contract. The petitioners counterclaimed for the balance of payments due under the contract.

The case was tried before the court between October 25 and October 27, 1983, and the trial court entered Findings of Fact, Conclusions of Law, and an Order on January 9, 1984. The court found that the respondents were entitled to rescission based on mutual mistake of fact and failure of consideration, and ordered the respondents to reassign the lease to the petitioners. The petitioners were ordered to pay the respondents $309,849.84 ($80,200 representing the down payment and $229,649.48 representing the cost of developing the property) together with costs and attorney's fees.

The petitioners appealed to the court of appeals, which affirmed the trial court by memorandum decision. *Renner v. Kehl,* 1 CA–CIV 7749 (filed December 17, 1985). The petitioners raise the same arguments before this Court, *viz.,* that rescission was not justified, or if rescission was appropriate petitioners are not liable for consequential damages.

RESCISSION

[1][2] Mutual mistake of fact is an accepted basis for rescission. *Amos Flight Operations, Inc. v. Thunderbird Bank,* 112 Ariz. 263, 540 P.2d 1244 (1975); *Mortensen v. Berzell Investment Company,* 102 Ariz. 348, 429 P.2d 945 (1967). *See* Restatement (Second) of Contracts § 152. In Arizona a contract may be rescinded when there is a mutual mistake of material fact which constitutes "an essential part and condition of the contract." *Mortensen v. Berzell Investment Company,* 102 Ariz. at 350, 429 P.2d at 947. The trial court found that the sole purpose of the contract was to enable respondents to grow jojoba, which depends upon an adequate water supply. The trial court specifically found that "There would have been no sale if both

sellers and buyers had not believed it was possible to grow jojoba commercially on the leased acres...." and that "[b]ased upon the factual data available, all parties were of the opinion that there would be sufficient good quality water for commercial jojoba production, and that it would be close enough to the surface that it would be economically feasible to pump it for irrigation of large acreages." Consequently, the trial court concluded that "[p]laintiffs are entitled to rescind the purchase agreement because of the mutual mistake of fact and because there was a total failure of consideration."[1]

1 The petitioner challenges the sufficiency of the evidence in support of the trial court's conclusions of fact and law, but failed to provide a record of the trial. The obligation for a complete record on appeal clearly lies with the appellant. *Visco v. Universal Refuse Removal Company*, 11 Ariz.App. 73, 462 P.2d 90 (1969); Rule 11(b), Ariz.R.Civ.App.P. Without a record we must presume that the trial court properly exercised its discretion and that there was substantial evidence in the complete record to support the findings of the trial court. *Auman v. Auman*, 134 Ariz. 40, 653 P.2d 688 (1982); *Visco v. Universal Refuse Removal Company, supra.*

[3] The belief of the parties that adequate water supplies existed beneath the property was "a basic assumption on which both parties made the contract," Restatement (Second) of Contracts § 152 comment b, and their mutual mistake "ha[d] such a material effect on the agreed exchange of performances as to upset the very bases of the contract." *Id.* comment a. The contract was therefore voidable and the respondents were entitled to rescission.[2]

2 The failure of the parties to make a thorough investigation of the water supply prior to signing the contract does not preclude rescission where the risk of mistake was not allocated among the parties and the mistake is material and relates to a basic assumption on which the contract was made. Restatement (Second) of Contracts § 152 comment a. *See id.*, illustration 1:

"A contracts to sell and B to buy a tract of land, the value of which has depended mainly on the timber on it. Both A and B believe that the timber is still there, but in fact it has been destroyed by fire. The contract is voidable by B."

DAMAGES

[4] The trial court also ordered that petitioners pay the respondents $309,849.84 together with costs and attorney's fees. Of the $309,849.84 awarded to the respondents, $229,649.84 represents reimbursement of the costs borne by the respondents in developing the property for jojoba production. The petitioners challenge the $229,649.84 awarded as an improper grant of "consequential damages".[3]

3 Consequential or "incidental" damages represent a plaintiff's expenses incurred in reliance upon the contract. *See Fousel v. Ted Walker Mobile Homes, Inc.*, 124 Ariz. 126, 602 P.2d 507 (App.1979). In *Fousel* these expenses included the cost of custom-made awnings, skirting and steps purchased for their mobile home, *see* discussion, *infra*; in this case they would represent the cost of developing the land for jojoba production.

The court of appeals upheld the full award "[b]ecause the plaintiffs have not received a double recovery in the award of rescission and consequential damages...." Slip op. at 4. The appeals court relied upon *Fousel v. Ted Walker Mobile Homes, Inc.*, 124 Ariz. 126, 602 P.2d 507 (App.1979), for the proposition that rescission can support an award of consequential damages.

In *Fousel* the plaintiffs purchased a mobile home from the defendants, who engaged in a series of misrepresentations which cost the plaintiffs considerable inconvenience and expense. The plaintiffs prevailed upon their claim for fraud and breach of contract and were awarded $2,705.26 in consequential damages and $10,000 in punitive damages. The sole issue on appeal was whether any damages could be awarded where the plaintiffs elected to sue for rescission. The court of appeals held that the doctrine of election of remedies does not necessarily bar an award of consequential or punitive damages, only "benefit of the bargain" damages. 124 Ariz. at 129, 602 P.2d at 510; *see Jennings v. Lee*, 105 Ariz. 167, 461 P.2d 161 (1969) (election of remedies). However, *Fousel* was predicated upon proof of breach of contract for fraud. The court stated that a party who has rescinded a contract may recover "any incidental or consequential damages resulting from *a breach of the contract.*" 124 Ariz. at 129, 602 P.2d at 510 (emphasis added). The court quoted from *Jennings v. Lee, supra,* wherein we stated that "[t]here is ample authority that a *defrauded* party may not only receive back the consideration he gave, but also may recover any sums that are necessary to restore him to his position prior to the making of contract." 105 Ariz. at 173, 461 P.2d at 167, cited at 124 Ariz. 129, 602 P.2d 510 (emphasis added).

[5][6] In this case there was no breach of contract for fraud. We are dealing with a rescission based upon mutual mistake, which implies freedom from fault on the part of both parties. *See* Restatement (Second) of Contracts § 152. There was no determination that fraud or misrepresentation occurred; indeed, the trial court concluded that "[t]here was no fraud or misrepresentation on the part of the defendants or their agents...." The reliance of the court of appeals upon

Fousel was misplaced; we hold that absent proof of breach for fraud or misrepresentation a party who rescinds a contract may not recover consequential damages. Accordingly, we reverse that portion of the trial court's order awarding consequential damages and vacate that portion of the court of appeals' decision which affirms the award of consequential damages.

[7][8] This does not mean, however, that the respondents are entitled only to recover their down payment. When a party rescinds a contract on the ground of mutual mistake he is entitled to restitution for any benefit that he has conferred on the other party by way of part performance or reliance. Restatement (Second) of Contracts § 376. Restitutionary recoveries are not designed to be compensatory; their justification lies in the avoidance of unjust enrichment on the part of the defendant. D. Dobbs, *Remedies* § 4.1 p. 224 (1973). Thus the defendant is generally liable for restitution of a benefit that would be unjust for him to keep, even though he gained it honestly. *Id;* Restatement (Second) of Contracts § 376 comment a. The issue we must now address is the proper measure of the restitutionary interest.

[9][10] The first step determining the proper measure of restitution requires that the rescinding party return or offer to return, conditional on restitution, any interest in property that he has received in the bargain. Restatement (Second) of Contracts § 384(1)(a). In Arizona this includes reimbursement for the fair market value of the use of the property. With respect to land contracts we have noted that "[i]t is of course essential to justify the rescinding of a contract that the rescinding party offer to place the other in status quo, and this includes the offer to credit the vendors with a reasonable rental value for the time during which the land was occupied." *Mortensen v. Berzell Investment Company,* 102 Ariz. at 351, 429 P.2d at 948. Earlier we stated that "[t]he offer to surrender possession of property received under the contract need not be unqualified, but may be made conditional upon the vendor's restitution of amounts paid on the contract, less proper allowances in respect of vendee's use of the premises." *Mahurin v. Schmeck,* 95 Ariz. 333, 341, 390 P.2d 576, 581 (1964). Thus the respondents were obliged to return the land to the petitioners in exchange for their down payment, and in addition to pay the petitioners the fair rental value of the land for the duration of their occupancy.

[11] However, to avoid unjust enrichment the petitioners must pay the respondents a sum equal to the amount by which their property has been enhanced in value by the respondents' efforts. The Restatement (Second) of Contracts § 376 provides that "[i]f [a party] has received and must return land ... he may have made improvements on the land in reliance on the contract and he is entitled to recover the reasonable value of those improvements.... The rule stated in this section applies to avoidance on any ground, including ... mistake...." comment a. The reasonable value of any improvements is measured by "the extent to which the other party's property has been increased in value or his other interests advanced." Restatement (Second) of Contracts § 371(b). Thus the petitioners must pay to the respondents that amount of money which represents the enhanced value of the land due to the respondents' development efforts. In short, the respondents are entitled to their down payment, plus the amount by which their efforts increased the value of the petitioners' property, minus an amount which represents the fair rental value of the land during their occupancy. They are not entitled to the $229,649.84 expended upon development, because that would shift the entire risk of mistake onto the petitioners, which is incompatible with equitable rescission.

CONCLUSION

The respondents were entitled to rescind the contract, but may not recover the costs of developing the land in the form of consequential damages. The respondents are entitled to restitution of their down payment and any amount by which the value of the land was enhanced, but in turn the respondents must pay petitioners the fair rental value of the tenancy. Accordingly, the trial court is affirmed in part and reversed in part and the court of appeals' decision is approved in part and vacated in part. The case is remanded to the trial court for further proceedings not inconsistent with this opinion.

HOLOHAN, C.J., and HAYS, CAMERON and FELDMAN, JJ., concur.

All Citations

150 Ariz. 94, 722 P.2d 262

Written but officially unpublished decisions from courts are increasingly common. As the notes explicitly spell out, this case cannot be cited as binding precedent. So why read it at all? What use can it have? A case dealing with the sale of a classic car and an "as is" clause seems significantly different from the matters at issue in Relich v. Leigh. Why do you think the judge's research assistant chose this as one of the few cases you should review?

2010 WL 682189

NOTICE: THIS DECISION DOES NOT CREATE LEGAL PRECEDENT AND MAY NOT BE CITED EXCEPT AS AUTHORIZED BY APPLICABLE RULES. See Ariz. R. Supreme Court 111(c); ARCAP 28(c); Ariz. R.Crim. P. 31.24

Court of Appeals of Arizona, Division 1, Department D.

Lori DELUCA; Jo-Ellen Doorn; Cheryl Kaminski, Plaintiffs/Appellants,

v.

Gregory McMAHON and Susan McMahon, husband and wife, Defendants/Appellees.

No. 1 CA-CV 09-0140.

|

Feb. 25, 2010.

Appeal from the Superior Court in Yavapai County; Cause No. P-1300-CV-0020060152; The Honorable David L. Mackey, Judge. AFFIRMED IN PART; REVERSED IN PART; REMANDED.

Attorneys and Law Firms

Eckley & Associates, PC By J. Robert Eckley, Kevin B. Sweeney, Phoenix, Attorneys for Plaintiffs/Appellants.

Shorall McGoldrick Brinkmann By Thomas J. Shorall, Jr., Asa W. Markel, Phoenix, Attorneys for Defendants/Appellees.

MEMORANDUM DECISION

JOHNSEN, Judge.

¶ 1 Lori DeLuca, Jo-Ellen Doom and Cheryl Kaminski ("Buyers") appeal from entry of summary judgment in favor of Gregory and Susan McMahon ("Sellers") on Buyers' complaint. We affirm in part, reverse in part and remand for further proceedings.

FACTUAL AND PROCEDURAL HISTORY

¶ 2 Sellers owned a duplex in Sedona but lived in Michigan and rented out the duplex. They engaged a property manager and visited approximately once per year. In March 2005, Sellers listed the property for sale. The following month, Buyers saw an advertisement for the duplex. They called the listing agent, Harry Christie, to make an appointment to see the duplex and spent approximately 20 minutes there. During their visit, Doorn, noticing a musty odor, asked Christie "if the house had ever taken on water."

Christie replied that the property had not taken on water and that the odor was caused by the prior tenant, who was a smoker and had large dogs.

¶ 3 Later in the day, Buyers made an offer on the property. They also executed a document entitled "Consent to Limited Representation," by which they agreed that Christie would represent them as well as the Sellers. The parties executed a purchase contract a few days later. The contract included the following advisory: "Buyer is advised by Broker to obtain inspections and investigations of the Premises." The contract also included the following warranties: "(a) Buyer warrants to Seller that Buyer has conducted all desired independent investigations and accepts the Premises and (b) Buyer acknowledges that there will be no Seller warranty of any kind, except as stated in Lines 280–286." Lines 280 to 286 stated in part: "Seller warrants that Seller has disclosed to Buyer and Broker(s) all material latent defects and any information concerning the Premises known to Seller, excluding opinions of value, which materially and adversely affect the consideration to be paid by Buyer."

¶ 4 Sellers completed a Seller's Property Disclosure Statement ("Disclosure"). In response to a question in the Disclosure about problems related to drainage, Sellers wrote, "Side yard to front drainage-pipe installed." In the Disclosure Sellers denied knowledge of "any water damage or water leaks of any kind" or "any past or present mold growth." The Disclosure included a seller's certification that the information it contained was "true and complete to the best of Seller's knowledge." It further included the following acknowledgement:

Buyer acknowledges that the information contained herein is based only on the Seller's actual knowledge and is not a warranty of any kind. Buyer acknowledges Buyer's obligation to investigate any material (important) facts in regard to the Property. Buyer is encouraged to obtain Property inspections by professional independent third parties and to consider obtaining a home warranty protection plan.

¶ 5 Buyers obtained an inspection of the property. With respect to grading, the inspection stated, "Drainage of site/slope of soil at foundation is proper based upon visual observation," "[s]ome visible signs of soil erosion were noted around the site," and "[s]igns of poor drainage/erosion." With respect to the roof, the report stated the roof appears "serviceable/within useful life" and appeared to be "typical for age of home," but showed "evidence of prior patching/repairs." The inspection report cautioned: "The inspection does not report on the possible presence of mold. If you have concerns for the presence of mold, we recommend hiring an independent [sic] specializing in mold testing and abatement." The parties closed escrow on the house on or about June 15, 2005. In September 2005, Buyers received a report based on an investigation conducted in August that "water intrusion has taken place in both the back wall cavities, resulting in microbial growth."

¶ 6 Buyers filed suit against Sellers and others, including Christie and his employer. The first amended complaint alleged Sellers breached a duty to disclose all known defects, including mold, waste and termite events. They asserted the duplex suffered a long history of water, mold and pest damage, which Sellers failed to disclose, and that Buyers had incurred repair costs. Buyers alleged breach of contract, negligent misrepresentation, mutual mistake and consumer fraud pursuant to Arizona Revised Statutes ("A.R.S.") sections 44-1521 *et seq.* (2003 & Supp.2009).

¶ 7 After the close of discovery, Sellers moved for summary judgment. Over Buyers' objection, the court granted Sellers' motion, reasoning that Christie's knowledge of issues with the duplex was imputed to Buyers as well as to Sellers. It concluded:

> Pursuant to Arizona law, "[t]he knowledge of a dual agent is normally imputed to both principals." *Manley v. Ticor Title Insurance Company of California,* 168 Ariz. 568, 573, 816 P.2d 225, 230 (1991) citing *Arizona Title Ins. & Trust Co. v. Smith,* 21 Ariz.App. 37[1], 376, 519 P.2d 860, 865 (1974).

> There is no material factual dispute that [Sellers] had no knowledge of the problems complained of by [Buyers].... [Sellers] can only be imputed with the knowledge of their agent Harry Christie. Since [Buyers] may be imputed with the same knowledge, they have no cause of

action against [Sellers] for breach of contract, negligent misrepresentation or consumer fraud.

> The Court also has considered [Buyers'] claim against [Sellers] for rescission based upon mutual mistake. The Court finds that the theory of "conscious ignorance" discussed in *Nelson v. Rice,* 198 Ariz. 563, 566, 12 P.3d 238, 241 (App.2000) precludes [Buyers'] claim of rescission based upon mutual mistake. The facts are undisputed that [Buyers] were put on notice that they should investigate the condition of the property as it related to water intrusion, drainage and mold; however, they chose to proceed with the sale even in the face of their limited knowledge. The Court finds as a matter of law, [Buyers] are not entitled to rescission based upon mutual mistake under the facts of this case.

¶ 8 Buyers moved for reconsideration. They argued that, under Arizona law, Christie's knowledge could not be imputed to them. The court denied the motion for reconsideration, concluding:

> Even if the Court were to accept the arguments of [Buyers], the Court's Ruling granting summary judgment for [Sellers] would still stand. In addition to the Court's Ruling regarding dual agency and imputed knowledge questioned by the [Buyers], the Court ruled that the theory of "conscious ignorance" precludes [Buyers'] claim of rescission. A review of the file reflects that [Buyers] have elected to pursue rescission and not damages. Therefore, the Court's Ruling, even if modified pursuant to [Buyers'] arguments, still disposes of [Buyers'] claims against [Sellers].

¶ 9 The court entered judgment in favor of Sellers, awarding them attorney's fees of $40,000 and costs. Buyers filed a timely notice of appeal. We have jurisdiction pursuant to A.R.S. § 12-2101(B) (2003).

DISCUSSION

A. Standard of Review.

¶ 10 Summary judgment may be granted when "there is no genuine issue as to any material fact and ... the moving party is entitled to judgment as a matter of law." Ariz. R. Civ. P. 56(c). Summary judgment should be granted "if the facts produced in support of the claim or defense have so little probative value, given the quantum of evidence required, that reasonable people could not agree with the conclusion advanced by the proponent of the claim or defense." *Orme School v. Reeves,* 166 Ariz. 301, 309, 802 P.2d 1000, 1008 (1990). In reviewing a motion for summary judgment, we determine *de novo* whether any genuine issues of material fact exist and whether the superior court properly applied the law. *Eller Media Co. v. City of Tucson,* 198 Ariz. 127, 130, ¶ 4, 7 P.3d 136, 139 (App.2000). We view the facts and the inferences to be drawn from those facts in the light most favorable to the party against whom judgment was entered. *Prince v. City of Apache Junction,* 185 Ariz. 43, 45, 912 P.2d 47, 49 (App.1996).

B. Mutual Mistake.

¶ 11 A party may be entitled to rescission based on mutual mistake concerning a "basic assumption" of the parties to the contract. *Renner v. Kehl,* 150 Ariz. 94, 97, 722 P.2d 262, 265 (1986) (quoting Restatement (Second) of Contracts ("Restatement") § 152 cmt. b (1981)). The mistake, however, may not be one on which the party seeking rescission bore the risk. *Nelson v. Rice,* 198 Ariz. 563, 566, ¶ 7, 12 P.3d 238, 241 (App.2000).

¶ 12 The superior court concluded Buyers' claim for mutual mistake was barred by their "conscious ignorance" of the facts about which Buyers asserted the parties were mutually mistaken. Under the Restatement, "A party bears the risk of mistake when ... he is aware, at the time the contract is made, that he has only limited knowledge with respect to the facts to which the mistake relates but treats his limited knowledge as sufficient." Restatement § 154(b). A comment to the Restatement further explains:

> *c. Conscious ignorance.* Even though the mistaken party did not agree to bear the risk, he may have been aware when he made the contract that his knowledge with respect to the facts to which the mistake relates was limited. If he was not only so aware that his knowledge was limited but undertook to perform in the face of that awareness, he bears the risk of the mistake. It is sometimes said in such a situation that, in a sense, there was not mistake but "conscious ignorance."

Restatement § 154 cmt. c.

¶ 13 Viewing the facts in the light most favorable to Buyers, we accept that Christie told them that the house had not "taken on water" and that Sellers did not disclose problems with drainage or roof leaks. Buyers acknowledged at the time of purchase their obligation to investigate the property, however, and the inspector they hired reported water and drainage issues. The inspection report disclosed evidence that the roof had been patched and that there were signs of poor drainage and erosion. The inspector also warned Buyers that the inspection did not address the possible presence of mold and recommended an independent inspection if mold was a concern. Doorn testified Buyers were provided a list of inspectors that included roofers and mold inspectors, and that despite knowing that they could have a mold inspection, they chose to purchase the property without one.

¶ 14 Buyers argue the principle of "conscious ignorance" does not apply because Sellers were obligated to disclose defects in the property, including drainage issues and roof leaks. But in their claim for rescission based on mutual mistake, Buyers assert that they and the Sellers were mutually mistaken about "substantial adverse conditions" of the property. That allegation is inconsistent as a matter of law with Buyers' argument that Sellers knew of the adverse conditions and should have disclosed them. On this record, we find no error in the superior court's conclusion that Buyers' conscious ignorance of the adverse conditions precluded their claim for rescission based on mutual mistake.

C. Other Claims for Relief.

1. The effect of "conscious ignorance" on the other claims.

¶ 15 Rescission is a remedy, not a cause of action, and may be sought based on various theories, including fraud and breach of contract. *See Jennings v. Lee,* 105 Ariz. 167, 461 P.2d 161 (1969) (action for rescission based on fraud); *Earven v. Smith,* 127 Ariz. 354, 621 P.2d 41 (App.1980) (breach of contract). As the superior court noted, Buyers elected to seek rescission on each of their claims. Sellers argue the court correctly dismissed each of Buyers' claims because Buyers' conscious ignorance precludes rescission on any theory of relief. Sellers contend that by attributing "conscious ignorance" to the Buyers, the court effectively found Buyers had unclean hands, which would bar their entitlement to rescission under any of their claims for relief.

¶ 16 The court, however, made no finding that Buyers were guilty of unclean hands, and Sellers offer no authority for the proposition that by itself, "conscious ignorance" constitutes a defense to rescission based on breach of contract, negligent misrepresentation or consumer fraud. Accordingly, we conclude the finding of conscious ignorance does not preclude Buyers' claim for rescission based on theories other than mutual mistake.

2. Imputation of Christie's knowledge.

¶ 17 The superior court also held Buyers could not prevail on their claims for breach of contract, negligent misrepresentation and consumer fraud because as a matter of law, Christie's knowledge was imputed to them.

¶ 18 As a general matter, the knowledge of an agent is imputed to the principal, and when an agent serves two principals, the agent's knowledge may be imputed to both. *Manley v. Ticor Title Ins. Co.,* 168 Ariz. 568, 572–73, 816 P.2d 225, 229–30 (1991). An exception to this general rule applies, however, in the case of misrepresentations by an agent who represents both the buyer and seller in a real estate transaction. *See Miller v. Boeger,* 1 Ariz.App. 554, 558–59, 405 P.2d 573, 577–78 (1965) (fact that agent was acting for both parties "is no defense" to action by one of them to hold the other liable for agent's misrepresentations) (quotation omitted). In *Jennings v. Lee,* one party sought to rescind a real estate transaction after discovering that the agent who had represented both parties provided her with false financial information about the property. 105 Ariz. at 168–70, 461 P.2d at 162–64. The other party argued the agent was acting as the plaintiff's agent when he gave her the false information. Adopting the principle applied in *Boeger,* the *Jennings* court concluded that the dual agency did not preclude rescission of the contract. *Id.* at 171, 461 P.2d at 165. *See also Miller v. Wood,* 188 Cal.App.2d 711, 714, 10 Cal. Rptr. 770 (1961) ("Where an agent common to two parties betrays one in favor of the other the second … cannot charge the first with the agent's knowledge.") (quotation and citation omitted).

¶ 19 In this case, Sellers and Buyers both engaged Christie, who Buyers assert misrepresented the condition of the property to the benefit of Sellers and the detriment of Buyers. Sellers contend Christie's knowledge is chargeable to Buyers so as to preclude their rescission claim. Under *Boeger, Jennings* and *Wood,* however, Sellers may not rely on the dual agency to defeat Buyers' claims.

¶ 20 Sellers argue *Jennings* and *Wood* do not apply because in those cases the agent was guilty of actual fraud. The cases, however, do not make the distinction Sellers urge. The rule the cases articulate applies broadly to misrepresentations by agents who represent both sides to a real estate transaction; the decisions do not purport to limit the rule to occasions in which the agent acts with some greater degree of culpability.

¶ 21 Sellers also argue that *Jennings* is undermined by *Manley,* which was decided 22 years after *Jennings* and applied the general rule that knowledge of a dual agent is imputed to both principals without recognizing the exception stated in *Jennings.* The facts in *Manley,* however, are unlike those in *Boeger, Jennings* and *Wood. Manley* involved a seller's claim against an escrow company. An employee of the escrow company observed circumstances suggesting fraud in a real estate transaction. 168 Ariz. at 570, 816 P.2d at 227. The employee informed the sellers' real estate agent but did not inform the sellers directly. *Id.* The court noted the general rule that knowledge acquired by an agent is imputed to the principal unless the agent is acting adverse to the principal. *Id.* at 572, 816 P.2d at 229. The sellers argued the knowledge of their agent should not be imputed to them because the agent also was the buyers' agent, but the court found that fact alone did not establish that the agent was acting adversely to the sellers. *Id.* at 572–73, 816 P.2d at 229–230. The court ultimately concluded that a question of fact remained as to whether the escrow company employee knew the agent had interests adverse to the sellers such that the agent was unlikely to convey the information to the sellers. *Id.* at 573, 816 P.2d at 230.

¶ 22 We do not understand *Manley* to alter the conclusion reached in *Boeger, Jennings* and *Wood* that the knowledge of a dual agent in a real estate transaction does not necessarily bar claims by one party to the transaction against the other. Accordingly, based on *Boeger, Jennings* and *Wood,* we hold that Buyers' rescission claims based on breach of contract, negligent misrepresentation and consumer fraud are not barred as a matter of law by Christie's knowledge.

D. Motion to Quash.

¶ 23 Buyers also argue the superior court abused its discretion in denying their motion to quash a subpoena for the deposition of one of their experts, whom they had withdrawn, and in allowing Sellers to use the expert. We decline to address this contention because the subpoena was issued at the request of the Christie Defendants, who are not parties to this appeal. In addition, the ruling on the motion to quash is not encompassed by the judgment from which the Buyers appeal. *See* A.R.S. § 12-2102(A) (2003).

E. Attorney's Fees.

¶ 24 Buyers and Sellers both seek their attorney's fees on appeal. Because neither side has yet prevailed, we deny both requests, but the superior court may grant attorney's fees incurred in this appeal in its determination of fees at the conclusion of the litigation.

CONCLUSION

¶ 25 We affirm the superior court's ruling that Buyers' conscious ignorance precludes their claim for rescission based on mutual mistake. We reverse its decision, however, that conscious ignorance of the Buyers also precludes their right to seek rescission on their other claims for relief. We further hold that Christie's dual agency does not as a matter of law preclude Buyers' claims for breach of contract, negligent misrepresentation and consumer fraud. Accordingly, we vacate the judgment, including the award of attorney's fees and costs, and remand to the superior court for further proceedings consistent with this decision. Buyers are awarded their costs of appeal, contingent on their compliance with ARCAP 21.

CONCURRING: PATRICIA A. OROZCO, Presiding Judge and JON W. THOMPSON, Judge.

All Citations

Not Reported in P.3d, 2010 WL 682189

Understand the Problem

What does the judge want in a bench memo?

Attorneys and law student interns who work in court chambers are frequently called upon to write legal memoranda for their judges. Usually these "bench memos" are intended to summarize the arguments on both sides of a point in contention, and to provide any additional research the judge may need to reach a decision or to write the opinion. In other words, at its best a bench memo can help the judge see past the advocacy of the parties' briefs to reach the most correct and just determination.[1]

Traditional bench memos have a structure similar to law office memos. They commonly feature sections laying out the history or main issues in the case, a statement of the facts, a summary of the parties' contentions or arguments, and the law clerk's analysis of the legal issues presented. If requested, they also include the law clerk's recommended outcome—some judges very much want to see their clerk's opinions, while others want only neutral information and prefer to make their own decisions without any outside influence.

Judges are busy people and many courts are overburdened. Therefore most judges encourage their clerks to make bench memos as brief as possible, yet still as long as needed to thoroughly analyze the issues at hand.

What does it mean for this memo to be "informal?"

Law students work hard to learn how lawyers present arguments and organize their ideas. Once you have been taught one way to write a law office memo or brief, it may be frustrating to find out that it is exactly that: *one* way to do this job. You may eventually find yourself employed in a professional setting that uses a slightly different form from the one you were taught. If so, you should of course adapt to the requested requirements. But what if there is no standardized way of presenting materials in your office? Does that mean that you automatically revert to doing exactly what you learned in your introductory legal writing class? Perhaps, but not necessarily.

Your job, always, is to present information in the best possible way to serve your purpose. Please understand that the parts of a law office memo that most of us learned were designed in essence to do just that (probably something akin to: Question/Issue Presented; Brief Answer; Factual Statement; Discussion/Analysis, and Conclusion). Lawyers tend to write in labeled sections so that readers remain oriented and documents can be easily scanned. The standard format accomplishes that. And the real point of legal memos is that busy people handling many cases need to be able to pick up a memo and quickly ascertain what it is intended to address and what conclusions it reaches, while still having the background analysis and support needed to delve further or to independently evaluate those conclusions. Do you see that the question and brief answer are intended to accomplish the first objective, while the discussion or analysis that makes up the body of the memo provides the second?

> One way lawyers often check their own documents is by scanning only through their headings without reading the accompanying text. If the headings alone convey the gist of what the document is trying to say then they are probably successful. If not, further revision might be in order.

The standard memo format was distilled so that much of the time it nicely serves the purpose of the assignment given to a junior attorney. But the form is generic, and should be adapted to the particulars of your practice or your project. If you know your supervisor is *very* familiar with the case and wants a quick turnaround on some research, for example, you might skimp on the Facts

---

1. For more detailed discussion see Mary Dunnewold et al., Judicial Clerkships: A Practical Guide 126 (2010).

section. If you are researching an issue concerning several complicated statutes, you might insert a separate section parsing the statutory language or history before delving into analysis of their application to your case in the Discussion section. If it would be more helpful to compare facts and allegations in a chart than to write them out in prose, then by all means do so. The point is that once you understand the purpose of your writing it becomes easier to adapt your methods of achieving that purpose to the specific needs of your projects. This is why the standard law office memorandum is something almost all law students are taught, yet may not be quite what most attorneys actually *do* most of the time.

> The judge does not precisely come out and say she wants something akin to the Discussion section of a more traditional legal memo, so how would her clerk know that? This is where you need to develop sound professional judgment and the ability to read and think a bit flexibly. The judge asks for a "readable discussion of your conclusions," "with a complete explanation of your reasoning and… authority." Isn't that basically what a good Discussion is?

In this case file, by asking for an "informal" memo your judge seems to be indicating that she wants a short, stripped-down document. Since legal analysis is always at the heart of what lawyers do, this usually means you should focus primarily on presenting your substantive consideration of the problem. In this instance the judge suggests she is looking primarily for a brief version of the Discussion portion of a traditional law office memo. You are therefore encouraged to include preliminary subsections as the Question Presented or a Statement of Facts *only* if they can be made very short, and if they make your brief paper significantly easier to understand and more helpful to the judge.

Nevertheless, everything you have learned about legal writing style still applies. Use topic or point headings where they will help break up your text. Spell out the relevant rules of law precisely, and carefully explain their applications to the facts as alleged in the complaint and supported in other case records. Consider counter-arguments where reasonable, and explain why your analysis is more correct.

Own every legal document you produce. Intentionally construct this one to be as clear and effective as possible for your reader, who understands general principles of contract law and the facts of this case and who wants your help puzzling through how to apply the law to these particular facts.

Utilize Legal and Non-legal Documents

How should you use the complaint?

Remember that a complaint is the pleading the plaintiff uses to initiate a lawsuit. Lawyers who draft complaints know that if their pleadings are incomplete or otherwise technically defective, defense counsel will immediately move to dismiss the case and will probably win. One goal of the writer is therefore to set forth enough information to survive any motion to dismiss. Yet most attorneys know that more facts will emerge in discovery, some of which may conflict with what they know or assume at the beginning stages of a case. For this reason, and also to maintain the tactical advantage of telling the other side as little as possible, complaint drafters may try to meet the requirement of providing adequate notice to defendants but stop giving details at a point just after reaching that threshold. Ask yourself whether the complaint in this case meets those objectives: does it provide factual allegations sufficient, in a bare-bones way, to support the legal claims it makes if the plaintiff's facts were found to be true? If not, then the complaint might be subject to outright dismissal.

In this case the judge says that defense counsel is moving to dismiss for failure to state a claim upon which relief may be granted. Defense sides almost always gain advantage in civil litigation by making cases take more time or be more hassle for plaintiffs. Therefore, in the usual order of things, a defense attorney's first step would probably be filing a motion to dismiss a complaint on purely technical grounds: improper pleading form, inadequate service of process, etc. Defense lawyers would save the more substantive question of whether there is a legal basis for granting relief if the facts alleged in the complaint are true for their next step, either after an improper complaint is dismissed or withdrawn and then refiled (gaining time and adding inconvenience to the plaintiff). Alternatively, they would move to the more substantive stage immediately upon concluding that there are really no purely technical failings that would be likely to result in a court throwing out the initial pleadings. That is probably the case here.

So in our case we are addressing what in federal court would be a Rule 12(b)(6) motion[2] (note that it shares that same designation under Arizona rules, which suggests that those state rules might track the federal rules fairly closely). As you have undoubtedly seen in Civil Procedure class and from learning generally how to read cases, for the purpose of deciding the motion this means the court has to act as if the facts alleged in the complaint are true. It doesn't at all mean that they *are* true, of course. Only that the court's job at this point is to ask if everything plaintiff claims is correct, "So what?" or more precisely, "Does the law provide any possible redress for Plaintiff's claims if they are true?"

What this means for your memo is that you must analyze the legal issues as if the facts in the complaint can be proven. You should be careful in your prose, however, to remember that they remain allegations, not yet actual "facts" that the defense may agree with. As you read the complaint please also take special note of what Ms. Relich is and is not claiming Mr. Leigh knew at the time of the sale. Those allegations will necessarily affect which facts can support which contract defenses.

What is effect of the seller advisory form?

Your initial scan of the judge's assignment memo in the case file should have alerted you that this case will hinge on what either or both parties knew about the property in question, and what the seller did or did not tell the buyer about it. At this pre-trial stage we do not yet have discovery or testimony from which to draw conclusions about what happened here. The only actual evidence the court has to work with (aside from what is alleged in the complaint and presumed for the moment to be true) will be found in the disclosure form. That means it requires pretty careful study.

Pay attention to the construction of the form itself. How is it organized, and what kinds of questions are asked? Based on the form's content, what would buyers and sellers reasonably assume were the goals of disclosure? How, if at all, would that affect what kinds of information the parties would expect to be included?

One issue you can definitely expect to arise is the fact that in the form's informational cover sheet the given title pretty assertively advises "When in doubt—disclose!" How should the parties read that?

Another issue predictably generated by that first cover page is the included note stating that by law (presumably some Arizona statute) "sellers are not obligated to disclose that the property … has been … the site of a homicide." Does this dispose entirely of any claim based on the long-ago double murder on the premises? If not, why not, and how might plaintiff argue that this particular case might be distinguished from that general disclosure rule?

Next, look closely at the information the seller actually provided in this form. What exactly did Mr. Leigh say about the house? Remember that lawyers' arguments may rest both on facts they can find, and upon what is *not* present but that the lawyers believe ought to have taken place (similar to the way that a party may be negligent either for unreasonable conduct or for a failure to take reasonable precautions).

---

2. And what might once have been called a demurrer.

Read the form critically and from the perspectives of both parties: If you had been advising Mr. Leigh when he was completing the disclosure form (and presumably very much wanting the sale to go through) would you have told him to fill it out exactly the way he did? Or, knowing what you do about the case, would you have suggested any alterations? If you were Ms. Relich and received the form, what would you expect to be true and not true about the house you intended to purchase?

Use Legal Authority

In this case we have secondary authority in the form of the Restatement of Contracts and primary authority from four Arizona cases. As always, you should use the secondary sources to familiarize yourself with the law generically, then fill in with the specifics drawn from your jurisdiction. In this particular instance those specifics really matter.

In your Contracts class you may have covered several defenses under the general heading of "deception," including not just misrepresentation but also concealment and nondisclosure. Concealment usually involves one party taking active steps to prevent another party from learning a given fact. We do not have any evidence or allegation that that's what happened in *Relich v. Leigh*, so even if that's a viable defense to contract enforcement in Arizona it probably would not work in this case. But what about nondisclosure? It may be a distinct contract defense in some states, but that's not quite how it operates in Arizona. If you believe that this case hinges on whether the seller had an obligation to provide certain information, you will need to be sure that you can precisely articulate how that defense works in our jurisdiction.

Pay careful attention, too, to the elements of the potential defenses. For example, a mistake must go to a "basic assumption" of the contract while a misrepresentation must be "material" to it. How do those standards differ? Use the exact elements required for each defense here—they are easy to confuse.

Apply Rules to Facts

Lawyers always say that we apply law to facts, but perhaps we should be clearer about the fact that it works in reverse, too. We apply facts to law in order to "spot the issues" and to know which rules to use. And then once we have decided on the appropriate legal principles we can take the more familiar step of closely examining what the rule does, and does not, tell us about how our facts should be decided.

This kind of reverse process is especially important for the case in this chapter, because part of the difficulty many law students and lawyers encounter in analyzing mistake and misrepresentation claims is that so often they both arise from the same factual nucleus. Just as prosecutors may bring multiple charges for the same offense ("we believe it was murder 2 but are also charging manslaughter in the 1st degree to ensure some form of homicide conviction") parties in civil cases are likely to bring any claim that can add or limit liability in the hopes that even if all aren't successful, one or more may work. A court need only find one defense compelling in order to void the contract, though of course it may also find multiple grounds for rescission if legally warranted.

The key way to avoid making mistakes in applying the contract defenses at issue here is to focus not just on what their elements are, but what their purposes are. Understanding the policy behind legal rules will make their application far more straightforward. It will also make it much easier for you to understand what you are doing, and consequently for you to write stronger arguments and analyses.

Articulate Policy Considerations

There is policy behind every rule

Law students sometimes talk about policy as if it is purely social, entirely opinion-based, or somehow not legal. Not only is that not true—public policy is a part of the law itself—but disregarding the significance of policy can get in the way of deep comprehension of legal rules. Without underlying rationales, rules of law would just be arbitrary decrees to be memorized and applied by rote. But that is not what law is, and it most certainly is not what we would want it to be.

Law is made by actual humans. Since laws are written and interpreted by people in order to govern ourselves, they are supposed to make sense to us. Most of the time they actually do. If you take a minute to understand the context, the policy considerations underlying most legal rules are pretty transparent. "Don't murder people" is a pretty universal and uncontroversial example. Most people would generally like to stay alive themselves and keep the people around them safe from harm, so we create rules against killing others.

And once we have established the broad outlines of policy principles the nuances and exceptions are also supposed to flow logically. This explains why there is usually a self-defense exception to homicide crimes: as a society we want to minimize death overall, but if there is no option but to take a life to protect your own, then doing so protects an innocent victim while not increasing the toll of the attempted crime.

Of course policy concerns are not always completely consistent with one another. The most vexing legal questions arise when there are tensions between competing policies. For example, American society very much values freedom of expression, including the right to express unpopular and even offensive positions. Yet we also want to protect ourselves from incitement toward violence. At what point does speech move from the protected realm into the potentially dangerous and therefore prohibited domain? Not an easy question to answer, always fact-specific and context-specific. And not ever truly resolvable without a deep engagement in both of the policy concerns that pull in opposite directions. This is why the most difficult questions in law (and the ones law professors love to test on!) tend to be ones where policies pull us in different directions. The more deeply you understand what is at issue and why, the more thoughtful you will be about how the issues may be resolved.

Policy helps decide close cases

If the rules applied to facts lead to one and only one reasonable conclusion, well then, that's the answer. Done. Policy considerations will not factor in at all, because there is only one possible legal outcome.

But how often are things that unequivocal? Sometimes, but not all that often. Any time there is room for interpretation of the meaning of the law, or where conflicting rules might apply (perhaps a general rule and its exceptions), then policy will matter—perhaps a great deal. Policy is, in the end, the *reason* for the rule. Understanding that rationale helps lawyers and judges determine how far it should be stretched and when it does or doesn't apply.

Suppose a six-year-old child has an 8:00 p.m. bedtime. Can he stay up past 10:30 p.m. for his cousin's wedding? Technically, no, that violates the rules, right?[3] So what does an advocate for letting the child stay up late to attend the wedding do? Let's start by asking what the reason is for establishing and enforcing a standard bedtime. Maybe it is that:

---

3. Of course a good advocate might invoke competing rules about participating in important ceremonial events with family. But for the sake of this example let's assume only the bedtime rule is at issue.

1. Getting enough sleep is important for small children's growth and development. Or

2. Routines are important for small children who respond best to predictable schedules. Or

3. Rules matter for their own sake; part of raising children is teaching them to follow rules rather than doing whatever they want. Or

4. The parents need time for themselves, and putting the child to bed early ensures that they can flourish as well.

Can we see that each of these rationales for the bedtime might lead to a slightly different approach to resolving the "should the kid stay up for the wedding?" question. If the primary concern is the child getting enough sleep, then a one-time exception may lead to an overly tired and cranky child the next day, but might arguably remain consistent with a general concern regarding overall sleep health. But if the "a rule is a rule" concern is the primary driver, then that purpose may be thwarted by permitting the child to attend the wedding. (Unless the parent is ready to introduce the added sophistication of "many rules have exceptions and here may be one.")

Policy, then, is not simply some added decoration to include in legal analysis after you have done the "real" legal work. It is an integral part of using the law itself. Giving sensible reasons for the rules will make your analysis stronger. It may even help you understand the rules themselves.

Consider the policies underlying the Mistake and Misrepresentation defenses

Why would we *ever* throw out an otherwise-valid contract just because one or both parties made a mistake about something? Chances are, you learned in your Contracts class that making private agreements binding as a matter of law is critical to the functioning of a market economy. Or that freedom to enter contracts, even *very* bad deals, is an important part of freedom overall. Courts are loath to throw out valid agreements. So what is the reason why this defense is recognized at all?

Everyone makes deals with imperfect knowledge. That is just the nature of business—parties may diligently gather as much information as they can, but it is absolutely not possible always to know everything. Yet taking this existential uncertainty into account, contracts are made, executed, and enforced every day. What distinguishes those deals with ordinary undiscovered information ("drat, the brakes on the car I just bought are more sensitive than I'm used to") from those that might be voided by newly found facts ("hey, I just found out that two owners ago this car was in a major collision which completely bent its frame!")?

The elements of the defense itself can help us understand the answer. Do you see how difficult it is to rescind a contract because of a mutual mistake? That it is harder still to do so based on just one party's error (why would that be?)? What do the elements of these defenses tell you about how to balance the uncertainties that come with all deal-making versus our concerns for fairness to the parties?

Next, think about the defense of misrepresentation. Here, what one party knows is directly affected by what another party says (or in Arizona at least, does not say but should have said). That seems different and less neutral when compared to a party's naturally occurring erroneous belief, doesn't it? Even though the defense does not require a finding of fault or intent, there is more activity, hence a stronger feeling of "faultishness," when one party is relying on what the other party said, did, or perhaps omitted. This whiff of undesirable conduct can help explain why the elements for rescinding a contract based on a misrepresentation are less stringent than they are for mistake. Knowing this distinction between mistake and misrepresentation defenses would help you learn and remember the rules more easily, of course. It would also help you apply them more thoughtfully, and explain your reasoning in a richer and more resonant way.

Demonstrate Reliable Legal Judgment

Lawyers are casually called "counselor" for a reason: at base, our job is often to provide professional guidance, advice, and expertise. This can be challenging for law students who have been, well, *students* for most of their lives, and may feel that it is not really their place to tell others what to do. That hesitation is valuable—the world does not need more bossy or arrogant lawyers—but reluctance to exercise good judgment can also get in the way of competently providing what judges, senior attorneys, or clients actually need from you. (In fact, many supervisors of young lawyers say that one of the ways to immediately stand out on the job is making well-considered decisions about assigned work rather than simply answering by rote whatever questions the boss asks.) Err on the side of providing sufficient information to allow others to reach their own independent conclusions, but try not to shy away from exercising your own judgement while doing so.

In this case file, for example, you should carefully consider any realistic contract defense that can be raised. One of those might be a unilateral mistake, presumably by the plaintiff here. But once you "spot the issue" by identifying this as a potential defense, please don't stop there. Does it really fit this case? To void a contract based on one party's mistake Restatement § 153 tells us that enforcing the contract must either be unconscionable, or the mistake must in some way be the fault of the non-mistaken party. Does either possibility fit our scenario? In a real stretch, possibly. But there are probably much better defenses.

Similarly, some lawyers seeking to void this contract for sale might be tempted to argue that a misrepresentation went to the "essential terms" of the agreement, hence no lawful binding agreement was ever formed. (Restatement of Contracts 2d § 163) But let's recognize that that's a difficult argument to win on these facts. We have not researched the point, but it isn't hard to imagine that the "essential terms" for residential property probably have to do with whether it can be lived in at all. Thus the sale of a house that turns out to be illegal to reside in because it is structurally unsound and has been condemned by the city might not meet the essential terms of a home purchase. But those are not quite the circumstances Relich and Leigh are facing.

Some attorneys would advise forgoing an argument that is very unlikely to succeed. Others would use every argument that can ethically be made in the hopes that at least one proffered argument will work. Reasonable minds can differ on these strategic decisions. Unless you have a boss telling you explicitly which of these postures to adopt, you will have to make your own determinations of the best approach, which may differ from case to case. But you cannot thoughtfully make *that* decision if you do not use your developing professional wisdom first to assess the strengths of each defense, and next to determine whether in your particular circumstances you should include even the weakest ones.

Apply the Rules to a New Problem

Contract defenses are frequently tested on both contract exams and on the bar. This makes perfect sense, because they are often at the heart of contract litigation.[4] A party that has breached an agreement or wants out of a deal essentially has only the options of trying to attack the formation of the contract itself ("we were never legally bound") or of saying the contract is for some other

---

4. Though this is not meant to say that contract enforcement or defense litigation is all, or even most, of the contracts work lawyers may do. Contract law factors heavily in negotiations and transactions (deal-making), and is therefore the specialty of many lawyers in a wide array of fields. But when anything goes wrong with an agreement defenses are usually one of the first topics considered. In anticipation of that eventuality, they should also be on the mind of any attorney drawing up a contract in the first place.

reason not enforceable.[5] In other words, contract defenses may often be one party's only potential shield against providing some form of compensation to the other party.

Make sure you can correctly analyze the defenses you have looked at by trying to apply them to a new fact pattern.

Sample exam question

Essay—45 minutes

In January 2014, Karen Jefferson saw a notice on a bulletin board at Arizona University that had been posted by defendant, Charles Chaus. In the poster Chaus indicated that he had for sale an Auguste Sebastien Philippe Bernardel violin made in 1835, with an appraised value somewhere between $20,000 and $28,000.

Jefferson called Chaus to ask about the violin. She then drove over to Chaus's home to see it in person, and played and inspected it for at least two hours. During Jefferson's visit Chaus again stated to Jefferson that the violin was an authentic 1835 Auguste Sebastien Philippe Bernardel violin worth somewhere between $20,000 and $28,000. He also showed her Certificate No. 5500 from one Robert Tipple dated September 21, 2006. The certificate indicated that the violin was an authentic Auguste Sebastien Philippe Bernardel violin, and listed the estimated value range that Chaus had repeated to Jefferson. (Tipple, who has since died, was a professional violin maker, authenticator, and appraiser in Tucson, Arizona.) Jefferson agreed to buy the violin for $22,000. The bill of sale signed by Chaus referred to the sale of "One Bernardel A.S.P. Violin."

From the date of purchase until the end of 2015 Jefferson played the violin for an average of eight hours a day. Sometime in April of 2015 Jefferson became aware that the violin might not be a genuine work of Auguste Sebastien Philippe Bernardel made in 1835. Shortly thereafter she contacted Charles Chaus, offering to return the violin and asking for her $22,000 back. Chaus refused to provide a refund, so Jefferson brought suit to rescind the contract of sale.

Jefferson supported her contention that the violin was not genuine by providing two expert violin authenticators. One of the experts signed an affidavit stating that in his opinion the violin was not an actual Bernardel, while the other testified similarly in a sworn deposition attended by counsel for both parties. Jefferson's experts appraised the violin as having a current value between $2500 and $4000. In opposition, Chaus offered only the support of his daughter, a professional concert violinist but not an expert in assessing or valuing violins.

Given the weight of the evidence the court agreed with Jefferson, concluding in a summary judgment that the violin in question was *not* an authentic Bernardel and that its value was far lower than $22,000.

Following this ruling by the court, plaintiff's attorney moved to void the violin's sale. Jefferson argues that there is no disputed issue for trial and that because of Chaus' misrepresentation, or a mistake by both parties, the court has no choice but to rescind the contract.

How should the court rule, and why?

Attacking the exam question

Before you go in to take the test, plan and strategize. You recall that misrepresentation and mistake defenses often arise from the same cluster of facts. You therefore expect that either or both may come up in this test. In the fog of test-taking, how will you know which defenses to analyze and what facts to consider? Key point for sorting these issues—remember that there cannot be a mis-

---

5. Everything else that contract lawyers might litigate would have to do with interpreting the terms of an agreement or determining what damages are owed for its breach.

representation without some (arguably) false statement by the seller. If the defense can point to an assertion it says is incorrect then you should analyze misrepresentation. If not, then chances are the defense will focus on a mistake. The operative question will then be whether both parties were mistaken or only the buyer.

Once you read this particular test question, you should see that there are several statements that the violin is an authentic Bernardel, which turns out not to be correct. Aha! Classic misrepresentation, so you will absolutely consider that issue.

Now, what to focus on in analyzing misrepresentation? This is where you think through all of the elements of the defense, yet also use good legal judgment to decide where to put most energy. There appears to be an expert consensus that the violin was not authentic, so the "not in accord with facts" element is easy and probably requires only a passing explanation. Status as a Bernardel was an overt statement rather than an omission, so failure to disclose seems not to be at issue here. Whether the statement was material may be more debatable, and is exactly the kind of question you could anticipate being argued in court. Accordingly, assume it will require more attention, and that you might need to consider any viable counterarguments. But materiality means relevance, and since the authenticity of this item has a demonstrably substantial impact on its value, in the end this is likely to be fairly easy for plaintiff to establish.

So what's left? Whether the buyer was *justified* in relying on seller's representations about the provenance of this antique violin. Running through the elements thoughtfully this way should suggest that this last issue is probably the most important one to consider carefully in your analysis. You'd want to organize your exam response to give yourself time to delve a little more deeply into that question.

Next, is there also a mistake defense here? Yes, probably, because it seems as if both parties thought the violin was a Bernardel. Both = mutual, you think to yourself, so we can dispense with discussion of unilateral mistake because it is not suggested by any of the facts we are given. Again, the test-taker should run through the elements of the defense, plan on covering all of them, but assess which ones the parties would actually be likely to debate. Can you guess that "basic assumption of the contract" is very subjectively bound up in the specific facts of any deal, and a pretty lofty standard to meet, so that it will almost *always* be a contested question? Chances are you should spend time on that for this particular fact pattern. In fact you could probably expect that this will be a central question to consider for any mistake defense.

Finally, here we have no information about either party being assigned risk in the sale, but we do have the buyer relying for a pretty big deal purchase on only a couple of sources that she did not herself double-check. So is there also maybe an issue of her bearing the risk of any mistake regarding the violin's authenticity?

Response with commentary

This sample below is certainly imperfect, but is reasonably strong. It is on the lengthy side, though, and may be more text than most people could produce in the time given. One thing to consider as you read through the sample is how the answer could be more succinct yet written as effectively.

> **Student Answer**
>
> The issue is whether the court should rescind the contract for the sale of the violin.
>
> *Misrepresentation*
>
> The elements to rescind a contract based on misrepresentation are: (1) a false statement; (2) the false statement is material to the contract and (3) the reliance is justifiable.

> Rescission of the violin sale is absolutely the question before the court. But it may not be very helpful to call it the "issue." That question is simply too broad, and it includes many possible questions to be resolved. Better to analyze a series of more narrowly framed "issues" along the way to answering this larger question.

The impulse to enumerate the specific facts that satisfy an individual element is a good one. In essence, it is a classic IRAC form. But in our test there are multiple elements to cover for several defenses, so this formula could quickly become unwieldy or burdensome. And the biggest payoff usually comes from diving deeply into the most genuinely complex questions. There is a real risk here of running out of time before reaching the most important issues. Try where possible to move swiftly through less debatable points.

Here, the statement that the violin was an authentic 1835 Auguste Sebastien Philippe Bernardel violin was false. The seller advertised and told buyer that it was an authentic violin, but the trier of fact found that the violin in question was indeed not the authentic Bernardel. Thus, element 1 is fulfilled.

A matter is material if a reasonable person would believe that it significantly induces a party to make the deal. Here, the fact that the buyer paid a high price for an authentic violin is material to the contract because the buyer paid a high value for a violin that was worth approximately 10% of what the buyer paid. This matter is material because if buyer had known that the violin was not the authentic one, the buyer would not have paid that much for the violin. Thus, element 2 is fulfilled.

Reliance is justifiable if the buyer actually and reasonably relied on the statement. Here, the Buyer reasonably and actually relied on the Seller's statement which he made in various forms and times: (1) advertised it on a poster, (2) while the Buyer was at his house, and (3) the Seller showed her a Certificate from a professional violin maker, authenticator, and appraiser. The buyer also only had two hours to play and inspect it and everything looked to be in order with what the seller was saying. Because it took her more than a year later to realize it was not the real violin, it was apparent that Buyer's reliance was justifiable. Thus, element 3 is fulfilled.

In form this paragraph seems to support and explain its thesis. But something seems missing. Do we know why the fact that the buyer took a long time to figure out the violin wasn't genuine would arguably support her side? Is it possible that she is just very bad at recognizing differences in instrument quality? Here is an instance where more complete explanation would make for much stronger legal analysis.

However, the seller may argue that the buyer did not only rely on the statement he made, but also her own assumptions because she played the instrument for two hours before agreeing to the contract. But the buyer's argument is stronger because it then took her more than a year to realize that the violin may not actually be genuine.

Therefore, the contract should be rescinded under misrepresentation.

Mutual Mistake

The elements to rescind a contract based on mutual mistake are: (1) both parties are wrong about something; (2) mistaken belief goes to basic assumption; (3) mistaken belief is material to the contract; and (4) the adverse party bears no assumption of risk.

Once again there is absolutely nothing wrong here. But it is worth brainstorming ways to accomplish this same objective more quickly, perhaps by combining several points or by using parenthetical phrases embedded within the list to apply easy elements to the fact pattern and get them out of the way. The more tools you have at your disposal for quick but complete written analysis, the better choices you can make while working fast and under pressure.

Here, both parties were wrong about the fact that the violin was actually made by Bernardel. Seller told buyer and the Seller was told by Robert Tipple, a professional violin maker, authenticator and appraiser. Therefore, element 1 is fulfilled.

The basic assumption is the reason why the party entered the contract. Here, the buyer entered the contract by paying a large sum of $22,000 for what she thought was an authentic violin. Because the authentic violin and the price were the reason why the buyer and seller entered into the deal, this is basic assumption, or the heart of the deal. The buyer ended up paying $22,000 for just a regular violin, which was actually appraised for between $2500 and $4000. Therefore element 2 is fulfilled.

This may be a missed opportunity. The analysis here looks a lot like the discussion of the "materiality" element, but the two standards are in fact quite different. Why is that, and what does it tell us about the nature of both defenses? Considering the nuances of law in that kind of depth is part of what distinguishes outstanding legal reasoning.

A matter is material if it significantly induces a party to enter into an agreement. Here, the buyer wanted an authentic violin and paid the money for an authentic violin. Instead, she received a violin that was not worth that amount of money. Therefore, this matter is material. Thus, element 3 is satisfied.

A party bears the assumption of the risk if she has reason to know of a particular danger and consciously ignores it. Here, the adverse party played the violin for almost two years. In that time she has come to bear the risk of the violin not being authentic because it should not take that amount of time for a regular everyday violin player to discover that the violin was not authentic. Therefore, the buyer assumed the risk. Thus, element 4 is not satisfied.

> Does this discussion persuasively explain why playing the violin after buying it is assuming the risk that it was in fact genuine back at the point of purchase? The writer seems not to fully understand this part of the law. If you aren't sure how the writer could make this stronger, take another look at Restatement 2d § 154 (b).

Furthermore, the seller may argue that the contract cannot be totally rescinded because the Buyer has been playing this violin for an average of eight hours a day for almost two years (from early 2014 to the end of 2015). Because over this time the value has been decreased and the current value of the violin is lower than what it would have been in January of 2014 when the deal was made. So, the court should rule that Buyer keeps violin and seller only has to pay a portion of the original deal back. Value should be determined by expert appraisers.

Therefore, the contract should not be rescinded under mutual mistake.

Contracts Project Checklist

Read your own drafts while looking carefully for each point raised below. If the points are included, please make sure that they are presented and explained to the best of your ability. If they are not, then consider whether your analysis can be made more complete.

1. Where does your analysis lay out the general elements of the mistake and misrepresentation defenses?

2. Does the analysis help the reader understand the similarities and differences between these two defenses? The reasons why they might be related, yet distinct? Does it help the reader understand why courts are generally reluctant to void properly formed contracts, yet might do so if the elements of these defenses are met?

3. Does the paper identify for the reader which elements are most at issue in your problem?

4. If you are contending that there was a misrepresentation in this case, where does your analysis explain:

   a. Exactly what assertion was made that is not in accord with the facts;

   b. If the assertion takes the form of an absence of disclosure rather than of a specific incorrect statement, how we know that Arizona law considers this to be a misrepresentation that may void a contract, and the circumstances under which it will be so considered;

   c. Why the misrepresentation is material to the contract (and accordingly, what it means for it to be "material");

   d. Why the purchaser was justified in relying on the seller's representation?

5. If you are contending that there was no misrepresentation, where does your analysis explain:

   a. The reason a court should conclude that there is no disputed assertion of fact; OR

    b. Why the assertion in dispute is actually correct; OR

    c. Why the incorrect representation was not material to the agreement; OR

    d. Why the buyer had no justification for relying on the seller's representation?

6. If you are contending that there was a mutual mistake that could void this contract, where does your analysis explain:

    a. What belief the parties had that was not in accord with the facts;

    b. Why the mistaken belief is a basic assumption of the contract (and accordingly, what it means for it to be a "basic assumption");

    c. How we know that the mistake had a material effect on the agreement;

    d. That the purchaser did not bear the risk of the mistake (we have no information that the parties allocated risk in the written agreement, so for the buyer to bear the risk she would either have had to consciously decided to proceed in the sale despite being aware of having limited knowledge, or it should be reasonable for the court to assign the risk to her)?

7. If you are contending that there was a unilateral mistake that could void this contract, where does your analysis explain:

    a. That all of the elements of mutual mistake may be satisfied; AND

    b. Either Leigh knew about Relich's mistake or somehow caused it, OR that enforcing the sale of the property would be unconscionable (recognizing and explaining that unconscionability is a very high legal standard and examining why it could possibly be met here)?

8. Is it clear from the analysis who knew what about the property when, and what evidence there is to support those conclusions? Are alternative interpretations of key events refuted either directly or indirectly?

9. Does the analysis carefully distinguish between the plaintiff's personal reasons for wanting to disavow the contract and the legal reasons why a court might deem it unenforceable?

10. Does the organization of the analysis fit the reasoning? Does it follow the traditional logic of applying rules of law to facts?

11. Is the discussion clearly presented, and would it make sense to the reader?

12. Was the analysis proofread, with technical errors and awkwardness eliminated?

Chapter 3

Criminal Law

Assignment: *Advise a Legislator about Current and Potential Legislation*

Based on the materials in the file, please draft a memo answering the Senator's questions and considering how the law would apply to the scenarios he is concerned about. Target length is fewer than ~~1200~~ words, exclusive of titles, headings, or other non-substantive organizational material. 1100

Analytical Skills to Focus On

✓ Understanding your advisory role

✓ Thinking conceptually about legal material

✓ Reading critically

✓ Meticulously analyzing both language and meaning

✓ Evaluating counterarguments

Case File

The materials in the case file are compiled in one complete set so you will have them all together. You should read them all carefully on your own before diving into the commentary and questions that follow. As you read through the materials, ask yourself the same basic questions a practicing lawyer would consider:

1. What is the state senator really concerned with? What information will help him decide what to do?

2. Why did the Senator choose the three examples you were asked to examine?

3. (Perhaps closely related to question #2) What principles and concerns underlie the legal rules at issue?

4. What do the materials in the case file add to your understanding of the problem, and how much should they guide your analysis of the hypotheticals the Senator has given you?

5. What materials are *not* included that would help you better understand your project? Are there ways to work around the realistic limitations of your time, experience, and information?

A project checklist is included at the end of the chapter. Use it to review and edit your drafts as you strive for maximal effectiveness.

··

Chapter 3 Case File

Your exercise packet contains the following:

- A project memo from the New Hampshire State Senator you work for, asking you to analyze three scenarios under the state's Theft by Extortion law
- A copy of Revised Statutes of the State of New Hampshire Annotated § 637:1 and § 637:5 consolidating crimes, including blackmail and extortion
- One of the many law review articles on the "blackmail paradox" that the Senator read in preparation for hearings on the proposed statutory revision
- *State v. Hynes*, 159 N.H. 187 (2009), in which the New Hampshire Supreme Court considered the scope of Theft by Extortion
- Copies of Yelp's Content Guidelines and Terms of Service to review if they are helpful in your analysis.

Thinking about Criminal Law

Criminal Law requires careful application of criminal codes. Most criminal law classes study either the Model Penal Code or their own state's criminal code, or some combination of both. For each crime potentially implicated in a factual circumstance, practitioners must carefully consider how the code applies. This requires breaking each crime into elements, analyzing each one, and judging which ones may be easier or harder for a prosecutor to prove. In a sea of common law first-year subjects, Criminal Law may be the most statute-driven of the traditional foundational courses. (In fact, it would not be unreasonable to outline an entire criminal law course simply by annotating the criminal code with the explanations, questions, and cases and hypotheticals considered in class.)

But the study of criminal law does not just consist of mechanically matching facts from column A to crimes in column B. It is profoundly concerned with justice, and usually explicitly emphasizes important theoretical questions like perpetrator's intent, and the social purpose of punishment. Where more than one charge is possible, such inquiries are crucial in guiding decisions about, for example, whether a homicide is murder, manslaughter, or not at all criminal. Students of criminal law should always consider these larger questions as a predicate to applying the statutory language, or as a means of determining which statutes are most appropriate to the given circumstances.

STATE OF NEW HAMPSHIRE
Offices of State Senator DeRoy Williams

MEMORANDUM

TO: Legislative Aide

FROM: Senator Williams

DATE: March 12, 20____

SUBJECT: Extortion

I recently took a meeting with the Business Leaders' Association board members. The brought in an online article about someone supposedly blackmailing a restaurant by threatening to post a bad review on the Yelp website (https://www.huffingtonpost.com/2012/05/30/yelp-extortion-sacramento_n_1556207.html). Some of their questions caused me want to take a careful look at our laws criminalizing extortion and blackmail. I want you to familiarize yourself with these issues so that you can advise me about whether our current law appropriately prohibits coercive behaviors without unduly restricting the freedoms that our citizens cherish.

> Who are the members of this organization? What concerns are they likely to have? The Senator is letting you know that he takes the issues these constituents raise seriously, so it may be helpful in your work to have some sense of what they are likely to be worried about and why.

I. Background on Blackmail and Extortion

In looking further into the issues our constituents raised I have learned a fair amount about blackmail and extortion that I did not recall from my early days as an assistant prosecutor. First, some terminology: in common parlance "blackmail" laws usually address threats to reveal hidden information, while "extortion" crimes tend to be grounded in coercion by way of threat to the victim's physical, emotional, or economic well-being. Other statutory schemes like New Hampshire's conflate the terms, and treat them together under the umbrella category of "Theft by Extortion." *See* **N.H. Rev. Stat. § 637:1; N.H. Rev. Stat. § 637:5.**

[handwritten: blackmail vs. extortion]

I have now also learned there is actually a great deal of scholarly controversy about these crimes that I had not previously been aware of. Apparently, commentators have referred to blackmail law as a "paradox," observing that it is "unique among major crimes: no one has yet figured out why it ought to be illegal." James Lingren, *Unraveling the Paradox of Blackmail*, 84 Colum. L. Rev. 670, 671 (1984). This is because the law takes two acts that are otherwise permissible—publicizing information and asking for a favor or payment—and makes them criminal when they are done in tandem. Some researchers have suggested that blackmail or extortion ought not to be a crime at all, though of course our history and traditions say otherwise.

> Knowing what employers, colleagues, and clients really want from you is an often overlooked but important professional skill. Note that the senator here is pretty directly telling you what he does not want to do. This is not to say you cannot use your own professional judgment when it differs from your boss's advice. But you should certainly try be aware of his preferences and the reasons for them, and pitch your advice accordingly.

Telephone (603) 658-4000
300 Capitol Ave.
Concord, NH 03302
http://www.nh.gov
Proudly Serving the 39ᵗʰ District

STATE SENATOR DEROY WILLIAMS

To my mind there is little question that extorting individuals or businesses with coercive threats ought to be illegal. And that it *is* illegal under our current law. The question I now have, though, is whether our statutes actually prohibit what they should, and permit what they ought to, when it comes to uses and abuses in online reviewing sites. That's what I would like you to look into. There are apparently very few published New Hampshire cases addressing the application of our extortion statute. I am attaching the one case I did find on the topic but I am not sure whether it will ultimately provide much guidance.

II. Our Constituents' Concerns

The Business Leaders' Association board brought me a copy of an article they had read about an extortion case in California based on the threat of negative Yelp reviews. They were worried about similar cases occurring in our state. Perhaps the workings of the free market meant that it has always been possible for businesses to be subject to inappropriate pressure in order to avoid negative publicity. But the advent of web searching and online reviews has changed the calculus substantially in the customer's favor.

The business owners I spoke with expressed fears that customers could essentially use the review sites to blackmail business owners by demanding favors in exchange for positive reviews. The reported that many of their members felt under pressure to cave in to nearly *any* consumer demands, no matter how outrageous, for fear of receiving a negative comment posted in online reviews of their companies. They also pointed out that this pressure might be especially acute for new businesses, particularly if they had not yet developed an established customer base or generated the many positive online reviews that could dilute the effect of one negative comment. They were also worried that the increasing importance of positive online reviews could open the door to the possibility of extortionate bargaining in their dealings with the review sites themselves.

> **Aha—a careful reader should see that even though it is somewhat buried in the middle of the Senator's memo, this paragraph really summarizes what you are being asked to do**

I want to respond to these concerns by making sure that our statutory scheme criminalizes coercive demands that unfairly target businesses' reputations. On the other hand, I recognize that the criminal law scholars have a point: we cannot turn every offer or request that has any teeth to it into a crime. That would erase the distinction between theft by blackmail or extortion and what we ordinarily consider the kind of "hard bargaining" that is, and should be, possible in a free society.

III. Examples to consider

In short, then, I want to know whether our current law criminalizes the kinds of behavior we think ought to be illegal while being narrow enough to exclude statements that are really more like negotiating than extortion. (If it does not, then our next task will be to craft a bill with newly drafted language for these statutes.)

I have asked the legislative counsel's office to consider the constitutional questions raised by the Theft by Extortion law, so you need not concern yourself with those matters. Instead, I would like you to focus

Telephone (603) 658-4000
300 Capitol Ave.
Concord, NH 03302
http://www.nh.gov
Proudly Serving the 39th District

STATE SENATOR DEROY WILLIAMS

on preparing a memo analyzing whether under the following scenarios the described conduct would be likely to violate New Hampshire law:

1. A customer threatens to write a negative review in a customer review website like Yelp unless the business makes up for unsatisfactory services.

2. Before being served, a customer approaches a business seeking specifically named upgrades or complimentary services in exchange for writing a favorable review on Yelp (or similar), or for not writing a negative one.

3. A business that is just starting out and wants to build a strong online profile decides to provide complimentary products or services (ones that are otherwise usually paid for) for its customers who will promise to post reviews on Yelp. *likely no harm, but harm to society*

Based on your legal analysis of these scenarios, please also let me know whether, in your opinion, the law properly protects the interests of both the small business owners whose companies may be subject to review, and the consumers and public who may find such reviews helpful.

If you believe any of the behavior in my scenarios is legally permissible by our state, but nevertheless should in some way be subject to restriction, please also consider whether the conduct is already prohibited by the site's user agreements. (If so, then perhaps that will be enough to reassure our business leaders that corrective legislation is not needed.)

Please make your memo as short and readable as possible while thoroughly and carefully explaining the legalities of our present statutory scheme.

Thank you.

DW

N.H. Rev. Stat. § 637:1
637:1 Consolidation.

Conduct denominated theft in this chapter constitutes a single offense embracing the separate offenses such as those heretofore known as larceny, larceny by trick, larceny by bailees, embezzlement, false pretense, extortion, blackmail, receiving stolen property. An accusation of theft may be supported by evidence that it was committed in any manner that would be theft under this chapter, notwithstanding the specification of a different manner in the indictment or information.

> The Senator's memo describes this New Hampshire statute and the ones that follow as conflating blackmail and extortion crimes under the umbrella category of theft. The Senator is your supervisor, and he seems like a pretty smart man. But that does not relieve you of an obligation to make sure that you agree with his understanding of these rules. Attorneys should be eager to soak up potentially valuable information from any source. But ultimately you have an ethical and professional obligation to provide your own well-considered professional guidance.

N.H. Rev. Stat. § 637:5

637:5 Theft by Extortion.

I. A person is guilty of theft as he obtains or exercises control over the property of another by extortion and with a purpose to deprive him thereof.

II. As used in this section, extortion occurs when a person threatens to:

(a) Cause physical harm in the future to the person threatened or to any other person or to property at any time; or

(b) Subject the person threatened or any other person to physical confinement or restraint; or

(c) Engage in other conduct constituting a crime; or

(d) Accuse any person of a crime or expose him to hatred, contempt or ridicule; or

(e) Reveal any information sought to be concealed by the person threatened; or

(f) Testify or provide information or withhold testimony or information with respect to another's legal claim or defense; or

(g) Take action as an official against anyone or anything, or withhold official action, or cause such action or withholding; or

(h) Bring about or continue a strike, boycott or other similar collective action to obtain property which is not demanded or received for the benefit of the group which the actor purports to represent; or

(i) Do any other act which would not in itself substantially benefit him but which would harm substantially any other person with respect to that person's health, safety, business, calling, career, financial condition, reputation, or personal relationships.

How frequently do you think lawyers in practice (or law students for that matter), read or rely on works of legal scholarship? Especially ones that are decades old? You would probably want to look this over simply because the Senator mentioned it in his memo. But as you read through this piece, ask yourself what it contributes to your assigned project. (Hint: you, and the Senator, are probably far less concerned with this particular author's personal theories of blackmail than he is.)

Unraveling the Paradox of Blackmail
James Lindgren
84 Colum. L. Rev. 670

Columbia Law Review
April, 1984

Copyright (c) 1984 by the Directors of the
Columbia Law Revision Association, Inc.;
James Lindgren

Most crimes do not need theories to explain why the behavior is criminal. The wrongdoing is self-evident. But blackmail is unique among major crimes: no one has yet figured out why it ought to be illegal. Recognizing the magnitude of the problem, one theorist wondered whether we can find "a principled distinction (or indeed any interesting distinction)"[1] between blackmail and permissible behavior that is not blackmail.

In blackmail, the heart of the problem is that two separate acts, each of which is a moral and legal right, can combine to make a moral and legal wrong.[2] For example, if I threaten to expose a criminal act unless I am paid money,[3] I have committed blackmail. Or if I threaten to expose a sexual affair unless I am given a job,[4] once again I have committed blackmail. I have a legal right to expose or threaten to expose the crime or affair,[5] and I have a legal right to seek a job or money, but if I combine these rights it is blackmail.[6] If both a person's ends—seeking a job or money—and his means—threatening to expose—are otherwise legal, why is it illegal to combine them? Therein lies what has been called the "paradox of blackmail."[7]

Possible rationales for blackmail have been presented by some of the leading legal scholars of this century, including Arthur Goodhart,[8] Robert Nozick,[9] Lawrence Friedman,[10] Richard Posner,[11] and Richard Epstein.[12] None, however, has successfully explained the crime. Not surprisingly, drawing the line between legitimate and illegitimate threats has proved impossible without an accepted theory. Most statutes broadly prohibit behavior that no one really believes is criminal and then rely on the good judgment of prosecutors not to enforce the statute as written.[13] It is unlikely that anyone will be able to bring order out of this confusion until we discover a theory of blackmail that explains the illegality of the paradoxical case.

This Article attempts to find such a theory. In Part I of this Article, I begin with a brief overview of the crime of blackmail. In Part II, I review and criticize eight existing theories of blackmail. One group of theories examines different parts of the blackmail transaction, postulating that the wrongfulness of blackmail consists in what the blackmailer threatens to do if not paid, in what he offers to do if paid, in what he is seeking or in what he is selling. These theories fail chiefly because no single part of the blackmail transaction, taken separately, is necessarily wrong. Since the conduct these theories identify may be wrong in blackmail but legitimate elsewhere, they fail to adequately distinguish legitimate from illegitimate behavior. A second group of theories centers on the purpose served by a law of blackmail—either to discourage invasions of privacy or to prevent the waste of economic resources. These theories fail because they do not explain either why blackmail is forbidden where these harms are absent or why we do not prohibit many other activities that create the same harms.

Finally, in Part III, I try to unravel the paradox and provide a coherent basis for distinguishing legitimate from illegitimate threats. In brief, I argue that the key to the wrongfulness of the blackmail transaction is its triangular structure. The transaction implicitly involves not only the blackmailer and his victim but always a third party as well. This third party may be, for example, the victim's spouse or employer, the authorities or even the public at large. When a blackmailer tries to use his right to release damaging information, he is threatening to tell others. If the blackmail victim pays the blackmailer, it is to avoid the harm that those others would inflict. Thus blackmail is a way that one person requests something in return for suppressing the actual or potential interests of others. To get what he wants, the blackmailer uses leverage that is less his than someone else's. Selling the right to go to the police involves suppressing the state's interests. Selling the right to tell a tort victim who committed the tort involves suppressing the tort victim's interests. And selling the right to inform others of embarrassing (but legal) behavior involves suppressing the interests of those other people.

Noninformational blackmail involves the same misuse of a third party's leverage for the blackmailer's own benefit. For example, when a labor leader threatens to call a strike unless he is given a personal payoff, he is using the leverage of third parties to bargain for his own benefit. Thus the criminalization of informational and noninformational blackmail represents a principled decision that advantages may not be gained by extra leverage belonging more to a third party than to the threatener. Recognizing the triangular structure of the blackmail transaction makes clear the parasitic nature of the blackmailer's conduct. Once this structure is understood, it becomes easier to find in blackmail the kind of behavior that concerns the other theorists: immorality, invasiveness, and economic waste.

I. AN OVERVIEW OF BLACKMAIL

A. Defining Terms

The terms blackmail and extortion are often used interchangeably,[14] which is how I use them in this Article. Broadly speaking, the terms blackmail and extortion can refer to nearly any crime where threats are used to gain an advantage or induce someone to do something.[15] Many modern statutes refer to behavior usually considered blackmail or extortion by other names, such as intimidation,[16] coercion,[17] theft[18] or stealing.[19] The most commonly prohibited threats are to injure person or property,[20] to accuse another of a crime[21] or to expose damaging information.[22]

Blackmail and extortion, however, may connote somewhat different behavior. Blackmail more commonly refers to a threat seeking hush money, while extortion usually refers to a threat of physical harm to persons or property or to a threat made by a public official. In the early eighteenth century, blackmail and extortion were different crimes. Both involved gaining property by threats, but extortion was committed by public officials,[23] while blackmail was committed by private citizens.[24] In addition, blackmail covered only threats of physical harm to persons or property.[25] There was nothing paradoxical in prohibiting these threats, which were to commit crimes. But in 1757, threatening to expose a capital offense or an infamous crime was made criminal in England.[26] It was not until 1843 that Parliament finally extended blackmail to cover threats to expose evidence of embarrassing but noncriminal behavior.[27] In the United States, the development of the law in some states anticipated the English statutes. In 1796, New Jersey passed the first statute prohibiting threats to expose any crime, not just a capital or infamous crime.[28] And in 1827, Illinois passed a statute prohibiting threats to expose "infirmities or failings," sixteen years before similar threats were made illegal in England.[29] As the crime of blackmail expanded from threats of physical harm to threats to expose damaging information, the paradox began to appear and the rationale for the crime became less clear.

B. Searching for a Theory

The paradox of blackmail is not merely an abstract philosophical question. A failure to understand or resolve the paradox has spawned a body of law that is in disarray—statutes that do not adequately describe the crime and court opinions that are poorly reasoned or just plain wrong.

Jurisdictions have enacted a wide variety of blackmail and extortion statutes, nearly all prohibiting blackmail of both the paradoxical and the nonparadoxical types. Modern statutes vary widely on what types of threats are prohibited,[30] whether the threat must succeed,[31] and what types of advantages must be sought for blackmail to have been committed.[32] But the most important differences are over the scope of the claim-of-right defense: when may a bargainer use a threat of harm to pursue a legitimate claim, even a threat to expose a crime or other embarrassing information? The statutes take three basic approaches—all inadequate.

First, many states try to define blackmail without mentioning a claim-of-right defense. A typical statute might flatly prohibit gaining property or inducing someone to do something by threats: (a) to inflict injury to person or property, (b) to reveal a crime, or (c) to expose damaging information.[33] Faced with such a statute, most courts have been unwilling to read in a claim-of-right defense. Thus defendants have been prevented from asserting that they were only trying to collect a lawful debt or that they were only seeking restitution for having been crime victims.[34] As interpreted by most courts, these statutes would seem to prohibit many legitimate activities, such as the threat of a disappointed customer to go to a consumer action reporter unless the merchant pays damages or restitution to the customer. On the other hand, when courts do try to create a claim-of-right defense, they may eviscerate the statute because they fail to understand the paradox of blackmail. For example, in Landry v. Daley,[35] a federal district court held that an Illinois blackmail statute did not apply to situations where the defendant threatened to do something he had a legal right to do.[36] Here the court did not recognize the paradox, that it can be criminal to threaten to do what you have a right to do while seeking what you have a right to seek. Such an analysis excludes from blackmail many traditional blackmail situations, such as where the blackmailer threatens to expose a criminal or other wrongdoer. Although this error would seem to be an obvious one, many courts have made it, generally under the guise of statutory construction.[37]

A second approach taken by state legislatures is to enact statutes with very limited claim-of-right defenses. For example, the Oregon coercion statute prohibits compelling action by a threat to expose a crime or secret.[38] The legislature provided a very narrow claim-of-right defense, allowing only threats seeking restitution.[39] In State v. Robertson,[40] the Oregon Supreme Court considered the statute's constitutionality. The court mentioned legitimate activities the statute appeared to prohibit, such as the threat: "If you don't quit making love to my wife, I'm going to tell your wife."[41] Finding the defense much too narrow, the state supreme court struck down the entire statute on first amendment grounds.[42]

Many statutes take a third approach, providing broad claim-of-right defenses.[43] These statutes often follow the Model Penal Code (Code), which divides the traditional crime of blackmail into two crimes, extortion[44] and criminal coercion.[45] Four separate claim-of-right defenses are provided,[46] most with multiple parts. Despite this profusion of statutory language, the Code still fails to adequately separate legitimate from illegitimate threats.

Under one of the Code's claim-of-right defenses, a threatener is permitted to make certain threats if the property obtained thereby is "honestly claimed as restitution or indemnification for harm done in circumstances to which such accusation . . . relates."[47] Thus under the Code, for example, a tort victim may threaten to expose the circumstances of the tort unless restitution is made. This defense applies to threats to reveal a crime, expose a damaging secret or cause official action to be taken or withheld.[48] It does not, however, apply to the most sweeping provision in the Code's theft by extortion section. This provision prohibits threats "to inflict any harm that would not benefit the actor,"[49] and is designed to proscribe gaining property by threats of gratuitous harm. Read literally, this provision would appear to prohibit many legitimate bargaining tactics—for example, threatening to walk away from a beneficial deal in order to extract more favorable terms.[50] Thus, by not applying this broad claim-of-right defense to the gratuitous harm provision, the Code appears to leave much ordinary bargaining open to prosecution. Obviously, the drafters never intended to criminalize this conduct,[51] but an adequate formulation eluded them.

Despite the difficulty of drafting a coherent blackmail statute, there are large classes of threats that nearly everyone agrees ought to be illegal and other large classes of threats that nearly everyone agrees ought to be permitted. The rest of this Article attempts to meaningfully distinguish those two types of threats.

II. THEORIES OF BLACKMAIL

By examining the existing theories of blackmail, we should gain not only an understanding of the complexity of the paradox, but a list of problems that any theory must resolve before it can be generally accepted. The existing theories can be divided into two general groups. The first group seeks to find something intrinsically immoral in the blackmail transaction, looking for wrongfulness either in the blackmailer's threatened conduct or in some other aspect of the transaction. The second group of theories explains the criminality of blackmail by looking at the harms blackmail causes. These theories argue that blackmail is forbidden because allowing it would either waste economic resources or create incentives to engage in other wrongful conduct.

*** Portions of this Article have been edited for brevity. In omitted portions of the Article, the author reviews numerous individual scholars' theories of blackmail while grouping them into two categories: A) theories concerned with what should be viewed as wrongful conduct by a blackmailer; and B) theories concerned with the societal purpose of criminalizing blackmail. The author then transitions to proposing his own way of looking at the crime:*

III. A NEW THEORY OF BLACKMAIL
A. Distinguishing Legitimate from Illegitimate Threats

We now turn to the main problem—distinguishing blackmail from legitimate bargaining. Merely identifying the element of threat will not solve the problem.[161] Even highly coercive threats are present in many types of legitimate economic bargaining.[162] For example, an injured potential plaintiff may threaten to sue unless a settlement is reached.[163] A seller may threaten to sell to someone else unless the buyer agrees to pay the price demanded.[164] Or a bank may threaten to foreclose on a loan that will destroy a business as well as someone's way of life.[165] The problem is to distinguish legitimate threats from illegitimate ones; we must explain why the same threat when made by one person can be permissible, but when made by another person in different circumstances can be blackmail.

Let us first examine informational blackmail. Here the blackmailer threatens to tell others damaging information about the blackmail victim unless the victim heeds the blackmailer's request, usually a request for money. The blackmailer obtains what he wants by using extra leverage. But that leverage belongs more to a third person than to the blackmailer. The blackmail victim pays the blackmailer to avoid involving third parties; he pays to avoid being harmed by persons other than the blackmailer. When the reputation of a person is damaged, he is punished by all those who change their opinion of him. They may "punish" him by treating him differently or he may be punished merely by the knowledge that others no longer respect him.

Thus when a blackmailer threatens to turn in a criminal unless paid money, the blackmailer is bargaining with the state's chip.[166] The blackmail victim pays to avoid the harm that the state would inflict; he pays because he believes that he can thereby suppress the state's potential criminal claim. Of course, this does not effect a legally binding settlement, but the leverage is effective precisely to the extent that the victim believes that he has reached an effective settlement. Likewise, when a blackmailer threatens to expose damaging but noncriminal behavior unless paid money, he is also turning third-party leverage to his own benefit. What makes his conduct blackmail is that he interposes himself parasitically in an actual or potential dispute in which he lacks a sufficiently direct interest. What right has he to make money by settling other people's claims?

At the heart of blackmail, then, is the triangular nature of the transaction, and particularly this disjunction between the blackmailer's personal benefit and the interests of the third parties whose leverage he uses. In effect, the blackmailer attempts to gain an advantage in return for suppressing someone else's actual or potential interest. The blackmailer is negotiating for his own gain with someone else's leverage or bargaining chips.

This misuse of another's leverage is perhaps seen most clearly in noninformational blackmail, in situations where a formal agency relationship exists—for instance, where a labor union leader threatens to cause a strike unless he is given a personal payoff.[167] There the labor leader is turning group power and a group dispute to personal benefit. The pressure on the blackmail victim would be the same if the blackmailer's agency relationship were merely informal—for instance, where an influential businessman threatens to cause a strike unless he is given a personal payoff.[168] Notice that the victim of blackmail probably does not care whether the threatener is a labor leader or an influential businessman, an authorized agent or an unauthorized one. What the victim fears is a strike. Whoever seeks a personal payoff by credibly wielding the power of a third party to harm the victim is a blackmailer.

The same misuse of representative or agency power can be seen where someone threatens to deny a public contract unless the contractor makes a payoff.[169] Again, it doesn't matter much to the victim whether the threatener is a government official or an influential citizen,[170] a formal representative or an informal one. Both would be turning group power to personal benefit, offering to suppress a potential interest of the government and the public for personal gain.

What emerges from these examples is the observation that blackmail is the misuse of an informal (or formal) power of agency or representation. Under my theory, blackmail is the seeking of an advantage by threatening to press an actual or potential dispute that is primarily between the blackmail victim and someone else. The blackmailer threatens to bring others into the dispute but typically asks for something for himself; he turns someone else's power, usually group power, to personal benefit. The bargaining is unfair in that the threatener uses leverage that is less his than someone else's.

Thus in a general sense, the law of blackmail promotes principled negotiations by outlawing a particular kind of unfair bargaining. A blackmailer uses a type of extra leverage to exact unearned payments, convert causes of action to cash, or resolve disputes other than on their merits. The law of blackmail tries to compel people to resolve their disputes by means the legal system provides or prefers, such as civil suits.[171] It also discourages the settlement of disputes by persons who are neither parties to those disputes nor agents for those parties. Thus blackmail law is a manifestation of a core principle of our legal system, the assignment of enforcement rights to the victim:[172] an individual enforces a private wrong and the state enforces a public wrong. This enforcement principle is extremely broad. It applies in civil law[173] and criminal law,[174] in public law and private law. It has been justified by economic analysis[175] and doctrines of individual liberty,[176] by natural law[177] and constitutional law.[178] It is fundamental to the organization of our courts and to our system of procedure.[179]

But the exclusive assignment principle is not monolithic—quite the contrary. It takes different forms in tort, contract and criminal law, and its configurations have changed over time. For example, in torts and contracts different people are assigned enforcement rights today than were assigned such rights before the decline of privity doctrines. Criminal claims are assigned to the state.[180] Tort and contract claims are assigned to the victim of those kinds of wrongdoing. And claims that would be nonredressable in court, such as the right to change one's opinion of someone, are assigned to the person who would change his mind.

B. Comparing Conceptions of Blackmail

*** * Portions of this section of the Article have been omitted for brevity. In the edited text, the author shows how his theory of blackmail compares to those put forth by earlier scholars. The Article then moves to consider whether the author's theory can be understood to be consistent with the approach in the Model Penal Code:*

In most important respects, the Model Penal Code seems to see blackmail in much the same light as my theory does. For example, the Code defines theft by extortion as follows:

A person is guilty of theft if he purposely obtains property of another by threatening to:

(1) inflict bodily injury on anyone or commit any other criminal offense; or

(2) accuse anyone of a criminal offense; or

(3) expose any secret tending to subject any person to hatred, contempt or ridicule, or to impair his credit or business repute; or

(4) take or withhold action as an official, or cause an official to take or withhold action; or

(5) bring about or continue a strike, boycott or other collective unofficial action, if the property is not demanded or received for the benefit of the group in whose interest the actor purports to act; or

(6) testify or provide information or withhold testimony or information with respect to another's legal claim or defense; or

(7) inflict any other harm which would not benefit the actor.

It is an affirmative defense to prosecution based on paragraphs (2), (3) or (4) that the property obtained by threat of accusation, exposure, lawsuit or other invocation of official action was honestly claimed as restitution or indemnification for harm done in the circumstances to which such accusation, exposure, lawsuit or other official action relates, or as compensation for property or lawful services.[207]

The first paragraph prohibits threats to inflict bodily injury or commit a crime. Because these cases do not raise the paradox, they do not trouble theorists. The next three paragraphs have long been found in one form or another in many blackmail or extortion statutes. The paradox is clearly raised by threats to expose a crime, expose a secret or cause the taking or withholding of official action, because such behavior is sometimes permissible. The Code handles this problem by setting out a very broad affirmative defense[208] for these threats, choosing not to prohibit many borderline cases that some jurisdictions would treat as blackmail. These cases involve a combination of both third-party leverage and leverage properly belonging to the threatener—for example, a threat to go to the authorities if the wrongdoer does not pay restitution.[209] Thus, if I am owed back pay by my employer, under the Model Penal Code I am allowed to threaten to go to the press as leverage to enforce my claim. Although this is borderline blackmail (since it involves both my leverage and the public's), the Code apparently reflects the belief that the public's interest in my getting relief sufficiently coincides with my own interest.

The last three paragraphs of the Code's provision on theft by extortion are less conventional. Significantly, the broad claim-of-right defense just mentioned does not apply to these threats.[210] The first of the three threats prohibited is the threat to cause a strike if the property is not received for the benefit of the group in whose interest the actor purports to act. As Ginsburg points out, the threat in this fifth paragraph is defined in terms of a breach of agency.[211] But it need not be a formal agency; a threat by an influential businessman is as illegal as one made by a union official. The criminality clearly arises from the disjunction between the leverage used and the advantage sought. Thus this fifth paragraph fits neatly into my rationale.

The sixth paragraph prohibits threats to testify or withhold information about another's legal claim. Threatening to testify about your own legal claim is apparently not prohibited, again reflecting the focus on whose claim is being suppressed. It is permissible to use leverage based on your own claim for your own benefit. But in this paragraph the drafters did not realize that there is another way for leverage to be congruent, the use of someone else's leverage for their benefit. For example, such behavior might consist of a threat to testify on behalf of an injured friend unless the wrongdoer paid the injured friend a fair settlement. The Model Penal Code appears to prohibit this behavior,[212] though it seems blameless; my theory suggests it ought to be permissible. Clearly, a broader claim-of-right defense must be applied to the threat to testify.

The last paragraph prohibits threats to "inflict any other harm which would not benefit the actor."[213] This very broad formulation is a strange one, not wholly consistent with either my theory or the general conception of blackmail. Indeed, even though this paragraph has been adopted in many states, I have never read a reported case of blackmail based on it. The paragraph was designed to get at a special problem in blackmail—that often the threatener would not benefit from carrying out the threat to expose the affair, report the crime, or whatever. The threatened infliction of harm is merely gratuitous.

The drafters consider this gratuitous harm provision as "the general principle on which other threats are to be included."[214] However, a number of problems inhere in the way the provision is drafted. Ginsburg offers two refinements that are necessary for the paragraph to make sense. We must exclude from the calculation two kinds of potential benefits to the threatener: the mere satisfaction of an appetite for spite and the enhancement of the threatener's reputation as someone who always carries out his threats.[215] But even with these limitations, the principle, as stated, is overbroad. There are many situations where someone may legitimately seek property in return for refraining from taking a course of action that would not benefit him. For example, a farmer may threaten to destroy his crop unless buyers pay a higher price for it. A seller may threaten not to sell to a buyer unless the buyer meets the seller's price, even when the seller would only lose by foregoing the deal. Both of these actions would appear to be prohibited by the Model Penal Code because they involve threats to inflict harm that would not benefit the actor; yet almost everyone would agree that they constitute legitimate bargaining behavior.[216]

Although the language of the provision is overbroad, the latest official commentary assumes that the paragraph covers only behavior entirely consistent with my theory:

The phrase "which would not benefit the actor" is thus meant to preclude a theft prosecution where the purpose of the threat is to secure economic benefit—the obtaining of property—for which the actor may have some claim. The claim need not be legitimate in the sense that the actor believes that he has a claim of right to the property that would trigger the provisions of Section 223.1(3). An actor whose behavior is reached only by Paragraph (7) would escape criminal conviction if he shows a legitimate interest even though his demand be excessive or unreasonable. The line is thus drawn between one who in an economic bargaining context attempts to maximize his own advantage and one who attempts to use his position, status, or knowledge, or any other unique characteristic of a situation, to his own personal advantage.[217]

The original comments on the gratuitous harm provision give only three examples of the kinds of situations the drafters believed this paragraph to prohibit:

(a) the foreman in a manufacturing plant requires the workers to pay him a percentage of their wages on pain of dismissal or other employment discrimination; (b) a close friend of the purchasing agent of a great corporation obtains money from an important supplier by threatening to influence the purchasing agent to divert his business elsewhere; (c) a professor obtains property from a student by threatening to give him a failing grade.[218]

All of these cases involve the misuse of someone else's leverage for personal gain and thus are consistent with my approach.

In most important respects, then, the Model Penal Code's extortion provisions are consistent with my theory of blackmail. Where the Code appears inconsistent with my theory (as in the gratuitous harm provision), the Code violates common sense if read literally. Yet the official commentary reveals an intent to formulate a rule entirely consistent with my own. The Code's apparent prohibition of clearly legitimate behavior seems to be wholly unintentional, probably stemming from the lack of a theory to guide the drafting of a broad, catch-all blackmail provision. To accord with a proper conception of blackmail, as well as the views of the Code's official commentators, the gratuitous harm provision should be replaced or redrafted to reflect a more coherent theory of blackmail.[219]

C. Looking at Borderline Cases

Where the threatener is using someone else's leverage for personal gain, he commits blackmail. Where he uses personal leverage for personal gain, his behavior is legitimate.[220] At one extreme, then, we have the use of someone else's leverage. At the other extreme, we have the use of personal leverage. In borderline cases, we have both.

The most common borderline blackmail cases are where a victim of wrongdoing threatens to go to the authorities or the press unless he is paid a settlement.[221] For example, assume a person believes he has been tortiously and criminally harmed by another person. All authorities agree that it is legitimate for the injured party or his lawyer to threaten to file a civil suit for damages.[222] But where the injured party threatens to go to the press or the police, he is adding someone else's chip (the state's or the public's) to his own and using both to press his claim. His threat goes beyond the exposure necessary to press his claim in court and thus straddles the border of blackmail. Is it blackmail because he has chosen a method that involves extra leverage? Or is it legal because he is settling a substantial claim of his own by a method related to that claim? Some statutes prohibit this behavior,[223] whereas some specifically allow it.[224] Some commentators assume that this behavior is criminal,[225] whereas some assume that it is legal.[226] My theory does not mandate that any one approach be taken to borderline blackmail; it leaves room for policy choices. It should, however, illuminate the principles involved and, at least to that extent, make the lines easier to draw. Under my theory, threats increasingly lose their legitimacy as the disjunction increases between the leverage used and the advantage sought, that is, between the blackmailer's personal interest and the interests of the third parties whose leverage he uses.

For example, assume that a woman threatens to reveal that a company is criminally polluting the air by secretly using a smokestack that is not properly equipped with pollution control devices. As a property owner who has suffered damage from the pollution, she possesses a small but legitimate claim against the company. If she threatens to report the polluter unless it turns itself in to the proper authorities, no blackmail has been committed. There is a perfect congruence between the advantage sought (the exposure and cessation of pollution) and the leverage used (the state's claim against the polluter). At the other end of the scale, if she asks for $1,000,000 to keep quiet about the pollution but seeks nothing for the public's benefit, the behavior is clearly blackmail. There is an almost total disjunction between the advantage sought and the leverage used. Any damages that she might be able to legitimately claim for the harm the pollution causes her are not likely to approach $1,000,000.

The cases in between raise closer questions. If she asks that the polluter stop using the smokestack in return for a promise not to expose, she is still asking for something that will benefit the public and the authorities. But she is an unauthorized agent for the public, who may prefer that she reveal the pollution. Although she may stop the pollution, she may be suppressing other people's claims for damages or the state's claim to fine or imprison the polluter. Still, because she is trying in good faith to use the public's leverage for public benefit, I doubt that anyone would consider this blackmail. If, however, she asks both that they stop polluting and that they pay her $1,000,000 to keep quiet, she has probably committed blackmail. Once again, her legitimate damages would not reach $1,000,000. Even though she is seeking something for the public, the cessation of pollution, she is also asking for a large payoff for herself, vastly exceeding any reasonable restitution. The lack of congruence between the leverage used and the benefit sought is probably substantial enough to make this behavior blackmail.

Most of the case law lead in one direction, toward prohibiting borderline blackmail involving threats to go to the police or the press. One authority summed up the consensus:

Although there are some decisions to the contrary, most of the courts have held that it is a criminal offense for a creditor to obtain money or property from a debtor by means of a threat to accuse the latter of a crime, although the creditor believes that the money or property is actually due him, and although he believes the debtor guilty of the crime which he is threatening to expose.[227]

Most recent statutory enactments, however, lead in the opposite direction, toward allowing most of this borderline blackmail behavior. For instance, statutes following the Model Penal Code permit one to threaten exposure of a tort or a crime when honestly seeking restitution in a matter related to the exposure. Under my theory, this may be an appropriate rule since the threatener's personal interest is likely to be substantial when the claim pressed is related to the information threatened to be exposed.[228]

If, however, the injured party threatens to expose an unrelated claim, the behavior is more suspect. Suppose, for example, that the wife in a divorce action threatens to expose her husband's income tax evasion unless he gives her a generous divorce settlement. Despite the legitimacy of her underlying divorce claim, she deliberately invokes extra leverage. The constituency who would be concerned about the terms of her divorce settlement differs from the constituency who would be concerned about the husband's tax evasion. Presumably, the latter would not think it fair to resolve the husband's potential tax dispute by paying the wife a larger divorce settlement. Thus the disjunction between the leverage and the benefit is greater than where the wife presses a related claim, for example, a threat to expose an extramarital affair unless paid money in a divorce settlement.

An examination of borderline cases thus confirms my basic approach. My theory finds difficult much the same cases the courts and legislatures do and illuminates why these cases are hard.[229] I do not pretend to resolve the difficult policy choices raised by borderline blackmail but my theory may make it easier to analyze these problems.

CONCLUSION

In this Article, I have examined eight existing theories of blackmail, theories that show striking variations. Some theories are based on the idea that it is wrong to hide private information;[230] while other theories are based on the idea that it is wrong to reveal it.[231] Both views cannot be right. Three theories offer analyses based explicitly on economic efficiency[232]—with little or no overlap in the inefficiencies they target.

Most of the theories give us insights into blackmail, but none of these theories successfully explains why conduct that is legitimate elsewhere suddenly becomes criminal in a blackmail transaction. One group of theories looks at only part of the transaction, leaving them unable to place the behavior encompassed by the crime in context. This, in turn, means that they cannot resolve the paradox of blackmail, which arises precisely because no single aspect of the blackmail transaction is necessarily wrongful when viewed in isolation. In one context a threat may be permissible, while in another the same threat would constitute blackmail. The other group of theories goes beyond the behavior itself to suggest other harms caused by blackmail, either privacy invasions or wasted resources. But as these theories move away from a focus on the behavior involved in blackmail, they increasingly lose their ability to distinguish blackmail from other conduct that causes the same harms.

In an attempt to overcome these problems I have offered a new theory of blackmail. In my view, to get what he wants, the blackmailer uses leverage that is less than someone else's. Blackmail is thus a way that one person requests something in return for suppressing or settling the actual or potential claims of others.[233] Selling the right to go to the police involves suppressing the state's claim, bargaining with the state's chip. Selling the right to inform the victim of a tort who committed the tort involves suppressing the tort victim's claim. And selling the right to inform others of embarrassing but legal behavior involves suppressing claims belonging to other people, even though those claims may be unredressable in court.

Similarly, noninformational blackmail involves the same misuse of another's power for the blackmailer's own benefit. For example, when a labor leader threatens to cause a strike unless he personally is paid off, he is suppressing the actual or potential claims of others for his own benefit.[234] And when a public official threatens to deny someone a public contract unless he is paid off, once again he is turning group or representative power to his own benefit.[235]

Thus blackmail differs from ordinary bargaining and threats because the leverage used belongs less to the threatener than to a third party. It becomes clear why, in the paradoxical case, otherwise legitimate conduct becomes illegitimate in blackmail. The problem is not with anything intrinsic to the threat, or any other aspect of the conduct, which may remain legitimate when taken in isolation. Rather, the problem essentially is that the wrong person is making the threat; the blackmailer's own interest is not sufficient to justify his using that leverage. Thus the leverage being used, while legitimate in the hands of another, is illegitimate in the hands of the blackmailer.

More than forty years ago Professor Campbell suggested that blackmail scholars have something in common with blackmail victims: they are allowed no peace of mind.[236] Like blackmail victims, scholars are met with one demand after another. In this Article, I have tried to meet the first demand, to unravel the paradox of blackmail by identifying what is wrong with blackmail that is not wrong with legal ways of obtaining advantages. Whatever the next demand might be, I hope that it is not as difficult to meet as the first.

Notes

a. Associate Professor of Law, University of Connecticut. B.A. 1974, Yale College; J.D. 1977, University of Chicago Law School. I would like to thank the many people who have read all or portions of earlier drafts or provided research or technical assistance: Franklin Zimring, Lori Andrews, Ray Solomon, Christine Kiley, Walter Andrews, Elizabeth Michelman, David Jones, Harry Dubnick, Phil Rudolph, Jan Brakel, Barbara Curran, Janet Gilboy, Norval Morris, Ronald Coase, Hans Zeisel, Spencer Kimball, James B. White, Francis Allen, Robert Levy, Robert Birmingham, Thomas Morawetz, Clements Ripley, Janet Spegele, Ellen Bowman and Jody Nelson. This Article is dedicated to Randy Block, who suffered severe brain damage in an automobile accident. Several days before, we spent hours in a little bar on the University of Chicago campus, discussing an embryonic version of the theory presented in this Article. As was usual with Randy, his comments were the most probing I received.

1. Murphy, Blackmail: A Preliminary Inquiry, 63 Monist 156, 158 (1980).

2. See Williams, Blackmail, 1954 Crim.L.Rev. 79, 163.

3. See, e.g., United States v. Merry, 514 F.2d 399 (8th Cir.1975) (threat to expose illegal activities at a massage parlor unless paid money); Eller v. State, 48 Ga.App. 163, 172 S.E. 592 (1934) (threat to expose opening of U.S. mail and forgery unless paid

money); People v. Clemens, 46 Ill.App.2d 363, 197 N.E.2d 482 (1964) (threat to arrest unless paid money).

4. See, e.g., N.Y. Times, Jan. 25, 1942, at 29, col. 4 (blackmailer sought a job as secretary and companion by threatening to expose an indiscretion); see also Salley v. United States, 306 F.2d 814 (D.C. Cir.1962) (blackmailer threatened to tell the victim's wife that the victim had caused the pregnancy of another woman); People v. Goldstein, 84 Cal.App.2d 581, 191 P.2d 102 (1948) (threat to expose an affair unless paid money).

5. Generally, threatening to accuse someone of a crime or regulatory infraction is not itself a crime. Landry v. Daley, 280 F.Supp. 938, 962–63 (N.D.Ill.1968) (The private citizen "has the power to initiate criminal prosecution against another and the right to give information and testimony against another. He may make statements injurious to another's reputation, provided he does not commit defamation."), rev'd on other grounds sub nom. Boyle v. Landry, 401 U.S. 77 (1971); Rex v. Pollock, [1966] 2 W.L.R. 1145, 1156 ("If an offence of indecency, of whatever sort, has been committed, or if a person bona fide believes that such an offence has been committed, he has a duty to report it. To say, in such circumstances, that one is going to report it, without any intention of using the threat of reporting as a means to extort

money or goods, is merely saying that one is going to fulfil a public duty and is not a criminal offence.").

Some statutes, however, prohibit the threat to accuse of a crime either by itself or when made with the intent to induce terror. See 3 R. Anderson, Wharton's Criminal Law and Procedure § 1399 (1957) [hereinafter cited as Wharton]; see also D. Ginsburg, Blackmail: An Economic Analysis of the Law 5 (unpublished manuscript on file at the offices of the Columbia Law Review).

6. Williams, supra note 2, at 163.

7. Id.; see also Murphy, supra note 1, at 156–57.

Most of the blackmail theorists have centered their theories on the paradoxical case, where the blackmailer has the right to do what he threatens to do. But there is another kind of blackmail, one that is neither paradoxical nor particularly troubling to theorists. Where what the blackmailer threatens to do is itself criminal, the criminality of blackmail is fairly easily justified. See, e.g., Stamatiou v. United States Gypsum Co., 400 F.Supp. 431, 433 (N.D.Ill.1975) ("an act forbidden by a statute cannot be the foundation of a legal contract in Illinois"), aff'd, 534 F.2d 330 (7th Cir.1976); Holcombe v. Whitaker, 294 Ala. 430, 436, 318 So.2d 289, 295 (1975); W. Prosser, Handbook of the Law of Torts 40 (4th ed. 1971) ("the defendant is not free to compel the plaintiff to buy his safety by compliance with a condition which there is no legal right to impose").

For example, assume a person threatens to damage a victim's house unless the victim pays the threatener money. Because generally no one has the right to destroy another's property, no one should be allowed to profit by selling a right the law prohibits. Conversely, no person should have to pay a potential wrongdoer to avoid being the victim of such a crime, since the law already protects victims from having their property destroyed. Here the blackmailer is selling something the law disallows and the blackmail victim is buying something that the law says should be his by right.

However, just because the criminality of this behavior is easily justified does not mean that there are no line-drawing problems. Should we prohibit threats to commit minor criminal offenses, quasi-criminal offenses, regulatory offenses, or torts—or even threats to breach contracts? See Landry v. Daley, 280 F.Supp. 938, 963 (N.D.Ill.1968), rev'd on other grounds sub nom. Boyle v. Landry, 401 U.S. 77 (1971); Note, A Rationale of the Law of Aggravated Theft, 54 Colum.L.Rev. 84, 91 (1954) [hereinafter cited as Columbia Note].

8. A. Goodhart, Essays in Jurisprudence and the Common Law 175-89 (1937).

9. R. Nozick, Anarchy, State, and Utopia 84–86 (1974).

10. Ball & Friedman, The Use of Criminal Sanctions in the Enforcement of Economic Legislation: A Sociological View, 17 Stan.L.Rev. 197, 205–06 (1965).

11. Landes & Posner, The Private Enforcement of Law, 4 J. Legal Stud. 1, 42–43 (1975).

12. Epstein, Blackmail, Inc., 50 U.Chi.L.Rev. 553 (1983).

13. In the words of one comment to a recently enacted statute:

> [N]o explicit exemption from liability is provided for a threat to charge another with a crime where there is an honest belief that the threatened charge is true and defendant's sole purpose is to induce reasonable action to correct the believed wrong; such instances may be left to prosecutive discretion. Ala.Code § 13A-6-25 commentary (1978) (emphasis added).

14. "In common parlance, the term 'blackmail' is equivalent to, and synonomous with, 'extortion,' within the non-technical meaning of the term." 3 Wharton, supra note 5, § 1396, at 795. "Though the word 'blackmail' may not be a word of art, it is a word of common parlance and popular usage, often defined as synonomous with extortion. . . ." Greenspun v. Gandolfo, 74 Nev. 16, 20, 320 P.2d 628, 630 (1958).

15. A distinction is traditionally drawn between robbery and blackmail or extortion: a criminal commits robbery when he threatens immediate bodily harm, whereas he commits blackmail or extortion when he threatens future bodily harm. See Winder, The Development of Blackmail, 5 Mod.L.Rev. 21, 25 (1941); 50 Am.Jur.2d Larceny § 34, at 191 (1970); see also People v. Moore, 184 Colo. 110, 518 P.2d 944 (1974) (robbery-theft distinction).

16. See, e.g., Ill.Ann.Stat. ch. 38, § 12-6 (Smith-Hurd 1979); Ind.Code Ann. § 35–45-2-1 (Burns 1979).

17. See, e.g., Ala.Code § 13A-6–25 (1978); Alaska Stat. § 11.41.530 (1983); Ark.Stat.Ann. § 41-1609 (1977); Conn.Gen.Stat.Ann. § 53a-192 (1972); N.J.Stat.Ann. § 2C-13-5 (West 1982); N.Y.Penal Law § 135.60 (McKinney 1975); N.D.Cent.Code § 12.1-17-06 (1976); Ohio Rev.Code Ann. § 2905.12 (Baldwin 1979).

18. See, e.g., Ark.Stat.Ann. §§ 41-2202, 41-2203 (1977 & Supp.1983); Ill.Ann.Stat. ch. 38, § 16-1 (Smith-Hurd 1979); S.D.Codified Laws Ann. § 22-30A-4 (1979).

19. See, e.g., Miss.Code § 97-3-81 (1972).

20. See, e.g., R.I.Gen.Laws § 11-42-2 (Supp.1980); Wyo. Stat. § 6-2-402 (1983); see also People v. Gallo, 54 Ill.2d 343, 353, 297 N.E.2d 569, 574 (1973) (lender threatened borrower that he would break borrower's legs "in three or four places" and that he would send "the west side boys" to see the borrower unless he repaid a loan);

Commonwealth v. De Vincent, 358 Mass. 592, 592, 266 N.E.2d 314, 315 (1971) (threat to cut out victim's tongue and shove it up his rectum along with dynamite and blow him up unless purported debt repaid); Brannon v. State, 164 Tex.Crim. 83, 84, 296 S.W.2d 760, 761 (1956) (threat that victim's life would not be "worth a plug nickel" unless victim produced the money requested).

Injury to person or property can sometimes include acts not involving the use of force by the blackmailer. See, e.g., Petersen v. Mayo, 65 So.2d 48 (Fla.1953) (en banc) (threat to cause deportation is a threat of injury to person); State v. McInnes, 153 So.2d 854 (Fla.Dist. Ct.App.1963) (threat to expose tax evasion is included, inter alia, under threat to injure property).

On the other hand, in some cases injury to person has been held not to include injury to reputation. See State v. Simmons, 114 R.I. 16, 327 A.2d 843 (1974); see also Freese v. Tripp, 70 Ill. 496 (1873) (injury to person under intoxicating beverages statute does not include mental anguish, disgrace, or loss of society); Calloway v. Laydon, 47 Iowa 456 (1877) (same); Commonwealth v. Mosby, 163 Mass. 291, 39 N.E. 1030 (1895) (threat to make a legitimate arrest is not a threat to injure, and therefore cause of action not sustained; criticized in Commonwealth v. Miller, 385 Mass. 521, 432 N.E.2d 463 (1982)); Mulford v. Clewell, 21 Ohio 191 (1871) (injury to person under intoxicating beverages statute does not include mental anguish, disgrace, or loss of society).

21. See, e.g., D.C.Code Ann. § 22-2305 (1981); Kansas Stat. Ann. § 21-3428 (1981); People v. Camodeca, 52 Cal.2d 142, 338 P.2d 903 (1959) (en banc) (extortionist falsely told bar owner that state regulatory agency had charges against the bar, which could be fixed if the bar owner paid the extortionist money); People v. Sexton, 132 Cal. 37, 64 P. 107 (1901) (threat to accuse another of a violation of federal laws in the sale of cigars), aff'd on other grounds, 189 U.S. 319 (1903); State v. Bassett, 151 Conn. 547, 200 A.2d 473 (1964) (threat to have stores prosecuted for violating Sunday closing laws unless they made an apparently bogus contribution to an organization supposedly lobbying against blue laws).

22. See, e.g., Okla.Stat.Ann. tit. 21, § 1488 (West Supp.1982); S.C.Code Ann. § 16–17-640(2) (Law.Co-op 1977); Brown v. State, 15 Ala.App. 180, 72 So. 757 (threat to publish information injurious to character), cert. denied, 198 Ala. 689, 73 So. 999 (1916); Horner v. State, 149 So.2d 863 (Fla.Dist.Ct.App.1963) (threat to expose an "unsavory characteristic").

The threat to expose damaging information can take the form of:

> (a) the threat to expose any matter that would damage personal or business reputation;

> (b) the threat of injury to reputation;

> (c) the threat to expose any secret;

> (d) the threat to expose any matter that would expose the victim to hatred, contempt, or ridicule; or

> (e) the threat to impair credit.

See, e.g., Ill.Stat.Ann. 38 § 15-5 (Smith-Hurd 1979); Ohio Rev.Code Ann. § 2905.11 (Page 1982); 18 Pa.Cons. Stat.Ann. § 3923 (Purdon 1983); R.I.Gen.Laws § 11-42-2 (1981).

23. In England extortion by a public official has been a misdemeanor at common law, as well as a statutory crime since 1275. According to Blackstone, extortion at common law was "an abuse of public justice, which consists in an officer's unlawfully taking, by colour of his office, from any man, any money or thing of value, that is not due to him, or more than is due, or before it is due." 4 W. Blackstone, Commentatires *141; see R. Perkins, Criminal Law 372–75 (2d ed. 1969); Statute of Westminster I, 3 Edw. ch. 26, 27, 30, 31 (1275), reprinted in 3 English Historical Documents 404–05 (H. Rothwell ed. 1975) (repealed by Theft Act, 1968, ch. 60, § 33(3), sched. 3, and Statute Law Reform Act, 26 & 27 Vict., ch. 125 (1863)); see also Statute of Westminster II, 13 Edw. ch. 13, 37, 42 (1285), reprinted in 3 English Historical Documents 440, 449–50, 452–53 (H. Rothwell ed. 1975) (repealed by Sheriff's Act, 50 & 51 Vict., ch. 55, § 39, and Statute Laws (Repeals) Act, 1969, ch. 52).

24. Blackmail, which is in effect extortion by a private person, was also a misdemeanor at common law. Regina v. Woodward, 11 Mod. *137 (1707); 1 L. Radzinowicz, A History of English Criminal Law and Its Administration from 1750, at 641 (1948); Campbell, The Anomalies of Blackmail, 55 L.Q.Rev. 382, 382 (1939). This common law misdemeanor, though apparently never widely invoked, fell into disuse as statutes were passed outlawing several forms of blackmail. See Campbell, supra, at 382–83.

The first British blackmail statutes were passed in Scotland. See 1567 Scot.Parl.Acts, ch. 27 (prohibiting payment, as well as extortion, of "black maill"); 1587 Scot.Parl.Acts, ch. 59, ¶ 13 (prohibiting "blak meill"). Then in 1601, a statute making blackmail a capital offense was passed, but it applied in only a few areas of England. 43 Eliz. ch. 13, § 2 (1601) (repealed by 7–8 Geo. 4, ch. 27, § 1 (1827)). In 1722, the repressive Waltham Black Act was passed making certain written threats demanding property illegal throughout the country. 9 Geo. 1, ch. 22, § 1 (1722) (repealed by 7–8 Geo. 4, ch. 27, § 1 (1827). Then, because blackmailers began sending extortionate letters without making any demands, Parliament passed a statute removing the requirement of demand. 27 Geo. 2, ch. 15 (1754); see 1 L. Radzinowicz, supra, at 641.

At least one authority has attributed the origin of the word "blackmail" to the targets of the 1722 English Black Act—the Waltham Blacks, a group who blacked their faces to avoid identification when they committed blackmail, poaching, and other crimes. See D. Ginsburg, supra note 5, at 4. However, this attribution is probably wrong since the word is used in Scottish sources as early as the 16th century. See, e.g., 1567 Scot.Parl.Acts, ch. 27; 1587 Scot.Parl.Acts, ch. 59, ¶ 13; see also 1 Oxford English Dictionary 224 (compact ed. 1971) (providing derivation of "blackmail"). The better explanation for the term "blackmail" is that it referred to mail, that is, tribute or rents, exacted in crops, work, goods, or a metal baser than silver (such as copper). This distinguished blackmail or black rents from white rents, which were tribute or rents exacted in silver. See id.

25. Some commentators have argued that the offense of blackmail was created by statute to plug a loophole in the law of robbery. E.g., R. Perkins, supra note 23, at 372–75. At common law robbery was the taking of property by actual force or the threat of imminent force. In the 18th century robbery was expanded case by case to include taking property by two other types of threats: (1) the threat to destroy the victim's house by mob violence; and (2) the threat to publicly accuse the victim of sodomy, whether or not the accusation was true. Some commentators have suggested that physical force is implicit in the accusation of sodomy because of the possibility of mob violence and in the threat to destroy a house because of danger to the occupants. Id. at 372.

26. 30 Geo. 2, ch. 24 (1757) (repealed by 30 & 31 Vict., ch. 59 (1867)). The earlier statutes had dealt with threats to do physical injury. This change broadened the statutes to cover anonymous letters threatening to accuse of an infamous or capital crime with an intent to gain. D. Ginsburg, supra note 5, at 5. An infamous crime is one punished by death, gallows, pillory, branding, whipping, or confinement at hard labor. See Ex parte Wilson, 114 U.S. 417, 428 (1885).

27. 6 & 7 Vict., ch. 96, § 3 (1843) (repealed by 6 & 7 Geo. 5, ch. 50 (1916)); see Winder, supra note 15, at 21, 24, 37–38. An earlier act, the Larceny Act, 7 & 8 Geo. 4, ch. 29, § 8 (1827) (repealed by Larceny Act, 24 & 25 Vict., ch. 95, § 1 (1861)), made illegal the demanding of property from any person with "menaces" and without probable cause. At the time, "menaces" apparently meant threats of physical injury to person or property. Winder, supra note 15, at 36–38. However, in the case of Regina v. Tomlinson, [1895] 1 Q.B. 706 (construing

Larceny Act, 24 & 25 Vict. ch., 96, § 44 (1861)), the word was unequivocally expanded to include the threat to expose damaging information. Winder, supra note 15, at 37–38.

28. Act of Mar. 18, 1796, § 57, 1796 N.J.Laws 108. Similar early statutes include Act of Dec. 19, 1817, div. 8, § 27, 1816 Ga.Laws 178; Act of Dec. 22, 1802, § 14, 1802 Ky.Acts 115; Act of Nov. 4, 1835, ch. 125, § 17, 1835 Mass.Acts 718; Act of Nov. 4, 1816, § 48, 1816 Mich. Laws 128; Act of Feb. 15, 1839, ch. 66, tit. 3, art. 5, § 58, 1839 Miss.Laws 138; Act of July 4, 1825, § 82, 1825 Mo.Laws 308.

29. Act of 1827, § 108 1827 Ill.Laws 145. In addition, a broad blackmail statute was drafted as part of a criminal code prepared at the request of the Louisiana legislature. It was published in 1833, but apparently the blackmail statute was never enacted. It would have prohibited threatening another "with any injury to . . . person, reputation or property, accompanied by a demand of property or of service." A System of Penal Law for the State of Louisiana (1833) (emphasis added).

30. Besides the threats mentioned supra notes 20–22 and accompanying text, some statutes prohibit:

    (a) the threat to commit any offense;

    (b) the threat to commit any felony;

    (c) the threat to physically confine or restrain;

    (d) the threat of physical harm to property;

    (e) the threat to cause or continue a strike or boycott, if the property is not demanded or received for the benefit of the group the threatener represents;

    (f) the threat to give or withhold testimony or information about another's legal claim or defense;

    (g) the threat of a public official to take or withhold action against anyone or anything or to cause a public official to do so; and

    (h) the threat to inflict any other harm that would not benefit the actor.

    See, e.g., Ohio Rev.Code Ann. § 2905.11 (Baldwin 1982); Ill.Ann.Stat. 38 § 15-5 (Smith-Hurd 1977); 18 Pa.Cons.Stat.Ann. § 3923 (Purdon 1983); R.I.Gen.Laws § 11-42-2 (1981).

31. Some American statutes require that the threat accomplish its purpose. See, e.g., Ill.Ann.Stat. 38 § 16-1(c) (Smith-Hurd 1977), described in Perkins, supra note 23, at 373–74. Under such a statute an unsuccessful blackmail threat may usually be prosecuted as a criminal attempt. E.g., Ill.Ann.Stat. 38 § 8-4 (Smith-Hurd 1972), described in Perkins, supra note 23, at 373–74. Most modern statutes do not require that the blackmail threat be successful; the making of the threat is enough. See, e.g., Mass.Ann.Laws ch. 265, § 25 (Michie/Law. Co-op.

1980), described in Perkins, supra note 23, at 373–74. The rationale for not requiring that the threat succeed is probably that successful blackmail typically requires the cooperation of the victim. Once the blackmailer has done his part by making the threat, why require another step by the victim?

32. Some statutes prohibit the obtaining of "property," "any precuniary advantage," "any valuable thing," or "any thing of value." See, e.g., Mass.Ann.Laws ch. 265, § 25 (Michie/Law.Co-op. 1980); Ohio Rev.Code Ann. § 2905.11 (Baldwin 1982); 18 Pa.Cons.Stat.Ann. § 3923 (Purdon 1983). Other statutes prohibit gaining "any advantage," inducing someone "to do or refrain from doing any act," or inducing someone "to do any act against his will." See, e.g., Colo.Rev.Stat. § 18-3-207 (1983); D.C.Code Ann. §§ 22-2306, 22-2307(3) (1981); Fla.Stat.Ann. § 836.05 (West 1976); Mass.Ann.Laws ch. 265, § 25 (Michie/Law.Co-op. 1980); Wyo.Stat. § 6-2-402 (1977).

33. Ill.Ann.Stat. ch. 38 § 15-5 (Smith-Hurd 1977).

34. [M]ost of the courts have held that it is a criminal offense for a creditor to obtain money or property from a debtor by means of a threat to accuse the latter of a crime, although the creditor believes that the money or property actually is due him, and although he believes the debtor guilty of the crime. . . .

31. Am.Jur.2d Extortion, Blackmail, and Threats § 11, at 909 (1967); Tooher, Developments in the Law of Blackmail in England and Australia, 27 Int'l & Comp.L.Q. 337, 367 (1978) (summarizing American law, Tooher states that "[t]he general rule is that a claim of right is not a defence to a charge of extortion"); see also Dennis v. Travelers Ins. Co., 234 So.2d 624 (Miss.1970) (threat to disclose criminal behavior unless restitution is made; civil suit by blackmail victim states a claim but is barred by statute of limitations); Lyons v. Zale Jewelry Co., 150 So.2d 154 (Miss.1963) (insulting language and a threat of criminal prosecution and jail unless a woman pays her son's debts; held that complaint states a claim for civil damages); Commonwealth v. Tucker, 187 Pa.Super. 61, 142 A.2d 786 (1958) (convicted for threat to keep in jail for larceny until victim paid his legitimate debt); Bianchi v. Leon, 138 A.D. 215, 226, 122 N.Y.S. 1004, 1012 (1910) (the "obtaining of a settlement under a threat of criminal prosecution is blackmail").

35. 280 F.Supp. 938 (N.D.Ill.1968), rev'd on other grounds sub nom. Boyles v. Landry, 401 U.S. 77 (1971).

36. Id. at 960–64. The court rejected a construction of the Illinois intimidation statute that would make criminal the threat to do lawful acts . . . [,] for example, . . . a threat to file legitimate criminal charges.

Given a reasonable and natural construction, the statute prohibits only threats to do any of the specified acts if the doing of that act would be unlawful . . . .

[A]ll the defenses that would have been available to the accused if he had carried out his threat and had been prosecuted or sued for doing so are available to him in a prosecution for intimidation.

Id. at 963; see also Ill.Ann.Stat. ch. 38, § 12-6 (Smith-Hurd 1979).

37. See United States v. Local 807, Int'l Bhd. of Teamsters, 315 U.S. 521 (1942); NLRB v. Karp Metal Prods. Co., 134 F.2d 954, 955 (2d Cir.1943) ("There can be nothing unlawful in the threatening to do that which it is lawful to do."); Hardie & Lane, Ltd. v. Chilton, [1928] 2 K.B. 306. In Hardie & Lane, Ltd. v. Chilton, Lord Scrutton argued that one may demand property without committing any offense where "you have a legal right to do the thing which you threaten to do." [1928] 2 K.B. at 319. In response to Lord Scrutton's argument, Sir Herbert Stephen wrote a letter to the London Times on April 26, 1928:

If this is really the test, some remarkable consequences follow. Suppose a man writes, "Unless you give me £100 I will show So-and-so your letter to Such-a-one", or "If you don't want me to prosecute you for the affair you know of, you must send me £100 by to-morrow's post." In each case the alternative to payment is something which the writer of the letter has "a legal right to do." In the latter case it might even be his legal duty to do it. I have known, I suppose, some dozens of cases where men have been sent to penal servitude, sometimes for long terms, for sending letters exactly to the above effect. If Scrutton, L.J.'s view of the law is correct, they would all seem to have been wrongly convicted.

A. Goodhart, supra note 8, at 178 (quoting Sir Stephen's letter in the London Times); see also Campbell, supra note 24, at 388.

In Enmons v. United States, 410 U.S. 396 (1973), the United States Supreme Court had trouble with the other side of the paradox—the legitimacy of what the threatener seeks. A divided Court held that even if a union blew up a utility power station to enforce its demands for higher wages, no extortion had occurred. The Court in effect asked: How could the union officials have committed extortion if they were seeking a legitimate labor objective, higher wages? Id. at 408–12.

38. Or.Rev.Stat. § 163.275 (1953).

39. Id. § 163.285.

40. 649 P.2d 569 (1982).

41. Id. at 580.

42. Id. at 587–90.

43. A number of states provide a defense when the threatener: (1) "honestly claims the property as restitution or indemnification for harm done in the circumstances to which the threat relates" or (2) is merely righting a wrong. See, e.g., Ala.Code § 13A-8-15 (1977); Alaska Stat. § 11.41.530(6)(b) (1978); Del.Code Ann. tit. 11, § 792 (1979); Iowa Code Ann. § 711.4 (West 1979); Ky.Rev.Stat. § 509.080(2) (Supp.1982); Mo.Ann.Stat. §§ 570.010, 570.030 (Vernon Supp.1982); N.J.Stat. Ann. § 2C:13-5 (West 1982); Ohio Rev.Code Ann. § 2905.11 (Page 1982); 18 Pa.Cons.Stat.Ann. § 3923(b) (Purdon 1983); Wash.Rev.Code Ann. § 9A.56.130(2) (1977).

44. Model Penal Code § 223.4 (Official Draft and Revised Comments 1980).

45. Id. § 212.5.

46. Id. §§ 212.5, 223.1(3), 223.4, 242.5.

47. Id. § 223.4.

48. Id.; see also infra notes 213–18 and accompanying text.

49. Model Penal Code § 223.4 (Official Draft and Revised Comments 1980).

50. Indeed, books on ethical negotiation encourage negotiators to threaten action that would harm the other side, even when actually taking that action would not benefit the threatener. R. Fisher & W. Ury, Getting to Yes 31–32 (1981).

51. Model Penal Code § 223.4 commentary at 223–24 (Official Draft and Revised Comments 1980); see also infra notes 207–19 and accompanying text.

* * * [text and accompanying footnotes have been omitted]

 161. A threat or an attempt to use fear is necessary for blackmail to have been committed. Works v. State, 295 Ala. 409, 411, 328 So.2d 624, 626 (1976) ("The essence of the offense of blackmail is the threat").

Under most statutes the threat may be communicated in any fashion, oral or written, explicitly or by innuendo. See Cape v. United States, 283 F.2d 430 (9th Cir.1960) (threat of damage to property was made merely by mentioning troubles that other contractors had had); People v. Massengale, 10 Cal.App.3d 689, 89 Cal.Rptr. 237 (1970) (no explicit threat was made, though behavior was menacing in obtaining contracts from elderly women to trim trees); People v. Oppenheimer, 209 Cal.App.2d 413, 26 Cal.Rptr. 18 (1962) (prisoner's inquiry in a letter whether judge's windows were insured constituted threat within extortion statutes, where threats were coupled with a demand that the judge pay the fines the prisoner had incurred); Iozzi v. State, 5 Md.App. 415, 247 A.2d 758 (1968) (threat was conveyed by pointing out what happened to another business, which had been bombed);

Columbia Note, supra note 7, at 87–88; 31 Am.Jur.2d Extortion, Blackmail, and Threats § 10, at 907–08. But the threat must be serious enough to coerce. Landry v. Daley, 280 F.Supp. 938, 963–65 (N.D.Ill.1968), rev'd on other grounds sub nom. Boyle v. Landry, 401 U.S. 77 (1971).

162. See L. Weinreb, Criminal Law 421 (1980) ("All bargaining situations have in them an element of matched 'threats' to withhold what one has to offer. . . ."); Columbia Note, supra note 7, at 90–91 ("The striking of a legitimate bargain often involves the threat to inflict economic harm if agreement is not reached."); see also United States v. Kramer, 355 F.2d 891 (7th Cir.1966) (contractor apparently threatened subcontractor that he would exercise his right to terminate the subcontract if the subcontractor did not have his men on the job on the following day; the subcontract was prevented by a labor union official from supplying workers and lost the subcontract).

163. See Kam Chin Chun Ming v. Kam Hee Ho, 45 Hawaii 521, 558–59, 371 P.2d 379, 402 (1962) (in action to set aside a family settlement agreement, court held that to avoid duress a threat to sue must be based on a bona fide claim); Campbell v. Parker, 209 So.2d 337, 339 (La.Ct.App.1968) ("But even if plaintiff did threaten defendant with suit in the event she defaulted in her payments on the note such action is not unlawful."); Williams, supra note 2, at 170.

164. See Anheuser-Busch, Inc. v. Jefferson Distributing Co., 353 F.2d 956, 962 (5th Cir.1965) (The trial court held that: "Plaintiff, being free to buy or not to buy Budweiser, and the defendant being free to sell or not to sell Budweiser, the court is of the opinion that a threat of the defendant not to sell Budweiser unless plaintiff engages in certain activities and plaintiff's subsequent engagement in such activities to its detriment, cannot constitute a cause of action against defendant"); Time, Mar. 14, 1983, at 64 (General Motors threatened to begin ordering supplies from foreign makers if no new steel contract was reached).

165. See People v. Babic, 7 Ill.App.3d 36, 287 N.E.2d 24 (1972) (homeowner threatened with mortgage foreclosure turns to blackmail to raise money); Campbell v. Parker, 209 So.2d 337, 339 (La.Ct.App.1968).

166. The situation is complicated somewhat when the threatener is the victim of the crime. Here, though he bargains with the state's chip, he also has a personal stake in restitution. For a discussion of such "borderline" cases, see infra notes 220–29 and accompanying text.

167. See, e.g., United States v. Kramer, 355 F.2d 891 (7th Cir.1966) (threat to send workers both few in number

and poor in quality unless paid off) vacated in part and remanded, 384 U.S. 100 (1966); United States v. Tolub, 309 F.2d 286 (2d Cir.1962) (union official asked for a one-third interest in the employer's business in return for avoiding labor trouble).

168. United States v. Kramer, 355 F.2d 891 (7th Cir.1966) (businessman influential with the union threatened continued union labor problems unless paid off) vacated in part and remanded, 384 U.S. 100 (1966); United States v. Feldman, 299 F.2d 914, 916 (2d Cir.1962) (extortion victims negotiated a deal with an influential businessman after a union official threatened a strike if they failed to give the businessman "whatever he works out with you people"); United States v. Postma, 242 F.2d 488 (2d Cir.1957) (a manager of a trucking company extorted money from other trucking companies to end a general strike by drivers against the local trucking companies); People v. Camodeca, 52 Cal.2d 142, 338 P.2d 903 (1959) (person falsely told bar owner that state regulatory agency had charges against the bar, which could be fixed if the bar owner paid the extortionist money).

169. See, e.g., United States v. Mazzei, 390 F.Supp. 1098 (W.D.Pa.), aff'd, 521 F.2d 639 (3d Cir.), cert. denied, 423 U.S. 1014 (1975); N.Y. Times, Mar. 25, 1977, at 26, col. 6; N.Y. Times, Aug. 13, 1976, at D13, col. 8; see also Columbia Note, supra note 7, at 91 ("No social purpose is served by allowing an agent to use his position of power for personal enrichment and the prevention of such exactions protects both the victim and the agent's principal.").

170. See N.Y. Times, Mar. 25, 1977, at 26, col. 6; N.Y. Times, Aug. 13, 1976, at D13, col. 8 (state senators threatened to instigate a legislative investigation that would lead to the loss of a public contract unless they were paid off); see also United States v. Margiotta, 688 F.2d 108 (2d Cir.1982) (local Republican Party chairman threatened to withhold public contracts unless insurance firm agreed to kick-back scheme), cert. denied, 103 S.Ct. 1891 (1983); United States v. Stirone, 311 F.2d 277 (3d Cir.1962) (union official threatened a businessman with the loss of a lucrative contract unless the union official received payoffs), cert. denied, 372 U.S. 935 (1963); Commonwealth v. Nevitt, 217 Pa.Super. 114, 268 A.2d 121 (1970) (bail bondsman offered to secure the dismissal of a drunk-driving charge in return for a payoff).

171. See State v. McCabe, 135 Mo. 450, 457, 37 S.W. 123, 125 (1896) (If the defendant's threats are permissible, "not only are the courts open to him to obtain a judgment for any sum due him, . . . [but] he may even collect an unjustifiable debt, or obtain an unconscionable

advantage. The law will not countenance or tolerate this method of collecting debts."); People v. Loveless, 84 N.Y.S. 1114, 1116 (Ct.Spec.Sess.1903) ("[T]here was an attempt to usurp the function of the courts, and to compel the complainant to satisfy a claim in controversy, not upon the merits of the claim, . . . [but] through fear of impairment to his credit.").

172. Epstein, Privacy, Property Rights, and Misrepresentations, 12 Ga.L.Rev. 455, 458 (1978) [hereinafter cited as Epstein, Privacy]; Landes & Posner, supra note 11, at 42–43.

Although blackmail law punishes threateners who settle other people's disputes for their own benefit, it does not go so far as to punish benevolent intermeddlers—those unauthorized agents who settle third-party disputes for the benefit of third parties (for example, a threat to report a criminal unless he stops committing the crime). See infra notes 220–27 and accompanying text.

173. Epstein has stated the principle for tort law: "One rule common to all theories of tort liability is that the party who has suffered the injury is the only party who is entitled to pursue the legal remedy against the person who wrongly caused the injury. The strength of this rule is universal." Epstein, Privacy, supra note 172, at 458.

174. Landes & Posner, supra note 11, at 42.

175. Id.

176. Epstein, Privacy, supra note 172, at 455; Landry v. Daley, 280 F.Supp. 938, 960–67 (N.D.Ill.1968), rev'd on other grounds sub nom. Boyle v. Landry, 401 U.S. 77 (1971).

177. H.L.A. Hart, The Concept of Law 158–62 (1961).

178. Brilmayer, The Jurisprudence of Article III: Perspectives on the "Case or Controversy" Requirement, 93 Harv.L.Rev. 297, 310–15 (1979) [hereinafter cited as Brilmayer, Juridprudence of Article III]; Brilmayer, A Reply, 93 Harv.L.Rev. 1727, 1731–32 (1980).

179. See J. Cound, J. Friedenthal & A. Miller, Civil Procedure, Cases and Materials 1–2 (3d ed. 1980); Brilmayer, Jurisprudence of Article III, supra note 178, at 306–10.

180. The criminal law has retained the principle that the state has the exclusive enforcement right, but the principle has taken on new dimensions over time. The traditional justification is that crimes are public wrongs, which the state enforces for the public. The private wrongs done to the victims of crime are supposed to be redressed in the tort system. Because of course they seldom are, the victim often has considerable influence over criminal law enforcement. Traditionally, police and prosecutors have deferred to the complaining witness's decision whether to press

charges, and more recently we have seen the growth of restitution and victims' rights.

* * * [text and accompanying footnotes have been omitted]

207. Model Penal Code § 223.4 (Official Draft and Revised Comments 1980). The Code's other main blackmail provision, the section on criminal coercion, applies to threats designed to induce action or inaction:

A person is guilty of criminal coercion if, with purpose unlawfully to restrict another's freedom of action to his detriment, he threatens to:

(a) commit any criminal offense; or

(b) accuse anyone of a criminal offense; or

(c) expose any secret tending to subject any person to hatred, contempt or ridicule, or to impair his credit or business repute; or

(d) take or withhold action as an official, or cause an official to take or withhold action.

It is an affirmative defense to prosecution based on paragraphs (b), (c) or (d) that the actor believed the accusation or secret to be true or the proposed official action justified and that his purpose was limited to compelling the other to behave in a way reasonably related to the circumstances which were the subject of the accusation, exposure or proposed official action, as by desisting from further misbehavior, making good a wrong done, refraining from taking any action or responsibility for which the actor believes the other disqualified.

Id. § 212.5. Because this section prohibits only four of the seven threats proscribed in § 223.4 (theft by extortion), the coercion section does not raise some of the problems inherent in the extortion section. Unfortunately, however, the coercion section is ambiguous concerning the purpose required. What is meant by the phrase "with purpose unlawfully to restrict another's freedom of action"? The official commentary suggests that it "means that the actor must intend to coerce conduct that he has no legal right to require." Id. § 212.5 commentary at 265.

208. The Code requires that the property obtained be "honestly claimed as restitution or indemnification for harm done in the circumstances to which such accusation . . . relates, or as compensation for property or lawful services." Id. A second claim-of-right defense also applies to this section. See id. § 223.1(3); see also infra note 210.

209. See infra notes 220–29 and accompanying text.

210. Only a much narrower defense applies, one tied to the threatener's belief in his right to claim the property: "It is an affirmative defense to prosecution for theft that the actor: . . . (b) acted under an honest claim of right to the property or service involved or that he had a right to acquire or dispose of it as he did. . . ." Model Penal Code § 223.1(3) (Official Draft and Revised Comments 1980). As the official commentary explains the defense, "The general principle is that the actor should have a defense where . . . he honestly believes that he is entitled to acquire [the property] and that his privilege extends to the use of force or other unlawful method of aquisition." Model Penal Code § 223.1 comment 4 (Official Draft and Revised Comments 1980). Thus, as to the three additional threats, the threatener's claim to the property must be so strong that he believes he could simply take it by force. Where you are seeking a legitimate end but not one that you honestly believe may be achieved by force, this defense does not apply.

Another, broader interpretation of this defense is possible, but unlikely. Perhaps a defendant need only show that he believed he had a right to act as he did. If such a broad reading were accepted, then political terrorists would be able to extort property without violating the theft by extortion statute. We would still have a law that did not conform to the common understanding of blackmail, but the particular deviations would be different from those discussed infra notes 211–19 and accompanying text.

211. D. Ginsburg, supra note 5, at 15.

212. The section prohibits obtaining the property of another. "Obtain" is defined in the Code as "to bring about a transfer or purported transfer of a legal interest in the property, whether to the obtainer or another." Model Penal Code § 223.0(5) (Official Draft and Revised Comments 1980) (emphasis added). Thus obtaining property of another would include inducing a transfer from one person to another. See also supra note 210.

213. Id. § 223.4(7) (Official Draft and Revised Comments 1980).

214. Model Penal Code § 206.3 commentary at 79 (Tent. Draft No. 2 1954) (Theft by Intimidation); see also Model Penal Code § 223.4 commentary at 223–24 (Official Draft and Revised Comments 1980).

215. See D. Ginsburg, supra note 5, at 26.

216. How would these examples be handled under my theory? Both the farmer and the seller are bargaining for their own benefit with their own chips—the farmer's crop, the seller's goods. As long as there is a congruence between the leverage used and the advantage sought, the behavior should be permitted.

217. Model Penal Code § 223.4 commentary at 223–24 (Official Draft and Revised Comments 1980). Notice that the comments even embrace my expanded

conception of a "claim," that it need not be a claim enforceable in court.

218. Model Penal Code § 206.3 commentary at 79 (Tent. Draft No. 2 1954) (Theft by Intimidation).

219. As a practical matter, these problems could be largely solved by simply extending the claim-of-right defense to cover threats of gratuitous harm. See supra notes 48–50 and accompanying text. But such a change would not address the underlying problem, the lack of a working rationale. This problem is best met by the reformulation of the gratuitous harm paragraph to reflect a more coherent approach to blackmail. Note that the Code provision on criminal coercion, which in many ways parallels the theft by extortion provision, omits altogether the problematic gratuitous harm provisions. Compare Model Penal Code § 212.5 (Official Draft and Revised Comments 1980) with id. § 223.4.

220. Sometimes a legitimate threatener is using group leverage for group gain. For example, a union leader may threaten to strike unless paid higher wages. See Columbia Note, supra note 7, at 91. Or a citizen may threaten a criminal with exposure unless the criminal stops committing the crime. In these situations there is a congruence between what is being sought and the constituency whose leverage is used.

221. See People v. Asta, 251 Cal.App. 64, 59 Cal.Rptr. 206 (1967); Dennis v. Travelers Ins. Co., 234 So.2d 624 (Miss.1970); Commonwealth v. Bernstine, 308 Pa. 394, 162 A. 297 (1932); Commonwealth v. Tucker, 187 Pa.Super. 61, 142 A.2d 786 (1958).

222. See, e.g., 3 Wharton, supra note 5, § 1397, at 796; Columbia Note, supra note 7, at 94.

Even where the possible lawsuit would be embarrassing to the tortfeasor, the threat to file a legitimate civil suit is treated as raising only the litigants' interests or leverage, and thus as not presenting a borderline case. Though the suit would involve the invocation of state power, it would be state power designed specifically to resolve disputes between private litigants. The courts are not only the preferred forum for settling private disputes, they are provided largely for that purpose. Invoking criminal processes, on the other hand, triggers state power designed not to settle private disputes but to protect the interests of the public at large.

223. See 31 Am.Jur.2d Extortion, Blackmail, and Threats, § 11, at 909 (1967). Many of the cases adjudicating this behavior seem harsh, often prohibiting even victims of crimes, torts or contract breaches from seeking restitution by threatening to expose the wrongdoing to the police or the press. See State v. Harrington, 128 Vt.

242, 260 A.2d 692 (1969) (lawyer for the wife in a fault-based divorce action was convicted of attempting to extort a settlement by threatening to expose the husband's extramarital affair); cf. Rex v. Dymond [1920] 2 K.B. 260 (female victim of a sexual assault convicted of blackmail for threat to tell whole town of the crime unless she was paid a small sum of money).

224. See, e.g., N.J.Stat.Ann. § 2C:13-5 (West 1982); Wash. Rev.Code Ann. § 9A.56.130 (1977); State v. Burns, 161 Wash. 362, 297 P. 212 (1931).

225. See Livermore, supra note 111, at 408; 31 Am.Jur.2d Extortion, Blackmail, and Threats, § 11, at 909 (1967).

226. See R. Fisher & W. Ury, Getting to Yes 143 (1981); Landes & Posner, supra note 11, at 42–43.

227. 31 Am.Jur.2d Extortion, Blackmail, and Threats § 11, at 909 (1967).

228. Another line of justification might be that where there is a legitimate claim for restitution, the people whose leverage is being invoked would generally want restitution to be made. Since those who would disapprove of the criminal's misconduct would want the injured party to recover, there is more congruence between the leverage and the benefit than might appear at first.

229. I would be disturbed if my theory mandated any particular approach to borderline cases, that is, if my theory were not subtle enough to explain why the cases are on the border. See J. Wilson, supra note 16, at 31.

230. See Epstein, supra note 12, at 562; Murphy, supra note 1, at 165 (concurring public officials).

231. See A. Goodhart, supra note 8; Ball & Friedman, supra note 10; Murphy, supra note 1, at 163–64 (concerning private citizens).

232. See D. Ginsburg, supra note 5; R. Nozick, supra note 9; Landes & Posner, supra note 11.

233. Of course, if that person is acting as an agent for those whose leverage he uses, no blackmail has been committed. Examples include a prosecutor's threat to prosecute unless the defendant accepts a plea bargain and a union leader's threat to cause a strike unless his workers are paid higher wages.

234. E.g., United States v. Kramer, 355 F.2d 891 (7th Cir.), vacated in part and remanded, 384 U.S. 100 (1966); United States v. Provenzano, 334 F.2d 678 (3d Cir.), cert. denied, 379 U.S. 947 (1964); United States v. Stirone, 311 F.2d 277 (3d Cir.1962), cert. denied, 372 U.S. 935 (1963), 262 F.2d 571 (3d Cir.1958) (same case in previous trial), rev'd, 361 U.S. 212 (1959).

235. See, e.g., N.Y. Times, Mar. 25, 1977, at A26, col. 6 (state legislators extorted $40,000 by threat of harmful committee report on investigation of company contract); N.Y. Times, Aug. 13, 1976, at D13, col. 8 (same).

236. Campbell, supra note 24, at 382.

159 N.H. 187

Supreme Court of New Hampshire.

The STATE of New Hampshire

v.

Daniel P. HYNES.

No. 2008-371.

Argued: March 12, 2009.

Opinion Issued: Aug. 5, 2009.

Synopsis

Background: Defendant was convicted in a jury trial in the Superior Court, Hillsborough–Northern Judicial District, Barry, J., of one count of theft by extortion. Defendant appealed.

Affirmed.

Dalianis, J., issued dissenting opinion.

Attorneys and Law Firms

Kelly A. Ayotte, attorney general (Elizabeth J. Baker, assistant attorney general, on the brief and orally), for the State.

Christopher M. Johnson, chief appellate defender, of Concord, on the brief and orally, for the defendant.

Opinion

HICKS, J.

The defendant, Daniel P. Hynes, appeals his conviction after a jury trial in Superior Court (*Barry,* J.) of one count of theft by extortion. *See* RSA 637:5, II(i) (2007). We affirm.

Background

The jury could have found the following facts. The defendant is an attorney who was admitted to the New Hampshire and Massachusetts Bars in 2006. In December of that year, he sent a "Cease and Desist/Demand Letter" to Claudia Lambert, the owner of Claudia's Signature Salon in Concord (the salon). The letter, written on "Daniel P. Hynes Esq." letterhead and noting his admission to the New Hampshire Bar, stated:

> I am writing in regards to your company's policy of pricing for different types of haircuts. It has been brought to my attention that your business charges $25 for haircuts but $18 for a

> Men's cut and $12 for a children [*sic*] haircut. Such a distinction in price based on gender and age is discrimination in violation of the law. Accordingly, I demand you immediately cease this unfair pricing and charge customers in a more appropriate manner, such as by the length of their hair or the amount of time it would take.

The letter claimed that the salon's practice was both unlawfully discriminatory in violation of RSA 354–A:17 (2009), and constituted an unfair trade practice in violation of RSA chapter 358–A (2009). The letter went on to state:

> I demand that you immediately cease your unlawful practice of charging for haircuts based upon age and gender. Should you not comply I will be forced to file a complaint with the State Commission for Human Rights while reserving all rights to remove and file in Superior Court. In addition, I demand payment in the amount of $1000 in order to avoid litigation. . . . I believe $1000 is a fair amount as it is the minimum that would be awarded for an unfair trade practice alone. You have ten (10) days to comply . . . . Should you fail to comply additional steps will be taken including filing with the State Commission for Human Rights and potential removal to Superior Court. If such action is necessary I will seek all remedies available including but not limited to an injunction, damages for discrimination, damages for the unfair trade practice, ill-gotten gains, punitive damages, attorney fees and costs. If you object or otherwise wish to discuss the above matter you may have your attorney contact me.

The letter was signed "Daniel P. Hynes Esq."

At some point after receiving the letter, Lambert's husband, Bernard Nardi, called the defendant to see if they could "work out a settlement." During the ensuing conversation, the defendant indicated he was not a client of the salon and had found it, along with its prices, on the Internet. Nardi offered, and the defendant accepted, $500 to settle the matter. The defendant then prepared settlement documents reflecting the agreement, which he faxed to Nardi's real estate business office. The documents indicated that, in consideration of five hundred dollars received, the defendant would discharge the salon from any claims and demands regarding its alleged discriminatory

> The court takes pains to note that the defendant was a licensed attorney. Is that fact material to the elements of the crime? If so, why?

practice. A meeting was scheduled to execute the documents.

Nardi subsequently contacted the New Hampshire Attorney General's Office, and it was determined that an investigator would attend the settlement meeting posing as Lambert's business partner. At the settlement meeting, the defendant again stated that he did not have a client. He further indicated that he, personally, would keep the $500 he received from Nardi, and that he was currently in negotiations with other attorneys in response to similar letters he had sent out. The investigator executed the settlement agreement, providing $500 to the defendant. After taking possession of the $500, the defendant was arrested and charged with theft by extortion. *See* RSA 637:5, II(i).

Prior to trial, the defendant moved to dismiss, arguing that his conduct is not prohibited by RSA 637:5, II(i), and, even if it is, the statute is unconstitutional. The trial court denied the motion, and the defendant was subsequently convicted. This appeal followed.

On appeal, the defendant argues that RSA 637:5, II(i) does not prohibit his conduct, either because it does not include a threat to sue, or because he stood to substantially benefit from the threatened conduct. In the alternative, he asserts that RSA 637:5, II(i) is unconstitutionally vague and overbroad. Finally, he argues that the trial court improperly instructed the jury. We address each argument in turn.

II. Scope of RSA 637:5, II(i)

[1] [2] RSA 637:5, I (2007) provides: "A person is guilty of theft as he obtains or exercises control over the property of another by extortion and with a purpose to deprive him thereof." The statute provides eight specific circumstances in which extortion occurs, as well as a catch-all provision, under which the State charged the defendant. RSA 637:5, II(a)-(i). The catch-all provision states that extortion occurs when a person threatens to "[d]o any other act which would not in itself substantially benefit him but which would harm substantially any other person with respect to that person's health, safety, business, calling, career, financial condition, reputation, or personal relationships." RSA 637:5, II(i).

The defendant argues that RSA 637:5, II does not prohibit his conduct because none of its eight specific provisions includes a threat to file a lawsuit. In addition, he asserts that the term "substantially benefit"

encompasses the kind of non-pecuniary satisfaction he would receive by ending the salon's alleged discrimination, and that this provision was satisfied by his standing to bring suit against the salon under RSA chapter 354–A (2009).

[3] [4] [5] [6] Resolution of this issue requires that we interpret RSA 637:5, II(i), which presents a question of law that we review de *novo. State v. Gallagher,* 157 N.H. 421, 423, 951 A.2d 130 (2008). In matters of statutory interpretation, we are the final arbiter of the intent of the legislature as expressed in the words of a statute considered as a whole. *Id.* at 422, 951 A.2d 130. We first examine the language of the statute, and, where possible, we apply the plain and ordinary meaning to the words used. *Id.* at 422–23, 951 A.2d 130. We interpret legislative intent from the statute as written and will not consider what the legislature might have said or add language it did not see fit to include. *State v. Langill,* 157 N.H. 77, 84, 945 A.2d 1 (2008). Further, we interpret a statute in the context of the overall statutory scheme and not in isolation. *Id.*

The defendant first asserts that we should interpret RSA 637:5, II(i) as excluding any threat to sue, regardless of whether there is a basis for the threatened suit, because it does not constitute the type of harm contemplated by the statute. In support of this assertion, he argues that this type of threat falls outside the core purpose of the extortion statute, and that including a threat to sue in the statute would chill the right of access to the courts. The defendant also argues that the rule of lenity supports his interpretation. We disagree.

> None of the scenarios provided by Senator Williams addresses litigation threats, and that does not seem to be a primary concern of the constituent group he met with. So will the court's reasoning on this point be helpful in your work? (Hint: probably yes, if you can understand the concepts underpinning the court's analysis and apply them flexibly.)

At common law, "extortion consisted of the corrupt taking of a fee by a public officer, under color of his office, where no fee is due, or not so large a fee is due, or the fee is not yet due." *State v. O'Flynn,* 126 N.H. 706, 709, 496 A.2d 348 (1985) (quotation and brackets omitted). "Beginning in the 19th century, many states enacted extortion statutes to criminalize conduct that was extortionate but did not fall within the ambit of the narrow crime of common law extortion." *Rendelman v. State,* 175 Md.App. 422, 927 A.2d 468, 474 (Ct.Spec.App.2007), *aff'd,* 404 Md. 500, 947 A.2d

546 (2008). This statutory form of extortion applied to both private individuals and public officials, and made criminal "the act or practice of obtaining something or compelling some action by illegal means, as by force or coercion." *Id.* (quotations and brackets omitted). In New Hampshire, the legislature has enlarged the scope of extortion to include "unlawful acquisitions of property by means of threats," *O'Flynn,* 126 N.H. at 709, 496 A.2d 348; *see* RSA 637:5, II (2007).

Here, the defendant suggests that a threat to sue is inconsistent with the purpose of the statute in part because the "threat of civil litigation . . . does not give rise to the kind of intimidation that constitutes extortion." While we agree that simply threatening to institute a lawsuit does not, standing alone, carry the inherent hallmarks of an extortionate act, our inquiry does not end there. Unlike the other provisions within RSA 637:5, II, the plain language of RSA 637:5, II(i) does not simply evaluate the type of threat that was made; that is, the substance of the threat. Rather, it requires us to consider both the threat's potential harm to the person threatened as well as its potential benefit to the person making the threat. Thus, contrary to the defendant's interpretation, we cannot simply evaluate the threat on its face and disregard the circumstances under which it was made. In order to make a proper determination as to these additional factors, we must consider all of the circumstances surrounding that threat on a case-by-case basis. We, therefore, cannot conclude, as a matter of law, that there are *no* circumstances under which a threat to sue would constitute extortion.

We recognize that several courts have drawn a contrary conclusion, finding that a threat to sue, even if baseless, does not constitute extortion. *See United States v. Pendergraft,* 297 F.3d 1198, 1207–08 (11th Cir.2002); *First Pacific Bancorp, Inc. v. Bro,* 847 F.2d 542, 547 (9th Cir.1988); *I.S. Joseph Co., Inc. v. J. Lauritzen A/S,* 751 F.2d 265, 267 (8th Cir.1984); *Rendelman,* 927 A.2d at 483. The focus in the majority of these cases is whether the threat constitutes a wrongful means to achieve a wrongful objective, as defined by the Hobbs Act, 18 U.S.C. § 1951 (2000). *See, e.g., Pendergraft,* 297 F.3d at 1205–06. For example, in *Rendelman,* the court stated:

> A wrongful purpose does not necessarily make the means threatened to accomplish it wrongful. The means threatened must be of a sort that

will instill fear. . . . The threat of litigation, being a lawful means in which a third party assigned by government to decide disputes will decide that very dispute, is not such a means.

Rendelman, 927 A.2d at 482. Similarly, in *I.S. Joseph Co.,* the United States Court of Appeals for the Eighth Circuit noted that "only the most liberal construction of the word 'fear' in the extortion statute could make it apply to" the threat to file a civil action. *I.S. Joseph Co.,* 751 F.2d at 267.

However, we find these cases distinguishable, because the courts' analyses considered the wrongful means—the threat—independent from the wrongful objective—the taking of property. As such, the type of threat made is a determinative factor. RSA 637:5, II(i) does not make such a distinction. Rather, as discussed above, it more broadly considers the consequences of the threat, both to the person making it and to its intended recipient. Furthermore, RSA 637:5, II(i) does not require there to be fear as a result of the threat, but, rather, only that there be substantial harm. We do not believe that these terms are interchangeable.

Further supporting our interpretation, other courts have held that an extortion conviction may be supported by the threat to bring a civil suit. The United States Court of Appeals for the First Circuit has indicated that, under federal law, an extortion charge may be based upon the threat of litigation if there is no basis for the threatened suit. *See United States v. Sturm,* 870 F.2d 769, 774 (1st Cir.1989) ("It would be unjust to convict A of extortion unless she knew she had no claim to the property that she allegedly sought to extort."). Additionally, in construing a statute almost identical to RSA 637:5, II(i), a New Jersey court upheld a conviction for theft by extortion based upon a demand for money coupled with a threat to sue. *See State v. Roth,* 289 N.J.Super. 152, 673 A.2d 285, 290–91 (App.Div.), *cert. denied,* 146 N.J. 68, 679 A.2d 655 (1996).

[7] We also disagree with the defendant's contention that this interpretation chills an individual's right of access to the courts. By no means does our holding imply that every demand for money, buttressed by a threat to sue, constitutes extortion. Rather, we are simply denying the defendant's contention that a threat to sue may *never* constitute extortion. Moreover, we decline to apply the rule of lenity in support of the defendant's interpretation. The rule of lenity "forbids interpretation of a federal statute so as to

increase the statutory penalty" when legislative intent is unclear and "is applicable only where statutory ambiguity has been found." *State v. Ravell,* 155 N.H. 280, 284, 922 A.2d 685 (2007) (quotation omitted). The statute at issue does not seek to increase a statutory penalty, and we have not found it ambiguous.

III. Constitutionality of RSA 637:5, II(i)

[10] The defendant next argues that, even if RSA 637:5, II(i) prohibits his conduct, we must vacate his conviction because the statute is unconstitutionally vague on its face and as applied to him under both the United States and New Hampshire Constitutions. In addition, the defendant argues that RSA 637:5, II(i) is unconstitutionally overbroad, both on its face and as applied.

[11] [12] We review questions of constitutional law *de novo. State v. MacElman,* 154 N.H. 304, 307, 910 A.2d 1267 (2006). We first address the defendant's claims under the State Constitution, and cite federal opinions for guidance only. *Id.* In reviewing a legislative act, we presume it to be constitutional and will not declare it invalid except upon inescapable grounds. *State v. Gubitosi,* 157 N.H. 720, 727, 958 A.2d 962 (2008). In other words, we will not hold a statute to be unconstitutional unless a clear and substantial conflict exists between it and the constitution. *Id.*

A. Vagueness

[13] "Where a defendant's vagueness claim does not involve a fundamental right, a facial attack on the challenged statutory scheme is unwarranted." *MacElman,* 154 N.H. at 307, 910 A.2d 1267. Here, the defendant argues that his claim involves fundamental rights because the statute implicates his rights to free speech and access to the courts under Part I, Articles 14 and 22 of the New Hampshire Constitution and the First Amendment to the United States Constitution. We assume, without deciding, that the defendant has articulated a fundamental or First Amendment challenge. We will therefore first review his facial challenge, and then consider his as-applied challenge. *See id.*

[14] [15] [16] [17] A statute can be impermissibly vague for either of two independent reasons: (1) it fails to provide people of ordinary intelligence a reasonable opportunity to understand the conduct it prohibits; or (2) it authorizes or even encourages arbitrary and discriminatory enforcement. *Id.* "A statute is not unconstitutionally vague as long as its prohibitions are

set out in terms that the ordinary person exercising ordinary common sense can sufficiently understand and comply with." *State v. Lamarche,* 157 N.H. 337, 340, 950 A.2d 172 (2008) (quotation omitted). "In addition, mathematical exactness is not required in a penal statute, nor is a law invalid merely because it could have been drafted with greater precision." *MacElman,* 154 N.H. at 307, 910 A.2d 1267 (quotation and brackets omitted). A party challenging a statute as void for vagueness bears a heavy burden of proof in view of the strong presumption favoring a statute's constitutionality. *Id.*

The defendant argues that RSA 637:5, II(i) is void on its face because the phrase "substantially benefit" is vague. Specifically, the defendant notes that the statute does not specify a required mental state or attach an objective measure in defining that phrase. He further notes that the phrase is not of the type that needs to be expressed in general terms. He argues it is the "absence of all of these saving characteristics" that makes RSA 637:5, II(i) vague on its face.

[18] We conclude that RSA 637:5, II(i) provides a person of ordinary intelligence a reasonable opportunity to understand the conduct it prohibits. It is well established that the necessary specificity required to uphold a statute "need not be contained in the statute itself, but rather, in the context of related statutes, prior decisions, or generally accepted usage." *State v. Porelle,* 149 N.H. 420, 423, 822 A.2d 562 (2003) (quotation omitted). Here, read in the context of generally accepted usage, the phrase "substantially benefit" is plain, unambiguous, and easily understandable. The term "substantial" is defined as "something having substance or actual existence . . .: something having good substance or actual value." *Webster's Third New International Dictionary* 2280 (unabridged ed. 2002). *Webster's* defines "benefit" as "to be useful or profitable . . .: become protected, aided, or advanced." *Id.* at 204. Taken together, the terms give clear notice to a person of ordinary intelligence that the statute prohibits a threat that would not provide him or her with some *actual* advantage that is real and definite.

[19] [20] Moreover, although "a scienter requirement in a statute ameliorates" a vagueness concern, *MacElman,* 154 N.H. at 308, 910 A.2d 1267, the lack of such a requirement does not necessitate invalidating the statute as unconstitutionally vague. The defendant argues that the legislature could have provided an illustrative list to help demonstrate the type of interests

encompassed in "benefit," or at least used a more specific phrase than "substantially benefit." A law is not invalid, however, merely because it could have been drafted with greater precision. *Id.* at 307, 910 A.2d 1267. We conclude that the phrase "substantially benefit" is sufficiently clear, and it therefore is not unconstitutionally vague on its face.

[21] Turning to the defendant's as-applied challenge, we conclude that the statute provided him with a reasonable opportunity to know that his conduct was proscribed by the statute. *See Porelle,* 149 N.H. at 424, 822 A.2d 562. The defendant asserts that it fails to give adequate notice that a threat to sue falls within the scope of extortion, arguing that the "disagreement [among courts] . . . evidences an ambiguity" in the statute as to whether it would apply under these circumstances. We find this argument unavailing. The plain language of the statute makes clear that it applies to a threat to "[d]o *any* act which would not in itself substantially benefit him but which would harm substantially" another person. RSA 637:5, II(i) (emphasis added). Thus, the statute neither explicitly, nor by implication, excludes a baseless threat to sue. The defendant also argues that the statute failed to provide him with adequate notice that his antipathy towards gender discrimination was insufficient to satisfy the "substantially benefit" requirement. For the reasons set forth more fully above, we find this argument equally unavailing. Reading the statute as a whole, the defendant had a reasonable opportunity to know that the term "benefit" would require, at the very least, standing to bring the threatened suit. Further, the defendant was not a client of the salon, nor did he represent one. Thus, he had not sustained even a nominal injury as a result of the salon's alleged discrimination to support his claim. We conclude that a person of ordinary intelligence would understand that RSA 637:5, II(i) applies to his conduct, and reject his as-applied claim.

Because the defendant does not argue that the statute may be subject to arbitrary enforcement, we do not address it. *Cf. Lamarche,* 157 N.H. at 340, 950 A.2d 172. Further, because the Federal Constitution offers no greater protection than does the State Constitution under these circumstances, *compare Gonzales v. Carhart,* 550 U.S. 124, 148–49, 127 S.Ct. 1610, 167 L.Ed.2d 480 (2007), *with MacElman,* 154 N.H. at 307, 910 A.2d 1267, we reach the same result under the Federal Constitution as we do under the State Constitution.

* * * [*Discussion concluding that the statute is not unconstitutionally overbroad is omitted.*]

IV. Jury Instructions

[29] The defendant asserts that the trial court inadequately instructed the jury as to the mental state elements of theft by extortion. Specifically, he argues that the court's instruction was flawed in that it "did not require the jury to make a finding as to whether [he] actually knew the [threatened] suit lacked a basis." This issue, however, was not preserved for appeal. · · · Here, the defendant made no objection to the court's jury instruction in this regard. In fact, the jury instruction proposed by the defendant on the elements of the crime charged does not raise the issue of the defendant's knowledge. Therefore, we conclude this issue has not been preserved for appeal, and we decline to address it.

Affirmed.

DUGGAN, J., concurred.

* * * [*Dissent omitted.*]

Yelp Terms of Service

Go online to: https://www.yelp.com/static?p=tos and review the Yelp Terms of Service. These terms of use may or may not have been drafted by lawyers for the corporation, but it's a certain bet that they were carefully reviewed by counsel before being finalized by the company. As you read through them, ask yourself what Yelp's lawyers appear to have been concerned with, and who the user agreement terms are designed to protect.

Understand Your Role in This Assignment

This assignment is different from the previous ones you have worked on in this text. It is far more policy-driven, and it demands conceptual expertise as well as rigorous legal reasoning. The more you think through *why* you are being asked to produce this memo and what purposes it may be put to, the more successful your draft is likely to be.

What does the Senator really want to accomplish?

The Senator has given you a difficult job. There are no clear answers to how we regulate and criminalize inappropriate coercion while entirely permitting the kinds of negotiations and consumer self-help that are hallmarks of the U.S. economy. The very fact that there is probably not a perfect solution here seems to be one important takeaway from the law review article you were given.

It is also worth remembering that Senator Williams is an elected official. Like many politicians, he might view his job as legislating for the public good while meeting the needs of his constituents—hoping ideally that there is no conflict between the two and he can achieve both simultaneously. He probably has a strong desire to spur the development of successful businesses in the state, so he may be especially inclined to support the interests of the Business Leaders' Association (whether or not they supported his campaign). The Senator does seem concerned with making sure the law applies appropriately to modern business practices. He also tells you that he is sensitive to the competing concerns of permitting bargaining and consumer advocacy while protecting businesses from undue or unfair pressure from online review aggregators.

Put that all together and it seems like the Senator is asking for both your legal analysis and your policy recommendations. That's an ambitious undertaking, and one a young legislative aide should be proud of taking on.

What will be most helpful to the Senator in accomplishing his objectives?

Your boss is asking you to draft a memo, so the document you will create for this assignment is likely most closely related to the law office memorandum you were probably introduced to at the outset of your law school career.

But here you are in a different setting. In this scenario you work in legislative chambers rather than in a law office, and the professional norms and expectations may be somewhat different. Moreover, the legislator is asking you for the shortest yet most thorough memorandum you can craft. You should therefore thoughtfully adapt the standard law office memo structure to best serve your specific purposes in this assignment: include any introductions, summaries, or sections that will make your document more helpful, and omit any that will bog it down. As Michael R. Smith observes, a crucial trait of the "intelligent legal writer" is "reader empathy."[1] By this Smith means that you should aim to put yourself in the position of the reader and try to appreciate what she or he really needs.[2]

At the beginning of your legal career you will have probably not written many professional documents in which you are genuinely being asked for your opinion. Keep in mind that the legislator's request is authentic—he really does want your advice. But as his legislative aide your job is to ground that advice in solid legal analysis rather than individual preference. So he will want objectively presented information, combined with enough background for him to decide whether he agrees with your recommendations.

---

1 MICHAEL R. SMITH, ADVANCED LEGAL WRITING (3d ed. 2012).

2. Note, too, that a smart staffer would be aware of his supervisor's style as exhibited in his own memos, and would perhaps use its format as a starting point. Not to the point of adhering to it blindly, though.

How do the Senator's three scenarios fit in to your task?

Why do you think the Senator asked you to analyze three specific situations under New Hampshire criminal law? Well, take a minute to consider what legal analysis of these hypotheticals will provide. Since legal analysis = rules of law applied to specific facts (with legal authority and effective explanations provided where needed),[3] reasoning carefully through these scenarios should give the Senator a feel for how the state's extortion laws may be applied in business review contexts. He probably decided, then, that examining concrete examples would be more helpful and grounded than an inchoate summary of the subject. (So much so, that had he given you this assignment but not provided these examples to work with, coming up with some of your own circumstances to analyze would have been an excellent way to set about your task.)

Think Conceptually about Legal Material

Legislators get to determine what the law should and will be

Practicing attorneys have to take the law as it is. Perhaps as advocates they might argue that it should be interpreted expansively or more narrowly than it is at present, and on rare occasions they might suggest to courts that the law should be changed altogether. But such circumstances are rare, and for the most part lawyers seek to apply established legal rules to their clients' unique problems. It is a different kind of freedom to work for a legislative body. The entire reason for its existence is to decide what the law ought to be and to make it so.

Of course that description grossly oversimplifies the committee processes and deal-making that actually goes into turning a bill into law, as well as the public commentary, lobbying, and frequently, agency implementation regulations that in reality may determine the rules' eventual effects. Still, being able to ask "Just what do I think the rules should permit and prohibit?" is a rare privilege, and an opportunity to be imaginative while thinking both abstractly and absolutely practically.

*Asking what the law **ought** to be is invaluable for lawyers (and law students), not just lawmakers*

Instructors in both law and non-legal fields still rely on the foundational research of Benjamin Bloom, an educational psychologist who studied learning in the 1950s and 1960s. Dr. Bloom's work generated several versions of what is commonly called *Bloom's Taxonomy*,[4] a hierarchical model of increasingly complex modes of thinking and learning.

Quick tip to understand and maybe raise your grades in law school classes: go over one of your exam answers to underline in one color anything you wrote that shows remembering/understanding, and another color showing your application/analysis. When you finish, if you do not have a lot more of the second color than the first then there's ample room to improve.

Bloom suggests that in the earliest stages, we strive simply to **remember** and **understand** what we learn (which, with complicated legal material, may already be plenty demanding). Intermediate thinking skills include **applying** and **analyzing** the material studied. When you think about what lawyers do all day, applying law and analyzing legal problems is likely to be the bulk of our work. Is it any surprise, then, that this is most of what is actually tested in law school classes? The person whose exam shows only that she has remembered and understood the doctrine taught in a particular course—no matter how difficult that law may have been to master—is unlikely to be very happy with her grade.

---

3. As noted in the *Introduction* to this text, perhaps this is an oversimplified formulation but it is the gist of legal reasoning. By now it should seem pretty familiar.

4. *See, e.g.*, Benjamin Bloom Et Al., Taxonomy Of Educational Objectives: The Classification Of Educational Goals (1956).

Bloom categorized the highest orders of thinking as **evaluating** and **creating**. Someone who can assess or build something necessarily has to understand it and be able to use it. She also has to be able to see how it fits into its larger context, and must deeply grasp the concepts and possess the imagination to compare it to what else might be, or perhaps *should* be. Thinking critically and creatively are pretty advanced skills.[5]

To put it more concretely, you probably can't start to apply the law until you know the rules, but the more you use the law the better you will understand it. And the more you think critically and conceptually about the law the more thoughtful and sophisticated your analysis will be. The Senator is directly asking you to think broadly and theoretically in this project, but that should become an important part of regular legal work no matter what assignment you are given.

Read Critically

We have already begun to consider what reading skills on the professional level should look like, but the topic is important enough to merit continued consideration.

One point that law professors keep making is that reading in law is not passive—it requires active critical engagement with the text. Assuming that's taken for granted, and that this is a message you have heard before, why is this so hard? Perhaps in part because reading law critically requires challenging authority. Elizabeth Fajans and Mary Falk point out that law students face a strong inhibition when reading legal materials: they are mostly reading enacted law and binding judicial opinions written by judges. Legislators and judges are important, and hopefully wise, and what they do directly affects the society we live in. This means that "talking back to the text" in law entails at least some comfort with talking back to power.[6] That may be hard to do both thoughtfully and without arrogance, particularly when we are well aware what judges and legislators do has the force of law.

Learning to read legal materials requires more than just courage, however. It also frequently demands a sophisticated understanding of legal principles and language, careful attention to the structure of texts, and awareness of the typical constraints and expectations of various legal genres. You are probably already attuned to some of this. For example, lawyers and law students automatically read statutes differently from the way we read cases even though both can have the force of primary authority. We should feel equally free to similarly sort the way we attend to secondary sources or nonbinding cases.

The law review article excerpt that the Senator gave you, for example: on first examination, did you skim it or pore over it meticulous detail? Did you read all of the footnotes? If so—why? When I ask law students about their reading, many sheepishly confess to having skimmed the article for its main points or having omitted the footnotes. Others say that they read every part of the piece with painstaking care. Both groups tend to be profoundly shocked when I suggest that the more experienced attorney could probably begin with the scanning approach rather than the more scrupulous one, and that the footnotes can be omitted almost entirely.

But look more closely at how the article fits into your project. It seems that this somewhat dated work of scholarship was given to you to quickly bring you up to speed on some of the tensions

5. Bloom's model might seem to suggest that people progress seamlessly and predictably from one step to another, but many other educational experts have found that learning and skills development is far messier than that. In fact, our basic grasp and recall of what we learn is strengthened by having to use it. And our ability to use complex ideas is enhanced by thinking conceptually about it.

6. Elizabeth Fajans & Mary R. Falk, *Against the Tyranny of the Paraphrase: Talking Back to Texts*, 78 Cornell L. Rev. 163, 165 (1993).

inherent in blackmail law. The Senator used it as background for his own education, and does not appear especially interested in the author's exact conclusions or recommendations. So what's wrong with skimming the article for its main ideas and only then returning to look more closely at points you find especially compelling or relevant?

So then why were the article's footnotes included at all? Because support matters to lawyers. Moreover, the footnotes would be valuable if you were researching the problem and wanted to see what authority the author relies upon. They also more fully document and elucidate the author's scholarly argument, but then, were we truly concerned with that in the first place?

Give yourself permission to be wise in your reading of law. You know that it can be hard, technical, and time-consuming. Good attorneys cannot take shortcuts to clear understanding of what they read. But we also can and must use good judgment to figure out what we really need to focus on.

Pay Attention to Both Language and Meaning

Just as he was probably taught to do in law school, the defendant in *State v. Hynes* paid pretty careful attention to language. He argued that N.H. Rev. Stat. § 637.5 enumerated various kinds of threats that could lead to a theft by extortion charge, and that nowhere on that list was a threat to pursue litigation—which is what he had been charged with doing. Defendant Hynes was making a reasonably shrewd statutory interpretation argument based on one of the core canons of construction: *expressio unius est exclusio alterius* ("express invocation of one thing suggests the exclusion of others").[7] So why didn't he succeed in having his conviction overturned on those grounds?

Maybe because even though wording matters enormously to lawyers and judges, wording cannot substitute for reasoning. The *Hynes* court uses history, persuasive authority, and the plain language of the statute itself to conclude that the purpose of the statute was to prohibit the taking of property by means of threatening substantial harm. The court consequently decides the pressure of facing a potential civil litigation might in *some* circumstances constitute an extortionate threat, even though there would be plenty of other situations in which a warned-of lawsuit would **not** meet that standard.

Now, reasonable legal minds can agree or disagree with the New Hampshire Supreme Court's holdings on these points. Indeed, whole fields of academic inquiry and litigation strategy turn on how closely we should hew to the specific language of enacted law versus how broadly we should consider the social context in which the law arose or might now be applied. The point here is not that either the defendant or the court was clearly incorrect, but simply that both language and broader meaning *matter*. The smart lawyer should be comfortable considering both, and with providing explanations for why in any given circumstance one of these should be given more weight than the other. (Keep in mind, too, that whenever they are in tension, one is quite likely to be invoked as a counterargument to the other!)

Evaluate Counterarguments

Considering counterarguments is uniquely important in legal analysis

Why do lawyers and law students have to spend so much time considering counterarguments to just about every position we take?

---

7. He actually seems to have referenced several different canons of statutory construction, including the rule of lenity (when in doubt, interpret in favor of protecting defendants). 159 N.H. at 193. The bulk of the court's analysis, however, seems aimed at his contention that the statute's list of potential threats is exhaustive and exclusive.

An obvious pragmatic answer is that law professors look for counterarguments (so erudite handling of them will almost always help your grades!) and that advocates can only prepare if they know what's likely to come at them (so better responses to counterarguments can help your case!). But this begs the question of why addressing counterarguments is so uniquely important in law. In other academic or professional disciplines, people may be expected to consider alternatives to their own views. Yet we do not automatically discount a piece of American history asserting that the United States was unprepared for the war in Vietnam just because it fails to directly consider the converse. In contrast to historians, law students are taught they are *never* done thinking through a question until they have carefully examined and somehow addressed alternative positions. Why is that?

A short answer may have to do with the adversarial nature of our legal system itself. Chances are good that in any future conflict, and certainly in active litigation, someone is probably going to make that counterargument if it has any validity at all.

But even when that is not quite the case, lawyers consider counterarguments carefully because it helps us gain multiple perspectives on vexing problems. Asking "What would I argue if I were on the other side?" helps us understand why the problem may be a difficult one, and tends to lead to much deeper comprehension of the issues at hand. In that way, then, perhaps we are not so different from other disciplines after all. Even if he doesn't attack countervailing views head-on in his historical article, don't we still want our Vietnam War scholar to read and thoughtfully consider the work of predecessors who hold different views? We know that his interpretation of events will be better for having done so.

How can you address counterarguments in this policy memo?

How is a legislative aide supposed to address counterarguments in an application and policy advice memo that no one is likely to be actively opposing?

By looking at the transactions in the given scenarios from the perspectives of both consumers and business owners. As consumers, most of us feel like we benefit from the free flow of opinions available from review consolidation apps like Yelp. But imagine you are starting up a small business—you probably legitimately fear the devastating reputational hit you could suffer from even one or a few negative reviews. With stakes that high, the temptation to acquiesce to an unsavory abuser of that review power might be overwhelming. It is only when you thoroughly understand these competing interests that you will be able to best help the Senator navigate the problems he hopes to address.

Competing Interests! (handwritten)

It may help to concede intellectually that all sides have a genuine point to make. We care about letting consumers share information, and we care about letting them advocate for good services for themselves. We also care about preventing coercive uses of power, including the power of negative reviews. The trick is in balancing those concerns. Consider all possible perspectives, but then use sound legal judgment and good sense to puzzle through them.

To get a deeper understanding of any legal issue, think through hypotheticals

Most law students quickly learn that one of the best ways to truly understand a rule of law, and to determine under which circumstances it should be extended or limited, is to apply it to hypotheticals. As hypotheticals to help you consider how to analyze your assigned scenarios, examine the following hypotheticals and ask what you think is the correct outcome and whether you think New Hampshire law *should* penalize the conduct involved:

> It's not much of an exaggeration to say that working through hypotheticals is what the Socratic method is. Students glean a rule of law from one or more cases that they have read, and then come to class ready to think about how it might be applied to new facts. Understanding that may help you better prepare for law school classes. Even more important, it may help you see that practicing to apply rules you are learning to new hypotheticals is one of the very best ways you can learn the materials well and get ready for law school exams.

1. **The original godfather.** Don Fanucci is known as the boss of the neighborhood. Storekeepers routinely give him 10% of their earnings as "tribute" or "protection." Shop owners who fail to pay Fanucci, or who undercount their profits, have been known to suffer serious injuries from beatings by street thugs who are presumed to work for Fanucci.

2. **"Nice doggie you got there. Would be a shame if …"** Your beloved pit bull Rocco escaped from your backyard. After 24 hours you are contacted by a neighbor who has him. The neighbor reminds you that pit bulls are often considered wild and potentially dangerous attack dogs, and they are frequently put down by animal control authorities. She says she would prefer to return Rocco to his owners rather than send him to an animal shelter. She simply wants $500 to cover her time and expenses in caring for the dog.

3. **Get me home!** Nyasha's flight was delayed for more than two hours. Once it finally boarded, her plane started to take off but at the last minute pulled up short on the runway. Apparently there was a mechanical problem. Deplaning and re-boarding took another two hours, during which Nyasha began tweeting about her experiences. Flight attendants approached her and offered to seat her in first class if she would tell her followers that the airline was doing everything it could to attend to its passengers' inconvenience.

When you look carefully at these hypotheticals it may become easier to see how the law can balance competing concerns. The first one provides a nearly textbook example of precisely the kind of extortion that we mean to prohibit. If the law doesn't cover that situation then it probably is not serving its purpose.

The second scenario is more subtle. If Rocco had been taken to a veterinarian, it is quite possible that he might have accrued $500 in medical expenses. But as far as we know he never went to a vet, there is no indication of any extraordinary expenditures on his behalf, and $500 seems to be an awful lot of money just to board an animal overnight. And the request for money juxtaposed with a heavily implied threat the dog could be killed by animal control authorities if the sum is not paid ramps up the sense of threat quite a bit, doesn't it? Suddenly the hypothetical illustrates Prof. Lindgren's argument that two things that are fine to say independently ("Pit bulls are frequently treated with suspicion and fear" and "Can I have $500 for taking good care of your beloved pet?") feel quite different when they become causally linked.

Which leads to the much more complicated third hypothetical. Nyasha just wants to get on her flight, and who wouldn't want to sit in first class if given the opportunity? Is it moral for her to be essentially bought off to say good things about the airline? Debatable—although it does lean further toward the ethical if she truly believes that the airline is making a good effort to handle some difficult circumstances. But even those who would believe it distasteful for Nyasha to send out a glowing tweet and accept the upgrade are likely to find it much harder to answer the legal question of whether Nyasha or the airline should face criminal sanctions for this transaction. Put yourself in Nyasha's shoes, the airline's, *and* those of her follow passengers and general Twitter followers. When you have done that, you have probably explored the meaning of extortion in a far richer way than you might just by reading the law more objectively. That deep thinking will get you ready to do your best work on this (and any) assignment.

Transfer What You Have Accomplished to a Law School Setting

Sample exam question

Essay – 40 minutes

<u>Via Email</u>

From: Speaker of the House, North York General Assembly
Sent: Thursday, March 15, 20___
To: Legislative Counsel
Subject: Needed quickly: Analysis of Extortion and Threats statute

I'm busy today in hearings with the committee reviewing some of our criminal statutes. Currently we're looking at 13 No.Y.S.A. § 1701:

> **North York:** a typical law professor's tactic to use a hypothetical jurisdiction so that there will be no common law you are expected to know. Notice, too, that North York's extortion statute is different from the statute in New Hampshire. How might that change your analysis?

Ch. 39 Extortion and Threats:

A person who maliciously threatens to accuse another of a crime or offense, or with an injury to his or her person or property, with intent to extort money or other pecuniary advantage, or with intent to compel the person so threatened to do an act against his or her will, shall be imprisoned not more than three years or fined not more than $500.00, or both.

Based on some comments that were made in this morning's session, what I need to find out from you is whether a person may be charged under this statute in the following kind of scenario:

An experienced music executive wants to become the new manager for Tutti Fruitti, a wildly successful and internationally recognized pop duo. The executive mentions in his pitch that although the general public seemed not to know, he was aware that the group was lip-synching during its performance of The Star-Spangled Banner during Game 5 of the World Series. He added that Tutti Fruitti "would probably be in some hot water if that one got out." He never explicitly connected his silence on the matter to his getting the job.

I know that you are traveling right now and will not be able to fully research this, and it may help to know that our intern could not find any cases directly on point in our jurisdiction. In the absence of controlling legal authority I simply need you to spell out your opinion of whether this sort of prosecution is likely to be permitted or not, and why. And if your answer would depend on how our courts interpreted parts of the statute, please explain which ones and how/why a court would rule one way or another.

Response needed asap before we reconvene. Please send your answer by email since I will not have time to stop by the office before we go back into the hearings. Thank you.

Attacking the exam question

Your first reaction to the test questions might be uh-oh, this extortion statute is not the same one that you were examining in New Hampshire. No fair—you haven't studied this one! But wait; the language of this statute looks very similar to the Model Penal Code that was discussed in the law review article you read, so you have actually had some guidance in applying it. And even if under the pressure of taking a test you didn't remember that, you already know how to attack the question.

First, break the statute into elements. There may be reasonable variations in doing this, but one version might look like:

1. Maliciously

2. Threatens to accuse another (of a crime/offense OR with injury to person/property)

3. With intent to extort money OR to compel unwilled action.

Next, proceed to consider each of the elements for the given facts.

An obvious problem for prosecution in the fact pattern will be that there does not seem to have been an unequivocal threat, at least not explicitly. The closest prosecutors may be able to come is to argue that the executive's comments about knowing a secret, in the context of his interview for a highly compensated position, implied a threat to reveal it if he was not offered the job. This seems like an ambiguous point, so is likely worth discussing in as much depth as you can, while including both arguments and counterarguments.

The rest of that element will be easier to prove: the executive might be suggesting that band members committed fraud. Even if not, there's more than a hint that publicizing the lip synching could cause them serious financial harm. A good response to the question can probably just briefly explain why the executive's conduct might be considered malicious, and what he might be trying to get the singers to do that is against their will (hire him even if he wasn't their top choice).

Sample answer with commentary

Below is a reasonably strong sample response.

Student Answer

The music executive's actions in his talks with TF can be prosecuted as criminal extortion.

The applicable rule is 13 No. Y. S.A. § 1701 Ch. 39 Extortion and Threats. Our case will focus on two central elements of the statute: "Maliciously threatens to accuse another of an offense," and "With intent to compel the person so threatened to do an act against his or her will."

> Starting with such a strong conclusion works well sometimes, but it does have its risks. A simple declarative thesis helps the writer clearly stake out a position to explain and defend. But it can make for one-sided analysis, and always runs at least some risk of being wrong. Most lawyers would hedge a bit more—maybe just by inserting a "probably" into this sentence.

> Good judgment. But would be even better if the writer included some explanation of why those two elements are most at issue.

"Maliciously threatens to accuse another of an offense"

The issue is whether the executive's comments during the meeting with TF can be considered a "malicious threat to accuse another of an offense." The ordinary meaning of "malicious" would be an action with negative intent. Further, the ordinary meaning of "threat" would be when someone has said something (with negative intent) that would insinuate that they would do some harmful act in the future.

In our case, during the executive's pitch to TF, he said to the duo that "TF would probably be in some hot water if that one got out," while pretty apparently referencing his earlier comments that the public seemed not to be aware of the lip synching. The executive never directly said that he would go public if he were not offered the job, but by saying "although the general public seemed not to know," he means that he has information that he can leverage against the group. When addressing an extortion issue, one of the determinative factors is the type of threat. In this case, the type of threat must be "malicious" — meaning an act with negative intent. When the executive mentioned that the group "would probably be in some type of hot water," he has used the malicious threat to accuse the group of an offense. The central reason why the executive mentioned this to the pop duo was because he wanted to leverage this offense against them. Further, this should constitute a "malicious threat to accuse another of an

> This author seems to understand the need to justify and fully explain conclusions. There is an obvious effort to lay out the reasoning for every point, which is excellent. But then, do you think every explanation here is equally successful? What could the writer do to improve?

offense," because the executive's intent was to provide this negative information about the group while he pitched them to be their manager. This type of conduct should constitute a "malicious threat" because the executive's intent was negative, and used that negative intent to try and leverage his power against the group.

From a policy standpoint, we should not allow this type of conduct. Allowing this type of conduct can promote extorting musicians (and others in the entertainment and sports industry where "employees" are represented by agents/managers), because it creates an unfair imbalance in bargaining power. If this type of conduct were promoted, rather than representing clients, music executives would be busy attempting to find "dirt" on them in hopes of getting more business from artists who might not otherwise select them as managers.

> In the call of the exam question this policy analysis was not directly requested. A law professor would probably still appreciate this student's impulse to include it. Why?

"With intent to compel the person so threatened to do an act against his or her will."

The next issue is whether the executive had *intent* to compel the person (TF) to do an act against his or her will. Intent is a mindset that must be proved for this element of the crime. The executive's intent in this case was to hopefully sign TF, and share in the proceeds of the band's successes. Further, the executive's conduct constituted an intent to "compel the person so threatened to do an act against his or her will."

In this case the executive hoped to corner TF so that they would feel they did not have any option besides signing with his music label. Although he never explicitly connected his silence about the lip synching issue on the matter to his signing TF, his conduct and its results showed attempt to leverage the group by force of threat to reveal embarrassing information about them. According to the statute, to be extortionate a threat must compel the person to act against their own will. Their "own will" would generally be seen as a decision they would not otherwise make. Here, because of the information TF were given with respect to their lip synching (the threat), they were compelled to choose the executive as their manager, which is a decision they otherwise might not have made.

> Again, this writer has very much absorbed the point that legal analysis should explicitly connect all of the dots to support conclusions. The rule is laid out in the prior paragraph, and the application to specific facts is carefully elucidated here. This important paragraph does get a bit wordy and repetitive, though. What could be cut without reducing the credit that the test-taker should earn?

If the North York legislature meant this statute as strict deterrent for extortion and threats, the executive's conduct should be condemned. Any type of conduct that constituted a "malicious threat" "with intent to compel the person so threatened to do an act against his or her will" should be punished under the statute to deter others from unsavory actions. Others might argue that the legislature's real objective was retribution for immoral decision-making. Applying the North York statute to this executive's actions would also accomplish that objective because the punishment is not overly severe, but appropriate given the executive's bad behavior that goes beyond regular business negotiation practices.

Overall, the executive's conduct was a violation of the statute and should be punished by law. We do not want executives in high positions to extort those with less bargaining power in hopes that they will make a decision against their will.

Criminal Law Project Checklist

Review your drafts while looking carefully for each point raised below. If the points are included, please make sure that they are presented and explained to the best of your ability. If they are not, then consider whether your analysis can be made more complete.

1. Where does your analysis explain the elements of theft by extortion?

2. Does the memo make it clear to the reader what is complicated about extortion law? Does it nonetheless justify why certain kinds of coercive conduct nonetheless remain criminal, and/ or why it probably should remain so?[8]

3. In your analysis of *each one* of the Senator's three examples, where does your reasoning explain:

   a. Exactly what property the defendant would be alleged to have obtained or sought control over;

   b. What threat was made;

   c. Why the threat rises to the level of "extortion" as the term is used in § 637.5 (II)— specifically, whether it falls within one of the enumerated examples of extortionate conduct; if so, which one(s) and why, and if not, why it should nonetheless be considered extortionate?

4. Where does your discussion consider whether your conclusions about the potential criminal culpability for actions in each example actually make sense?

5. Where does the discussion acknowledge the concerns and perspectives of both consumers and business owners?

6. If you argue that any of the Senator's scenarios are legally permissible, yet nonetheless troubling, where does your memo analyze the Yelp user agreements to see whether the behavior in question may already be contractually prohibited?

---

8. Unless, of course, the memo takes the fairly extreme position that verbal coercion should never be criminalized. That would certainly be a viable (though very minority) viewpoint, but it is not one that seems compatible with the Senator's approach.

Chapter 4

Property[1]

Assignment: *Prepare an Advice Letter for Your Client*

Based on the materials in the file, please draft a letter to your clients providing the advice and information they seek. In doing so, you should explain the law as it pertains to their situation, and outline the legal options if the clients choose to proceed with filing a nuisance lawsuit. Target length is fewer than 1000 words exclusive of letterhead, salutations, subheadings, or other standard non-substantive organizational material.

Analytical Skills to Focus On

✓ Understanding the problem to be solved

✓ Thinking deeply about the legal rules implicated

✓ Stating rules precisely

✓ Evaluating counterarguments

✓ Demonstrating sound professional judgment

Case File

The materials in the case file are compiled in one complete set so that you will have them all together. You should read them all carefully on your own before diving into the commentary and questions that follow. As you read through the materials, ask yourself:

1. What do the clients really want to accomplish, and what options would help them achieve their objectives?

2. What rule or legal principle is implicated in the problem? What policy concerns are implicated?

3. What narrative can you construct about the facts at issue? What counter-narrative can the other side offer? Do the narratives seem more related to the strict legal question or to competing policy considerations?

---

1. This title is slightly misnamed because nuisance law intersects property and tort. It arises from property principles protecting the right to use and enjoy one's space, but lawsuits alleging nuisances ordinarily originate in tort.

4. What does each document in the case file add to your understanding of the problem?

5. How authoritative is each document as a source of fact or law?

6. What materials are *not* here that you would want to review to better understand your case?

A project checklist is included at the end of the chapter. Use it to review and edit your drafts as you strive for maximal effectiveness.

....

Chapter 4 Case File

Your exercise packet contains the following:

- A letter from your clients asking for information and advice
- Map showing the properties at issue, which your clients included with their letter
- Your memo to your boss and your file outlining the work you plan to undertake in response to your clients' letter
- Sections of secondary sources outlining the various types of nuisance
- Relevant cases to use in your analysis

Thinking about Property

Law students sometimes comment that the topics covered in their Property classes feel more "random" or thematically disconnected than those in some of their other courses. And students are not necessarily wrong: intellectual property, estates in land, landlord/tenant rules, and the law pertaining to finders of personal property do not seem on their face to have a whole lot to do with one another. So what unites these "property" matters beyond the fact that they are traditionally covered in property law courses?

One answer may be that whether we are dealing with real property, personal property, or more inchoate intellectual property, we are addressing matters of private ownership. One core aspect of ownership is control—the ability to do what we want with our own stuff. Much of property law is designed to protect the rights of owners. Yet ownership control cannot be absolute. Sometimes the government must intervene in private ownership for the public good (eminent domain), or one person's chosen use of property affects another's (nuisance), or there is a societal benefit to use of property that can outweigh an owner's right to leave it fallow (adverse possession and prescriptive easement). Navigating the boundaries of individual ownership and the rights of others or the collective good is arguably at the heart of issues in property law.

You may find it easier to understand how the various topics covered under the umbrella subject of "Property" connect if you think of property law as encompassing an overarching theme: how do people relate to *one another* and respect each other's rights to their own private things?

Sharon and John Michael Osgood

1414 Leafside Road

Quogue, New York 11954

Dear Mr./Ms. [Your name],

We are writing to you out of desperation. You and your law firm were so helpful when we bought our house, and then again when we had that unpleasantness with our former employee. We are hoping that you can once again help us with what we believe may be a legal matter.

As you probably remember, we own and operate the Osgood Doggie Emporium located at 648 Montauk Highway (also called Rt. 27). Ours is a very successful kennel and grooming boutique which offers temporary care for animals and obedience and training classes as well as high-end grooming services and pet care products. After starting out with just a small grooming shop we have managed to build a compound spread over two separate properties, and we now provide a wide variety of services to our elite clientele. As you can imagine, we are proud of our business and have worked very hard to ensure its success. We also rely on the income from the Emporium to make our living.

About three months ago the family living next to one part of our Emporium (we are enclosing a map screenshot to give a sense of their proximity to us) agreed to let a new television drama film on their property. For months now the filming has been nothing but annoying and disruptive. When we asked around, we found out that it is for a new TV drama called *Starshine*. They are shooting 22 episodes now, which is expected to take another two months or so. If the show is successful they plan to continue filming the majority of their episodes at this location for as long as the program airs!

Frankly, we are already at our wits' end with this show. There are trucks going back and forth at all hours of the day and night bringing food and equipment and whatnot. As you probably know, Route 27 is the main—really only—thoroughfare through this end of Long Island. The actual driveway for the location branches off of a small side road rather than Route 27 itself, but this doesn't end up helping much at all. The heavy traffic to and from the filming location seems to constantly tie up traffic on the highway. The constant jams mean that our drop-in business has drastically decreased. Kennel and training business is still basically ok, but revenue from product sales in the boutique is down about 45% from the same period last year.

There are other problems in addition to traffic: the production is noisy, with loud electrical generators running at all hours, and the bright lights for the cameras are frequently on past 10:00 at night. These sights and sounds are very upsetting to the animals in our kennels. They whimper far more than usual, and seem nervous and agitated when we attend to them throughout the day. We are very worried that we will lose boarding customers if the dogs go home more anxious and unhappy than they were when they came to us.

Of course we went over and tried speaking to the *Starshine* people. The ones we could find were brusque and, in my opinion, rude. Furthermore, they seemed primarily to be production assistants who did not have real authority to alter the filming operation. Our requests to speak to the producers in charge of the film crew were met with roadblocks and stony silence. We then tried to contact some of our local officials. Once again, this avenue was not very helpful in resolving our complaints. We were able to learn that there was no permit for this filming, but apparently permits are not required here when the filming takes place entirely on private property. And no one seemed especially eager to help us out, which puzzled us until we realized how eager the government is to encourage film productions. Why, the state has a whole office set up just to provide incentives for movie and television productions! http://www.nylovesfilm.com. I guess the continued success of our local business just doesn't matter as much to them as this big TV show.

Since we were not able to resolve this informally, our next step seems to be to take some sort of legal action. We looked on the internet, and from what we can tell it seems like we should have a claim against the *Starshine* production for either public or private nuisance. But of course we aren't lawyers, so we are writing to find out what you think our legal options are and whether you can help us. Do you think we have a good case? Is this something you and your firm can work on?

Very truly yours,

Sharon Osgood

Sharon Osgood

> This paragraph and the two prior ones provide a lot of facts, all of which clearly matter a great deal to your clients. The challenging task for you will be to figure out which facts matter most for their legal questions, which they care about the most (not necessarily the same thing at all), and how you will address the clients' problem in light of those concerns.

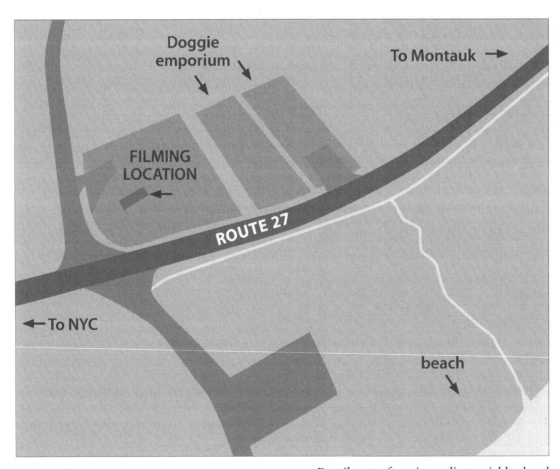

Detail map of our immediate neighborhood

Memo

To: File

Cc: Supervising attorney

From: [Your Name]

Date: April 14, 2016

Re: Osgood Letter

Work plan for Osgood letter. Potential nuisance suit.

Received letter yesterday from long-standing clients asking about legal options to limit filming operations on a property adjacent to their dog boutique. Clients have asked about public and private nuisance law, and seem to have done some online reading about the issue.

Next steps:

1. Consider information that clients are likely to have seen: research first few pages of online search for "nuisance" to see what they may currently understand/believe.

2. Research actual law of nuisance in New York state

    a. Start with NY encyclopedia for quick background

    b. Find analogous cases in both public and private nuisance.

3. Prepare letter explaining law to clients, and offering to act on their behalf if both warranted and desired.

> This memo lays out your own work plan. The materials in the case file suggest that so far this plan has been followed. Look thoughtfully at "your" plan: did it make sense? Is it what you would actually do if this were your case in practice? If so, why, and if not, why not?

3 Lawyers Desk Reference 10th § 14:4
Lawyers Desk Reference 10th Edition | October 2017 Update
Harry M. Philo

Chapter 14. Environmental Sources
B. Types of Actions

§ 14:4. Nuisance
References

Public nuisance is an act or omission which obstructs or causes inconvenience or damage to the public in the exercise of rights in common to all citizens. Public nuisance usually involves a criminal prosecution, and a private right of action is generally held to accrue only if there is a showing of interference with the rights of the general public as well as the individual plaintiff's special damage which must be distinguishable in kind and not in degree from that sustained by others.

A private nuisance occurs when an activity on one's own property, which activity over a substantial length of time or on successive and repeated occasions, causes significant and substantial interference with the person, property, health, safety or comfort of others. Nuisance centers around the damages inflicted rather than any particular kind of act or omission which has led to the invasion.

Thus, nuisance can result from negligent or intentional conduct or from abnormally dangerous activity. There must be a substantial interference with the interest involved, which is more important where injunctive relief is sought rather than damages. The defendant's conduct must also be unreasonable. Remedies for nuisance include abatement by self-help in addition to damages or injunction.

In certain limited situations, ultrahazardous activity may be cause for the imposition of strict liability for "absolute nuisance." The controlling factor is the relation of the activity to its surroundings. In states where this theory is used it might have contemporary application considering the recent escape of nerve gas or the continued shipment of highly toxic and explosive substances across the country.

Proving damages is often difficult in pollution cases and this is especially true where it is hard to prove the concentration necessary to cause the damage, or where the defendant is guilty of aggravating a pre-existing condition. Damages should be sought for the following:

1. property damage
2. pain and suffering
3. medical expenses, including future medical expenses
4. loss of consortium
5. loss of companionship where such damages are allowed
6. the diminution of property value occasioned by the nuisance where nuisance is permanent
7. loss of use and enjoyment of property
8. punitive damages where allowed

Problems of proof also arise when the nuisance is a result of multi-source pollution. This is particularly true in regional pollution suits where the cost and difficulty of investigation are important factors. Creative thinking and familiarity with governmental and technological developments is necessary. Although the specific damages may be difficult to prove in the multi-source nuisance action, it should be remembered that the fact that other polluters are guilty of the same acts as defendant is not a defense to the action. Common defenses which must be considered are the statute of limitations, forms of assumption of the risk and even assertions of prescriptive rights.

This NY-specific legal encyclopedia is likely to be a more specific secondary source than the preceding generic LAWYERS DESK REFERENCE entry, isn't it? As you read it, compare the contents and style to the prior article to decide what this adds to a lawyer's comprehension and decide why an attorney might review both or one over the other.

Excerpts from 81 N.Y. Jur. 2d Nuisances

New York Jurisprudence, Second Edition

May 2016 Update

Nuisances

John A. Gebauer, J.D.

I. In General
B. Classification of Nuisances

---

§ 4. Generally; distinction between public and private nuisances

West's Key Number Digest, Nuisance 🗝 1, 59

While all nuisances are either public[i] or private,[ii] they are further classified as nuisances *per se* or *per accidens*[iii] or as absolute or qualified.[iv]

The difference between a public and private nuisance does not depend on the nature of the thing done but on the fact that one affects the public at large and the other a limited number only.[v] In other words, if the danger or damage threatens the public, the nuisance is classified as common; if it threatens one person or a few, it is then called a private nuisance.[vi] Another distinction between public and private nuisances is that a private nuisance occurs when defendant interferes unreasonably with plaintiff's right to use and enjoy his or her property whereas, in contrast, a public nuisance exists when there is an interference with a public right.[vii]

Do the problems described by the Osgoods affect just them or the public at large? Obviously both can be alleged on our facts, but consider carefully whether one of these claims is more credible or practical in your case. Or alternatively, whether the two claims in tandem might bolster one another.

The difference between a public and a private nuisance is significant, primarily because only a public nuisance may be made the basis for a criminal prosecution; and only the public, through the proper officer, may sue to enjoin or abate a public nuisance whereas only a private individual may sue to abate a private nuisance.[viii] In some situations, however, a public nuisance may so violate private rights as to constitute also a private nuisance, giving rise to a right of action by a private individual.[ix]

---

§ 5. Public nuisances

West's Key Number Digest, Nuisance 🗝 59 to 62

A public, or as sometimes termed a common, nuisance has been defined as a conduct or omission which offends, interferes with, or causes damage to the public in the exercise of rights common to all[x] in a manner such as to offend public morals, interfere with use by the public of a public place,[xi] or endanger or injure the property, health, safety, or comfort of a considerable number of persons.[xii] Whether conduct constitutes a public nuisance must be determined as a question of fact under all the circumstances.[xiii] A public nuisance is an offense to the public of a neighborhood or community in the enjoyment of its common rights as distinguished from activity which results merely in injury even to large numbers of persons in the enjoyment of private rights, not shared by members of the community or neighborhood at large.[xiv] The nuisance is a common or public nuisance, as distinguished from a mere private nuisance, when the particular offensive act is conducted in such a manner that it causes substantial annoyance and discomfort indiscriminately to many and divers persons, who are continually, or may from time to time be, in the vicinity.[xv] A nuisance is public also where it is committed in such place and in such manner that the aggregation of private injuries becomes so great and expensive as to constitute a public annoyance and inconvenience and a wrong against the community, which may properly be the subject of a public prosecution.[xvi]

To establish a public nuisance, it is always essential to show the injury in fact.[xvii] A public nuisance is actionable by a private person only if it is shown that the person suffered special injury beyond that suffered by the community at large.[xviii] Consequently, the operation of a lawful business may not be deemed to constitute a public nuisance unless something is done in the operation thereof which is unlawful, or its operation is negligent or improper in some degree or respect as to work an unreasonable obstruction or injury to the public.[xix]

Other specific definitions of public nuisances are found in a number of statutes considered in another part of this article.[xx]

§ 6. Private nuisances

West's Key Number Digest, <u>Nuisance</u> 🔑 1 to 6

Private nuisance is established by proof of intentional action or inaction that substantially and unreasonably interferes with other people's use and enjoyment of their property.[xxi] A private nuisance has been defined as one which violates only private rights and produces damages to but one or a few persons.[xxii] Although a private nuisance frequently has been defined as anything done to the hurt or annoyance of the lands, tenements, or hereditaments of another,[xxiii] and the essence of a private nuisance has been said to be interference with the use or enjoyment of land,[xxiv] this definition embraces not a mere physical injury to the realty but any injury to the owner or possessor as respects his or her dealing with, possessing, or enjoying it.[xxv] Liability for private nuisance extends to injury to the person, as well as to the lands, tenements, and hereditaments of another.[xxvi]

One is liable for a private nuisance if his or her conduct is a legal cause of the invasion of the interest in the private use and enjoyment of land, and such invasion is intentional and unreasonable, negligent or reckless, or actionable under the rules governing liability for abnormally dangerous conditions or activities.[xxvii] The interference must not be fanciful, slight, or theoretical but certain and substantial and must interfere with the physical comfort of an ordinarily reasonable person.[xxviii] The elements of a private nuisance involving intentional and unreasonable invasion of use and enjoyment of another's land are:

(1) an interference substantial in nature;
(2) intentional in origin;
(3) unreasonable in character;
(4) with a person's property right to use and enjoyment; and
(5) caused by another's conduct in acting or failing to act.[xxix]

What constitutes a reasonable use of one's property depends upon the circumstances of each case.[xxx]

The fact that acts or conditions may not be a public nuisance, because they are lawful, does not necessarily prevent such acts or conditions from constituting a private nuisance.[xxxi] On the other hand, a nuisance may be both public and private in character, or in other words, a public nuisance becomes also a private nuisance as to any person who is specially injured by it to any extent beyond the injury to the public.[xxxii]

Notes

i. § 5

ii. § 6

iii. § 7

iv. § 8

v. *Melker v. City of New York*, 190 N.Y. 481, 83 N.E. 565 (1908).

vi. *Copart Industries, Inc. v. Consolidated Edison Co. of New York, Inc.*, 41 N.Y.2d 564, 394 N.Y.S.2d 169, 362 N.E.2d 968 (1977); *Khoury v. Saratoga County*, 267 N.Y. 384, 196 N.E. 299 (1935); *Nalley v. General Elec. Co.*, 165 Misc. 2d 803, 630 N.Y.S.2d 452 (Sup 1995); *Malerba v. Warren*, 108 Misc. 2d 785, 438 N.Y.S.2d 936 (Sup. 1981), *judgment modified on other grounds*, 96 A.D.2d 529, 464 N.Y.S.2d 835 (2d Dep't 1983); *Town of Preble v. Song Mountain, Inc.*, 62 Misc. 2d 353, 308 N.Y.S.2d 1001 (Sup. 1970); *Canfield v. Quayle*, 170 Misc. 621, 10 N.Y.S.2d 781 (Sup. 1939).

vii. *Andersen v. University of Rochester*, 91 A.D.2d 851, 458 N.Y.S.2d 404 (4th Dep't 1982) (holding, in a personal injury action by one who was injured when their motorcycle struck railroad ties on defendant-university's property, that they would not be entitled to amend the complaint by adding a second cause of action for public nuisance where the proposed amendment had failed to state a cause of action for public nuisance absent any allegation of interference with a public right); *Nalley v. General Elec. Co.*, 165 Misc. 2d 803, 630 N.Y.S.2d 452 (Sup 1995).

viii. *Copart Industries, Inc. v. Consolidated Edison Co. of New York, Inc.*, 41 N.Y.2d 564, 394 N.Y.S.2d 169, 362 N.E.2d 968 (1977) (stating that a private nuisance is actionable by the individual person or persons whose rights have been disturbed while a public, or as sometimes termed a common, nuisance is an offense against the State and is subject to abatement or prosecution on application of the proper governmental agency).

ix. § 6

x. *Haire v. Bonelli*, 57 A.D.3d 1354, 870 N.Y.S.2d 591 (3d Dep't 2008); *Burns Jackson Miller Summit & Spitzer v. Lindner*, 59 N.Y.2d 314, 464 N.Y.S.2d 712, 451 N.E.2d 459 (1983); *Copart Industries, Inc. v. Consolidated Edison Co. of New York, Inc.*, 41 N.Y.2d 564, 394 N.Y.S.2d 169, 362 N.E.2d 968 (1977); *Andersen v. University of Rochester*, 91 A.D.2d 851, 458 N.Y.S.2d 404 (4th Dep't 1982); *People v. HST Meth, Inc.*, 43 A.D.2d 932, 352 N.Y.S.2d 487 (1st Dep't 1974).

xi. *Agoglia v. Benepe*, 84 A.D.3d 1072, 924 N.Y.S.2d 428 (2d Dep't 2011); *Haire v. Bonelli*, 57 A.D.3d 1354, 870 N.Y.S.2d 591 (3d Dep't 2008); *City of New York v. Smokes-Spirits.Com, Inc.*, 12 N.Y.3d 616, 883 N.Y.S.2d 772, 911 N.E.2d 834 (2009).

The condition of monkey bars on a school playground, which allegedly should have had additional surfacing material on the ground beneath them, was not an actionable public nuisance absent any showing that the alleged omissions interfered with the public's right to make proper use of the playground. *Grandeau v. South Colonie Cent. School Dist.*, 63 A.D.3d 1484, 881 N.Y.S.2d 549, 246 Ed. Law Rep. 334 (3d Dep't 2009).

xii. *Wall Street Garage Parking Corp. v. New York Stock Exchange, Inc.*, 10 A.D.3d 223, 781 N.Y.S.2d 324 (1st Dep't 2004); *532 Madison Ave. Gourmet Foods, Inc. v. Finlandia Center, Inc.*, 96 N.Y.2d 280, 727 N.Y.S.2d 49, 750 N.E.2d 1097 (2001); *Burns Jackson Miller Summit & Spitzer v. Lindner*, 59 N.Y.2d 314, 464 N.Y.S.2d 712, 451 N.E.2d 459 (1983); *Copart Industries, Inc. v. Consolidated Edison Co. of New York, Inc.*, 41 N.Y.2d 564, 394

N.Y.S.2d 169, 362 N.E.2d 968 (1977); *Andersen v. University of Rochester*, 91 A.D.2d 851, 458 N.Y.S.2d 404 (4th Dep't 1982).

xiii. *City of Rochester v. Premises Located at 10–12 South Washington Street*, 180 Misc. 2d 17, 687 N.Y.S.2d 523 (Sup 1998).

xiv. *New York Trap Rock Corporation v. Town of Clarkstown*, 299 N.Y. 77, 85 N.E.2d 873 (1949); *People v. Rubenfeld*, 254 N.Y. 245, 172 N.E. 485 (1930); *State v. Waterloo Stock Car Raceway, Inc.*, 96 Misc. 2d 350, 409 N.Y.S.2d 40 (Sup 1978); *State v. Wright Hepburn Webster Gallery, Limited*, 64 Misc. 2d 423, 314 N.Y.S.2d 661 (Sup 1970), *order aff'd*, 37 A.D.2d 698, 323 N.Y.S.2d 389 (1st Dep't 1971).

The sine qua non of an action for public nuisance is the interference by a defendant with a public right. *Reid by Reid v. Kawasaki Motors Corp., U.S.A.*, 189 A.D.2d 954, 592 N.Y.S.2d 496 (3d Dep't 1993).

xv. *People v. HST Meth, Inc.*, 43 A.D.2d 932, 352 N.Y.S.2d 487 (1st Dep't 1974); *State v. Waterloo Stock Car Raceway, Inc.*, 96 Misc. 2d 350, 409 N.Y.S.2d 40 (Sup 1978); *Town of Mount Pleasant v. Van Tassell*, 7 Misc. 2d 643, 166 N.Y.S.2d 458 (Sup 1957), *judgment aff'd*, 6 A.D.2d 880, 177 N.Y.S.2d 1010 (2d Dep't 1958).

To establish a public nuisance the annoyance, discomfort or interference experienced by a considerable number of persons must be substantial. *State v. Fermenta ASC Corp.*, 238 A.D.2d 400, 656 N.Y.S.2d 342 (2d Dep't 1997).

Homeless shelter, alcohol crisis center, and aftercare program operated by not-for-profit corporation was not a public nuisance despite claim that the corporation's operation induced violent or unstable nonresidents to reside in city without proper screening or supervision, burdening city's resources and threatening public safety; alleged interference with the public right was not substantial or unreasonable. *DeStefano v. Emergency Housing Group*, Inc., 281 A.D.2d 449, 722 N.Y.S.2d 35 (2d Dep't 2001).

xvi. *People v. Rubenfeld*, 254 N.Y. 245, 172 N.E. 485 (1930) (so many are touched by the offense and in ways so indiscriminate and general that the multiplied annoyance may not unreasonably be classified as a wrong to the community); *Hoover v. Durkee*, 212 A.D.2d 839, 622 N.Y.S.2d 348 (3d Dep't 1995); *State v. Waterloo Stock Car Raceway, Inc.*, 96 Misc. 2d 350, 409 N.Y.S.2d 40 (Sup 1978); *Sullivan County v. Filippo*, 64 Misc. 2d 533, 315 N.Y.S.2d 519 (Sup 1970).

A village's dredging work on a brook and attendant sheathing did not create a public nuisance as such work was not unreasonable in character, resolved the worsening problem of flooding in the immediate vicinity, and posed no harm to the community as a whole. *Kaplan v. Incorporated Village of Lynbrook*, 12 A.D.3d 410, 784 N.Y.S.2d 586 (2d Dep't 2004).

Defendant did not, by parking his automobile so that it partially extended across opening for driveway, in violation of local traffic ordinance, create public nuisance. *Harvey v. Platten*, 33 A.D.2d 724, 305 N.Y.S.2d 182 (3d Dep't 1969).

xvii. *State v. Wright Hepburn Webster Gallery, Limited*, 64 Misc. 2d 423, 314 N.Y.S.2d 661 (Sup 1970), *order aff'd*, 37 A.D.2d 698, 323 N.Y.S.2d 389 (1st Dep't 1971); *People, on Complaint of Green, v. Willis*, 173 Misc. 442, 17 N.Y.S.2d 784 (Spec. Sess. 1940) (holding that the obstruction of a drainage system did not necessarily constitute a nuisance).

xviii. *Baity v. General Elec. Co.*, 86 A.D.3d 948, 927 N.Y.S.2d 492 (4th Dep't 2011), leave to appeal denied, 87 A.D.3d 1416, 930

N.Y.S.2d 170 (4th Dep't 2011); *Agoglia v. Benepe*, 84 A.D.3d 1072, 924 N.Y.S.2d 428 (2d Dep't 2011).

xix.   *State v. Wright Hepburn Webster Gallery, Limited*, 64 Misc. 2d 423, 314 N.Y.S.2d 661 (Sup 1970), *order aff'd*, 37 A.D.2d 698, 323 N.Y.S.2d 389 (1st Dep't 1971); *People on Complaint of Lawrence v. Abbro Metallics, Inc.*, 125 N.Y.S.2d 69 (Magis. Ct. 1953).

xx.   § 25.

xxi.   *Nemeth v. K-Tooling*, 100 A.D.3d 1271, 955 N.Y.S.2d 419 (3d Dep't 2012).

xxii.   *Id.*

xxiii.   *Heeg v. Licht*, 80 N.Y. 579, 1880 WL 12421 (1880); *Swords v. Edgar*, 59 N.Y. 28, 1874 WL 13552 (1874); *Nalley v. General Elec. Co.*, 165 Misc. 2d 803, 630 N.Y.S.2d 452 (Sup 1995).

xxiv.   *Molander v. Pepperidge Lake Homeowners Ass'n*, 82 A.D.3d 1180, 920 N.Y.S.2d 201 (2d Dep't 2011); *Haire v. Bonelli*, 57 A.D.3d 1354, 870 N.Y.S.2d 591 (3d Dep't 2008); *Copart Industries, Inc. v. Consolidated Edison Co. of New York, Inc.*, 41 N.Y.2d 564, 394 N.Y.S.2d 169, 362 N.E.2d 968 (1977); *Blessington v. McCrory Stores Corporation*, 305 N.Y. 140, 111 N.E.2d 421, 37 A.L.R.2d 698 (1953) (stating that if the alleged nuisance does not involve interference with the use or enjoyment of land, then the nuisance, if any, must be in the category of a public nuisance); *Queens County Business Alliance, Inc. v. New York Racing Ass'n, Inc.*, 98 A.D.2d 743, 469 N.Y.S.2d 448 (2d Dep't 1983) (holding that plaintiffs stated no cause of action in private nuisance since they failed to allege an essential element of a private nuisance, that is, an interference with the use or enjoyment of land).

Abutting landowner could not recover damages for a nuisance based on the city's repair of a public sidewalk where the landowner did not prove that the city's reconstruction work substantially interfered with the landowner's use and enjoyment of its property. *Seril v. Bureau of Highway Operations of Dept. of Transp., City of New York*, 245 A.D.3d 233, 667 N.Y.S.2d 42 (1st Dep't 1997).

xxv.   *Kavanagh v. Barber*, 131 N.Y. 211, 30 N.E. 235 (1892); *De Moll v. City of New York*, 163 A.D. 676, 148 N.Y.S. 966 (2d Dep't 1914).

xxvi.   *Swords v. Edgar*, 59 N.Y. 28, 1874 WL 13552 (1874); *Walkowicz v. Whitney's, Inc.*, 178 Misc. 331, 34 N.Y.S.2d 175 (Sup 1942).

xxvii.   *Caldwell v. Two Columbus Ave. Condominium*, 92 A.D.3d 441, 940 N.Y.S.2d 15 (1st Dep't 2012); *Copart Industries, Inc. v. Consolidated Edison Co. of New York, Inc.*, 41 N.Y.2d 564, 394 N.Y.S.2d 169, 362 N.E.2d 968 (1977); *Benjamin v. Nelstad Materials Corp.*, 214 A.D.2d 632, 625 N.Y.S.2d 281 (2d Dep't

1995); *Theofilatos v. Koleci*, 105 A.D.2d 514, 481 N.Y.S.2d 782 (3d Dep't 1984); *Nalley v. General Elec. Co.*, 165 Misc. 2d 803, 630 N.Y.S.2d 452 (Sup 1995); *State v. Fermenta ASC Corp.*, 162 Misc. 2d 288, 616 N.Y.S.2d 702 (Sup 1994).

xxviii.   *Matteliano v. Skitkzi*, 85 A.D.3d 1552, 925 N.Y.S.2d 276 (4th Dep't 2011), *leave to appeal denied*, 17 N.Y.3d 714, 933 N.Y.S.2d 654, 957 N.E.2d 1158 (2011).

xxix.   *Berenger v. 261 West LLC*, 93 A.D.3d 175, 940 N.Y.S.2d 4 (1st Dep't 2012); *Matteliano v. Skitkzi*, 85 A.D.3d 1552, 925 N.Y.S.2d 276 (4th Dep't 2011), *leave to appeal denied*, 17 N.Y.3d 714, 933 N.Y.S.2d 654, 957 N.E.2d 1158 (2011); *Gedney Commons Homeowners Ass'n, Inc. v. Davis*, 85 A.D.3d 854, 925 N.Y.S.2d 181 (2d Dep't 2011); *Doin v. Champlain Bluffs Development Corp.*, 68 A.D.3d 1605, 894 N.Y.S.2d 169 (3d Dep't 2009); *Copart Industries, Inc. v. Consolidated Edison Co. of New York, Inc.*, 41 N.Y.2d 564, 394 N.Y.S.2d 169, 362 N.E.2d 968 (1977).

A village's dredging work on a brook and attendant sheathing did not support landowners' private nuisance claim as the village's superintendent of public works testified that the work was accomplished in the most reasonable manner possible with limited encroachment upon the landowners' exclusively owned property, and the landowners failed to show that their use and enjoyment of their land was substantially and unreasonably interfered with. *Kaplan v. Incorporated Village of Lynbrook*, 12 A.D.3d 410, 784 N.Y.S.2d 586 (2d Dep't 2004).

Two of the necessary elements of a private nuisance are an interference that is intentional in origin and unreasonable in character. *Higgins v. Village of Orchard Park*, 277 A.D.2d 989, 716 N.Y.S.2d 845 (4th Dep't 2000).

In the absence of negligence or intent, a cause of action to recover damages arising from a private nuisance cannot be maintained. *State v. Fermenta ASC Corp.*, 238 A.D.2d 400, 656 N.Y.S.2d 342 (2d Dep't 1997).

xxx.   *Benjamin v. Nelstad Materials Corp.*, 214 A.D.2d 632, 625 N.Y.S.2d 281 (2d Dep't 1995).

xxxi.   *Vincent v. Hercules Powder Co.*, 228 A.D. 118, 239 N.Y.S. 47 (3d Dep't 1930) (holding that the fact that the maintenance of a powder magazine is not a public nuisance, since it is maintained by authority of law, does not prevent it from constituting a private nuisance where it causes damages to individual rights and private property).

xxxii.   *Ackerman v. True*, 175 N.Y. 353, 67 N.E. 629 (1903); *Kavanagh v. Barber*, 131 N.Y. 211, 30 N.E. 235 (1892).

As to the right of action by a private person in relation to a public nuisance, see § 56.

24 A.D.3d 400

Supreme Court, Appellate Division, Second Department, New York.

Eugene R. ANDERSON, et al., appellants,

v.

Gordon ELLIOTT, et al., respondents, et al., defendants.

Dec. 5, 2005.

Attorneys and Law Firms

Van DeWater & Van DeWater, Poughkeepsie, N.Y. (Janis Mary Gomez of counsel), for appellants.

Pavia & Harcourt, LLP, New York, N.Y. (Victor Genecin of counsel), for respondents Gordon Elliott, Gordon Elliott Productions, Inc., Millbrook Media Corp., Follow Productions, Inc., and 63 Willow Lane Corp.

Baker & Hostetler, LLP, New York, N.Y. (Ona T. Wang of counsel), for respondents Food Network and Scripps Networks, Inc. (no brief filed).

BARRY A. COZIER, J.P., GABRIEL M. KRAUSMAN, GLORIA GOLDSTEIN, and PETER B. SKELOS, JJ.

Opinion

In an action, inter alia, to recover damages for private nuisance, the plaintiffs appeal, as limited by their notice of appeal and brief, from so much of an order of the Supreme Court, Dutchess County (Brands, J.), dated July 28, 2004, as amended, as, upon converting the motion of the defendants Gordon Elliott, Gordon Elliott Productions, Inc., Millbrook Media Corp., Follow Productions, Inc., and 63 Willow Lane Corp., joined in by the defendants Food Network and Scripps Networks, Inc., to dismiss the complaint pursuant to CPLR 3211(a)(7), into a motion for summary judgment, pursuant to CPLR 3211(c), granted those branches of the motion which were to dismiss the second cause of action to recover damages for private nuisance and the claim for punitive damages, and denied their cross motion for leave to serve an amended complaint.

ORDERED that the order is affirmed insofar as appealed from, with one bill of costs to the defendants Gordon Elliott, Gordon Elliott Productions, Inc., Millbrook Media Corp., Follow Productions, Inc., and 63 Willow Lane Corp.

The defendant Gordon Elliott is an officer of the defendants Gordon Elliott Productions, Inc., Millbrook

Media Corp., Follow Productions, Inc., and 63 Willow Lane Corp. (hereinafter the Elliott defendants). The defendant Food Network is a cable television network operated by the defendant Scripps Networks, Inc.

The defendant 63 Willow Lane Corp. purchased a residential property at 63 Willow Lane for the purpose of filming a television program. Willow Lane is located in the plaintiffs' residential neighborhood in the Town of Clinton, Dutchess County. The Town's Zoning Laws prohibit commercial use of the property.

The filming occurred on the property over the course of several months on four separate occasions. After each of the first two filmings, the Town Zoning Enforcement Officer informed Gordon Elliott about the zoning violations and ordered him to cease and desist.

The plaintiffs, as taxpayers and owners of property on Willow Lane, brought an action alleging a violation of the Town's zoning laws, to recover damages for private nuisance, and seeking punitive damages. They claimed that the presence of an excessive number of cars, a dumpster, mattresses, and flood lights diminished the values of their properties and their use and enjoyment of the properties. Shortly after the plaintiffs commenced this action, the defendants filmed on one additional occasion. Subsequently, the defendants ceased their filming, removed all of their equipment and materials, and listed the property for sale.

[1][2] The Supreme Court properly granted that branch of the motion which was to dismiss the second cause of action to recover damages for private nuisance. To recover damages based on the tort of private nuisance, a plaintiff must establish an interference with the use or enjoyment of land, substantial in nature, intentional or negligent in origin, unreasonable in character, and caused by the defendants' conduct (*see Copart Indus. v. Consolidated Edison Co. of N.Y.*, 41 N.Y.2d 564, 568, 394 N.Y.S.2d 169, 362 N.E.2d 968; *Ward v. City of New York*, 15 A.D.3d 392, 789 N.Y.S.2d 539; *Weinberg v. Lombardi*, 217 A.D.2d 579, 629 N.Y.S.2d 280). The alleged disturbance that was caused by the defendants' television filming on several occasions did not, as a matter of law, rise to the level of substantial interference with the plaintiffs' use and enjoyment of their properties as to constitute a private

nuisance (*see Ruscito v. Swaine, Inc.,* 17 A.D.3d 560, 561, 793 N.Y.S.2d 475, *lv. denied* 5 N.Y.3d 704, 801 N.Y.S.2d 2, 834 N.E.2d 781, *cert. denied* 546 U.S. 978, 126 S.Ct. 557, 163 L.Ed.2d 461; *Pearlman v. Simons,* 276 A.D.2d 762, 714 N.Y.S.2d 767; *cf. Zimmerman v. Carmack,* 292 A.D.2d 601, 739 N.Y.S.2d 430).

Furthermore, the Supreme Court properly dismissed the claim, inter alia, based on the alleged private nuisance, seeking punitive damages. The complaint failed to allege facts demonstrating such a high degree of moral culpability as to warrant such damages. Moreover, there was no allegation that the acts complained of were calculated or done with a malicious intent to injure the plaintiffs (*see Kelly v. Defoe Corp.,* 223 A.D.2d 529, 530, 636 N.Y.S.2d 123; *Jakobsen v. Wilfred Labs.,* 99 A.D.2d 525, 527, 471 N.Y.S.2d 306).

Since the proposed amended allegations did not add any information of significance, the cross motion for leave to serve an amended complaint was properly denied (*see Flynn v. Sinclair Oil Corp.,* 14 N.Y.2d 853, 251 N.Y.S.2d 967, 200 N.E.2d 633). Although the Supreme Court erred in considering the affidavit of the Elliott defendants' real estate agent without giving notice to the parties (*see* CPLR 3211[c]; *Rovello v.*

Orofino Realty Co., 40 N.Y.2d 633, 635, 389 N.Y.S.2d 314, 357 N.E.2d 970; *Sopesis Constr. v. Solomon,* 199 A.D.2d 491, 492, 605 N.Y.S.2d 402), the Supreme Court had an additional ground for determining that there was no factual basis that the defendants' activities caused a decrease in the plaintiffs' property values. It was undisputed that the activities "were short lived and [had] ceased" and that the defendants removed all of their materials and equipment without leaving any permanent changes to the property. Accordingly, the plaintiffs failed to allege sufficient facts to support a cause of action for special damages in order to maintain their proposed amendment for a private action to enjoin a zoning violation (*see Guggenheimer v. Ginzburg,* 43 N.Y.2d 268, 275, 401 N.Y.S.2d 182, 372 N.E.2d 17; *Allen Avionics v. Universal Broadcasting Corp.,* 118 A.D.2d 527, 499 N.Y.S.2d 154, *affd.* 69 N.Y.2d 406, 515 N.Y.S.2d 418, 508 N.E.2d 130; *Guzzardi v. Perry's Boats,* 92 A.D.2d 250, 253, 460 N.Y.S.2d 78).

All Citations

24 A.D.3d 400, 807 N.Y.S.2d 101, 2005 N.Y. Slip Op. 09264

> **Uh-oh.** This case presents a very similar set of facts to your clients'—problems stemming from months of filming a television show—and here the private nuisance claim was dismissed as a matter of law. Is there a way that you can distinguish the Osgoods' circumstances from those of the plaintiffs here? If not, would there be any way to ensure that this precedent is not dispositive if your clients brought suit?

73 A.D.3d 1105, 901 N.Y.S.2d 688, 2010
N.Y. Slip Op. 04530

John Aristides et al., Respondents

v

Phillip Foster et al., Appellants.
Supreme Court, Appellate Division,
Second Department, New York
May 25, 2010

CITE TITLE AS: Aristides v Foster

Attorneys

Congdon, Flaherty, O'Callaghan, Reid, Donlon, Travis & Fishlinger, Uniondale, N.Y. (Gregory A. Cascino of counsel), for appellants.

MARK C. DILLON, J.P., RUTH C. BALKIN, THOMAS A. DICKERSON, and PLUMMER E. LOTT, JJ

Opinion

In an action, inter alia, to recover damages for private nuisance, the defendants appeal from an order of the Supreme Court, Suffolk County (Sgroi, J.), dated May 22, 2009, which denied their motion for summary judgment dismissing the complaint.

Ordered that the order is affirmed, without costs or disbursements.

The defendants Phillip Foster and Kathy Foster operate a 7-Eleven store franchise on Laurel Road in East Northport, Suffolk County. The defendant 7-Eleven, Inc., is the franchisor. The plaintiffs own and reside in a house on Laurel Road, separated from the 7-Eleven store by one commercial building. The 7-Eleven store existed at the time the plaintiffs purchased their home in 1978. The plaintiffs commenced this action, inter alia, to recover damages for private nuisance. Primarily, their claims were based on allegations that, beginning in 1999, vendors making deliveries at all hours parked their tractor-trailer vehicles on the roadway, blocking access to the plaintiffs' home, emitting pollution and noise as the trucks idled; that patrons of the store also parked in front of their residence, blocking access thereto; and that patrons loitered on and near the 7-Eleven store, creating noise and disturbances. The defendants moved for summary judgment dismissing the complaint. The Supreme Court denied the defendants' motion. We affirm.

The elements of a private nuisance cause of action are an interference (1) substantial in nature, (2) intentional in origin, (3) unreasonable in character, (4) with a person's property right to use and enjoy land, (5) caused by another's conduct in acting or failure to act (*see Copart Indus. v Consolidated Edison Co. of N.Y.*, 41 NY2d 564, 570 [1977]; *Donnelly v Nicotra*, 55 AD3d 868, 868–869 [2008]; *JP Morgan Chase Bank v Whitmore*, 41 AD3d 433, 434 [2007]; *Vacca v Valerino*, 16 AD3d 1159, 1160 [2005]; *Zimmerman v Carmack*, 292 AD2d 601, 602 [2002]). Here, the defendants failed to establish their entitlement to judgment as a matter of law by eliminating all triable issues of fact as to whether the conditions alleged constituted a private nuisance and whether they caused the alleged nuisance. The defendants claim that the plaintiffs "seek to blame [them] for their general dissatisfaction with the commercial nature of the neighborhood," and assert that the plaintiffs cannot prove that the vehicles which park in front of their property, obstructing their access thereto, are not associated with the many other commercial establishments in the immediate area. However, the defendants failed to refute the plaintiffs' statements in their deposition testimony, submitted by the defendants in support of their motion, that trucks delivering goods to the 7-Eleven store, as well as patrons of the store, frequently, even daily and multiple times during the course of some days, park their vehicles in front of the plaintiffs' home, blocking the plaintiffs' access thereto, and leave the vehicles idling, emitting noise and fumes. Moreover, while the 7-Eleven store existed and received deliveries by truck when the plaintiffs purchased their home, according to the testimony of the plaintiff Susanne Aristides, in 1995, 1996, or 1997, she observed that the trucks delivering goods to the 7-Eleven store began to be larger, 80- or 85-foot-long tractor-trailer trucks, as opposed to the "small little tiny trucks" that previously made these deliveries. Additionally, given the plaintiffs' descriptions of the conditions created by these circumstances, contrary to the defendants' contention, they failed to establish that the conditions were not sufficiently substantial in nature and unreasonable in character as to constitute a private nuisance. In this regard, Susanne Aristides testified that she photographed vehicles parked in front of the plaintiffs' home as frequently as 10 to 15 times per day. She stated that she is "out just about every day taking pictures." She also estimated that she had recorded approximately 1,000 license plates of offending vehicles. Accordingly, the Supreme Court properly denied the defendants' motion for summary judgment dismissing the complaint.

The defendants' remaining contention is raised for the first time on appeal, and, accordingly, is not properly before this Court (*see Wilner v Allstate Ins. Co.*, 71 AD3d 155 [2010]). Dillon, J.P., Balkin, Dickerson and Lott, JJ., concur.

3 Misc.3d 1014

Supreme Court, New York County, New York.

WALL STREET GARAGE PARKING CORP.,
Plaintiff,

v.

NEW YORK STOCK EXCHANGE, INC.,
Defendant.

March 12, 2004.

Attorneys and Law Firms

Jenkens & Gilchrist Parker Chapin LLP, New York City (Stephen F. Harmon of counsel), for plaintiff.

Milbank, Tweed, Hadley & McCloy LLP, New York City (Douglas Henkin and Anthony J. Rotondi of counsel), for defendant.

Michael A. Cardozo, Corporation Counsel (Janet V. Siegel of counsel), for City of New York.

Opinion

WALTER B. TOLUB, J.

By this proceeding, plaintiff seeks to enjoin the defendant from blocking access to Exchange Place in lower Manhattan and to prevent the stop and inspection of vehicles exiting from plaintiff's parking garage.

Plaintiff owns and operates a parking garage located at the rear of a building at 45 Wall Street. The entrance and exit ramps to plaintiff's garage are located on Exchange Place between William Street and Broad Street. The defendant is the New York Stock Exchange, Inc. (NYSE), the oldest and largest of all United States stock exchanges. The NYSE operates offices located at 11 Wall Street, 18 Broad Street, 20 Broad Street and 30 Broad Street.

History

In recent years, the issue of security surrounding major corporate entities and prominent New York landmark locations has become of increased importance. Many of New York City's most recognizable businesses and buildings have worked diligently to increase security in the hopes of keeping their tenants and visitors safe from any harm that might befall them.

> And now in addition to a distinctively important landmark, the opinion must consider what were probably unique security concerns due to unprecedented threats to this national institution. Again, careful legal analysis will require considering how narrowly or broadly to understand this particular case.

The New York Stock Exchange is no stranger to the implementation of security measures. As one of the oldest and most famous financial institutions, the NYSE is home to several thousand employees and traders, and receives countless business visitors annually. Tourists flock to it, film makers have immortalized it, and unfortunately but undoubtedly, there are people in this world that would like to destroy it.

> The opinion itself is acknowledging that the NYSE is unique. It is historically and symbolically significant as perhaps the most widely-recognized financial institution in the world. Which raises the question for case readers: how situationally-specific were the determinations in this case?

In response to security concerns, in the Spring of 1996, the New York Police Department (NYPD) implemented several major traffic changes around the perimeter of the NYSE that were designed to thwart attacks by vehicles carrying explosive devices. In particular, the intersection at Wall Street and Broadway was closed to traffic, as was New Street between Wall Street and Exchange Place. Traffic patterns were then rerouted so as to only allow traffic northbound on the eastern side of Broad Street. The western side of Broad street, blocked by a metal fence running from Exchange Place to Wall Street, was closed to vehicular traffic (Affidavit of James C. Esposito, ¶¶ 5–7).

In the fall of 1998, in response to security concerns following a bomb scare adjacent to 2 Broad Street, the NYPD implemented additional security measures in the area surrounding the NYSE. Most notably, the NYPD closed the sidewalks surrounding the NYSE's building at 11 Wall Street to pedestrian traffic from 6:00 p.m. to 8:00 a.m. (Affidavit of James C. Esposito, ¶ 8).

With security an ever-growing concern, in March, 2001, the NYSE increased NYPD presence in the vicinity through their utilization of the NYPD Paid Detail Program.[1] Under this program, off-duty uniformed police officers were deployed outside of NYSE buildings in an effort to maintain a police security presence.

1 [Omitted]

In response to the terrorist attacks on September 11, 2001, the NYPD effectuated a multi-block security zone surrounding the NYSE. Upon further assessment, the NYPD closed the intersections of Wall Street and Broadway; Nassau Street and Pine Street; Wall Street and William Street; William Street and Exchange Place; Broad Street and Beaver Street; Beaver

Street and New Street; and Broadway and Exchange Place, thereby creating a "secure zone" around the NYSE. These intersections were initially blocked using concrete "jersey barriers", which were later replaced by weighted pickup trucks, and have since been enhanced through the placement of additional vehicles and concrete planters designed to deter improvised vehicle bomb attacks in New York City's financial center.[2]

2 Both the addition of vehicles at the blocked intersections as well as the concrete planters were added at the direction of the NYPD Police Commissioner (Affidavit of James C. Esposito ¶ 12).

Indeed, the NYPD's Counter–Terrorism Bureau has concluded that the security measures implemented in the area surrounding the NYSE since the September 11 attacks should be maintained (Affidavit of John Colgan, ¶ 4). However, while the NYPD created and patrolled the initial security zone, and although the NYPD maintains a heavy presence in this area through general patrols and Hercules Teams, it is the NYSE security team that currently maintains the perimeter and street closures surrounding the NYSE.[3] Thus, at the present time, a private police force controls the public streets in the vicinity of the New York Stock Exchange.

3 The multi-block security zone created after September 11, 2001 was created by the NYPD and staffed by NYPD officers, NYSE security officers, NYPD Paid Detail Officers, and NYSE contracted security teams (Affidavit of James C. Esposito, ¶ 11).

Notwithstanding the security issues, which all parties concede are extremely important, the fact remains that many businesses have suffered as a result of post-September 11, 2001 security measures. In this case, plaintiff owns and operates a parking garage located on Wall Street with entrance and exit ramps located on Exchange Place between William Street and Broad Street, bordering the NYSE security zone.[4]

4 Plaintiff's business was initially located within the no-vehicle security zone. However, in April, 2002, the NYSE agreed and the NYPD approved moving the perimeter of the security zone further west on Exchange Place, so as not to prevent vehicles from using plaintiff's garage (Affidavit of James C. Esposito ¶ 15; Affidavit of James C. Esposito Exhibit A). In addition to this measure, the NYPD altered the traffic pattern by allowing cars to turn left onto Exchange Place from William Street so as to be able to avoid entering any part of the NYSE security zone.

Prior to September 11, 2001, plaintiff enjoyed a lucrative parking business, housing on average, 150 to 160 vehicles per day. Following both the attacks and the implementation of the subsequent security measures in 2001, plaintiff's business dropped significantly. Although plaintiff did not offer an estimate of lost business for the time period from September 11, 2001 to December 31, 2002, plaintiff claims that in 2003 an average of 68 cars parked daily in the garage.

In February, 2004, the City of New York notified the NYSE of necessary construction at the corner of Exchange Place and William Street that would require the closure of that intersection for approximately six to eight weeks (Affidavit of James C. Esposito, ¶ 17). As a result of the construction, vehicles using plaintiff's garage would no longer be able to enter or exit the garage without entering the secure zone surrounding the NYSE and being subjected to inspection by NYSE security.[5]

5 Each vehicle entering the NYSE secure zone is searched by NYSE security and bomb-sniffing canine teams.

In an effort to accommodate the patrons utilizing plaintiff's garage and to minimize the wait time for vehicle inspection, the NYSE relocated one of its two canine bomb-sniffing teams to a position outside of plaintiff's garage between 3:00 p.m. and 6:00 p.m. Notwithstanding this effort, plaintiff claims that his business has continued to suffer; patrons often have to endure longer waiting periods for security checks prior to being able to leave the garage, and many have not returned. Plaintiff estimates that between February 1 and February 20, 2004, an average of 65 patrons parked their vehicles daily. From February 21 to March 2, 2004, that number dropped to an average 38 vehicles daily, and on March 3, 2004, plaintiff reported only 25 vehicles parked in his garage (Affidavit [of Joseph Vassallo] in Support of Preliminary Injunction and Temporary Restraining Order, ¶¶ 6, 7, 11).

Plaintiff brings the instant action seeking relief from what is characterized in the complaint and supporting motion papers as the unlawful security system implemented by the New York Stock Exchange (Complaint at ¶ 12, Plaintiff's Memorandum of Law, p. 3).

Discussion

The instant application arose after access to plaintiff's parking garage was drastically limited when the City of New York commenced road construction at the only publicly accessible means of ingress and egress currently available to plaintiff. As a result of this construction, all vehicles wishing to park in plaintiff's garage must enter and exit the garage by traveling through the NYSE "secure zone", and consent to searches made by NYSE security personnel and bomb-sniffing canine teams.

The essence of plaintiff's complaint twofold: (1) the security zone maintained by the NYSE constitutes a public nuisance, has caused special damages, and thus entitles plaintiff to a preliminary injunction; and (2) the NYSE's operation of a private police force that controls and conducts searches on public thoroughfares is illegal.

Preliminary Injunction

[1] [2] [3] [4] A preliminary injunction is a provisional remedy designed to maintain the status quo between the parties during the course of litigation (*Uniformed Firefighters Association of Greater New York v. City of New York,* 79 N.Y.2d 236, 581 N.Y.S.2d 734, 590 N.E.2d 719 [1992]; Barr, Altman, Lipshie and Gerstman; *New York Civil Practice Before Trial* [James Publishing 2001–2002] § 17:03; CPLR 6301). The remedy lies within the sound discretion of the trial court, but is one that is considered drastic (*Borenstein v. Rochel Properties, Inc.,* 176 A.D.2d 171, 574 N.Y.S.2d 192 [1st Dept.1991]). As such, the remedy is only appropriate where the moving party has established (1) a likelihood of success on the merits of the action; (2) irreparable harm absent issuance of a preliminary injunction; and (3) a balancing of the equities in favor of the movant (*Aetna Insurance Company v. Capasso,* 75 N.Y.2d 860, 552 N.Y.S.2d 918, 552 N.E.2d 166 [1990]; *Doe v. Axelrod,* 73 N.Y.2d 748, 750, 536 N.Y.S.2d 44, 532 N.E.2d 1272 [1988]). Allegations that are bare or merely conclusory are deemed insufficient for this purpose (*Doe,* 73 N.Y.2d 748, 750, 536 N.Y.S.2d 44, 532 N.E.2d 1272; *Business Networks of New York, Inc. v. Complete Network Solutions, Inc.,* 265 A.D.2d 194, 696 N.Y.S.2d 433 [1st Dept.1999]).

Public Nuisance

[5] [6] [7] It is well established that a public nuisance under contemporary New York law "consists of conduct or omissions which offend, interfere with or cause damage to the public in the exercise of rights common to all, in a manner such as to offend public morals, interfere with use by the public of a public place or endanger or injure the property, health, safety or comfort of a considerable number of persons" (*Copart Industries, Inc. v. Consolidated Edison Company of New York, Inc.,* 41 N.Y.2d 564, 568, 394 N.Y.S.2d 169, 362 N.E.2d 968 [1977](citations omitted), *reargument denied,* 42 N.Y.2d 1102, 399 N.Y.S.2d 1028, 369 N.E.2d 1198 [1977]). Success on a claim of public nuisance requires that plaintiff prove by clear and convincing evidence "(1) the existence of a public nuisance; (2) conduct or omissions by a defendant that create, contribute to or maintain that public nuisance; and (3) particular harm suffered by plaintiff different in kind from that suffered by the community at large as a result of the public nuisance" (*N.A.A.C.P. v. Acusport, Inc.,* 271 F.Supp.2d 435, 483 [E.D.N.Y.2003]). In addition to these requirements, plaintiff, as a private individual seeking redress under a claim of public nuisance, must also establish that the type of harm suffered is a "special injury beyond that suffered by the community at large" (*532 Madison Avenue Gourmet Foods, Inc. v. Finlandia Center, Inc.,* 96 N.Y.2d 280, 292, 727 N.Y.S.2d 49, 750 N.E.2d 1097 [2001], *reargument denied in, 5th Ave. Chocolatiere, Ltd. v. 540 Acquisition Co., LLC.,* 96 N.Y.2d 938, 733 N.Y.S.2d 377, 759 N.E.2d 376 [2001]; *see also N.A.A.C.P.,* 271 F.Supp.2d 435, 482; *Leo v. General Electric Company,* 145 A.D.2d 291, 538 N.Y.S.2d 844 [2nd Dept.1989]; *Graceland Corp. v. Consolidated Laundries Corp.,* 7 A.D.2d 89, 180 N.Y.S.2d 644 [1st Dept.1958], *judgment aff'd,* 6 N.Y.2d 900, 190 N.Y.S.2d 708, 160 N.E.2d 926 [1959]).

> **Note carefully who may assert a claim of public nuisance, and what a private plaintiff must show in NY to have a cause of action under this claim.**

[8] It is well established under New York law that the primary purpose of streets is use by the public for travel and transportation, and consequently, the unlawful obstruction of a public street without express authority is not only a violation of § 19–107 of the New York City Administrative Code, but also constitutes a public nuisance (*Callanan v. Gilman,* 107 N.Y. 360, 365, 14 N.E. 264 [1887]; *O'Neill v. City of Port Jervis,* 253 N.Y. 423, 428, 171 N.E. 694 [1930]. *See also 532 Madison Avenue Gourmet Foods, Inc.,* 96 N.Y.2d 280, 292–293, 727 N.Y.S.2d 49, 750 N.E.2d 1097; *Village of Stillwater v. Hudson Valley Railway Company,* 255 N.Y. 144, 174 N.E. 306 [1931]; *Cassel v. City of New York,* 167 A.D. 831, 841, 153 N.Y.S. 410 [1st Dept.1915]; *The Broad Exchange Co. v. The Curb Stock and Bond Market of New York, Inc.,* 117 Misc. 82, 191 N.Y.S. 534 [Sup.Ct. N.Y. Co. Special Term 1921]). Moreover, assuming *arguendo* that a landowner had a right to obstruct part of a sidewalk in front of their premises, courts have held that the "obstruction of a public street or sidewalk beyond the reasonable uses permitted to abutting owners" also constitutes a public nuisance (*Graceland Corp.,* 7 A.D.2d 89, 90–91, 180 N.Y.S.2d 644).

[9] This case presents a situation where a private entity, the New York Stock Exchange, has assumed responsibility for the patrol and maintenance of truck blockades located at seven intersections surrounding the NYSE. Although these blockades were created by the NYPD in the aftermath of September 11, no formal authority appears to have been given to the NYSE to maintain these blockades and/or conduct security searches at these checkpoints.

The court is loathe to characterize the need for heightened security around the NYSE, or for that matter, any location throughout this great City as being a public nuisance. Nonetheless, the fact remains that there are legal methods by which these closures could have been effectuated, and in failing to do so, the closure of these intersections by the NYSE is tantamount to a public nuisance. Having established the existence of a public nuisance, this court now turns its attention to whether plaintiff is entitled to injunctive relief.

[10] At first blush it would appear that the plaintiff fails to meet one of the most essential requirements to warrant injunctive relief, the requirement of irreparable harm. While it is true that plaintiff has suffered a loss of business due to both the current construction on William Street and the security checkpoints currently controlled by the NYSE, those damages, though perhaps difficult to calculate, are compensable in money and therefore not irreparable (*Scotto v. Mei*, 219 A.D.2d 181, 184, 642 N.Y.S.2d 863 [1st Dept.1996]; *SportsChannel America Associates v. National Hockey League*, 186 A.D.2d 417, 589 N.Y.S.2d 2 [1st Dept.1992]).

[11] However, an analysis of cases involving the obstruction of public thoroughfares reveals that injunctive relief will lie notwithstanding that money damages are obviously calculable (*Flynn v. Taylor*, 127 N.Y. 596, 28 N.E. 418 [1891]; *Callanan v. Gilman*, 107 N.Y. 360, 14 N.E. 264; *Graceland Corp.*, 7 A.D.2d 89, 180 N.Y.S.2d 644; *The Broad Exchange Co.*, 117 Misc. 82, 191 N.Y.S. 534; *Bleichfeld v. Friedenthal*, 49 Misc.2d 584, 268 N.Y.S.2d 192 [Sup.Ct. Kings Co.1966]). As the Appellate Division in *Graceland* explained,

> one who suffers damage or injury beyond that of the general inconvenience to the public at large, may recover for such nuisance in damages or obtain injunction to prevent its continuance. This is old law. (*Callanan v. Gilman*, 107 N.Y. 360, 14 N.E. 264; Prosser, Torts [2d ed.], p. 403 et seq.; 10 McQuillin, Municipal Corporations

[3d ed.], § 30.128; 66 C.J.S., Nuisance, § 78) (*Graceland*, 7 A.D.2d 89, 91, 180 N.Y.S.2d 644).

Thus, the final inquiry, and perhaps the most difficult, is the consideration of the balancing of the equities. Plaintiff's business is proximate to a world-renown landmark financial center. Following the 2001 terrorist attacks, it came as no surprise to anyone, including plaintiff, that security would be tightened in the area surrounding the NYSE (Affidavit [of Joseph Vassallo] in Support of Preliminary Injunction and Temporary Restraining Order). In fact, the original secure zone as created by the NYPD initially included plaintiff's garage. Only after plaintiff approached defendant was the original security zone modified so as to lessen the burden on plaintiff's business. To that end, the NYPD and NYSE moved the security perimeter westward on Exchange Place, allowing Plaintiff's patrons unfettered access to William Street until the City commenced construction at the intersection (Affidavit of James C. Esposito ¶¶ 14, 15; Ex. A).

Clearly, the City's closure of William Street coupled with the nuisance created by the NYSE security zone compounded plaintiff's economic losses, and clearly, plaintiff is entitled, to recover on those losses. Nonetheless, defendant argues that even if the plaintiff has demonstrated a prima facie showing that defendant's maintenance of the subject road blockades constitutes a public nuisance, while plaintiff may be entitled to monetary compensation, in balancing the economic losses of a private business against the security of several thousand people, an injunction, under these circumstances, cannot lie (*Spring–Gar Community Civic Association, Inc. v. Homes for the Homeless, Inc.*, 135 Misc.2d 689, 516 N.Y.S.2d 399 [Sup.Ct. Qns. Cnty. 1987] *rev'd other grounds*, 149 A.D.2d 581, 540 N.Y.S.2d 453 [2nd Dept.1989]; *Chatham Green, Inc. v. Bloomberg*, 1 Misc.3d 434, 440, 765 N.Y.S.2d 446, 451 [Sup.Ct. N.Y. Co.2003]).

However, plaintiff has presented, and the court perceives, a more complex and more troublesome issue, and that is the NYSE's "occupation" of a security zone that encompasses a substantial portion of lower Manhattan, without any authorization or supervision by a governmental body.

The parties in this matter concede that the original security zone established around the NYSE as it currently exists was created by the NYPD in direct response to the terrorist attacks on September 11, 2001.

As previously indicated, the initial patrolling and monitoring of the security zone was conducted by a combination of NYPD Officers, members of the NYPD Paid Detail Program, NYSE security, and outsourced security hired by the NYSE. At some point thereafter, and it is unclear as to when this happened, the control of the security posts at each of the blocked intersections were transferred to NYSE security.

There is no question that under New York law, the New York City Police Department has the authority to temporarily shut down public streets when it deems that there is a necessity for their closure, and that those closures may become permanent.[6] However, this court questions whether the NYPD may delegate the maintenance and control of those blockades to a private security force without formally delegating some kind of police authority, or even if that authority may be delegated at all.

6 [Omitted]

The NYSE has yet to provide this court with any evidence of an agreement giving them the authority to maintain the security perimeter and/or conduct the searches that their private security force conducts daily. As such, the NYSE's actions are unlawful[7] and may be enjoined as they violate plaintiff's civil rights as a private citizen.

7 The court emphasizes that it is not of the opinion that the barricades themselves are unlawful, it is the operation of those barricades by a private security force that renders the practice unlawful.

The necessity for heightened security in today's world is apparent, and in this City, we are acutely aware of this need. As a result, it is often necessary for public and private entities to employ extraordinary measures, some of which are cumbersome and clearly overreaching, in an effort to ensure public safety. However, those steps must be taken in accordance with applicable law. The spectre of private police forces patrolling public streets is unacceptable, and private entities may not take the law into their own hands, no matter how well intentioned. As such, if the City is prepared to delegate the authority and responsibility of patrolling and searching the perimeter of the secure zone surrounding the New York Stock Exchange to the NYSE, it should do so in compliance with applicable law. Failing that, the NYSE must be enjoined from maintaining and patrolling the blockades at each of the subject intersections.

Accordingly, it is

ORDERED that the NYSE is preliminarily enjoined from maintaining the security blockades and conducting vehicle searches at the intersections of Wall Street and Broadway; Nassau Street and Pine Street; Wall Street and William Street; William Street and Exchange Place; Broad Street and Beaver Street; Beaver Street and New Street; and Broadway and Exchange Place; and it is further

ORDERED that said injunction shall become effective within five (5) business days after service of this Order upon defendant with Notice of Entry.

This memorandum opinion constitutes the decision and order of the Court.

All Citations

3 Misc.3d 1014, 779 N.Y.S.2d 745, 2004 N.Y. Slip Op. 24097

10 A.D.3d 223
Supreme Court, Appellate Division,
First Department, New York.

WALL STREET GARAGE PARKING CORP.,
Plaintiff–Respondent,

v.

NEW YORK STOCK EXCHANGE, INC.,
Defendant–Appellant.

Aug. 5, 2004.

Attorneys and Law Firms

Milbank, Tweed, Hadley & McCloy, LLP, New York (Douglas W. Henkin and Anthony J. Rotondi of counsel), for appellant.

Jenkens & Gilchrist Parker Chapin LLP, New York (Stephen F. Harmon and Eric L. Unis of counsel), for respondent.

PETER TOM, J.P., RICHARD T. ANDRIAS, MILTON L. WILLIAMS, GEORGE D. MARLOW, LUIS A. GONZALEZ, JJ.

Opinion

TOM, J.P.

At issue on this appeal is whether defendant New York Stock Exchange (NYSE) created a public nuisance by restricting vehicular access to a security zone around the Stock Exchange devised by closing seven traffic intersections in the aftermath of the terrorist attacks of September 11, 2001, thereby entitling plaintiff, a business entity in the area, to preliminary injunctive relief. We find the motion court erred in granting plaintiff a preliminary injunction because enjoining defendant Stock Exchange from inspecting vehicles entering the security zone surrounding NYSE premises changes, rather than preserves, the status quo and because plaintiff has not otherwise satisfied the prerequisites for obtaining preliminary injunctive relief.

Even prior to the events of 9/11, concern that the NYSE, the largest stock exchange in the United States, might

> In this case, NY's intermediate appellate court overruled the trial court's granting of a preliminary injunction. The question for readers is why, and how that decision will apply to subsequent cases. (Another question critical readers should consider is why the earlier case was included in the case file in the first place if it does not represent the current state of NY law.)

be vulnerable to an explosive device hidden in a vehicle prompted the New York City Police Department (NYPD) to close New Street between Wall Street and Exchange Place and the intersection of Wall Street and Broadway to vehicular traffic in May 1996. A bomb hoax in September 1998 resulted in the closure of the sidewalks surrounding the premises occupied by the NYSE to all pedestrian traffic from 6:00 P.M. to 8:00 A.M. daily. In March 2001, the Stock Exchange began participating in the NYPD Paid Detail Program, in which off-duty police officers, in uniform and acting with full power and authority of regular on-duty police officers, provide security at the expense of a participating entity rather than the New York City taxpayers.

The center of the NYSE's economic activity is its trading floor, which extends across buildings located at 11 Wall Street and at 18, 20 and 30 Broad Street. After the terrorist attacks of September 11, 2001, the area was patrolled by members of the NYPD, including police officers participating in the Paid Detail Program as well as those on regular duty, and including members of NYPD's heavily armed "Hercules Teams," by NYSE's own security personnel and by personnel provided by T & M Protection Resources, Inc. The Police Department blocked access to NYSE's premises from the seven intersections that surround the trading floor, placing barriers on Wall Street at Broadway and at William Street, on Exchange Place at Broadway and at William Street, on Nassau Street at Pine Street, on Broad Street at Beaver Street and on New Street at Beaver Street. The barriers were later replaced by trucks loaded with sand.

Plaintiff parking garage, which was formerly located within the security zone, claims that its business is being adversely impacted by security measures implemented by defendant NYSE in response to the events of September 11, 2001. Plaintiff garage is located on Exchange Place near the intersection with William Street. As an accommodation to plaintiff, the original security zone was modified and the truck barrier on Exchange Place at William Street was moved west towards Broad Street to permit vehicular access to and from the garage from William Street and Exchange Place. Garage patrons were then able to avoid entering the security zone, thus obviating the need for a search. However, on or about February 21, 2004, the William Street access point was once again blocked when the City began road construction on said street, and plaintiff's customers were again required to enter the security area to gain access to the garage.

The impact on plaintiff's business was substantial. Plaintiff asserts that from an average of 150 to 160 vehicles a day prior to 9/11, patronage dropped to 68 cars a day thereafter, further declining to 65 a day by February 2004. With the commencement of road construction, usage dropped to a mere 38 vehicles daily by the beginning of March, causing plaintiff to commence this action seeking damages as well as preliminary and permanent injunctive relief. Plaintiff sought to prohibit defendant NYSE "from obstructing, blocking or closing in any way ingress or egress to or from Exchange Place or the flow of vehicular traffic thereon, at or near where plaintiff conducts its business, and from stopping, arresting and searching vehicles exiting plaintiff's parking garage on Exchange Place between Broad Street and William Street."

Defendant NYSE took issue with the allegation that its security force had completely taken over the control of security posts located at the blocked intersections. The affidavit of NYSE's Senior Vice President of Security, James Esposito, states that "NYPD officers" are "directly involved in the security zone." Photographs of the area submitted by defendant depict NYPD officers stationed at pedestrian checkpoints with NYSE security personnel, as well as the deployment of the "Hercules Team and other NYPD personnel and vehicles within the security zone." Defendant opposed the application for preliminary relief on the ground that the garage is located outside the secured area and that the unrestricted access to plaintiff's premises available from William Street was subject only to temporary curtailment by street construction by the City at the intersection.

By order entered March 12, 2004, Supreme Court granted plaintiff's motion for a preliminary injunction, enjoining NYSE from blocking access to Exchange Place and from stopping and inspecting vehicles exiting the garage. Expressing doubt as to the authority of the City to delegate responsibility for security to a private entity, the court concluded that subjecting garage customers to search and blocking public streets constitute a public nuisance in violation of New York City Administrative Code § 19–107. In balancing the equities, the court reasoned that the nuisance represents a sufficient threat both to "plaintiff's civil rights as a private citizen" and to public order to warrant injunctive relief.

Several days after Supreme Court issued its order, defendant applied to this Court for a temporary stay of the injunction. Mr. Esposito's accompanying affidavit, dated March 15, states that, "as of this morning a lane had already been re-opened to vehicular traffic on William Street at Exchange Place to allow access to [defendant's] garage from outside the NYSE security zone (as was the case before the construction began at the intersection of William Street and Exchange Place)." This Court granted the application, lifting the injunction during the pendency of this appeal. We now reverse.

As an initial consideration, "[a] preliminary injunction is a provisional remedy. Its function is not to determine the ultimate rights of the parties, but to maintain the status quo until there can be a full hearing on the merits (*Gambar Enters. v. Kelly Servs.*, 69 A.D.2d 297, 306 [418 N.Y.S.2d 818])" (*Residential Bd. of Mgrs. of Columbia Condominium v. Alden,* 178 A.D.2d 121, 122, 576 N.Y.S.2d 859). At the time plaintiff commenced this petition for a preliminary injunction, the status quo was represented by established security measures, including a series of vehicular and pedestrian checkpoints, that had already been in place for some 2 ½ years. Questions concerning supervision and control notwithstanding, the security measures are not alleged to have undergone any substantial change so as to warrant judicial restoration of established procedures. Rather, the precipitous decline in plaintiff's business is attributed to the total closure of the intersection of William Street and Exchange Place due to construction work by the City. With the completion of the road construction at the intersection, which plaintiff does not materially dispute, the status quo ante has been restored, rendering academic plaintiff's application for preliminary relief.

[1] [2] To be entitled to a preliminary injunction, the proponent is required to demonstrate a probability of ultimate success on the merits, irreparable injury in the event that injunctive relief is denied and a balancing of the equities in its favor (*Grant Co. v. Srogi,* 52 N.Y.2d 496, 517, 438 N.Y.S.2d 761, 420 N.E.2d 953; *see also Aetna Ins. Co. v. Capasso,* 75 N.Y.2d 860, 862, 552 N.Y.S.2d 918, 552 N.E.2d 166). However, because a public nuisance is inherently a condition for which the law provides a remedy, the proponent of the injunction is relieved from the general requirement to show that it lacks an adequate remedy at law (*see Graceland Corp. v. Consolidated Laundries Corp.,* 7 A.D.2d 89, 93–94, 180 N.Y.S.2d 644, *affd.* 6 N.Y.2d 900, 190 N.Y.S.2d 708, 160 N.E.2d 926).

[3] It is unlikely, however, that plaintiff will be able to establish its right to recover on the ground that it sustained injury as the result of a public nuisance, the

single theory advanced in the complaint. As stated in *532 Madison Ave. Gourmet Foods v. Finlandia Ctr.,* 96 N.Y.2d 280, 292, 727 N.Y.S.2d 49, 750 N.E.2d 1097:

A public nuisance exists for conduct that amounts to a substantial interference with the exercise of a common right of the public, thereby offending public morals, interfering with the use by the public of a public place or endangering or injuring the property, health, safety or comfort of a considerable number of persons. A public nuisance is a violation against the State and is subject to abatement or prosecution by the proper governmental authority (*Copart Indus. v. Consolidated Edison Co.,* 41 N.Y.2d 564, 568 [394 N.Y.S.2d 169, 362 N.E.2d 968]).

Where, as here, a claim for recovery is predicated on a public nuisance, the claimant must show that it has "suffered a special injury beyond that of the community" (*532 Madison Ave.,* 96 N.Y.2d at 293, 727 N.Y.S.2d 49, 750 N.E.2d 1097). As a general rule, "one who suffers damage or injury, beyond that of the general inconvenience to the public at large, may recover for such nuisance in damages or obtain injunction to prevent its continuance" (*Graceland Corp.,* 7 A.D.2d at 91, 180 N.Y.S.2d 644).

Plaintiff's claimed economic injury is only partly attributable to the security procedures implemented in the area surrounding the NYSE. The further decline in its business commencing in February 2004 was precipitated by the City's road construction, a condition that has since abated. Furthermore, as Supreme Court noted in its order, "many businesses have suffered as a result of post-September 11, 2001 security measures." The security zone surrounding the New York Stock Exchange covers several square blocks containing large buildings, many of which house businesses that can claim some measure of harm as a consequence of the security measures imposed. Plaintiff, which operates a business located outside the security zone, has not demonstrated a special injury beyond the disruption experienced by the community as a whole (*532 Madison Ave. Gourmet Foods,* 96 N.Y.2d at 293, 727 N.Y.S.2d 49, 750 N.E.2d 1097). Any impediment to plaintiff's right to operate its garage will not support recovery of damages on a public nuisance theory where the same circumstances have impeded the similar rights of a large number of other businesses located in the area (*cf. Flynn v. Taylor,* 127 N.Y. 596, 600, 28 N.E. 418; *Leo v. General Elec. Co.,* 145 A.D.2d 291, 538 N.Y.S.2d 844).

On balance, the equities favor defendant NYSE. Plaintiff does not dispute the need for heightened security in the area. Defendant took steps to accommodate plaintiff by moving a checkpoint so as to place the access ramp to the garage outside the secured area. Plaintiff concedes that, as a result, many of its customers were unaffected by the security measures. The abatement of any public nuisance created by alleged improprieties in defendant's security procedures is a governmental prerogative, and the substantial police presence in the vicinity suggests that defendant's security operations are subject to some degree of official scrutiny.

Since plaintiff is unable to establish its right to recover on the ground that it has sustained special damages as the result of a public nuisance, its application for injunctive relief cannot stand because plaintiff is unable to persuasively argue that it has sustained irreparable injury. Its action against the NYSE is predicated on economic loss, compensable by monetary damages. Plaintiff has documented the decline in its patronage as the result of the security measures undertaken by defendant and does not contend that it is impossible to calculate the extent of that loss. Thus, plaintiff cannot demonstrate that it lacks an adequate remedy at law so as to warrant injunctive relief (*see 1659 Ralph Ave. Laundromat Corp. v. Ben David Enters., LLC,* 307 A.D.2d 288, 289, 762 N.Y.S.2d 288). Moreover, it is clear that plaintiff's loss of business was predominantly caused by the City's construction work, a temporary condition that no longer exists. Therefore, there is no need to enjoin any conduct by defendant NYSE to avoid speculative future damages consequent to a continuing harm (CPLR 6301; 6312[a]).

Accordingly, the order of the Supreme Court, New York County (Walter B. Tolub, J.), entered March 12, 2004, which granted plaintiff's motion for preliminary relief and enjoined defendant from maintaining security blockades and conducting vehicle searches in the immediate vicinity of the New York Stock Exchange, should be reversed, on the law and the facts, without costs, and the motion denied.

Order, Supreme Court, New York County (Walter B. Tolub, J.), entered March 12, 2004, reversed, on the law and the facts, without costs, and plaintiff's motion for preliminary injunctive relief denied.

All concur.

All Citations

10 A.D.3d 223, 781 N.Y.S.2d 324, 2004 N.Y. Slip Op. 06307

Understand the Problem To Be Resolved

What is the purpose of an advice letter?

Practicing attorneys commonly refer to the kind of client letter you are drafting as an *opinion letter* or *advice letter*. In these kinds of letters, lawyers offer their expert assessment of a given situation. Frequently such letters also provide a prediction of what might happen in ensuing litigation or transactions, so that the clients have guidance when deciding what next steps to pursue. In function, then, the analysis in an advice letter is often substantively similar to what would be found in a typical law office memo. Naturally, though, the tenor and structure are likely to be quite different.

Remember your audience for this letter and strike the right tone. Your clients are educated laypeople: they will need you to translate legal concepts into common language and make your advice understandable. But that does not mean that you should talk down to your clients, or worse, oversimplify the law just to make it comprehensible. Keep in mind, too, what they are seeking from you—they want answers to their questions, and they want to solve their actual problems with the current filming arrangements. This does not mean that you should not hedge your predictions or fail to present valid counterarguments. But you are unlikely to satisfy your clients' desires simply by laying out all possible sides to an issue without offering any specific options or making concrete recommendations.

To understand the format for your letter it is important to remember that in the end it is a type of business correspondence. It should follow the conventions of a business letter in terms of salutations and closings, and will ultimately be printed on your professional letterhead. And as with all professional communications, it should thoughtfully balance the concerns of conciseness and brevity with those of thoroughness and clarity.

What is your role in your clients' decision-making?

Attorneys perennially struggle with how we should fit into helping clients address their problems. Obviously, lawyers are there to provide expertise regarding the law. That part of our responsibility is pretty straightforward and unequivocal. But does it end there? Lawyers' fiduciary obligations are to generally foster their clients' best interests. And clients rarely come to their lawyers seeking *only* information about the law. They come with particular problems that usually have both legal and non-legal dimensions. Ultimately, clients are almost always seeking assistance in solving those problems. The problems belong to the clients and not the lawyers, though. And the clients should have the final say in what happens in their lives; ultimately they will have to live with what happens long after their attorneys have moved on to attend to other matters.

Given these complexities, it should not be surprising that there has been a great deal written about the extent to which lawyers do and should assist their clients' decision-making. But none of this writing will definitively tell you what to do in any given situation. As authorities on client counseling summarize: "[cl]ients hire experts because they believe that experts know what to do."[2] Ultimately it is the clients' concerns, businesses, and welfare at stake, however, and most lawyers are more comfortable guiding their clients' own problem-solving rather than dictating specific solutions.

The Model Rules of Professional Conduct tell you that lawyers must "exercise independent professional judgment and render candid advice."[3] The rule also indicates that attorneys can include non-legal considerations in their advice, including important moral, ethical, and social considerations. Even more significantly, the rule does not parse the crucial line separating lawyerly assistance

---

2. Stephen Ellmann et al., Lawyers and Clients: Critical Issues in Interviewing and Counseling 366 (2009).

3. American Bar Association MRPC Rule 2.1, Advisor.

and respect for client autonomy. If an attorney believes a case is winnable, does that mean she should advise her client to file it? Or should she instead simply indicate that she is willing to move forward with litigation if the client chooses to proceed? Similarly, if she believes a case is a long shot, the rule is clear that she has a professional obligation to present that information to the client. But if the client nonetheless wants to proceed, should the attorney try to talk him out of it?

There are no clear answers here. Different lawyers approach their advisory roles differently—and perhaps they view their duties differently depending on the needs and desires of individual clients. You must decide for yourself whether you understand your role to be just offering your information and experience, giving opinions about the array of options that your client should consider, or more vigorously influencing the client's final decisions about the best course of action.

Think Deeply about Nuisance

What does nuisance law actually protect?

Property scholars would probably explore the concept more precisely, but essentially nuisance law addresses the fact that private ownership of land is intended to confer on each owner the privilege to enjoy property in any way he sees fit.[4]

The problem comes from people owning real property in proximity to one another, and the simple reality that some of the ways people might use their land necessarily affects the experiences of their neighbors. Nuisance law is meant to offset the competing concerns of incompatible landowners within the same community.

Immediately then, this should set off a few bells: is one of your first thoughts that the rules in this area are going to have to balance competing policy considerations? It should be; anyone who owns real property could likely imagine themselves on either side of a nuisance case. ("My neighbor's cat yowls at all hours of the night!" "Why does my neighbor get to decide whether I can have a pet?")

Even before you review the specific legal rules used to determine what constitutes an actionable nuisance, your legal training should compel you to guess that you are about to encounter a "rule"

> This explains why determining what is "reasonable" has vexed countless generations of lawyers and law students.

that is pretty subjective to apply. An astute law student expects that in an area where the law has to weigh two or more equally compelling perspectives, it will probably generate guiding principles that are heavily context-driven and hence quite fact-specific. Do you see why? If so, the insight that the kind of issues to be addressed can help predict the form of legal rules governing a particular topic may help you gain a deeper comprehension of *all* of the law you encounter.

Lawyers are also a doubting people, so be sure to double-check any prediction. In New York, is your prediction true that nuisance laws are comparatively flexible and leave room for latitude based on specific factual context?

What are the differences between private and public nuisance?

On its face, the answer to this question is a simple one.

To understand the distinction it may help to remember that some of our sources refer to public nuisances as common ones; that is, as problems shared more broadly by others in the community. How many people does that actually mean, though? It would defy logic to conclude that *everyone* in a community must be negatively impacted for something to be considered a public nuisance—some

---

4. Those researchers might also want to situate current nuisance law in historical context. Property law experts point out that standards for nuisance arise from fairly ancient common law, but have changed substantially with the move from a primarily agrarian society to an industrialized urban economy. Can you see why changes in how and where people lived would affect legal notions of what does, and does not, interfere with others' property rights?

subset of the populace would have to be enough. But then, does everyone in that subset have to be equally affected? Do they all have to find the effects troublesome? If not, what is the relationship between what percentage of the community they constitute and just how bothered they actually are?

There are probably no exact answers to these metaphysical inquiries. But they do help us understand in a deeper way how private and public nuisances differ. In the private action, a court is essentially asked to consider the competing rights of two[5] equally situated parties to use their own property. In the public claim, the rights of members of the community at large are pitted against the whole community's concerns for health, safety, or general comfort.

That structural imbalance of one particular land user versus the rest of population suggests that claims of public nuisance may come into court with some inherent advantages. And that may well be so. But there are difficulties in making such a claim. First, it does indeed have to be true that the public as a whole is affected by the alleged nuisance. And the public must generally find the alleged nuisance harmful. Gathering collective support for such a claim is much more complicated and challenging than simply pursuing a private party's concerns.

Even more crucially, public nuisance claims are typically pursued by representatives of the public, which frequently means some kind of governmental body. New York and other jurisdictions do permit affected private actors to pursue public nuisance claims, but consider carefully the limits the law imposes on those actions and whether or not your clients are likely to fall within the established parameters for bringing such a case.

Read cases critically

Since nuisance suits arise from the common law, the cases in your jurisdiction will serve two purposes. First, they should articulate the precise rule or rules to be applied in your state. Second, since we have already noted that application of nuisance rules is likely to be very fact-bound, research into case law should be especially helpful to a lawyer who is trying to predict what a court might do in the future by surveying what courts have done in the past. This kind of predictive survey requires sound professional judgment (more on that in a minute), which means looking at the case law thoughtfully and with a practiced eye.

The cases included in this file address both private and public nuisance law.

> Note that this means one of the first things you should have done when reading those opinions was to sort them by which cause of action each was considering. You need to do this to fully understand the doctrine, but also to ensure that you would not unknowingly import concepts from one cause of action into the other. Do your notes on the cases lead with those categorizations?

1. Private nuisance cases

Lawyers usually reason by analogy, so it makes sense that a lot of what we do is search for similar facts to compare. But just what is it that makes facts similar? One of the less intuitive parts of "thinking like a lawyer" is that for us, "similar" connotes facts that are materially comparable *because they interact with the rule in the same way*. In other words, the purpose of the rule itself helps us understand what facts may be easily analogized. Earthworms and elephants are both animals, but otherwise may not seem to have very much to do with one another. For rules governing scientific testing of potentially lifesaving medications, they might be treated exactly the same way. On the other hand, for rules determining what pets ordinary citizens may be permitted to keep in their backyards, they may be treated quite differently.

---

5. That is a bit of an oversimplification. A private nuisance claim can certainly have multiple plaintiffs. But once the alleged intrusion rises to the level of affecting a significant group of landowners rather than just a few neighbors, the specter of an alternative or additional public nuisance case is raised.

To really test your comprehension of both legal rules and legal analysis, it is an old law professors' trick to give students hypothetical facts that look almost exactly like those in a memorable case they have read. If you ever see this on an exam, beware! Chances are pretty good that the facts differ just enough in some material way that the applicable rule might yield a different result. Why? Because we are really looking for *legally* analogizable facts, not simply similar ones. Do not make the mistake, then, of assuming that a case about alleged nuisance in a television production is necessarily dispositive for the Osgoods' potential claim. Go further, and consider carefully why that case and the *7-Eleven* case were decided the way they were, and to which circumstances the Osgoods' issues seem most comparable.

2. Public nuisance case(s)

There's an old saying that "hard cases make bad law." A great deal of writing has explored what that phrase might mean, but the gist is that situations involving extreme circumstances are less likely than others to generate the most helpfully and generally applicable legal rulings. We can leave it to academics to consider whether this maxim is actually true,[6] but it should make us take a closer look at cases whose facts seem unusually distinctive or passion-inspiring.

In the Wall Street parking garage cases we seem to have both emotionally compelling circumstances and rarely duplicated conditions. The cases deal with post-9/11 protective measures for a site of incalculable symbolic significance. Understanding that makes it easier to empathize with the difficult issues the courts were wrestling with. But it makes it harder to evaluate how to use the case going forward. At the very least, remember the appellate decision *is* binding precedent in your jurisdiction. And both the trial court decision and the appeal seem to agree upon the legal standard for establishing a public nuisance in New York, so an advocate should certainly be able to use that rule of law in any subsequent case.

Apply Rules

What do we really mean by "rules"?

Legal novices might assume that it would be easy to figure out what a legal rule is, yet by now you have probably realized that it can actually be surprisingly complicated. Lawyers use the term "rule" to mean a number of related but subtly different things. Any of them may serve the purpose of a "rule" to apply to facts for legal analysis, but the shrewd law student needs to be sensitive to these small but crucial differences.

1. Settled rules

Enacted statutes and promulgated regulations unquestionably set out legal rules. ("A person commits the offense of theft when he unlawfully takes or appropriates any property of another with the intention of depriving him of the property.") Well-settled common law serves the same function. ("**Suit for false imprisonment** may be maintained in our jurisdiction when a person is constrained against his or her will within any area without justification or consent.")

Even when we deal with settled black-letter law, though, there may be small differences in how rules are stated. Did you learn negligence as the four-part test (breach, duty, causation, damage) that was laid out in Chapter 1? In some instances negligence is presented as a five-element test: causation is separated into **actual cause** (or perhaps **direct cause**) and **proximate cause**. Occasionally,

---

6. One renowned scholar of English law called the phrase clichéd, but seemed at least in part to agree with it by suggesting that cases that moved judges emotionally were more likely to "make bad law." GLANVILLE WILLIAMS, THE SANCTITY OF LIFE AND THE CRIMINAL LAW 105 (1957).

negligence torts are presented as having three distinct elements because the first two are merged into **breach of a legal duty.** So which "rule" should you use? That's easy—the one that applies in your jurisdiction. And when you are taking a course in law school, your "jurisdiction" is whatever your professor taught your particular section or class.

Aside from the numbering of elements, there may be differences in their language. One important (and challenging) question for lawyers and law students alike is whether small differences in rule statements are substantive or merely semantic. (E.g.: does it change the substance of the rule if the final element of negligence is phrased as **harm** rather than **damage**?)

They can be either. Doing a theft analysis is probably the same whether the statute refers to "acquiring" or "appropriating" someone else's property. You will have to ask and consider the exact same questions no matter where they fall on your internal elemental chart. But for our false imprisonment example, can you imagine circumstances that might lead to different outcomes depending on whether the rule is phrased as "confining" the plaintiff versus "restraining" him? Perhaps there would be the same outcome in most factual circumstances, but in more marginal cases the nuances in specific language could have a meaningful effect on the legal analysis. This is exactly why it is so important to state rules accurately and precisely.

> To be clear: for the false imprisonment example the outcome could well be the same no matter which language the statute adopts. But for some facts—say a person asked to remain alone in a large unlocked gymnasium—the connotations of the operative words could well lead to different outcomes.

2. Constructed rules

Since we are now discussing legal principles that lawyers may *contend* are settled law, it would be more accurate to title this section **Constructed "rules."** Or perhaps **Constructed sub-rules,** because this category of rules often consists of interpretations of what one part or element of an established rule actually means.

That last description probably sounded a little complicated or unclear, so let's unpack it a bit. Suppose you have a jurisdiction that has adopted the rule for the intentional tort of false imprisonment set out in the section above. OK then, what exactly does the state mean by the alleged tortfeasor having acted "without consent" in a case that feels somewhat coercive, but where no verbal objection to confinement was offered by the plaintiff? So for example, imagine you read a case in which a mall security guard wearing both a weapon and badge approached a teenager and said "You just shoplifted! Come with me right now." The teenager knew she was innocent and did not want to go into a back room with the guard, but was intimidated and felt as if she had no choice. She didn't say anything as she glumly walked into the store's lounge, where she was kept and questioned for 40 minutes. The court's opinion concluded that the lack of an open objection did not mean that as a matter of law the plaintiff consented to being detained. Instead, the judge wrote, a jury could find that the plaintiff reasonably believed any protestations would be futile.

If you had a similar case, just citing "without consent" as an element for false imprisonment would be insufficient. You would probably start there, but should then go on to consider this precedent and others like it in more depth to develop a sense of what the statute means by "no consent" where there is an absence of complaint, but a sensation of duress. You would explain what "without consent" legally consisted of in such circumstances, support your interpretation with legal authority, and then use that explanation as a **rule** to apply to your particular facts. In other words, you are treating your interpretation as a rule of law to be applied, and expecting (hoping?) your readers would agree. And if a court does so, then hey, it *becomes* an unequivocal rule of law!

Chances are you performed this kind of interpretation of sub-rules in some of your first-year legal writing exercises. Law students often struggle to reconcile that work with learning the settled rules of law (established elements or factors) they are taught in many of their other courses.

Understanding the difference between settled rules and constructed rules, and knowing that advocates for the latter usually try to hide their efforts and make their interpretations seem both correct and resolved, may help you resolve a common confusion.

Use both settled rules and constructed rules in your nuisance analysis

Back to Legal Analysis 101: state the rule to be applied, and state it precisely. For the Osgoods this will mean accurately describing what both public and private nuisance consist of in the state of New York (remembering to rely upon primary authority from that jurisdiction as your first resource).

But your clients here need *advice*, not just information. They want your professional judgement about how the law will apply to their particular circumstances. For that kind of predictive reasoning you may well find that you need more than the bare elements of nuisance. You will likely have to use the case law to support principled conclusions about what kinds of things tend to be found nuisances, and what sorts of things do not. In other words, you may need to construct some (tentative) rules to help you analyze the Osgoods' case.

Consider Counterarguments and Demonstrate Sound Judgment

We have already observed that nuisance law is pretty contextual and situation-driven. Here's a helpful hint that probably should not surprise you: whenever a question is that factually specific, it is very unlikely to have only one possible right answer.[7] In both practice and law school, whenever you encounter a situation in which there is only one correct answer, you should simply and directly say what it is. Use solid legal authority and clear explanations to justify your conclusions, and do so completely, but as efficiently as possible so you can move on to more challenging issues.

Where there is more than one possible interpretation, however, you must thoughtfully consider all sides. Look at the question from every legitimate perspective, imagine the best possible version of that legal analysis, and present each side thoughtfully.

Are you done then? No! If you truly want to assist your clients (or get As in your law classes) you will need to use good legal judgment to assess these competing counterarguments. Are the two positions essentially equally viable? Say so. But if one can be articulated yet is dubious or a genuine long shot, say that too, and justify your conclusions. Law schools are preparing you to help your future clients solve problems that intersect with law. Naturally, then, your professors want you to practice employing that kind of judgment when looking at simulated or hypothetical problems along the way.

---

7. Sometimes law students, and even law professors, will shorthand the indeterminacy of legal analysis to conclude that "in law there are no right answers." That isn't quite true, though. If we want to know what the penalty is in South Carolina for a first-time offender convicted of manslaughter, then that is absolutely knowable information. We simply have to look up the answer. But when we do, we are likely to find that judges have some discretion to impose sentences within an assigned range. It takes genuine expertise to predict or to argue what penalty within that range is appropriate for a certain defendant. And it may also be true that at least before the defendant was convicted there was a possible debate about whether her actions were best categorized as manslaughter, justifiable homicide, or murder. Law schools aim to teach students to consider those distinctions carefully and consequently emphasize them, which is why it is probably somewhat more accurate to conclude that "*on law school* exams there are (frequently) no right answers."

Transfer What You've Done to a Law School Setting

Sample exam question

Essay — 45 minutes

Homeowners in the Hilltop Manor residential subdivision in Westchester, NY, filed a complaint alleging both public and private nuisance against Acme Cement Manufacturing Co. The suit was brought by 32 residents of Hilltop Manor (out of the approximately 1000 persons living in the subdivision, and 12,000 residents living within a 3-mile radius of the cement plant). Most of the plaintiffs live on the northern side of the subdivision, which is the one closest to the recently opened cement plant.

Plaintiffs allege that "volumes of white dust" emanate from the plant. They contend that the dust covers their homes and cars, and requires regular (even daily) dusting. A few have even installed special windows in their homes in an effort to keep the dust out. In a pre-trial deposition Acme's CEO acknowledged that volumes of dust were a necessary byproduct of cement manufacturing, but insisted that his plant possessed state-of-the-art filtering equipment that nearly eliminated any dust pollution.

Defendant Acme now moves for summary judgement and dismissal of the complaint on two points:

1. Plaintiffs have no "special injury" that would permit them to maintain an action for public nuisance; and

2. Even assuming plaintiffs' allegations were true, the presence of dust is not sufficiently "substantial in nature" or "unreasonable in character" to find a private nuisance and warrant closing the plant.

How should the court rule on the motions?

Attacking the exam question

Law school examinations tend to require "issue spotting," but is that what this particular question demands? Probably not. There are two rather specific queries at the end, one of which deals with a key issue in public nuisance and the other with what will probably be the central questions for a private nuisance claim. The question drafter has done the work of defining the issues in your response for you. Does that mean you can leap unreflectively into responding to these questions? By now I hope you assume the answer to anything that suggests you could be unreflective about your legal work simply has to be "no."

First, check to see whether there are any related but unnamed issues that have to be settled to analyze the specific questions posed. If there are none (and there don't seem to be any here but there certainly could have been, which is why it was worth looking for them), then move on to assessing the issues you know you have to talk about. Decide which ones are the most complicated and multifaceted. Apportion your time so that you can devote as much of it as possible to the most complicated and debatable points.

In this problem, there are probably good arguments and counter-arguments to both questions posed. But that does not automatically mean that you should give equal time to both. There is certainly ambiguity about whether the facts support a special injury for public nuisance, for example, so you should absolutely analyze both sides of that issue. But the "substantial" and "unreasonable" questions pertaining to private nuisance just seem to provide more fodder for argumentation, don't they? If that's your perception then by all means find a way to show that legal judgment in the way that you construct a response.

Sample answer with commentary

Below is an example of what might be a fairly high-scoring student response. It is certainly not a perfect answer, and though it would probably garner a score on the higher side it would not necessarily earn an A. This response is a little longer than some students might be able to draft in the time limit, but not unreasonably so. The question to consider as you review is answer is whether the student used the volume of text most effectively.

Student Answer

Did the plaintiffs suffer a special injury?

The issue here is whether plaintiffs have sufficient evidence to prove a "special injury" in order to maintain an action for public nuisance. Under a public nuisance action, a plaintiff must prove a "special injury," which means that their injury suffered from the nuisance was different than the harm suffered by the rest of the community. In our case, plaintiffs have presented triable issues with respect to whether there was a special injury.

The injury experienced by the plaintiffs differs from the injuries suffered by the rest of the community. First, out of the 1,000 residents who live in the subdivision near the concrete plant, only 32 have brought an action. Although the remaining 968 people in the subdivision may experience dust in the air, causing breathing issues and potential health risks, the 32 who brought the action will experience that as well. However, one of the main reasons why the 32 people who brought the action have suffered a different kind of injury is because their homes and cars are regularly covered with "volumes of white dust." Plaintiffs have stated that the dust has caused them to have to regularly (sometimes daily) need to dust off of their cars. Compared to the 968 people in the immediate community near the concrete plant where everyone will experience the effects of the dusty air, the 32 plaintiffs have regularly experienced a different kind of injury to their houses and vehicles. A "special injury" must be distinct from what others in the community are experiencing. These 32 plaintiffs have clearly experienced a unique injury that the other 95% of the community has not been subjected to.

> One nice thing about this paper is that its structure directly parallels the "call" in the exam question. Many law school or bar exams are not that direct in telling you what points to analyze, but when they are, listen. But even while responding directly to this specifically asked question, should the student/writer have circled back somewhat to situate this issue more generally within the elements of public nuisance? Different graders might vary in their responses to that question, but most would agree that it would be at least a little better to do so if that were possible without bogging down the focus on the exact questions asked.

> When you think about what the student is doing in this paragraph, you should see that an advocate in this case must carefully thread a needle. On the one hand, to be "public" the alleged nuisance has to affect a lot of people. But on the other hand, to have a private right of action for a public nuisance a plaintiff must show a special injury not shared widely in the community. Do these contradict each other? They can't, completely, or it would be impossible ever to bring a private case for public nuisance. But there is certainly a tension there. What does that tell you about how to understand these legal rules? Has this student addressed this tension well? Would you?

Another reason why the 32 plaintiffs' action is triable is because some of the plaintiffs installed special windows in an effort to keep out the dust. Although everyone close to the concrete plant may experience poor air quality because of the dust, none of the others (as far as we know) have had to go to the expense and inconvenience of putting in special windows to keep the dust out. Also, the fact that "most of the plaintiffs" live on the northern side of

> Is this an instance where there really are no viable counterarguments, or should some have been considered and addressed here?

the subdivision also proves that their injuries should be considered different from the harm caused to the rest of the community. The dust has arguably created a special injury for these particular plaintiffs because they have experienced unique injuries compared to the rest of the community.

Acme's motion for summary judgment with respect to plaintiffs› public nuisance claim (specifically whether it was a "special injury") should be denied.

Was the presence of dust "substantial in nature" and "unreasonable in character?"

The first issue is whether the interference from the dust was "substantial in nature." For an interference to be substantial, it must lessen real worth or value. In our case, the plaintiffs have presented sufficient evidence to prove that the interference was "substantial in nature."

Although we do not have the prices of the special windows some plaintiffs installed to keep out the dust it is fair to assume that putting them in was not free. Without Acme's presence it is highly unlikely that these plaintiffs would have installed windows to keep dust out. Since these plaintiffs have gone out of their way to address the offending dust by purchasing special windows, it should be uncontested that the dust has created an interference that was "substantial in nature."

> Are we dealing now with elements of public nuisance or private? The call of the exam question actually tells us, but this heading doesn't. Best practice for the student response would be to spell out the exact cause of action at issue and its elements. And ideally, to explain why defense counsel focused the motion to dismiss on these in particular elements.

> Uncontestable is a pretty strong statement. It essentially asserts that there is no reasonable counterargument on this point. Do you agree? How might the student have handled this differently?

Plaintiffs have triable issues of fact with respect to Acme's interference being "substantial in nature."

Second, if a person had to wipe "volumes of white dust" off of their car daily, or even regularly, this should be considered unreasonable. Although Acme has stated that this dust is a "necessary by-product" of cement manufacturing and that their equipment "nearly eliminated any dust pollution," it is simply untrue. The fact that Acme's cement plant emanates dust which covers houses and cars regularly (sometimes daily) shows that their machines have not come close to nearly eliminating the dust pollution. The cement manufacturing has obviously affected these people substantially. In order to clean volumes of dust off of your house you either have to do a lot of work yourself, or hire someone.

> Is this discussion really answering why the dust is legally unreasonable? If not, it is conclusory even if it is right.

However, Acme will likely dispute this point because, of the 1,000 residents around the plant, only 32 people have argued that the pollution is "unreasonable in character." Further, Acme will reiterate that they have "nearly eliminated" the dust pollution because less than 5% of the residents have been affected by the pollution. Acme may also say that concrete plants have to operate somewhere, and dust is a common product of the industry. If the defense can show that Acme's equipment is really is "state of the art," and is thus the best equipment on the market, they may be able to prove that there is nothing the manufacturer can do about the problem. The country needs concrete plants, so their conduct should not be considered unreasonable as a matter of law or we could have to cut back substantially on concrete production, which would hurt the U.S. economy.

> Perhaps these points could be better developed or fit more seamlessly within the legal analysis, but this does seem like a solid and helpful policy point. Do you think it makes the arguments more powerful?

There are triable issues of fact with respect to whether Acme›s interference was "unreasonable in character." For all of these reasons, the case should proceed to trial.

Learn From Your Work

One of the most helpful things law students can learn is to look critically at even fairly effective legal analysis. Ask yourself: "What does this student do that works, and why?" "How could it be better?" What strengths would you tell this student to keep capitalizing on? What should the student work to develop further?

Now, the harder part is casting the same critical look on your own efforts. Go back and look at an earlier paper for this course or for a different one, and ask yourself how the analysis could be improved.

Property Project Checklist

Read your own drafts while looking carefully for each point raised below. If the points are included, please make sure that they are presented and explained to the best of your ability. If they are not, then consider whether your analysis can be made more complete.

1. Where does your analysis lay out the general elements of private nuisance?

2. Where does your analysis lay out the general elements of public nuisance?

3. Does the letter help the clients understand that in nuisance cases the courts will balance the interests of both parties?

4. If you are concluding that the Osgoods have a viable claim for private nuisance, where does the letter explain in lay terms:

    a. What it means for *Starshine* to have interfered with their use or enjoyment of their land;

    b. Why the interference meets the legal standard for being considered "substantial";

    c. Why the interference can be deemed "unreasonable";

    d. That *Starshine*'s interference with their property was either intentional or negligent (this one's pretty easy, right?);

    e. How *Starshine* caused the problems the Osgoods are experiencing?

5. Even if you are concluding that the Osgoods have a cause of action for private nuisance, where does the letter explain what the most difficult parts of that case would be and why? Was the letter careful to make no promises or guarantees of success even if the attorney expressed confidence?

6. If you are arguing that the Osgoods do not, or may not, have a viable claim for private nuisance, where does the letter explain which elements will be especially difficult to maintain and why?

7. If you are concluding that the Osgoods have a viable claim for public nuisance, where does the letter explain in lay terms:

    a. What common right of the public *Starshine* may have interfered with;

    b. Why that interference meets the legal standard for being considered "substantial";

    c. Why the interference offends public morals, interferes with the use of a public facility, or endangers/injures the property, health, safety, or comfort of a considerable number of persons (and how many people or what percentage of the community is required to constitute "a considerable number of persons");

    d. Why the Osgoods have suffered a special injury such that they have a private right of action for public nuisance, despite the fact that the municipality has taken no action against *Starshine*?

8. If you are concluding the Osgoods have a cause of action for public nuisance, where does the letter explain what the most difficult parts of that case will be and why? Is the letter careful to make no promises or guarantees of success even if the attorney expressed confidence?

9. If you are arguing that the Osgoods do not, or may not, have a viable claim for public nuisance, where does the letter explain which elements will be especially difficult to maintain and why?

10. Does the organization of the letter fit its reasoning? Does it follow the traditional logic of applying rules of law to facts?

11. Is the discussion presented readably and in ways that the Osgoods would understand? Does it avoid patronizing the clients while also steering clear of unnecessary legal jargon?

12. Was the analysis proofread, with technical errors and awkwardness eliminated?

13. If you were to receive the letter, would you find it helpful in addressing your problem and in making a final decision about how to proceed?

Chapter 5

Evidence

Assignment: *Draft the Argument Section for a Pre-trial Brief*

Based on the materials in the file, please draft the Argument section of the reply brief opposing the motion to preclude the evidence in question—in other words, in permitting it. Target length is fewer than 1000 words excluding point headings.

Analytical Skills to Focus On

✓ Reading critically what is, and *is not*, on the page

✓ Thinking strategically

✓ Comprehending statutes and exceptions

✓ Framing strong legal arguments

✓ Explaining analysis persuasively

Case File

In this case file you will act as an Assistant District Attorney ("ADA") in Arapahoe County, Colorado. Assume you graduated from law school about 18 months ago, and have only recently moved from prosecuting misdemeanors to handling felony cases. You are working under the supervision of a more senior ADA on *People v. Eng*, a drug trafficking case you fully expect may actually go to trial, rather than settling on a guilty plea for lesser charges as most criminal cases do. Your job in this instance is to persuade the court that the emails defendant Eng sent to his lawyer fall within the "crime-fraud" exception for attorney-client privilege. As such, that they are not privileged communications and may be used as evidence against Eng at trial.

The materials in the case file are given to you in one complete set so that you will have them all together. As you read through the materials, ask yourself:

1. How do the prosecution and the defense sides see the contested emails? Which facts are generally agreed upon, and what is disputed by the different sides?

2. What exactly is the rule in question, and how does the rule operate?

3. What do the documents in the case file contribute?

4. Are there any materials *not* here that you would want to review to better understand your case? If this were an actual case, how would you work to build the evidence you need? Are there ways to work around what you do not know?

A project checklist is included at the end of the chapter. Use it to review and edit your drafts.

....

Chapter 5 Case File

Your exercise packet contains the following:
- Instruction memo from a senior ADA in your office
- Notice of Motion to preclude evidence submitted by defendant's counsel
- Brief in support of motion to preclude
- Relevant excerpt of the Colorado Revised Statute pertaining to attorney-client privilege
- Relevant cases to use in your analysis

Thinking about Evidence

Evidence courses are often hybrids. Like many other law school courses, they emphasize studying and applying codes, usually the Federal Rules of Evidence, while thinking conceptually about legal doctrine. But far more than most of canonical law school classes, they also tend to highlight the practical aspects of how these rules are used. That's because trial lawyers must frequently make spontaneous legal arguments about testimony at issue. That is not the only way evidence issues arise, of course—litigators may spend significant time researching and considering evidentiary questions in far more detail in pre-trial motion practice or in appeals. But the need to quickly cry "Objection!" and immediately provide justifications or counter-arguments (if asked) is certainly on the minds of most Evidence professors. You will probably understand your own evidence class better if you take some time to think about how it balances deep consideration of rules and policies of evidence law with preparation for hands-on employment of the rules.

Evidence rules are also fairly intricate. They require exacting understanding, and they require precise application to specific facts. This may make them uniquely well-suited to multiple-choice testing, which tends to emphasize precision in knowing and applying rules. If your class uses multiple-choice problems then you should certainly practice with as many sample questions as you can. But if it doesn't? Do some anyway. Good multiple-choice questions are often crafted so that you will select the wrong answer if you almost—but don't quite—understand something. As a result, seeing what you get right and wrong will deepen your comprehension in a different way than practicing essay-style analysis does.

In fact, this kind of "cross-training" in reasoning through both multiple-choice and prose responses will probably be useful to refine your skills in all law school subjects, irrespective of the courses' specific assessment methods.

MEMO

To: [your name]
From: Bob
Re: People v. Eng
Date: 2/23/20___

We just received a copy of defense counsel's motion to exclude the emails we are going to need to prosecute the Eng case.

As you know, Eng was instrumental in constructing the website that drove traffic to the DJT Medical Group, which was essentially a clearinghouse website where customers could order "prescriptions" for whatever opiates they wanted and have them delivered by mail or courier. We had a confidential informant who let us know that the company was operating out of our county. We were investigating the company for months as an illegal distributor of schedule 1 narcotics, and were just closing in on the main players when they got wind of our investigation. They tried to quickly shut everything down and destroy evidence. As a result, their employee Eng ended up being the only person we were able to charge in what we know was a much larger drug distribution conspiracy. We need to win this motion so that we will be able to support our most serious charges against him. Without those charges against Eng we won't have the leverage we need to try to get him to name the bigger players.

I think it is pretty clear that the emails to his lawyer should fall within the "crime-fraud" exception to attorney-client privilege. Please look into the matter and prepare a draft of the Argument section of our brief. Don't worry about the Statement of Facts and so forth. They are pretty standard and we have a short deadline, so right now I'm asking one of our paralegals to prepare everything except the legal argument itself.

Please remember Judge Cooper is always going on about how "briefs have to be *brief*!" Keep it as short as you possibly can while still making a winning argument.

> The judge presiding over this case may be especially vocal on this point, but it is a good one for all law practice. Concise materials are most likely to be thoroughly read and absorbed, so may be especially influential, assuming they are nonetheless complete and credible.

A Notice of Motion is a fairly formulaic cover document. Its purpose is to inform the court and opposing party of a request for a ruling by the court. The documents accompanying the notice are where an attorney provides materials to show why that request should be granted. In most jurisdictions, such materials generally include a brief (Memorandum of Law) to set forth legal arguments. New factual information might be included in sworn affidavits, but if there has already been discovery in the case the lawyer can just reference the established record.

18th JUDICIAL DISTRICT COURT

ARAPAHO COUNTY COLORADO

--X

People of the State of Colorado

- v. -

Darrell Eng,

                                  Defendant.   Docket Number 52019

--X

SIR or MADAM:

PLEASE TAKE NOTICE that upon the annexed Memorandum of Law, and upon all of the proceedings herein, the undersigned will move before the Honorable Gordon Cooper, a Judge of this Court, located in the Criminal Courthouse, 1790 West Littleton Road, on March 21 at 9:00 a.m. or as soon thereafter as counsel can be heard, for an order precluding the prosecution from offering evidence of any and all electronic communications between defendant Darrell Eng and his retained counsel Lucas S. Hemet, Esq., and/or any other person preparing attorney work product in the Law Offices of Lucas Hemet, and for such other and further relief as to this Court seems just and proper.

DATED this 22nd day of February, 20____.

LAW OFFICES OF LUCAS HEMET

Lucas S. Hemet

Lucas S. Hemet, Esq.
1427 W. Littleton Rd.
Littleton, CO 80120

Attorney for Defendant

18th JUDICIAL DISTRICT COURT

ARAPAHO COUNTY COLORADO

--x

People of the State of Colorado

- v. -

Darrell Eng,

                              Defendant.   Docket Number 52019

--x

MEMORANDUM OF LAW

IN SUPPORT OF DEFENDANT'S MOTION TO PRECLUDE Evidence

DATED this 22nd day of February, 20_____.

LAW OFFICES OF LUCAS HEMET

Lucas S. Hemet

Lucas S. Hemet, Esq.
1427 W. Littleton Rd.
Littleton, CO 80120

Attorney for Defendant

18ᵗʰ JUDICIAL DISTRICT COURT

ARAPAHO COUNTY COLORADO

---x

People of the State of Colorado

- v. -

Darrell Eng,

Defendant.   Docket Number 52019

---x

INTRODUCTION

Defendant Darrell Eng submits this memorandum in support of his Motion to Preclude email correspondence, copies of which are annexed hereto as Exhibits A and B. The evidence was obtained through a search and seizure of a laptop computer in Defendant's possession. The evidence is inadmissible because the communication is protected by attorney-client privilege under Colorado Revised Statute § 13-90-107.

> This entire Introduction and much of the brief that follows is in passive voice. Active constructions are usually clearer, and they tend to be more engaging to readers. Why is this attorney so pervasively adopting passive constructions? It could be unintentional (or just weak writing), but there may instead be a subtle purpose to his choices. Passive voice tends to emphasize the objects rather than the subjects of sentences. It also obscures who is doing the acting, which in turn focuses more attention on the action itself. Do either of these rationales explain Hemet's decisions here?

STATEMENT OF FACTS

Darrell Eng is a college graduate and trained information architect who has spent eight years working in the technology sector. He worked as a professional website manager for DJT Medical Group for approximately three years before his employment was unexpectedly terminated on or about December 4, 20____. Prior to this termination Mr. Eng's annual performance reviews were satisfactory, and he had been promoted to his present position only five months prior. Eng Aff. ¶ 5. During the time he was employed by DJT Mr. Eng worked primarily off-site and rarely traveled to DJT's offices. *Id.* at ¶ 8.

On or about December 11, 20____, Colorado State Police entered and searched DJT's offices. As part of that investigation, police also searched Mr. Eng's home despite his no longer being employed by DJT. At that time, Police Officers removed a laptop computer from Mr. Eng's kitchen. The laptop contained email correspondence from an account that Mr. Eng maintained.

Included in Mr. Eng's email correspondence were exchanges between Mr. Eng and Meg Davis, Esq., an Attorney-at-Law working for the Law Offices of Lucas Hemet. (Copies of emails are attached hereto as Ex. A and Ex. B.) Meg Davis had been previously retained as counsel by Mr. Eng.

Notice that the most important factual support is attached to the memo. First, that probably means you should immediately flip to the attachments and read them. Second, it's helpful to observe how lawyers put court papers together. The attorney would probably have included the emails as an attachment even if they were already in the case's records. Making life more convenient for the judge is never a bad decision!

The contents of the emails included questions pertaining to the lawfulness of Mr. Eng's employment termination, and were prepared in the course of Ms. Davis's representation of Mr. Eng. Davis Aff. ¶ 7. Mr. Eng believed at the time of the correspondence that the contents of those emails were protected by attorney-client privilege. Eng Aff. ¶ 10.

ARGUMENT

"The attorney-client privilege is the oldest of the privileges for confidential communications known to the common law. Its purpose is to encourage full and frank communication between attorneys and their clients and thereby promote broader public interests in the observance of law and administration of justice." *Upjohn Co. v. United States*, 449 U.S. 383, 389 (1981). The privilege protects all confidential communications made in in the course of an attorney-client relationship. *See United States v. Richard Roe, Inc.* (*In re Richard Roe, Inc.*), 68 F.3d 38, 39 (2d Cir. 1995).

In Colorado the legislature has codified this common law privilege, stating explicitly that it did so "to encourage confidence and to preserve it inviolate." C.R.S.A § 13-90-107. The state's rationale for preserving attorney-client privilege is to secure justice by ensuring open communication between a client and his attorney. *People v. Tucker*, 232 P.3d 194, 198 (Colo. App. 2009).

Advocates know their structures send important subliminal signals to readers. Why is there a paragraph break here? A primary school English teacher introducing paragraphing might suggest that the ideas here are not so distinct from those above that they required a new paragraph. But it is certainly not incorrect to treat this material as a new thought. Moreover, doing so has the strategic advantage of emphasizing Colorado's commitment to the common law privilege, and drawing attention to the specific statute on point. If you pay careful attention to these kinds of nuances in writing it will make your own legal analysis stronger.

I. Mr. Eng's emails actively sought legal advice regarding his employment termination, and were consequently protected by attorney-client privilege.

To establish attorney-client privilege a client must simply seek counsel from his lawyer in regards to his legal rights. *People v. Tucker*, 232 P.3d 194, 198 (Colo. App. 2009). Once the relationship begins, the privilege extends to any communications made directly between the client and attorney with respect to the client's rights or obligations under the law. *Id.*

In *Ryskamp v. Looney*, for example, the officers of an investment fund discussed their legal rights regarding their management functions directly with the company attorneys. No. 10-cv-00842-WJM-KLM, 2011 U.S. Dist. LEXIS 98644, at *6 (D. Colo. Sep. 1, 2011). The court found that the communications showed on their face that the parties were discussing rights and related issues, and thus the emails sought and included legal advice and were protected by attorney-client privilege. *Id.*

Mr. Eng's emails are similarly protected by attorney-client privilege because they show that Eng was seeking legal advice while discussing his rights and related issues. As was the case in *Ryskamp*, Eng's emails unmistakably show that his primary concern was learning more about his legal rights after he was unexpectedly fired. He asks directly: "can they really just [terminate me] with no notice

Do you see the implicit IRAC in this section of the brief? The author does not call attention to the Rule + Application + Explanation formulation, yet nonetheless is guided by its inherent logic. That's part of what makes this a pretty persuasive and well-crafted brief.

and no cause?" (Exhibit A, attached) Eng also forwarded the termination email from his former employer for his attorney to review. There would have been no reason for him to do so other than to seek information regarding the legality of the termination.

The attorney's response further corroborates that the subject of the communication was legal counsel regarding Eng's rights. The subject line on the lawyer's emailed response was "termination questions." (Exhibit B, attached) The emailed reply then proceeds to provide advice to Mr. Eng regarding the termination. The character of this consultation is precisely equivalent to the kind of advice sought and protected by the state of Colorado in *Ryskamp. Id.* at 6.

II. Mr. Eng reasonably expected his emails with his attorney to be confidential because of his ongoing protected lawyer-client relationship.

Attorney-client privilege applies to statements a client makes when the client reasonably expects the statements will be treated confidentially. *Tucker,* 232 P.3d at 198. A reasonable belief of confidentiality arises when a client shares information with his attorney while receiving legal advice. *See, e.g., Ryskamp,* 2011 U.S. Dist. LEXIS 98644, at *7 (concluding there was no evidence presented to support a finding that defendant did not expect emails to attorneys to be treated confidentially).

Mr. Eng reasonably expected courts to treat his email with his attorney confidentially because he believed he had an attorney-client relationship. Mr. Eng expressed intent that Ms. Davis provide legal services, and Ms. Davis replied in her professional capacity with legal information, and did so using her law firm's email with its standard professional disclaimers included. (Exhibits A and B, attached) Davis even made plans to schedule a meeting for further consultation on the matter. (Exhibit B, attached)

It should be dispositive that Mr. Eng had used Ms. Davis as his attorney in the past and that there is no indication either party ever terminated the attorney-client relationship. Mr. Eng intended to consult with his lawyer on a new matter in the course of that ongoing attorney-client relationship, and his expectation of privilege is therefore justifiable and reasonable.

This last paragraph is framed as concluding wrap up, which is probably why it contains no citations. But does it introduce any new ideas? If so, what do you think of the lawyer's choice not to reference authority?

III. The crime-fraud exception does not apply because defendant Eng's disclosures were merely adjacent to his inquiries about legal rights and obligations and he was not acting in furtherance of a crime.

The crime-fraud exception to attorney-client privilege negates the privilege only when the communications between a client and his attorney seek actively to further a crime or fraudulent act. *Tucker,* 232 P.3d at 199 (*citing Law Offices of Barnard D. Morley, P.C. v. MacFarlane,* 647 P.2d 1215, 1220 (Colo. 1982)). The party attempting to apply this narrow exception must meet the burden of proof

This entire section of the brief represents an important tactical decision on the attorney's part.

It could easily have been omitted. The motion papers would then simply assert that the emails were privileged and wait to see how opposing counsel responded. For tactical reasons many lawyers would not want to "make the other side's case." Of course the DA is almost certain to raise the crime-fraud exception, and defense counsel would then raise the arguments included here in a subsequent reply brief. Eventually this gets the same questions before the court.

But there could be good reasons for doing so here. It's more straightforward, of course, to get right to the real issue that the court will have to address. And there is essentially no realistic likelihood that the prosecutors would fail to assert the exception if it weren't brought up by the defense. The judge may appreciate the efficiency of having the real issue immediately on the table. The lawyer may want to have the first shot at framing the central question. Finally, if the defendant is awaiting trial in jail rather than on bail, speediness in resolving pretrial issues may matter to him a great deal.

by showing facts sufficient to support a good faith belief that wrongful conduct has occurred. *Id.*

The Colorado Court of Appeals looks to the Second Circuit for guidance on the proper test to determine whether the crime-fraud exception applies. *Tucker*, 232 P.3d at 200 (*citing In re Richard Roe, Inc.*, 68 F.3d at 40). Both courts place a substantial persuasive burden on the party seeking to pierce the privilege, requiring a showing that the communications in question must themselves be "in furtherance" of a future or ongoing crime. *See In re Richard Roe*, 68 F.3d at 40–41 (finding error in stripping communications of attorney-client privilege merely because they were relevant to a crime and determining instead that the party seeking to use the crime-fraud exception must state the factual basis of the alleged crime).

The crime-fraud exception does not apply to Mr. Eng's emails because his actions were not in furtherance of a crime. The primary purpose for his emails was to inquire about the legality of his employment termination. Any disclosures about alleged criminal activities were merely related to this ultimate objective of seeking legal counsel regarding his rights and obligations upon suddenly losing his livelihood.

CONCLUSION

For the reasons set forth above, this honorable Court should preclude any and all of the attorney-client communications from being accepted into evidence at trial, and grant such other and further relief as may be warranted.

Respectfully submitted,

LAW OFFICES OF LUCAS HEMET

Lucas S. Hemet

Lucas S. Hemet, Esq.
1427 W. Littleton Rd.
Littleton, CO 80120

Attorney for Defendant

Exhibit A
[copy]

Eng, Darrell P.

From:	Eng, Darell <deng@gmail.com>
Sent:	Thursday, December 05, 20_____ 10:42 AM
To:	Davis, Meg
Subject:	Fw: Notice

Hi Meg,

I wish I could say something good today but I just got fired!

I guess that means I have some questions. First, can they really just do this with no notice and no cause? And second, this prescription business has been an incredible money-maker for them and my search-optimization work in site building is probably a big part of the reason why. Without me most of their "patients" would never have been able to find them. Can I get any portion of their profit that's due to my efforts? I mean, I drove all those customers to the business in the first place! Last then, I'm going to have to find another gig. Would you be able to help me set up a similar company on my own? I don't need those guys anyway.

---------- Forwarded message ----------

From:	DJT Medical <djtmedicalgroup@fcas.com>
Date:	Wed, Dec 4, 20_____ at 4:15 PM
Subject:	Notice
To:	deng@gmail.com

Good afternoon.

We are writing to notify you that due to legal restraints DJT Medical Group has decided to move its operations in a different direction, and your services will no longer be needed. We are therefore electing to terminate your employment effective immediately.

DJT Management Team

Exhibit B
[copy]

Davis, Meg

From:	Davis, Meg <megdavis@hemetlaw.com>
Sent:	Friday, December 06, 20_____ 3:20 PM
To:	Eng, Darrell
Cc:	Veronica Luce
Subject:	Termination questions

Dear Mr. Eng,

I am terribly sorry to hear about your employment situation. Of course I am happy to assist. Copying my secretary here so that she can work with you to set up an appointment.

I do want to caution you that it is difficult to challenge the termination of at-will employment, so I cannot promise that you will have recourse against your employer. Nonetheless it is certainly worth a discussion to fully explore your options. I should note, too, that while I can assist with incorporation of any lawful business, I would be unable to help in the creation of a company with the purpose of avoiding or violating any state or federal laws.

NOTICE: The information contained in this e-mail message and any attachments may be legally privileged or otherwise protected by law. This message is intended only for the individual(s) named herein or other contacts of The Law Offices of Lucas Hemet specifically authorized to receive this communication. If you are not the intended recipient please notify the sender and promptly delete this message. Please do not read, store, copy or otherwise disseminate or distribute this e-mail or any part of it. Any communication about the contents of this email to unauthorized parties is strictly prohibited.

C.R.S.A. § 13-90-107

§ 13-90-107. Who may not testify without consent—definitions

Effective: March 16, 2017

(1) There are particular relations in which it is the policy of the law to encourage confidence and to preserve it inviolate; therefore, a person shall not be examined as a witness in the following cases:

. . .

(b) An attorney shall not be examined without the consent of his client as to any communication made by the client to him or his advice given thereon in the course of professional employment; nor shall an attorney's secretary, paralegal, legal assistant, stenographer, or clerk be examined without the consent of his employer concerning any fact, the knowledge of which he has acquired in such capacity.

68 F.3d 38
United States Court of Appeals,
Second Circuit.

In re RICHARD ROE, INC., and John Doe, Inc.
UNITED STATES of America,
Petitioner–Appellee,

v.

RICHARD ROE, INC., Richard Roe, John Doe,
Inc., and John Doe, Respondents–Appellants.

No. 669, Docket 95–6142.

|

Argued Sept. 7, 1995.

|

Decided Oct. 13, 1995.

Appeal was taken from an order of the United States District Court for the Eastern District of New York, Thomas C. Platt, Jr., J., holding officers of two corporations in contempt for refusing to produce certain documents to grand jury after the court found that documents fell within the crime-fraud exception to the attorney-client privilege. The Court of Appeals, Winter, Circuit Judge, held that district court employed incorrect test to determine whether crime-fraud exception to attorney-client privilege applied and thus remand was necessary for application of correct "in furtherance" test for crime-fraud exception.

Remanded.

Attorneys and Law Firms

David M. Zornow, New York City (Keith D. Krakaur, Lawrence S. Spiegel, Skadden, Arps, Slate, Meagher & Flom, New York City, of counsel) for Respondents–Appellants John Doe, Inc. and John Doe.

Laura A. Brevetti, New York City (Robert A. Culp, of counsel) for Respondents–Appellants Richard Roe, Inc. and Richard Roe.

Sean F. O'Shea, Assistant United States Attorney, Brooklyn, New York (Zachary W. Carter, United States Attorney, Eastern District of New York, David C. James, Lee G. Dunst, Assistant United States Attorneys, of counsel) for Petitioner–Appellee.

> A critical reader should be asking: what jurisdiction is this set in and what body of law does the case address? Is it binding or persuasive in your case? How will that affect how you use it?

Before: WINTER, ALTIMARI, and McLAUGHLIN, Circuit Judges.

Opinion

WINTER, Circuit Judge:

This appeal concerns the scope of the so-called "crime-fraud" exception to the attorney-client privilege and attorney work product immunity (collectively "the privileges"). Appellant corporations John Doe, Inc. and Richard Roe, Inc.[1] asserted the privileges with respect to four grand jury subpoenas seeking documents and testimony from the corporations and from attorneys who jointly represented the firms at one time. The government subsequently moved to compel production, arguing that the matters sought fell within the crime-fraud exception to the privileges. Based on an *ex parte* affidavit submitted by the government, the district court concluded that there was a factual basis to believe that the exception applied and thereafter conducted an *in camera* inspection of the documents at issue. In a sealed opinion, the court found that

1 Because this appeal involves proceedings currently before a grand jury and the briefs and record on appeal are under seal, we employ pseudonyms.

although many [of the documents] may enjoy the privilege claim, [the court was] in no position to say that one or more or all of them may not prove to be relevant evidence of activity in furtherance of contemplated or ongoing criminal or fraudulent conduct in this case. Furthermore, this Court does find that these documents, read collectively, have the real potential of being relevant evidence of activity in furtherance of a crime.

The district court thus held that the documents fell within the crime-fraud exception and issued two orders compelling the production of those documents. The court further ordered that unspecified witnesses, clearly including the corporations' joint attorneys, give virtually unlimited testimony concerning: (i) the documents, (ii) an investigation performed by appellants' counsel, and (iii) opinions rendered by counsel during the time frame of the subpoenaed documents. At a hearing on June 21, 1995, John Doe and Richard Roe, two officers of the corporations, refused to produce the subpoenaed documents and were held in contempt. This expedited appeal followed. Because the district court employed an incorrect test to determine whether the crime-fraud exception applies, we reverse and remand with directions.

[1] [2] [3] The attorney-client privilege is "the oldest of the privileges for confidential communications known to the common law." *Upjohn Co. v. United States,* 449 U.S. 383, 389, 101 S.Ct. 677, 682, 66 L. Ed.2d 584 (1981). The privilege applies so that

> (1) [w]here legal advice of any kind is sought (2) from a professional legal adviser in his capacity as such, (3) the communications relating to that purpose, (4) made in confidence (5) by the client, (6) are at his instance permanently protected (7) from disclosure by himself or the legal adviser, (8) except the protection be waived....

United States v. Kovel, 296 F.2d 918, 921 (2d Cir.1961). The attorney-client privilege is designed to promote unfettered communication between attorneys and their clients so that the attorney may give fully informed legal advice. *In re John Doe, Inc.,* 13 F.3d 633, 635–36 (2d Cir.1994) ("*John Doe 1994* "); *In re Grand Jury Subpoena Duces Tecum Dated September 15, 1983,* 731 F.2d 1032, 1036 (2d Cir.1984) ("*Marc Rich* "). The protection given to attorney work product serves a similar purpose: "to avoid chilling attorneys in developing materials to aid them in giving legal advice and in preparing a case for trial." *In re John Doe Corp.,* 675 F.2d 482, 492 (2d Cir.1982) ("*John Doe 1982* "). *See generally Hickman v. Taylor,* 329 U.S. 495, 67 S.Ct. 385, 91 L.Ed. 451 (1947).

[4] Nevertheless, "[i]t is well-established that communications that otherwise would be protected by the attorney-client privilege or the attorney work product privilege are not protected if they relate to client communications in furtherance of contemplated or ongoing criminal or fraudulent conduct." *Marc Rich,* 731 F.2d at 1038 (citations omitted). Although there is a societal interest in enabling clients to get sound legal advice, there is no such interest when the communications or advice are intended to further the commission of a crime or fraud. The crime-fraud exception thus insures that the secrecy protecting the attorney-client relationship does not extend to communications or work product " 'made for the purpose of getting advice for the commission of a fraud' or crime." *United States v. Zolin,* 491 U.S. 554, 563, 109 S.Ct. 2619, 2626, 105 L.Ed.2d 469 (1989) (quoting *O'Rourke v. Darbishire,* [1920] A.C. 581, 604 (P.C.)).

[5] We have recently reiterated that a party seeking to invoke the crime-fraud exception must at least demonstrate that there is probable cause to believe that a crime or fraud has been attempted or committed and that the communications were in furtherance thereof. *John Doe 1994,* 13 F.3d at 637. In the instant case, the district court, after considering the government's *ex parte* submission and reviewing the subpoenaed documents *in camera,* premised its holding that the crime-fraud exception applied on a finding that "these documents, read collectively, have the real potential of being relevant evidence of activity in furtherance of a crime." The government argues that this formulation reflects the proper legal standard. We disagree.

[6] [7] The "relevant evidence" test departs from the correct "in furtherance" test in two respects. First, the crime-fraud exception does not apply simply because privileged communications would provide an adversary with evidence of a crime or fraud. If it did, the privilege would be virtually worthless because a client could not freely give, or an attorney request, evidence that might support a finding of culpability. Instead, the exception applies only when the court determines that the client communication or attorney work product in question was *itself* in furtherance of the crime or fraud. *See In re Grand Jury Subpoenas Duces Tecum,* 798 F.2d 32, 34 (2d Cir.1986) (crime-fraud exception inapplicable where the documents themselves in combination with government proffer did not support a finding "that those communications were in furtherance of those crimes"). Second, the crime-fraud exception applies only where there is probable cause to believe that the particular communication with counsel or attorney work product was intended in some way to facilitate or to conceal the criminal activity. *Id.* at 34 (reversing compulsion order for failure "to show the requisite purposeful nexus"); *Marc Rich,* 731 F.2d at 1039 (the crime or fraud must "have been the objective of the client's communication"); *United States v. White,* 887 F.2d 267, 271 (D.C.Cir.1989) ("[t]o subject the attorney-client communications to disclosure, they must actually have been made with an intent to further an unlawful act"). *See also* John William Gergacz, *Attorney–Corporate Client Privilege* 4–16 (1990) ("The client's intention in communicating with counsel is controlling under the crime-fraud exception and, therefore, must be established as a part of the prima facie case.").[2] Because a simple finding of relevance does not demon-

strate a criminal or fraudulent purpose, it does not trigger the exception.

2   This court and others have generally enunciated the requirement of a criminal or fraudulent purpose in discussions of the attorney-client privilege and not the work product immunity. Where, as here, the attorney-client privilege and the work product immunity substantially overlap, we see no reason to apply a different standard for attorney work product. See In re Grand Jury Proceedings, 604 F.2d 798, 803 (3d Cir.1979).

There are loose ends remaining. For example, the precise factual basis of the alleged crime or fraud is unclear. Moreover, the government apparently claims that only one of the two corporate privilege-holders was involved in a crime or fraud. This raises the very difficult issue of whether the crime-fraud exception applies where one of two joint privilege-holders is innocent. However, because the district court used a "relevant evidence" test, rather than an "in furtherance" test, it did not need to reach this issue.

[8] We therefore remand this matter to the district court for an examination of each document under the proper standard. The district court shall determine which, if any, of the documents or communications were in furtherance of a crime or fraud, as discussed above. If production is ordered, the court shall specify the factual basis for the crime or fraud that the documents or communications are deemed to have furthered, which of the parties asserting claims of privilege possessed a criminal or fraudulent purpose with respect to those documents or communications, and, if appropriate, whether the crime-fraud exception applies to an innocent joint privilege-holder.

In addition, should the district court require grand jury testimony on the ground that the documents or other communications fall within the crime-fraud exception, it shall specify the witness or witnesses required to give testimony, the scope of the examination permitted, and the basis, as described above with regard to the documents, for applying the crime-fraud exception. Where appropriate, the district court may examine these witnesses *in camera* before ordering testimony before a grand jury.

One further matter remains. Appellants ask that, in the event of remand, we direct that this case be assigned to a different judge. This request is based largely on events subsequent to the appeal, and we decline to consider it until a recusal motion has been presented to, and ruled upon by, the district court. This proceeding can also occur on the remand.

Further proceedings should remain under seal. The remand will utilize the procedures set out in *United States v. Jacobson,* 15 F.3d 19, 22 (2d Cir.1994). The mandate shall issue forthwith. Jurisdiction will be automatically restored to this panel without a new notice of appeal if and when appellants inform the clerk of this court that the district court has ordered the disclosure of documents or presentation of testimony to the grand jury based upon the crime-fraud exception or has denied a recusal motion. Any subsequent briefing can be by letter on an expedited schedule to be set by the clerk.

Remanded for further proceedings in accord with this opinion.

232 P.3d 194

Colorado Court of Appeals,

Div. II.

The PEOPLE of the State of Colorado,
Plaintiff–Appellee,

v.

Justin TUCKER, Defendant–Appellant.

No. 06CA2580.

|

Oct. 1, 2009.

Synopsis

Background: Defendant was convicted in the Alamosa County District Court, Pattie P. Swift and Frank Plaut, JJ., of attempt to influence a public servant, forgery of a government-issued document, impersonating a peace officer, criminal impersonation to gain a benefit, and theft under $100. Defendant appealed.

Affirmed.

Attorneys and Law Firms

John W. Suthers, Attorney General, Katherine A. Aidala, Assistant Attorney General, Denver, Colorado, for Plaintiff–Appellee.

Douglas K. Wilson, Colorado State Public Defender, Nathaniel E. Deakins, Deputy State Public Defender, Denver, Colorado, for Defendant–Appellant.

Opinion

Opinion by Judge RICHMAN.

Defendant, Justin Tucker, appeals the judgment of conviction entered on jury verdicts finding him guilty of attempt to influence a public servant, forgery of a government-issued document, impersonating a peace officer, criminal impersonation to gain a benefit, and theft under $100. We affirm.

I. Background

During the summer of 2004, defendant, a first-year law student, was an intern for Peter Comar, the District Attorney for the 12th Judicial District of Colorado. In the spring and summer of 2004, defendant and his wife were parties to a domestic relations case pending in Montana, in which Montana District Court Judge Gregory Todd had entered a permanent restraining order against defendant and in favor of his wife. Defendant subsequently was charged with vio-

lating the order, and, in June 2004, he was criminally charged in Montana with stalking. Attorney Solomon Neuhardt was appointed to represent defendant in the criminal case. Although a different judge was assigned to the criminal case, Judge Todd conducted the initial advisement.

In August 2004, Neuhardt received a letter that purported to have been written and signed by Comar. The letter was printed on the letterhead of the Alamosa District Attorney. The salutation read "Dear Mr. Neuhardt" and the letter went on to state, in pertinent part:

> Mr. Tucker has requested that we forward to you the criminal charges we will be filing on Judge Todd. It is not our policy to do so, but I will be totally frank with you. I am very upset with the situation. Mr. Tucker's grandfather was on the 10th circuit court of appeals for many years and his brother-in-law is the attorney general of Colorado. I have promised Mr. Tucker and his family that if Mr. Tucker is affected adversely in any way[,] Judge Todd's career will end. A judge has a moral obligation to find out the facts. Judges are not there to rubber stamp whatever a woman says. If Todd had even been willing to look at the facts he would have known that Mrs. Tucker is an accomplished liar. No judge in the state of Colorado or Arizona would have issued a restraining order in this case.... I personally think it is time to do the right thing and protect Mr. Tucker.... It is reprehensible that the State of Montana is willing to further this harassment. If Mr. Todd and the State of Montana want to ignore the totality of circumstances in this case[,] ... we will act in kind. If they continue to do so we will use all the resources of the State of Colorado to protect him.

> The state of Colorado will also review every thing the [Montana prosecutor] does with a fine tooth comb. This may seem harsh to you but our office has dealt with [defendant's wife] quite frequently and am [sic] amazed any state would try to protect such a deviant.

> We are also prepared to charge [defendant's wife] criminally. We have also been in contact with the district attorney's office in Maricopa County Arizona. They are equally tired of [defendant's wife] and will be filing criminal perjury charges against her.

Neuhardt called Comar and asked him whether he had written the letter. Comar stated he had not written it. Concerned about Judge Todd's safety, Neuhardt called the judge's office to inform him of the letter's content. Neuhardt later faxed a copy of the letter to the judge. He mailed the original to Comar.

Defendant was subsequently charged in Colorado with the four offenses as set forth above, and, after the jury found defendant guilty on all counts, the trial court sentenced him to four years on probation. This appeal followed.

II. Motion to Preclude Evidence

Before trial, defendant filed a motion to preclude the use of the letter at trial, as well as Neuhardt's testimony about the letter, asserting these communications were shielded by the attorney-client privilege. At the hearing on this motion, the parties stipulated that defendant had (1) drafted the letter and sent it to Neuhardt, and (2) attempted to reproduce Comar's signature on the letter. Other than the stipulations and background facts set forth above, no evidence was adduced at the hearing.

The court denied defendant's motion, relying on the Colorado statutory definition of the attorney-client privilege, as codified by section 13–90–107(1)(b), C.R.S.2009, which states: "An attorney shall not be examined without the consent of his client as to any communication made by the client to him or his advice given thereon in the course of professional employment...."

The trial court found that on its face, the letter in question does not "purport to be a communication from [defendant] to Mr. Neuhardt; it purports to be a communication from Mr. Comar to Mr. Neuhardt." Thus, the court concluded, it does not meet the threshold requirement of a privileged communication. On appeal, defendant contends that the trial court erred in denying his pretrial motion to exclude the letter and Neuhardt's testimony pursuant to the attorney-client privilege. We disagree.

The trial court also rejected defendant's argument that the letter should be excluded because Neuhardt violated the Montana Rules of Professional Conduct when he disclosed the letter. Because defendant does not reassert this argument on appeal, that issue has been abandoned, and we do not address it here. *See People v. Malloy*, 178 P.3d 1283, 1285 (Colo.App.2008).

A. Standard of Review

[1] In reviewing a trial court's ruling on a motion to exclude evidence, we defer to the court's factual findings if competent evidence in the record supports them, and we review the court's legal conclusions de novo. *People v. Bonilla–Barraza*, 209 P.3d 1090, 1094 (Colo.2009).

B. Applicable Law

[2] [3] [4] As the trial court correctly concluded, the common law attorney-client privilege is now codified in Colorado by section 13–90–107(1)(b). Although codified, the privilege originated in the common law, and much of the common law jurisprudence pertaining to the privilege is retained. Thus, the privilege is established by the act of a client seeking professional advice from a lawyer and extends only to confidential matters communicated by or to the client in the course of gaining counsel, advice, or direction with respect to the client's rights or obligations. *Losavio v. Dist. Court*, 188 Colo. 127, 132–33, 533 P.2d 32, 35 (1975); *People v. Trujillo*, 144 P.3d 539, 542 (Colo.2006). The purpose of the attorney-client privilege is to secure the orderly administration of justice by ensuring candid and open discussion between the client and the attorney without fear of disclosure. *Losavio*, 188 Colo. at 132, 533 P.2d at 34. Furthermore, the privilege "applies only 'to statements made in circumstances giving rise to a reasonable expectation that the statements will be treated as confidential.'" *Wesp v. Everson*, 33 P.3d 191, 197 (Colo.2001) (quoting *Lanari v. People*, 827 P.2d 495, 499 (Colo.1992)); *see also D.A.S. v. People*, 863 P.2d 291, 295 (Colo.1993) (noting that there must be circumstances indicating the intention of secrecy for a communication to be privileged); *People v. Tippett*, 733 P.2d 1183, 1192 (Colo.1987) (stating that communications must be "private or secret" to be privileged).

C. Analysis

[5] Here, we see no error in the trial court's finding that, on its face, the letter in question does not "purport to be a communication from [defendant] to Mr. Neuhardt; it purports to be a communication from Mr. Comar to Mr. Neuhardt." Thus, the court concluded, it does not meet the threshold requirement of a privileged communication. We agree with that conclusion. *See* § 13–90–107(1)(b); *Gordon v. Boyles*, 9 P.3d 1106, 1123 (Colo.2000) ("attorney-client privilege extends only to matters communicated by or to the client in the course of gaining counsel, advice, or direction

with respect to the client's rights or obligations"). Defendant cites no authority, and we have found none, holding that a fraudulent letter with a forged signature, but nonetheless sent to an attorney, is treated as an attorney-client communication for purposes of applying the privilege.

In addition, we note that even if a lawyer reading the letter realized that defendant drafted, signed, and sent the letter, nothing in the letter purports to seek legal advice, counsel, or direction from the lawyer. *See Losavio*, 188 Colo. at 132–33, 533 P.2d at 35; *Trujillo*, 144 P.3d at 542. Rather, the letter expresses the writer's intention to file criminal charges against the judge, to take unspecified action to end the judge's career, and, possibly, to file criminal charges against defendant's wife.

Moreover, the letter does not meet the confidentiality requirement of a privileged communication. To the extent the letter seeks to have a threat conveyed to Judge Todd, or to defendant's wife, the letter cannot be understood to be a communication made in circumstances giving rise to a reasonable expectation that the statements will remain confidential. Further, the letter indicates that the matters discussed therein had already been shared with other people, specifically, with Comar and other personnel at the district attorney's office in Maricopa County, Arizona. *See Tippett*, 733 P.2d at 1193 (communication was not confidential because its contents were known to third parties). In such circumstances, it was unreasonable for defendant to expect that the letter would be kept confidential. *See Wesp*, 33 P.3d at 197 (to be privileged, statements must be made under circumstances giving rise to a reasonable expectation that they will be treated as confidential). Even assuming defendant intended the letter as a "joke," as he later testified at trial, it was unreasonable for him to expect the recipient of the letter to have perceived it as such and kept it confidential.

[6] Finally, even if the letter could be construed as a confidential client communication from defendant to his lawyer, it is not protected by the attorney-client privilege due to the crime-fraud exception.

In *A. v. District Court*, 191 Colo. 10, 22, 550 P.2d 315, 324 (1976), the court held that the attorney-client privilege must give way when the communication with the attorney is made for the purpose of aiding the commission of a future crime or of a present continuing crime. In *Caldwell v. District Court*, 644 P.2d 26, 31

(Colo.1982), the court held that "[a]lthough the exception to the attorney-client privilege created for future illegal activity was at one time limited to criminal activity, it is now well-settled that this exception is also applicable to advice or aid secured in the perpetration of a fraud." (Citation omitted.) Now referred to as the "crime-fraud" exception to the attorney-client privilege, this doctrine has been applied in Colorado and elsewhere to negate the application of the attorney-client privilege to communications with an attorney that seek to further criminal activity or perpetrate a fraud. *See Law Offices of Bernard D. Morley, P.C. v. MacFarlane*, 647 P.2d 1215, 1220 (Colo.1982) (under the "crime-fraud exception," communications between an attorney and client are not privileged if they are made for the purpose of aiding the commission of a future or present continuing crime); *People v. Board*, 656 P.2d 712, 714 (Colo.App.1982) (defendant's attorney allowed to testify against defendant because communication to attorney from defendant pertained to the commission of a crime); *Lahr v. State*, 731 N.E.2d 479, 483–84 (Ind.Ct.App.2000) (attorney permitted to testify as to two forged documents tendered by client with intent they be submitted as evidence in pending criminal case); *State v. Hansen*, 122 Wash.2d 712, 862 P.2d 117, 121–22 (1993) (defendant's statement to his attorney that he was going to get a gun and shoot the judge, prosecutor, and public defender falls under the crime-fraud exception to the attorney-client privilege).

[7] Despite defendant's argument to the contrary, the parties' stipulated facts do not establish the attorney-client privilege, nor do they undermine application of the crime-fraud exception. *See Morley*, 647 P.2d at 1221–22 (party asserting crime-fraud exception has burden of establishing foundation in fact for assertion of ongoing or future criminal conduct). A prima facie showing that the crime-fraud exception applies removes the protection of the attorney-client privilege. *Board*, 656 P.2d at 714. This burden is met by showing facts "adequate to support a good faith belief by a reasonable person that wrongful conduct sufficient to invoke the crime or fraud exception to the attorney-client privilege has occurred." *Caldwell*, 644 P.2d at 33.

While the crime-fraud exception is not yet so refined by Colorado law, other courts have held that it is not enough to show only that the communication is "relevant" evidence of a crime. *See In re Richard Roe, Inc.,*

68 F.3d 38, 40 (2d Cir.1995). Rather, the party seeking to invoke the crime-fraud exception must at least demonstrate probable cause to believe that a crime or fraud has been attempted or committed and that the communication was in furtherance thereof. *Id.*

Evidence that defendant forged Comar's signature, thereby impersonating a peace officer, and criminally impersonated Comar to gain a benefit by deceitfully attempting to influence the judge, demonstrate probable cause to believe that defendant was attempting or committing a crime or fraud and that the letter was in furtherance of those crimes.

Thus, because the letter was not a privileged communication, or was admissible pursuant to the crime-fraud exception, the trial court did not err in denying the pretrial motion to suppress it or in permitting the prosecution to introduce it and Neuhardt to testify about it at trial.

III. Sufficiency of the Evidence

[* * * Omitted]

IV. Preclusion of Expert Testimony

[* * * Omitted]

A. Relevance

To be admissible, evidence must be relevant. CRE 402; *People v. Greenlee,* 200 P.3d 363, 366 (Colo.2009); *People v. French,* 141 P.3d 856, 860 (Colo.App.2005), *vacated and remanded,* 165 P.3d 836 (Colo.App.2007). Evidence is relevant when it has "any tendency to make the existence of any fact that is of consequence to the determination of the action more probable or less probable than it would be without the evidence." CRE 401.

[16] Here, at a pretrial hearing on the prosecutor's motion to exclude the expert's testimony, defense counsel argued that the testimony was admissible because it was relevant to negate the criminal intent element of the charged offenses. More specifically, counsel argued that the testimony might show that defendant had a reasonable expectation that the letter would not be disclosed without his permission, thereby negating his "culpable mental state." The trial court, however, questioned how such testimony could be relevant "without some information or evidence concerning [defendant's] understanding of what his lawyer's duties" were. Defense counsel did not state that defendant would so testify, explaining that the opinion was relevant because

what [Neuhardt] will testify to is that he knew [defendant] was a law student and knew more than the layperson. So I will then be able to present, perhaps without calling [defendant], inferentially, that certainly a law student has a better understanding of what an attorney-client relationship should be and how communications should be handled as opposed to a normal layperson.

Nevertheless, we agree with the trial court's conclusion:

Whether Mr. Neuhardt should or should not have disclosed the defendant's letter does not make it more or less probable that the defendant committed the acts or that he had the required mental state.... Evidence that Mr. Neuhardt violated the Montana [R]ules of [P]rofessional [C]onduct, however, is not relevant to prove what the defendant expected his lawyer would do with the letter.... Evidence concerning the Montana [R]ules of [P]rofessional [C]onduct and their requirement that attorneys maintain client confidences is irrelevant *unless the defense first puts forward evidence that the defendant was familiar with the rules of professional conduct and relied upon them in sending the letter to Mr. Neuhardt.* The fact that the defendant is a Colorado law student is not sufficient to provide a foundation that he would have knowledge of the Montana code of professional conduct or even the Colorado code of professional conduct.... Thus, evidence that Mr. Neuhardt may have violated the Montana [R]ules of [P]rofessional [C]onduct is simply irrelevant to prove any fact of consequence in this case. *Evidence of the client confidentiality requirements of the Montana code of professional conduct is irrelevant without a foundation that the defendant was aware of those requirements and relied upon them in sending the letter.*

(Emphasis added.) *See also People v. Simmons,* 182 Colo. 350, 354–55, 513 P.2d 193, 195–96 (1973) (in vehicular homicide case, trial court properly excluded attorney's testimony for the defense about the victims' pending lawsuit alleging police officers were negligent in pursuing the defendant; testimony was irrelevant to impeach officers' credibility absent an offer of proof that the officers had actual knowledge of the pending lawsuit).

At trial, defendant testified that he expected his lawyer would not give the letter to anybody else or disclose it, claiming, "It's common sense." The defense made no further effort to present the expert opinion.

[17] Expert testimony is admissible when it is useful to the jury. *People v. Shreck,* 22 P.3d 68, 79 (Colo.2001). Usefulness to the jury depends on whether the proffered expert testimony is "relevant to the particular case: whether it 'fits.' Fit demands more than simple relevance; it requires that there be a logical relation between the proffered testimony and the factual issues involved in the litigation." *People v. Martinez,* 74 P.3d 316, 323 (Colo.2003). The admissibility must be evaluated in light of its offered purpose. *Id.*

Here, the purpose of offering the proposed expert testimony to support defendant's assertion of lack of intent to influence a public servant or to defraud does not "fit" absent evidence of defendant's knowledge of or reliance upon the Montana Rules of Professional Conduct. At the time of the pretrial hearing, defendant did not tender evidence of his knowledge and reliance, nor did he advise the court as to whether such evidence would be offered as a foundation at trial. Therefore the proposed expert opinion did not "fit" and was properly excluded by the pretrial ruling.

When defendant later testified at trial as to his expectation that the attorney would not disclose the letter, he did not state that such expectation was based on the Montana Rules of Professional Conduct or any other ethical rule, but simply relied on his "common sense." Moreover, no further effort was made by defendant to proffer the expert testimony. In closing, defendant's counsel argued that Neuhardt had an obligation not to disclose the letter and that defendant believed the letter was confidential. Under such circumstances, there was no error in the exclusion of the proposed expert opinion and no prejudice to defendant.

B. Res Gestae

Given our conclusion that the expert's testimony was not relevant under CRE 401, we necessarily reject defendant's argument that it was admissible as res gestae evidence. *See People v. Skufca,* 176 P.3d 83, 86 (Colo.2008) ("[t]o be admissible, res gestae evidence must also be relevant under CRE 401"); *see also People v. Ramirez,* 155 P.3d 371, 378 (Colo.2007) (to be admissible under CRE 702, expert testimony must be both relevant and reliable).

The judgment is affirmed.

Judge CARPARELLI and Judge MÁRQUEZ* concur.

* Sitting by assignment of the Chief Justice under provisions of Colo. Const. art. VI, § 5(3), and § 24–51–1105, C.R.S.2009.

2011 WL 3861437

United States District Court, D. Colorado.

Denis RYSKAMP, Derivatively on Behalf of
BOULDER GROWTH & INCOME FUND,
Plaintiff,

v.

Joel W. LOONEY, Dean L. Jacobson, Richard I.
Barr, Susan L. Cociora, and John S. Horejsi,
Defendants,

and

Boulder Growth & Income Fund, Inc., Nominal
Defendant.

Civil Action No. 10-cv-00842-WJM-KLM.

|

Sept. 1, 2011.

Attorneys and Law Firms

Jeffrey P. Harris, Brian Thomas Giles, Statman Harris
& Eyrich, LLC, Cincinnati, OH, Kip Brian Shuman,
Rusty Evan Glenn, Shuman Law Firm, The, Boulder,
CO, for Plaintiff.

Christian Heath Hendrickson, Sherman & Howard,
L.L.C., Denver, CO, Joshua G. Hamilton, William F.
Sullivan, Daniel Scott Carlton, Paul Hastings LLP, Los
Angeles, CA, for Defendants.

ORDER ON MOTION TO COMPEL

WILLIAM J. MARTÍNEZ,
District Judge.

THIS MATTER is before the
Court on Plaintiff's Motion
to Compel Production of
Court–Ordered Documents
under Fed.R.Civ.P. 37(a)
("Motion to Compel"), ECF
No. 110, filed on June 13,
2011. For the foregoing rea-
sons, the Motion to Compel is
GRANTED in part and DENIED in part.

> This case seems to be the one defendant's counsel relies on most heavily in his brief. Why did he make that choice? Consider carefully whether you agree with his characterizations of the decision or will portray it differently.

BACKGROUND

This is a shareholder derivative action brought by Denis Ryskamp ("Ryskamp" or "Plaintiff") on behalf of
Boulder Growth and Income Fund, Inc. (the "Fund")
and against the Fund's Board of Directors (the
"Board"): Richard Barr ("Barr"), Susan Ciciora ("Ciciora"), John Horejsi, Dean Jacobson ("Jacobson"),
and Joel Looney ("Looney"), for breach of fiduciary

duty and unjust enrichment. (Am. Compl., ECF No. 11
at ¶ 1.)

The following facts established in the record, unless
otherwise noted, do not appear to be in material dispute. The Fund is a closed-end fund with the stated
objective of concentrating investment in real estate
investment trusts and other registered closed-end income funds. (*Id.* at ¶ 4.) Defendants are members of
the Board. (*Id.* at ¶¶ 5–9.) The Fund is managed by
Boulder Investment Advisers LLC ("BIA") and Stewart
Investment Advisers ("SIA") (collectively the "Advisers"), which are paid a combined fee of 1.25 percent of
the Fund's assets under management. (*Id.* at ¶ 15.)
Stewart Horejsi ("Horejsi"), father to Defendants Ciciora and John Horejsi (collectively the "Interested
Directors"), is an employee and investment manager
for both B IA and S IA. (*Id.* at ¶ 19.)

On February 20, 2008, the Board announced a rights
offering of common stock to existing shareholders. (*Id.*
at ¶ 23.) Shortly after the rights offering was completed
in June 2008, Doliver Capital Advisors, L.P. ("Doliver"), a competing closed-end fund adviser, filed a
Schedule 13–G with the Securities and Exchange Commission ("SEC") announcing that it was the Fund's
largest shareholder, holding 16.9% of the outstanding
stock. (*See id.* at ¶¶ 30–31.) Plaintiff alleges that after
discovering that Doliver was now the Fund's largest
shareholder, the Board and its advisers caused $50 mil-
lion of the $76,166,466.08 raised in the rights offering
to be invested in cash equivalents, increasing assets
under management. (*See id.* at ¶¶ 28, 35, 49.) In November 2008, the Board suspended the Fund's level-rate distribution policy, which eliminated previous-
ly-paid monthly payments to shareholders. (*Id.* at
¶52.)

Plaintiff alleges the level-rate distribution suspension
and investment in cash equivalents caused the Fund's
share price to drop. (*Id.* at ¶ 53.) Simultaneously with
the Board's suspension of distributions, an entity
known as the Ernest Horejsi Trust No. 1B ("EH Trust")
allegedly began purchasing the allegedly artificially
depreciated Fund shares in a bid to regain its control
position. (*Id.* at ¶ 45.) Plaintiff alleges that the Fund's
controlling shareholder is the EH Trust, and that Defendant Ciciora is a trustee of the EH Trust. (*Id.* at
¶14.) Plaintiff also alleges that Defendants Ciciora and
John Horejsi are, among other things, Affiliates (as defined by the Securities Exchange Act of 1934) of the EH
Trust. (*Id.* at ¶¶ 16–20.) According to Plaintiff, the

Board took aggressive action to drive down the share price of the Fund, so the EH Trust could purchase the Fund's stock at artificially reduced prices in order to fight off Doliver's bid for control. (*Id.* at ¶ 50.)

On September 22, 2009, Plaintiff sent the Board a demand letter requesting that the Board institute an action by the Fund against its directors to redress the conduct Plaintiff later alleged in his Amended Complaint. (*Id.* at ¶ 41.) On December 14, 2009, counsel for the Board wrote that a Review Committee had been convened to review Plaintiff's demand. (*Id.* at ¶ 41.) The Review Committee members and the Fund were, and are, represented by Paul, Hastings, Janofsky & Walker LLP ("Paul Hastings"). (Dec. 14 Ltr., ECF No. 34–5 at 2.) Defendants Barr, Jacobson, and Looney (the "Independent Directors") comprise the Review Committee. (ECF No. 11 at ¶ 41.) The Review Committee was granted full authority to act on behalf of the Board. (Jan. 29 Ltr., ECF No. 34–8 at 2.) On January 29, 2010, Paul Hastings issued a letter stating that the Review Committee had investigated Plaintiff's claims and decided not to take legal action. (*Id.* at ¶ 43.) On December 17, 2009, Plaintiff sent a letter requesting information about the Review Committee and the scope of its investigation. (*Id.* at ¶ 42.) On December 22, 2009, the Board refused to provide any of the information requested. (Dec. 22 Ltr., ECF No. 34–7 at 2.)

On February 23, 2010, Plaintiff again requested that the Board provide certain information and documents pertaining to the content, manner and scope of the Review Committee's investigation. (ECF No. 11 at ¶ 82.) The Board again refused to provide any of the requested information. (*Id.*) Plaintiff then brought this action alleging claims for breach of fiduciary duty and unjust enrichment. (*See* Compl., ECF No. 1.)

On June 25, 2010, Defendants filed a Motion to Dismiss pursuant to Rules 8(a), 12(b)(6), and 23.1 of the Federal Rules of Civil Procedure, claiming, *inter alia,* that Plaintiff failed to allege with requisite particularity that the Fund wrongfully refused his demand. (ECF No. 32 at 2.) Plaintiff filed a Motion to Stay Consideration of Defendants' Motion to Dismiss to Allow for Limited Discovery on the Independence and Investigation of the Review Committee ("Motion to Stay Consideration") on July 16, 2010. (ECF No. 38.) On September 14, 2010, Defendants filed Nominal Defendant Boulder Growth and Income Fund, Inc. and the Review Committee Members' Motion to Stay Discov-

ery ("Motion to Stay Discovery") pending a ruling on their Motion to Dismiss. (ECF No. 54.) Plaintiff wanted to proceed with discovery while Defendants wanted to stay discovery. Defendants' Motion to Stay Discovery was granted, and Plaintiff's Motion to Stay Consideration was denied. (Order on Mots. to Stay, ECF No. 61.)

Finding that oral argument would assist the Court in the determination of Defendants' Motion to Dismiss, a hearing was held on April 13, 2011. (Min. Entry for Mtn. Hr'g, ECF No. 84.) Defendants renewed their argument that Plaintiff did not plead with sufficient particularity that demand was wrongfully refused and that the Review Committee failed to act independently. (*See* Order on Mtn. to Dismiss, ECF No. 85 at 5.) The Court, however, found that this lack of factual specificity was due in large part to Defendants' refusal to provide Plaintiff with information and documentation relevant to the Review Committee's independence and the scope and content of its investigation. (*Id.*) The Court denied the Motion to Dismiss without prejudice to being re-filed, and ordered Defendants to provide Plaintiff with initial disclosures required by Fed.R. Civ.P. 26(a)(1)(A) and all information and documents sought in the February 23, 2010 letter from Plaintiff's counsel to Defendants' counsel. (*Id.* at 7–8.)

In response to this Court's Order, Defendants provided Plaintiff with more than 11,000 pages of documents reviewed by the Review Committee, Rule 26(a)(1) Initial Disclosures, the 51–page report of the Review Committee's investigation, and a 25–page privilege log. (ECF No. 127 at 2.) On June 13, 2011, Plaintiff filed a Motion to Compel Production of Court–Ordered Documents Under Fed.R.Civ.P. 37(a), seeking production of those documents withheld by Defendants and set forth in Defendants' privilege log. (ECF No. 107). This matter is now before the Court.

LEGAL STANDARD

"A shareholder derivative suit is governed by the law of the state of incorporation." *Bender v. Schwartz,* 917 A.2d 142, 151 (Md.Ct.Spec.App.2007). The parties agree that the Fund's state of incorporation is Maryland. Under Maryland law, a plaintiff in a derivative action must either make a demand on the board of directors that the corporation bring the suit, or show that demand is excused as futile. *Bender v. Schwartz,* 917 A.2d 142, 152 (Md.Ct.Spec.App.2007), citing *Kamen v. Kemper Fin. Svcs. Inc.,* 500 U.S. 90, 96 (1991);

Waller v. Waller, 187 Md. 185, 192 (1946). After demand is made, the corporation's board of directors must conduct an investigation into the allegations in the demand and determine whether pursuing the demanded action is in the best interests of the corporation. *Bender v. Schwartz*, 917 A.2d at 152. If the board fails to take the action demanded following an investigation, the shareholder may sue on behalf of the corporation. *Id.* The shareholder may defeat a motion to dismiss by showing the board did not act independently or demand was wrongly refused. *Id.*

To determine whether demand was wrongly refused, the court reviews the board's investigation under the business judgment rule, which calls for deference to the board unless the plaintiff can show that the investigation was not conducted independently and in good faith, or that the board's decision was not within the realm of sound business judgment. *Id.* Plaintiff has the burden of setting forth facts to rebut the presumption that the board acted reasonably and in the corporation's best interests. *Aronson v. Lewis*, 473 A.2d 805, 812 (Del.1984). "A stockholder must show more than mere suspicion and must state a claim in particular, rather than conclusory terms." *Bender*, 917 A.2d at 152–53. Plaintiff's pleading burden for establishing wrongful refusal of his demand is higher than that required under Rule 8. *Burns v. Friedli*, 241 F.Supp.2d 519, 525 (D.Md.2003). Rule 23.1 requires a Plaintiff "state with particularity" the facts of the case. Fed.R. Civ.P. 23.1(b)(3).

The Order on Defendants' Motion to Dismiss allowing for limited discovery was intended to provide a clearer picture of whether the Review Committee's investigation into Plaintiff's demand was properly conducted under a reasonable application of the business judgment rule to the facts of this case.

DISCUSSION

This present dispute arises from Defendants' refusal to produce all of the Court-ordered documents referenced above, including records of interviews conducted, e-mail correspondence, "Confidential Memoranda", and other information purportedly relied upon by the Review Committee during its investigation of Plaintiff's claims. Defendants claim that they have properly withheld some of the documents within the description of documents ordered by this Court to be produced on the basis of the attorney-client privilege and application of the work product doctrine. (ECF No. 128.) In his Motion to Compel, Plaintiff argues for the production of all documents withheld by Defendants (ECF No. 107).

I. Attorney–Client Privilege

Plaintiff points out that many of the withheld communications include Horejsi and/or other non-attorney employees of the Fund or the Advisers ("Multi–Party Communications"). As a result, Plaintiff argues the attorney-client privilege does not apply because these communications extend beyond Paul Hastings and its clients, the Fund and the Independent Directors. (ECF No. 107 at 9–10.) Defendants, however, argue these communications are necessary for the purpose of operating the Fund because any advice given by Paul Hastings to the Fund or the Independent Directors must also be communicated to the Advisers and the Interested Directors for the advice to be effectuated. (ECF No. 127 at 10.)[1]

1   Attached to this Order is a Court–Annotated Privilege Log. On this Court–Annotated Privilege Log, each document at issue in the Motion to Compel has been numbered from 1 to 243 to aid in accurately identifying such documents in this Order. As best the Court can determine, Plaintiff here contests the applicability of the attorney-client privilege to the following documents: 1, 2, 11–35, 37–73, 75–108, 111–68, 170–210, 213, 215–22, 224–27, 230–31.

In a diversity matter such as this where the case is based on a state cause of action, state law controls the determination of the attorney-client privilege. *White v. American Airlines, Inc.*, 915 F.2d 1414, 1424 (10th Cir.1990). In Colorado, the attorney-client privilege is "established by the act of a client seeking professional advice from a lawyer and extends only to confidential matters communicated by or to the client in the course of gaining counsel, advice, or direction with respect to the client's rights or obligations." *People v. Tucker*, 232 P.3d 194, 198 (Colo.App.2009) (citing *Losavio v. Dist. Court in and for Tenth Judicial Dist.*, 533 P.2d 32, 35 (Colo.1975)). Communications between attorney and client are protected to "facilitate[ ] the full development of facts essential to proper representation of a client." *Alliance Constr. Solutions, Inc. v. Dep't of Corr.*, 54 P.3d 861, 864 (Colo.2002) (citation omitted). The privilege applies only to communications under circumstances giving rise to a reasonable expectation that the communications will be treated as confidential. *Tucker*, 232 P.3d at 198 (citing *Wesp v. Everson*, 33 P.3d 191, 197 (Colo.2001)). The attorney-client privilege encompasses confidential communications made by the client to an attorney, and communications from the attorney to the client. *Shriver v. Baskin–Robbins Ice Cream Co., Inc.,* 145 F.R.D. 112, 114 (D.Colo.1992) (citing *People v. Tippett,* 733 P.2d 1183 (Colo.1987)).

The application of the attorney-client privilege presents certain problems in the context of a corporation as client. While the attorney-client privilege applies to corporations, a corporation cannot speak directly to its lawyers. *See Upjohn Co. v. United States,* 449 U.S. 383, 390 (1981); *Genova v. Longs Peak Emergency Physicians, P.C.,* 72 P.3d 454, 462 (Colo.App.2003). Because "a corporation can only act through its officers, directors, agents, and employees, ... communications between corporate counsel and company personnel are privileged so long as they concern matters within the scope of the employees' corporate duties." *Shriver,* 145 F.R.D. at 114 (citing *Upjohn,* 449 U.S. at 394–95); *accord Genova,* 72 P.3d at 462. Such privileged communications remain privileged even when a corporate agent shares the communication with another agent charged with acting on such issues. *Genova,* 72 P.3d at 462 (citing *Shriver,* 145 F.R.D. at 114).

In *Alliance Construction Solutions,* the Colorado Supreme Court created a four-part test to determine whether a communication between a corporation's counsel and an officer, director, agent, or employee is privileged: (1) the communication must be with "an employee, agent, or independent contractor with a significant relationship not only to the [corporate] entity but also to the transaction that is the subject of the [corporate] entity's need for legal services"; (2) the entity "must demonstrate that the communication was made for the purpose of seeking or providing legal assistance"; (3) "the entity must show that the subject matter of the communication was within the scope of the duties provided to the entity by its employee, agent, or independent contractor"; and (4) the entity "must show that the communication was treated as confidential and only disseminated to those persons with a specific need to know its contents." *Alliance Constr. Solutions,* 54 P.3d at 869–70.

In *Alliance Construction Solutions,* the court addressed the issue of whether communications between an independent contractor and counsel to a governmental entity were privileged. *Id.* at 867. Following the four-part test, the court found that the independent contractor had a significant relationship to the project at issue and the governmental entity asserting the privilege; the purpose of the communication was to gain or provide legal assistance; the subject matter was within the indepen-

dent contractor's duties; and the communication was shown to have been treated as confidential. *Id.* at 870–71. Therefore, the court held that such communication was privileged. *Id.* at 871.

Here, Plaintiff contests the application of the attorney-client privilege as applied to (1) communications by Paul Hastings or other outside counsel where Horejsi, the Interested Directors, or other non-attorney employees of the Fund were present; (2) communications by and between Paul Hastings and the Adviser Counsel where Horejsi or the Interested Directors are present; (3) communications by and between the Advisers' counsel and/or Horejsi's counsel (Stephen Miller ("Miller") and Joel Terwilliger ("Terwilliger")) (the "Adviser Counsel") and Advisers; and (4) communications where no attorneys were present.[2] (ECF No. 107 at 9.)

2 In his Motion to Compel, Plaintiff also contests Defendants' claim of attorney-client privilege as applied to communications by the Adviser Counsel which were disclosed to the Fund ("Adviser Documents"). (ECF No. 107 at 9.) However, pursuant to the parties' Stipulated Motion for Entry of Second [Proposed] Protective Order Pursuant to Federal Rule of Evidence 502(d), ECF No. 129, and the subsequently-issued protective order, ECF No. 132, Plaintiff has withdrawn its Motion to Compel with respect to these Adviser Counsel Documents.

In determining whether the Multi–Party Communications are protected by the attorney-client privilege, the Court begins by considering the relationship between the parties. In review of the August 2, 2011 Privilege Log ("Aug. 2 Privilege Log"),[3] the Court notes that the individuals participating in the allegedly privileged communications are Fund management, the Fund's compliance officer, the Interested Directors, Horejsi, Adviser portfolio managers, and Adviser Counsel. (Aug. 2 Privilege Log, ECF No. 143-2 .) The Court finds that each of these parties has a significant relationship to the Fund. It cannot be reasonably disputed that the Fund, as an inanimate entity, must act through its agents. *Genova,* 72 P.3d at 462. In this regard, the Fund's management, compliance officer, and all directors, including the Interested Directors, clearly have the duty to act for the Fund. Similarly, the Fund is managed by the Advisers, which serve as independent contractors to the Fund and are necessary for the management of the Fund. Horejsi and other Adviser portfolio managers are responsible for investing the Fund's assets, implementing investment strategy, and managing day-to-day transactions. (Zwickel Decl., ECF No. 127-8 at ¶ 7.) The Adviser portfolio managers were very closely involved with the management and investment decisions of the Fund and the issues involved in this litigation. Similarly, the Advisers Counsel were relied on by the Adviser portfolio managers to ensure regulatory and other compliance issues involving the Fund's investments, they communicated with the Fund's counsel, and were involved in decisions which are the subject of this litigation. (*See Id.* at ¶¶ 6–7.) Accordingly, the relationship between the Fund, Fund management, the Fund's compliance officer, the Interested Directors, Horejsi, Adviser portfolio managers, and Adviser Counsel satisfies the first prong of the *Alliance Construction Solutions* test. 54 P.3d at 869–70.

3 This version of the privilege log was filed with the Court as Exhibit B to Defendants' Response to Plaintiff's Notice of Clarification Re: Documents Produced to Plaintiff Pursuant to a Federal Rule of Evidence 502(d) Protective Order. (ECF No. 143.) This privilege log is updated from the privilege log filed as Exhibit A to Plaintiff's Motion to Compel, and does not include the Adviser Documents recently provided by Defendants following the entry of the Second Protective Order, ECF No. 132.

Second, the Court looks to whether the communications were made for the purpose of seeking or providing legal assistance. *Id.* As the Supreme Court noted in *Upjohn,* corporations "constantly go to lawyers to find out how to obey the law." 449 U.S. at 392 (quotation omitted). Here, a declaration submitted by Paul Hastings counsel indicates that the Fund management, the Fund's compliance officer, the Interested Directors, Horejsi, Adviser portfolio managers, and Adviser Counsel regularly served as contacts for the Fund's counsel, and followed the advice of the Fund's counsel on many of the issues related to the rights offering and investment of the subsequent profits which are at issue in this litigation. (*See* Zwickel Decl., ECF No. 127–8.) The Aug. 2 Privilege Log further indicates that the parties discussed the rights offering compliance issues, SEC Rules, and other compliance issues with the Fund's counsel in managing the Fund. (ECF No. 143-2.)

Further, there are instances on the Aug. 2 Privilege Log where Paul Hastings was not a participant in the communication, but advice given by Paul Hastings was discussed. Colorado courts recognize that "[a]n otherwise privileged communication by a lawyer to a corporate agent does not lose its protected status simply because the agent then conveys the attorney's opinion to corporate management charged with acting on such issues." *Genova,* 72 P.3d at 462. Here, a declaration submitted by Paul Hastings counsel indicates that communications not listing counsel from Paul Hastings or other

attorneys as parties to said communications indeed involved the conveyance of underlying legal communications by Paul Hastings. (Carlton Decl., ECF No. 127–1 at ¶ 13.) The Court notes that the description of such communication on the Aug. 2 Privilege Log clearly indicates that the parties were discussing legal advice provided by Paul Hastings. Because the parties associated with the contested communications are each charged with the management of the Fund, the Court finds that communications regarding legal advice provided by Paul Hastings to an agent or officer within the scope of corporate duties does not destroy the communication's protected status. The Court further finds that those communications either directly with Paul Hastings or which discussed advice given by Paul Hastings[4] regarding the rights offering and related compliance issues satisfy the second prong of the *Alliance Construction Solutions* test.[5]

4 As noted on the Aug. 2 Privilege Log, ECF No. 143–2.

5 As best the Court can determine, with regard to the second step of the Alliance Construction Solutions test, the Court finds that the following contested documents contain a description giving rise to a prima facie claim of attorney-client privilege: 1, 2, 11–35, 37–73, 75–87, 111, 115–19, 121–22, 124, 136–42, 144–68, 170–74, 177–210, 213, 215–22, 224–27, 230–31.

Third, the Court looks to whether the subject matter of the communication was within the scope of the duties provided to the entity by its agents. *Alliance Construction Solution,* 54 P.3d at 869–70. As discussed above, the Fund management, the Fund's compliance officer, the Interested Directors, Horejsi, Adviser portfolio managers, and Adviser Counsel are all tasked with ensuring that their management of the Fund complies with the law. This regulatory compliance with respect to the rights offering and subsequent investment of the profits was the topic of conversation for many of the communications between Paul Hastings and the parties at issue, as well as between the parties at issue in discussion amongst each other regarding advice from Paul Hastings.[6] Thus, the third prong of the *Alliance Construction Solutions* test is satisfied. 54 P.3d at 869–70.

6 The following documents appear to be subject to attorney-client privilege under the Alliance Construction Solutions test: 1, 2, 11–35, 37–73, 75–87, 111, 115–19, 121–22, 124, 136–42, 144–68, 170–74, 177–210, 213, 215–22, 224–27, 230–31.

Finally, the Court looks to whether the communications were treated as confidential. Through declaration, Defendants' counsel indicates that counsel understood the Fund management, the Fund's compliance officer, the Interested Directors, Horejsi, Adviser portfolio managers, and Adviser Counsel served as representatives of the Fund for purposes of communicating facts necessary to provide competent legal assistance. (Zwickel Decl., ECF No. 127–8 at ¶ 8.) Counsel stated that such communications were made with an expectation of confidentiality and that those communications would remain subject to the attorney-client privilege. (*Id.* at ¶ 7.) Further, and most importantly on this point, the Court does not have evidence to the contrary. Therefore, the fourth prong of the *Alliance Construction Solutions* test is satisfied. 54 P.3d at 869–70.

Accordingly, with respect to the Multi–Party Communications here contested by Plaintiff, the Court finds the attorney-client privilege applies to these communications despite the inclusion of the Fund management, the Fund's compliance officer, the Interested Directors, Horejsi, Adviser portfolio managers and Adviser Counsel in these communications. The Court thus finds that the following communications are protected by the attorney-client privilege and their production to Plaintiff will not be compelled: 1, 2, 11–35, 37–73, 75–87, 111, 115–19, 121–22, 124, 136–42, 144–68, 170–74, 177–210, 213, 215–22, 224–27, 230–31.

A. Common Interest Doctrine

[* * * Omitted]

B. Crime–Fraud Exception

Plaintiff argues that while the attorney-client privilege may apply, certain documents are not protected based on the crime-fraud exception. (ECF No. 107 at 10.) Plaintiff alleges that Horejsi, as an adviser to the Fund, manipulated the timing of the rights offering so that he could use his insider knowledge to make a personal profit at shareholder expense. (*Id.*) Further, Plaintiff alleges that the Adviser Counsel assisted in this alleged fraud. (*Id.*) Plaintiff asks the Court to compel production of all communications dated October 2007 through June 2008 where Horejsi is a participant and the description of the communication relates to either rights offering compliance or share sale compliance. (*Id.*)[9]

9   As best the Court can determine, in this regard Plaintiff is requesting the Court compel documents 206, 208, 213, 215–217, 219–221, 225–227.

Defendants argue that Plaintiff lacks probable cause on which to base his claims. (ECF No. 127 at 18.) Defendants allege that all of the Fund's stockholders acquired and disposed of the Fund's stock during the 2007 and 2008 rights offerings, and that there is no evidence that Horejsi traded his securities on the basis of material, nonpublic information. (*Id.*)

In Colorado, the attorney-client privilege gives way when the communications between a client and attorney are made for the purpose of aiding the commission of a future crime or a present continuing crime. *A. v. Dist. Court of Second Judicial Dist.*, 550 P.2d 315, 324 (Colo.1976) (citation omitted). This limitation was extended to cases involving civil fraud in *Caldwell v. District Court in and for City & County of Denver*, 644 P.2d 26 (Colo.1982) and is now known as the "crime-fraud" exception to the attorney-client and work product privileges.

Application of the crime-fraud exception requires "a prima facie showing that the exception applies to each document before the document is actually stripped of its privilege and admitted into evidence." *A. v. Dist. Court*, 550 P.2d at 326. To invoke the exception, the party opposing the privilege has the burden to present a prima facie showing of "facts 'adequate to support a good faith belief by a reasonable person that wrongful conduct sufficient to invoke the crime or fraud exception to the attorney-client privilege has occurred.'" *People v. Tucker*, 232 P.3d 194, 199 (Colo.App.2009) (quoting *Caldwell*, 644 P.2d at 33); *see also Wesp*, 33 P.3d at 200 n. 16 ("[t]he party asserting that the privilege is pierced by the crime-fraud exception must make a prima facie showing that provides a foundation in fact for the assertion of ongoing or future criminal conduct."). Thus, the movant "must at least demonstrate probable cause to believe that a crime or fraud has been attempted or committed and that the communication was in furtherance thereof." *Tucker*, 232 P.3d at 200 (citing *In re Richard Roe*, 68 F.3d 38, 40 (2d Cir.1995)).

In *Tucker,* the court held that where the defendant admitted to forging a district attorney's signature and where there was evidence that the defendant impersonated the district attorney to gain a benefit by deceitfully attempting to influence a judge in a criminal case, there was probable cause to believe defendant was attempting to commit or committing a crime or fraud. *Tucker*, 232 P.3d at 200. In *Tara Woods,* however, the court held there was not probable cause to believe defendant was attempting to commit or committing a crime or fraud where the plaintiff relied on mere conclusory allegations. *Tara Woods Limited Partnership v. Fannie Mae*, No. 09–cv–00832–MSK–MEH, 2010 WL 3322709, at *3 (D.Colo. Aug. 19, 2010).

Here, Plaintiff's allegations provide facts, which if true, would cause a reasonable person to believe wrongful conduct has occurred. Plaintiff alleges a pattern whereby Fund Advisor Horejsi communicated with his personal attorney and Adviser Counsel Miller and with Adviser Counsel Terwilliger to manipulate the timing of rights offerings in order to allow Horejsi affiliates to sell Fund shares in advance of the 2008 rights offering at a premium price, purchase a greater number of Fund shares at net asset value during the rights offering, then resell the shares again at a premium price following the rights offering. (*See* Harris Decl., ECF No. 135–1 at ¶ 6.)

Plaintiff further alleges that Horejsi communicated with Miller and Terwilliger in order to have inside knowledge of and control over the timing of the 2008 rights offering. (*Id.*) These allegations are supported in considerable detail by communications already in Plaintiff's possession indicating that Horejsi and Terwilliger were attempting to manipulate the date of the rights offering for Horejsi's maximum benefit. (BIF008194, BIF010816, ECF No. 107–3.) Moreover, it is undisputed that Horejsi, as an Adviser, profits from management of the Fund's assets, and his children are members of the Board. The motivation for Horejsi to act in the manner alleged by Plaintiff is thus amply present. Finally, while the current complaint does not directly assert a claim of fraud against Defendants, following the limited discovery ordered by the Court on April 15, 2011, Plaintiff has indicated an intent to file a second amended complaint to include a claim sounding in fraud against one or more Defendants. (ECF No. 135 at 10.)

Because Plaintiff's allegations are supported in the record through information from initial disclosures and through counsel declaration, the Court finds that Plaintiff has met his burden in demonstrating "probable cause to believe that a crime has been attempted or committed" necessary to invoke the crime-fraud exception to the attorney-client, common interest, and work product privileges. *See, e.g., Tucker,* 232 P.3d at 200. The Court therefore orders that the following documents be produced to Plaintiff: 206, 208, 213, 215–217, 219–221, 225–227.

C. Fiduciary Exception

[* * * Omitted]

CONCLUSION

For the foregoing reasons, it is hereby ORDERED that Plaintiff's Motion to Compel, ECF No. 107, is GRANTED in part, DENIED in part, and HELD IN ABEYANCE in part as follows:

1) Plaintiff's Motion to Compel with regard to documents excluded from the attorney-client privilege pursuant to the crime-fraud exception is GRANTED. Defendants shall produce to Plaintiff all such documents in their entirety;

2) Plaintiff's Motion to Compel with regard to the Interview Memoranda is HELD IN ABEYANCE. Defendants shall produce to Chambers, on or before September 7, 2011, unredacted copies of the Interview Memoranda which remain in dispute as discussed in Part II above; and

3) Plaintiff's Motion to Compel with regard to all other documents listed on the Aug. 2 Privilege Log is DENIED.

Understand the Problem

The legal questions in this case arise in one of the pretrial motions defense attorneys frequently file to keep potentially harmful evidence from being used against their clients at trial. These types of motions are very common. They often have multiple purposes: for example, here the goals may be to limit the evidence shown eventually at trial while simultaneously seeking significant advantage that could force the prosecutor to negotiate a favorable plea bargain.

If defense counsel wins this motion there may be little to no evidence to prosecute Eng. Even the possibility of losing the motion might therefore be enough to induce a prosecutor to offer a generous plea agreement before the judge's ruling rather than risk losing. That last possibility is especially likely if, as would seem probable to an experienced criminal defense attorney, the DA's ultimate goal was primarily to secure Eng's cooperation against others who worked at DJT Medical Group.

Both prosecutors and criminal defense attorneys typically carry heavy caseloads, as do the judges who oversee the cases. It is not surprising, then, that the supporting papers for these motions may be fairly standardized and brief. That does not mean that your argument must be formulaic, of course—only that you would be wise to remember the adage that generally the lower you are in the court system, the shorter and more to-the-point your submissions should be.

Think Strategically About the Motion

What will make the judge decide in your favor?

Judges must follow the law. Tautologically, that means that what will make your side win this motion is having the better legal argument. "Better" can mean a lot of things, though, and often the strongest advocacy takes into account that judges are human, and will probably prefer outcomes that feel satisfyingly correct.

Experienced practitioners know wherever there is room for judges' interpretation, there is also an opportunity to try to convince the judge to *want* to rule in your client's favor. No one wants judges to be biased by their own emotions. Yet scholars of law and emotion[1] point out that denying that emotion plays *any* role in legal decision-making is not only overly mechanical, it is also inaccurate. Most judges expect their determinations to make not just legal sense but common sense. Thus, providing legal analysis that ruling in your favor would be legally "correct" is crucial, but showing the judge that such a decision would be "right" also helps your case.

Some lawyers go about this in ways that are pretty transparent. They may try to make their clients look like the good guys, or try to make their opponents seem like the bad guys. Sometimes such approaches to generating sympathy on the facts, even if clumsy, work. But direct appeals to compassion are not the only ways to influence the court. Advocates can also use broader policy concerns or methods of understanding and interpreting law to help persuade the judge to find a particular outcome both legally justified and correct. For example, an advocate might suggest that ruling against their position could create a dangerous slippery slope, or would in some other way generate bad law.

None of these tactics will succeed if the law and the facts do not support your client's position. And most often, persuasive techniques are more convincing when deployed with a soft touch rather than a heavy hammer. Strategic advocates use every tool at their disposal to present their legal analysis both accurately *and* persuasively. Can you find some instances where Mr. Hemet is doing that in his brief?

---

1. E.g., Susan Bandes and Terry Morony, each of whom has written extensively on the topic of emotion in law.

Read the Law Carefully

What does the statute protect?

Even if you had never heard of attorney-client privilege before tackling this problem (which seems unlikely) you should be able to sense that it is pretty important and broadly construed just by reading the Colorado rule.

The statute says on its face that there are certain relationships in which "it is the policy of the law to encourage confidence and preserve it inviolate." That's pretty strong stuff. Laws do not always include explicit policy objectives. Even fewer employ words like "inviolate" that carry a whiff of the sacrosanct. These rhetorical choices suggest the topic is an important one to the lawmakers who drafted it, which might in turn imply that courts will interpret it generously.

The substantive provisions of the rule are pretty definitive as well. "An attorney *shall* not be examined …" does not offer the kind of situational wiggle room that the word "may" would provide.[2] Observe too that a plain reading of the statute would suggest a purpose of protecting clients—the protection is automatically in place but the client may consent to waiving it. Compare that to the lawyer, who is given no such option.

The statute's wording suggests the protection is afforded expansively as well. It applies to "*any communication* made by the client" in the course of employing a lawyer's "professional services." Not much room for hedging there.

Is all of this what you see when you read C.R.S.A. § 13-90-107? If some of these points were not visible to you as you read the statute, there may be more you can do to develop your skills in critically reading legal materials. The point is not that you can (or should) pick up every single thing a lawyer or law student would need to know about this privilege just by carefully reviewing the statutory language.[3] But as we have noted repeatedly, an important part of developing your analytical skills in law is learning how lawyers read text. Keep aiming to find what your mentors and professors see in legal materials before they point it out. If more experienced practitioners make inferences you overlooked, go back to the text and try to figure out where they are getting them from. (And whether you agree with them.)

What communications does Colorado exclude from privilege under the crime-fraud exception?

The Colorado statute we've examined only sets out the attorney-client privilege. It does not specify any exceptions. We certainly know there *are* exceptions, however, so for those rules we will need to look to the case law. But the three cases you have read do not seem to provide a single standardized articulation of the crime-fraud exception. (Question to consider: are there meaningful differences in the phrasing of the rule, or is each court essentially stating the rule substantially similarly in the absence of set and routinely agreed-upon language? Both happen in law, and the answer matters enormously to determine how you will understand and apply the rule in your case.)

---

2. Most lawyers believe that "shall" unambiguously means "must." Legal linguistic expert Bryan A. Garner (editor of BLACK'S LAW DICTIONARY) has suggested that the word "shall" sows confusion and promotes litigation, and he encourages writers to avoid it. According to the 2010 Federal Plain Language Guidelines, to indicate that a rule is truly mandatory drafters of statutes should only use the word "must." However, many statutes, regulations and other legal rules using "shall" nevertheless remain, and courts do still generally treat the word as if it creates a binding obligation.

3. Moreover, you may have already known more about this area of the law than a quick read of the statute would have gleaned. Perhaps you studied the attorney-client privilege in an Evidence class, or were simply familiar with the concept from your general knowledge. Your time in law school should also have taught you that just reading the statute would not be enough to fully understand its nuances; you would also want to see how it is understood and used in case law.

An astute reader of law should see that both the attorney-client privilege and the crime-fraud exception emerged from the general corpus of common law, which means that even persuasive authority is likely to be helpful in understanding the Colorado rule. Still, when the language is inexact, it will certainly be preferable to rely on inside-the-jurisdiction statements of the rule. This suggests leaning most heavily on the explanation of the crime-fraud exception in *People v. Tucker* and *Ryskamp v. Looney* rather than *In re Richard Roe*.[4] Those cases formulate the crime-fraud exception as pertaining to communications with the attorney **made for the purpose of aiding the commission of a future crime or of a present continuing crime.** So this is probably the language you should adopt to state the rule.

> Note that this does not automatically mean you will have to rely heavily on Ryskamp just because opposing counsel seems to. Do not make the mistake of non-lawyers or legal novices and assume opposing legal arguments will always mirror one another ("Did not!" "Did too!"). That is often not how it works at all—good lawyers on different sides of a problem can frame their positions by focusing on different sources of authority, or by emphasizing dissimilar points.

> Quick—try sketching a timeline showing which kinds of communications are protected by attorney-client privilege and which may not be. You do not have to be an artist, or even especially visually oriented, for this kind of illustrative representation to be useful to you. (Learning research suggests that it may actually be more valuable to try this if graphic images are not your preferred way of comprehending information.) But if you struggle to create a timeline at all, it is possible that you do not yet fully understand the rule. If so, keep on it!

But for your case, what does that actually mean? Let's assume for the moment the district attorney can prove DJT Medical Group engaged in a conspiracy to illegally distribute narcotics, and Darrell Eng actively and knowingly participated in that conspiracy. If Mr. Eng's emails to his attorney concerned only his *past* involvement in these crimes, then the rule is clear: attorney-client privilege exists for the exact purpose of protecting his ability to communicate with his lawyer to prepare an effective defense for the case against him. Naturally, that is precisely the argument Mr. Hemet's motion brief appears to be making (not that he concedes that DJT was actually a criminal enterprise or that Eng was knowingly involved in illegal activity; those facts are for the People to prove at trial).

To succeed in this motion you will have to convincingly argue that the emails were seeking to aid a future crime, or to continue an ongoing one, or both. And that's possible given your facts. So how, exactly, will you explain and support that position?

Frame Strong Legal Arguments

Virtually every law school in the country offers both introductory and advanced writing courses that drill down expertly into particular practices of effective legal writing. This text focuses more narrowly on the skills of legal reasoning, so the craft of writing persuasively is adjacent to our project but does not have exactly the same goals. Still, legal analysis is the core of effective writing in law, and it never hurts to consider how it is constructed.

Look closely at how opposing counsel fashioned his arguments

Mr. Hemet's brief in this case may not be perfect, but it is pretty solid. It is worth taking some time to deconstruct a few of the things he has done. We examine some of these choices because it always helps to see how a clever tactician can try to make every decision advantageous. Note, too, that the more subtle the choices are the more likely they may be to unconsciously affect the reader.

---

4. *Ryskamp* was decided by federal court sitting in diversity jurisdiction, so it would not be final authority on Colorado law—that power is reserved to the courts of the state. Therefore if there were conflicting interpretations of the privilege, the state courts' version would supersede. But in this instance Tucker and Ryskamp seem to state the rules congruently. Most advocates might have at least a small preference for relying on the most directly-controlling in state cases, but Ryskamp can also be seen as a reliable source of law.

1. Organization and structure

Hemet's large-scale organization uses the first two points to position his facts favorably. In Point I he characterizes Eng's emails as being about the employment termination. If his depiction is persuasive, even before we get to the actual arguments this signal helps portray the case as *not* being about an ongoing or future criminal endeavor. But of course to portray the emails this way Hemet makes the choice to obscure (ignore, really) Eng's request for assistance in setting up his own business to compete with DJT. Is that omission successful? Is it wise?

In Point II the brief situates the email conversation as part of an ongoing representation. Just by making this a separate point heading Mr. Hemet made a smart decision. First, that choice means there are two points explaining why the attorney-client privilege applies and only one raising and refuting the counterpoint. That construction subliminally reinforces the idea that the points in the defense's favor outnumber and outweigh those on the People's side. It also permits Hemet to use two short, direct and, most important, *readable* point headings: one to emphasize the purpose of the email chain and represent it as seeking employment advice, and another to suggest an uninterrupted ongoing lawyer-client bond. (By the way—we have few facts either way, but based on what we do know do you think it is necessarily true that the Eng's relationship with his attorney was a continuing one, or could he have been seeking to reopen a connection to his counsel in an earlier matter?)

2. Attention to detail

Mr. Hemet's Argument opens with two paragraphs characterizing the attorney-client privilege as a vital and historically important one. Since this introduction is posed as a short general introductory background it can get away without including a point heading. Should it have had one nonetheless? Well, one major advantage of a well-crafted point heading is that it allows the writer to succinctly frame a thesis. But a disadvantage is that a law-trained reader is probably well acquainted that purpose. To lawyers and judges reading briefs, point headings sort of automatically *feel* argumentative. Omitting one here suggests that what follows is inarguable foundational background that everyone would agree upon. That implication is entirely consistent with the perception of the privilege Mr. Hemet wants to encourage.

Look, too, at how Mr. Hemet constructed Point I of his argument. His contention is that the emails were purely seeking legal advice about the employment termination.[5] This section of the Argument has an IRAC-like structure; it describes what Hemet says is the rule from *Ryskamp*, and then moves ever more specifically into applying that version of the rule to his client's situation. Hemet devotes his entire last paragraph in this short section to the lawyer's subject line in her email. Why? Likely it is because he wants to add factual support to his argument. The subject line in the client's initial email simply forwarded the one from the employer, so that is of no help. But in response the attorney went to the trouble to *change* the subject line rather than just to hit the "reply" button. Hemet clearly believes that the change supports his idea that the consultation was seeking legal advice regarding termination. That may be a lot of weight to place on one small change. Perhaps it will not work. But finding and using small details favorably is precisely how lawyers develop facts to support their cases.

> Did you see all of these things when you read defense counsel's brief? If not, then Hemet probably accomplished what he set out to do. Chances are, he wanted these decisions to appear natural and unnoticeable.
>
> But if you strive to become skilled at recognizing how good lawyers refine the presentation of their cases, you will improve your own ability to do so yourself.

Mr. Hemet has also paid attention to how he positions the law. In the second paragraph of Point III of his Argument, notice how he uses two cases, *In re Richard Roe* and *Tucker*. *Richard Roe* is probably most helpful to his position, but it is not binding in his jurisdiction.

---

5. Is he right? In part, certainly, but Eng does seem to have been asking about something else, too.

Hemet takes pains to show that *Tucker* adopted its standards for Colorado. He also describes the holding of the case in an explanatory parenthetical rather than in the text of the paragraph. Why would he do that? We can only speculate, but Argument text tends to seem like . . . argument, whereas citations give an impression of neutrality and authority. So assuming the characterization of the case in its citation is reasonably accurate, including the parenthetical can be an effective way to make the description of the holding feel more unassailable.

Not all advocates would make the same choices Hemet does in drafting this brief. Perhaps you would have made different decisions than he did in these examples. The point here is not that Hemet was always brilliant. Instead, and more important, it's that if you carefully and critically identify the kinds of small determinations that help lawyers frame effective arguments you will have more tools at your disposal for your own legal analysis.

Put together your own narrative

Technically you are crafting a reply brief to defendant's motion. It may be tempting and easy, then, to respond directly to defense counsel's points. But reacting point-by-point is usually a mistake. You will generally be the most persuasive when you have a coherently developed narrative of your own position: one that can stand on its own irrespective of defendant's points. As Steven D. Clark puts in in *Writing to Win* (2d ed. 2012), "[t]he more attention you pay to answering the allegations of the other side, the less you will devote to making your own case." *Id.* at 147.

In addition to being pithy, good arguments are those presented calmly and without a demanding or argumentative tone. As Stark notes: "the more you call attention to the fact that you're advocating, the more you lose credibility in the eyes of the court." *Id.* at 149. In other words, your aim is to convince the court that your *position* is especially strong, rather than your argument.

So what *is* your position? Defense counsel's story is that this case involves a routine legal consultation about employment law that is protected by attorney-client privilege. Is that the DA's understanding of what happened? Probably not, so make sure that you do not inadvertently support their version of events. Rather than adopting a purely "no, that's not right!" posture, explain the rules of law and the facts of the case in ways that seamlessly support your viewpoint. One option might be to begin by focusing on the purpose of the crime-fraud exception and why it has always coexisted and been an important part of the privilege itself. Next you could look closely at the emails to suggest that there was some criminal purpose in the communication itself. Yet this is merely an example of one possible way to come at the narrative. There are undoubtedly others.

No matter how you tell your client's story, please always remember: once you have positioned the rule and facts as favorably as you (credibly) can, the explanation part of your legal analysis equation will always be easier.

Explain Analysis Persuasively

Fiction writers are constantly exhorted to "show, don't tell." What people giving this advice mean is that stories work better when they convey information, attitudes, and character though their own actions, feelings, or dialogue rather than by narrative exposition.[6] It feels more natural that way; it allows readers to believe they have formed their own conclusions rather than being told what to think, and it therefore draws the reader into the story. In other words, showing rather than telling *persuades* the reader to believe that the story and characters are somehow more real. As members of

---

6. The genesis of the phrase is usually attributed to classic playwright Anton Chekov, who is reputed to have said "don't tell me the moon is shining; show me the glint of light on broken glass."

professions deeply invested in persuasion, law students and lawyers can draw a great deal from this advice.

Lawyers' professional and ethical obligations (and just maybe our sometimes argumentative natures) usually require us to be more direct than fiction writers. We must both show *and* tell.

If legal analysis equals rules, applied to facts, carefully explained, then **show** how each of those steps works. Don't just recite a rule. State it accurately, then explain what it is, where it comes from, and why it is the way it is. Help the reader know not just what the rule says, but what you (from your advocate's viewpoint) understand it to mean. Don't just **tell** the reader what the outcome is when the rule is applied to your facts. Lead the reader step-by-step through the application of the rule to each specific factual detail to show the reader why your legal argument is correct. This is why the explanation part of legal analysis is so crucial—it's where the real work of a legal argument is done.

> An astute reader should notice immediately that this case appears to be about civil claims between two private parties. In contrast to the case file assignment, then, the setting suggests that the issues at hand may apply the "fraud" part of the crime-fraud exception. Would that change how the rule operates or not?
>
> Is this something you picked up on as you were reading? If so, terrific. If not, work more on critically questioning what you read. One way to do that might be to practice reading sample exam questions with several of your classmates and each writing down 3–4 things that you observed as you read through the fact pattern. Compare what each of you wrote with a goal of helping everyone in your group improve their ability to read questions carefully.

Your ultimate goal is to explain your side's reasoning so carefully and methodically that it feels to your reader not just correct, but incontrovertible and inevitable.

Now, Transfer What You've Done to a Law School Setting

Once again, we switch gears and address related issues under the crime-fraud exception in a sample law school essay exam question.

Sample exam question

Essay – 40 minutes

Buchanan Management Corp. ("Buchanan") filed a civil suit against Raul Dawkins, Jr. ("Dawkins"). Buchanan's multiple causes of action, including fraudulent misrepresentation, fraudulent inducement, breach of contract and unjust enrichment, stemmed from the company's contention that Dawkins had misrepresented a commitment to hire Buchanan to manage the golf course at the Lee Valley Country Club that Dawkins was preparing to purchase at auction. Buchanan alleged that Dawkins made false promises to offer an extended management contract to Buchanan in an effort both to have Buchanan assist in initially setting up the golf course and to block Buchanan from purchasing the Club itself.

Buchanan charges that Dawkins, with help from his lawyers at the Law Firm of Hooper & Vinnick, was secretly recruiting a different golf course management company while simultaneously reassuring Buchanan that it would be contracted to manage the golf course once the purchase was completed. Buchanan alleged it did not learn until months later that someone else, Jasper White, would be hired to manage the course. This information came out only after Buchanan ended its own efforts to purchase the Club, sold its nearby lot to Dawkins at a discount, and began the initial steps of organizing the management of Dawkins's golf course after Dawkins purchased the Club.

Neither party disputes that throughout the period in which Dawkins was negotiating for the purchase of the Club, his attorneys at Hooper & Vinnick were in regular communication with

Jasper White. Buchanan contends that it is entitled to discover the contents of that communication because the crime-fraud exception to attorney-client privilege applies.

What will Buchanan need to show in order to be successful in its requests for discovery of correspondence between Hooper & Vinnick and Jasper White?

Attacking the exam question

Important advice for critically reading exam questions: always look *very carefully* at what the call of the question is asking.[7] In this question the use of specific character names may make it seem at first glance that the required analysis is very fact-specific. But do you see that the question essentially just asks the test-taker to explain the crime-fraud exception, and to backfill those explanations by showing how it would operate in this particular case? In other words, this test provides what beginning law students often expect to encounter on law school exams but rarely find: an opportunity to straightforwardly explain what they know about the law they have studied.

So a good law student who has diligently prepared for this test should find it easy, right? Perhaps, but not necessarily. First, not all students will carefully read or understand what the question is asking, so some may approach their responses is non-optimal ways. Even more likely, though, is the fact that it is not always easy to do especially well in law school on simpler or more straightforward exams.

Uncomplicated questions provide more opportunity, hence more obligation, to be exacting and nuanced in your analysis. Students who do well will produce responses that may not differ enormously from those of their classmates, but do everything just a little more carefully or with a little more detail. Practice providing that level of excellence on this kind of clear-cut question, and then use those skills to add the same thoughtfulness even where the questions are more demanding.

Sample answer with commentary

Below is an example that could be a reasonably high-scoring student response. The sample is far from perfect but it is typical of what a strong law student might be able to complete in the short time given for the problem.

Student Answer

To be successful in Buchanan's request for discovery of correspondence between Hooper & Vinnick ("Hooper") and Jasper White ("White"), Buchanan needs to show first that Jasper White's correspondence was with his attorneys and then that the crime-fraud exception applies.

First, attorney-client privilege applies to communications between an attorney and a client regarding the client's legal rights and obligations.

Here, White and Hooper were in regular communication, so any emails or written correspondence could be subject to attorney-client privilege if that communication pertains to the management of the golf course, and White and Hooper have an attorney-client relationship.

Importantly, attorney-client privilege applies to communications made between an attorney and a client. So, Buchanan would have to establish that White was a client of the firm. From the facts, it seems

> This text keeps emphasizing that a hallmark of good legal reasoning is careful explanation of rules applied to fact. But good judgment in doing that work matters, too. Is anyone really challenging the existence of a protected attorney-client relationship between Dawkins and his lawyers here? Since the answer seems to be no, the writer might have been wiser to move more expeditiously into analyzing the applicability of the crime-fraud exception.

---

7. The "call of the question" is usually thought of as the part actually asking you something specific with respect to the fact pattern. It is usually the final phrase or sentence of an essay question or the last part before the answer options in a multiple-choice question. But beware and read carefully; sometimes it comes at the beginning or is mixed into the provided facts.

as though Dawkins is the client and Hooper was retained to assist in negotiating the purchase of the golf club. Buchanan would have to point to facts that support an attorney-client relationship between White and Hooper, such as a retainer agreement or contract. Buchanan could also attempt to establish that White intended to seek legal advice from Hooper, and that Hooper, acting in an official legal capacity, counseled White regarding his legal rights as manager of the golf club. For example, Buchanan could depose White and the attorneys from Hooper to determine whether White thought Hooper represented him and whether Hooper counseled White, thus establishing an attorney-client relationship.

If Buchanan can establish an attorney-client relationship existed between White and Hooper, then he must next show that the communications between White and Hooper were in furtherance of an intent to defraud Buchanan.

The crime-fraud exception is a narrow exception that applies to communications between an attorney and a client, where the client intends to commit a crime, and the communications are in furtherance of a crime. In contrast, communications that are merely relevant to a crime is insufficient to strip communications of attorney-client privilege. Furthermore, the party seeking to prove crime-fraud exception must present evidence to support a reasonable belief that the communications were in furtherance of a fraudulent plan.

> Why is the exception "narrow"? Many law students avoid referencing policy at all when analyzing exam fact patterns, or at most they may tack some policy point on to the end of an essay after the "real" legal analysis has been done. That is a mistake. Considering policy and the purpose of legal rules is an important part of good legal reasoning. If the reader were told here that the exception is narrowly drawn because of the historic importance placed on protecting attorney-client relationships, but not when they are used as a smokescreen for immoral or illegal schemes, it would actually be much easier for the test-taker to explain which kinds of conduct were and were not protected.

Here, Buchanan would have to show that White intended to defraud Buchanan and that the communications with Hooper were in furtherance of that scheme. The facts show that Dawkins was making the false promises. So, if Buchanan can show that Dawkins and White planned to defraud Buchanan together, then Buchanan can establish that White intended to defraud Buchanan. For example, Buchanan could request texts, email, and other written communication between White and Dawkins to establish that they conspired to defraud Buchanan.

> Nothing is incorrect, but so far the paper is a little thin in explaining the rule. It would be helpful for the writer to spell out that in at least some jurisdictions "in furtherance" means more than just related to a crime or fraud—the communications(s) must actually be assisting an ongoing or planned future crime/scheme. And explaining why the crime or fraud had to be concurrent or future rather than past would show that the writer truly grasped both the attorney-client privilege and this particular exception. These small additions could well be the difference between earning a perfectly fine grade and an excellent one.

Next, Buchanan would have to show that the correspondence between White and Hooper was in furtherance of that crime. That would be a difficult standard to prove because the communications have to be more than relevant. Here, Buchanan would have to show that White's communications with Hooper were used to misrepresent and defraud Buchanan. For example, if White communicated with Dawkins that he learned from his lawyer that lying to someone about a management contract to induce them to act would be difficult to prove, then perhaps Buchanan could argue that White's communications with Hooper were used to further a crime.

Learn From Your Work

Why? No, but really—*why*?

In my experience teaching, I find that virtually every time I point to something a law student has written or said and ask "Why?" or "How do you know?" I get back better and better explanations. It is always impressive to see what students can come up with in response to just a little prodding, but it is frustrating, too. What if they had included all of those excellent ideas and explanations the first time around?

The student-writer of our sample exam above seems to have absorbed this lesson reasonably well for a novice. There are many examples of the "why" being explained and developed, and these make the analysis stronger. There could be more, or perhaps some better decisions about which points to explain in what depth, but the impulse is there. Under the tight 40-minute time limit given for the assignment, what is included here isn't too bad. Re-read the sample answer and find some points either where the author is answering "why" pretty well, or where you think more would be helpful.

Next, look at a few paragraphs of some of your own legal analysis. After every sentence as yourself "Why?" And when you answer that question, ask "Why?" again. And keep going until you really cannot think of anything more to add. Completing this exercise will help you see what more *you already know but did not think to say*, which can then be added in to strengthen your legal analysis.

Now, go include it the first time around. Every time.

Evidence Project Checklist

Read your own drafts while looking carefully for each point raised below. If the points are included, please make sure that they are presented and explained to the best of your ability. If they are not, then consider whether your analysis can be made more complete.

1. Where does your analysis establish what attorney-client privilege is, and that it has a crime-fraud exception?

2. Do you identify for the reader what the purpose of the privilege is, and why fraudulent or criminal schemes do not further that purpose?

3. Where does the analysis explain that the exception applies to only those allegedly criminal or fraudulent schemes that are presently ongoing or contemplated for the future at the time the communications take place, and does not apply to events that have already taken place?

4. If you are arguing that the crime-fraud exception applies, where does your explanation of the applicable rules of law make clear:

    a. That the otherwise-privileged communications in question must have been "in furtherance" of a contemplated or continuing criminal/fraudulent scheme;

    b. What "in furtherance" legally consists of?

5. If you are arguing that the crime-fraud exception applies, where does your explanation of the applicable rules of law make clear:

    a. What subject matter Mr. Eng's and his lawyer's emails concerned;

    b. How we know that this was the subject matter;

    c. Why those communications may be considered part of a current or planned crime?

6. Are specific points in the emails or in their larger factual contexts examined and used to support your Argument's contentions?

7. Are alternative interpretations of the purpose of the emails refuted either directly or indirectly?

8. Is every thought sufficiently completed and developed such that there is no room for any further development in response to a "Why?" prompt?

9. Does the organization of your Argument fit its reasoning? Does it follow the traditional logic of applying rules of law to the facts at hand?

10. Is the discussion clearly presented? Will it be persuasive to readers?

11. Was the analysis proofread, with technical errors and awkwardness eliminated?

Chapter 6

Professional Role Problem

Assignment: *Draft an Affidavit and Explanatory Memo*

Based on the materials in the file please draft both an affidavit for your client to be submitted in opposition to the motion to dismiss, and a very brief cover email to your boss explaining the applicable legal standard and why the affidavit you have crafted is helpful in constructing an effective narrative to defeat defendant's motion. Target length for the two documents is fewer than 1200 words (excluding caption and signature), with the affidavit likely taking up somewhere around 40–60 percent of the word count.

Analytical Skills to Focus On

✓ Extract material facts

✓ Use legal authority

✓ Understand and craft legal documents

✓ Frame legal issues strategically

Case File

Put simply, an affidavit is a statement of specific facts attested to by someone with sufficient personal knowledge to confirm their veracity. It is generally sworn to and notarized, and may therefore be treated as testimony subject to penalties for perjury. Affidavits are frequently used to provide facts a court can use when deciding motions, particularly before or during the earliest stages of discovery when a full factual record has not yet been developed.

The materials in the case file are given to you in one complete set so that you will have them all together. As you read through the materials, ask yourself:

1. What exactly is the rule in question about when attorney-client relationships are terminated, and how does the rule operate? (Also, not central to the problem but worth thinking about—why does Ohio have such a short statute of limitations for legal malpractice suits, and who does that protect?)

2. What is the relationship between Kaliman's two plans of attack:

   a. not time barred as a matter of law; and

   b. time of severing the attorney-client relationship is a factual question?

Are there any points in which the two claims are inconsistent or incompatible?

3. What do each of the documents in the case file contribute?

4 Are there any materials *not* here that you would want to review to better understand your case? If this were an actual case, how would you work to build the evidence you need? Are there ways to work around what you do not know?

A project checklist is included at the end of the chapter. Use it to review and edit your drafts.

· ·

Chapter 6 Case File

Your exercise packet contains the following:

- Notes from your supervising attorney
- Transcription of client interview
- Affidavit in Support of Motion to Dismiss from opposing counsel
- Relevant Ohio statute
- Relevant Model Rule for attorneys' professional conduct
- Relevant cases to use in your analysis

Thinking about Lawyer's Responsibilities

Law students are usually required to take a course in Professional Responsibility or Legal Ethics. Is there a difference between the two? In substance, courses with either name (or any similar variation) are likely to cover the same body of rules and obligations that govern licensed law practice. And in both titles the modifiers are particularly important: these classes teach students about their legal responsibilities as professional *lawyers*, and the rules regarding ethical requirements in the *legal* profession. Neither moniker denotes a class truly about excellent or moral conduct as an attorney. Why is that? In part it is regulatory—accredited U.S. law schools mush teach the code of conduct for forbidden and permissible behavior of lawyers, and licensed attorneys must take and pass a national examination on the subject (MPRE).

But every good lawyer knows that the Model Rules of Professional Conduct (and the Code of Judicial Conduct for judges) define minimum conduct required or allowed. The rules certainly exhort lawyers to aim higher, but they do not impose professional discipline when we meet only the basic standards.

Odds are good, though, that your professors want more from you. They want you to be both legally ethical and morally principled. And they hope you will make every effort to excel every day you practice law. That explains why your PR/LE class probably covers more than just the bare minimum rules, and similarly why this Chapter asks you to combine rules of professional conduct with strategic considerations of effective lawyering.

· ·

134 Bridge Street
Akron, Ohio 44308
330-231-9800
www.KalimanFirm.com

Kaliman Law Firm, LLP

Memo

To:	Associate
From:	P. Kaliman
Re:	Foster case
Date:	August 13, 20_____

☒ Assignment   ☐ Please Comment   ☒ Time Sensitive   ☐ Urgent

We represent the widow in *Foster v. Wallace*. I am working on response papers to defendant Wallace's motion to dismiss, and I need you to draft the client affidavit in support.

Foster lost her husband several years ago in a car accident. To compound her tragedy, Foster was forced to sue the husband's life insurance company to collect on his policy (we did not represent her in that case). Gerald Zimet died in a one-vehicle crash when his car hit a highway overpass while traveling an estimated 65 mph on a two-lane highway zoned for 50. The automobile was totaled on impact and badly burned, making it difficult to gather evidence from the incident. Zimet was a 61-year-old manufacturing executive in good health. He had recently been indicted for embezzlement from his company. He was covered for $2,000,000 in life insurance from Cincinnati Fidelity, with a triple indemnity for accidental death. The insurance company contended Zimet's death was a suicide and refused to pay more than the face value of the policy.

Foster sued Cincinnati Fidelity for breach of contract, with the assistance of her counsel Joya Wallace. That case was referred to pre-trial mediation where Wallace advised Foster that the circumstantial evidence for suicide was overwhelming. Wallace told Foster that she would be exceedingly unlikely to collect more than the $2 million if the case went to trial, and that if she did not settle the case she would likely face significant delay and expensive accrued legal fees, probably to no avail. Based on that advice Foster took the insurance company's offer of $2.25 million dollars.

> The stakes here are high for both sides—almost $4 million in triple indemnity payments!
>
> Note to ponder: Law students from economically disadvantaged backgrounds are sometimes uncomfortable with the wealth at stake in many of the cases they encounter. It is certainly not true that only prosperous people use the American legal system, though there are genuine critiques about opportunities for meaningful access to justice. But litigation is very expensive. Is it any surprise that it may pursued especially vigorously by both sides when there is a great deal of money involved?

> Whether Ms. Wallace's advice was so off-base that it could be considered malpractice will be an important issue if this case goes to trial. (Remember too that for Foster to succeed, Wallace's recommendations must have been worse than simply mistaken; they must have failed to meet the ordinary standard of care expected of a licensed attorney.) But does the quality of Wallace's advice actually matter for the narrower procedural question at issue for the moment?

At the conclusion of the mediation session Foster signed a memorandum of settlement in full satisfaction and release of all claims against Cincinnati Fidelity. The settlement memorandum referenced the filing of a voluntary dismissal with prejudice of the lawsuit. Nine days later Foster went to Wallace's office to sign a release form that the insurance company had prepared. Wallace then mailed an original of the release to the Clerk of the Court for filing. A formal court order of order of dismissal with prejudice was entered into the record two days after that.

Sometime after the case ended Foster read up on the difficulty of proving suicide in ambiguous car crashes. She learned that uncertainty about causes and motivations in one-car crashes is actually quite common, and that researchers suspected many "asleep at the wheel" cases were probably suicides. But theorizing and proving are two different things, she found out, and one difficulty investigators have encountered in studying this phenomenon is the absence of definitive proof either way. Thus for good reason, Foster now believes the burden of proving suicide would have been a hard one for the insurance company to meet, and that her lawyer's advocacy on her behalf fell short of the standards required under our state's ethical rules. She instituted a complaint with the bar association (currently stayed pending resolution of this litigation) and has retained us to bring a claim against Wallace for the $3.75 million difference in life insurance recovery.

Knowing the Ohio statute of limitations on malpractice actions is a *very* short one year, we immediately commenced this suit against Wallace. Unfortunately, even with our haste the complaint ended up being filed a year and six days after the preliminary settlement was agreed to in mediation. Nonetheless we believe our case is timely because it was commenced less than a year after the signing and filing of the final release and dismissal of the lawsuit against Cincinnati Fidelity.

Wallace has moved to dismiss our case as time-barred. I plan to respond by arguing that as a matter of law it is not, or in the alternative that the date of termination for Wallace and Foster's attorney-client relationship is a factual question to be resolved at trial.[1] I'm working on my brief now, but meanwhile would like you to very quickly prepare:

1. An affidavit for the client to support our response to the motion to dismiss. This can be based on the transcription from my client interview; attached.

2. A cover email with just a couple of paragraphs explaining the legal rule in Ohio for determining when an attorney/client relationship is considered terminated, and therefore why you drafted the affidavit as you did (this will be helpful both to explain your reasoning to me and to double-check my own legal analysis as I prepare the brief).

Thank you.

PK

---

1. I'm toying with adding a third contention based on Ohio's "discovery rule" tolling statutes of limitation until an injury is discovered, which arguably wasn't until the client consulted with us. I don't really think that claim would add much, though. The lawyer's pessimism about the case was made clear at the time of the settlement, and the only really new information here is that we think Wallace's judgment was terrible.

Kaliman Law Firm, LLP

Internal transcript
Attorney work product

Facts

File:	Foster v. Wallace
Present:	PK; client Karen Foster
Duration:	0:25:05
Date:	07/27/__
Transcriber:	Suzanna Choi

Kaliman: Good morning Ms. Wallace. After the traffic snarl last time I hope you were able to get here easily today?

Foster: It was fine, thanks.

Kaliman: And would you like any coffee or pop?

Foster: No thank you. I'm fine. Just tired.

Kaliman: Ok then, I'll try to be brief. You don't mind if I record this today? The questions I'm asking could be crucial so I want to make sure to get the details down exactly right.

Foster: Okay.

Kaliman: All right then. So as I explained when we first met, there is a very short statute of limitations in Ohio for malpractice cases. If we are past the one year time period then that's it, game over even if your case is very strong and you would have—should have—won. That's why we were in such a hurry to file right away once you came in. As I predicted, the defendant is arguing that we've passed the time limit and has asked the court to dismiss the case….

Foster: But we can win that, right?!

Kaliman: Well I said that if we acted right away then we would have a reasonable argument that the time had not run, and I still believe that. As I mentioned initially, I do think this malpractice case won't be easy. If we win this motion to dismiss we'll still have a tough road ahead. But at the moment our concern is surviving this motion. If we do, then Wallace's malpractice insurer may encourage her to try to settle with us.

Foster: Yes. What do you need to know?

Kaliman: Why don't we start with you telling me again what happened on the day of the mediation?

Foster: Well we talked for hours, sometimes with the insurance company and sometimes just us with the mediator…

> Professionalism side note: this would be a difficult conversation to have with any client, let alone one who is grieving a lost spouse while trying to plan for her financial future. Kaliman wants to give Ms. Foster some hope, but not overpromise the likelihood of success. Do you think this statement strikes the right balance?

Internal transcript
Attorney work product

Kaliman: I'm sorry, I meant just at the end when you signed the agreement. What did your lawyer say that it meant?

Foster: She explained that since the case was over the insurance company would cut the settlement check right away, and I could expect it in about a month or so.

Kaliman: [Jumping in] Wait, sorry, did she actually *say* that the case was over?

Foster: I don't remember exactly. We were certainly talking like it was done. Or at least about to be finished. That's why they were willing to prepare the check.

> Q: Why does Kaliman seem especially excited about clarifying this point? How could Foster's answer affect the legal analysis in the motion to dismiss?

Kaliman: What happened that made you believe the case was, as you say, "about to be finished" rather than fully completed?

Foster: I guess because I hadn't been paid.

Kaliman: Of course. Was there anything else?

Foster: My lawyer said I would still have to come back to her office in a few more days to sign some papers.

Kaliman: Can you remember anything specific that she said about those papers?

Foster: That in a week or so the insurance company would send something for me to sign. And that as soon as I did, they would begin the process of cutting the check for the payment. I remember asking about the timing because I planned to pay for my daughter's graduate school tuition, and the bill for fall was about to come in.

Kaliman: Thanks. Now with respect to the memorandum of settlement you signed on that day, what did your lawyer tell you it would do to the case?

Foster: She said it would settle it "favorably" to me. Since she convinced me that I couldn't get the full amount at trial, and I was worn down, I agreed.

Kaliman: Did she at any point tell you that her representation of you was concluded?

Foster: No.

Kaliman: Say that you were no longer her client?

Foster: No, nothing like that.

Kaliman: Did she ever give you anything in writing to indicate your professional relationship with her had come to an end?

Foster: No.

> Professionalism side note: can you see that the attorney started off asking more general and less leading inquiries, and is now beginning to follow up with more directed questions? Lawyers call starting broad and open-ended and then refining more specifically "funneling." It helps provide an undirected vision of the client's overall impressions, while allowing the lawyer to home in on the key legal questions she needs to explore further.

Kaliman Law Firm, LLP

Internal transcript
Attorney work product

Kaliman: Then let's look at what happened when you went to her office on June 14. What did you understand to be the purpose of that visit?

Foster: To sign the final paperwork to wrap up the case. I think she may have even used those words: "wrap up."

Kaliman: What did you think that meant?

Foster: Well I understood that the insurance company wasn't going to issue payment on Gerald's policy until I signed their paper, so I guess I thought that this was a formality needed to settle the case in a final way.

Kaliman: Can you recall anything in particular your lawyer said or did that caused you to believe that?

Foster: Not really; sorry, it was just the general environment.

Kaliman: Okay then. Was there ever a time in that June 14th meeting in which Ms. Wallace indicated that she was no longer acting as your attorney?

Foster: Not at all! I thought what she was doing was finishing everything up with the case.

Kaliman: Can you recall what either of you said when you parted that day?

Foster: She said she had to send copies of the paper I'd just signed to the court and back to the insurance company, and that then they would send my check. I still thought she had been on my side in the case so I thanked her for her work. That was it.

Kaliman: I think this is all I need. Thank you. Is there anything else about when the lawsuit ended that you are aware of that I haven't asked about?

Foster: I can't think of anything.

Kaliman: Ok I appreciate your time. We'll get to work on responding to their motion to dismiss. As I said before, I cannot promise that we will win this. It's a tricky question but I believe we have a decent shot. If so then we will be able to proceed toward trial or settlement negotiations. Either way we should know pretty quickly, so at least you won't be left hanging for a long time.

Foster: Thank you.

Common Pleas Court   Index No. 245
Summit County, Ohio

Karen Foster

                    Plaintiff,

          V.

Joya Wallace, Esq.

                    Defendant.

State of Ohio
Summit County

AFFIDAVIT

Joya N. Wallace, an attorney licensed to practice law in the state of Ohio, and being duly sworn, under penalty of perjury hereby deposes and says:

1. I am a principal partner of Wallace & Phelps, a law office located at 56 Pine Way, Akron, Ohio. I am the defendant in the above-captioned proceeding.

2. In my professional capacity, I provided legal counsel to Karen Foster in her lawsuit against Cincinnati Fidelity Insurance Co. (hereinafter "Fidelity") seeking to enforce a life insurance policy held by her deceased husband Gerald Zimet.

3. Upon Ms. Foster's instructions I commenced suit on her behalf against Fidelity on October 4, 20__.

4. On June 5, 20__ I assisted Ms. Foster in court-mandated mediation with Fidelity.

5. At the conclusion of the June 5, 20__ mediation session the case was fruitfully resolved. The parties both signed a memorandum of agreement which included a release of all legal claims (annexed hereto as Exhibit A).

6. On June 5, 20__ I informed my client Ms. Foster that the case was successful and had been fully concluded. I asked her to come to my office in a few days for the paperwork in the case.

> Notice the effect here of Ms. Wallace's word choice: calling the case "settled" at the in the mediation session might have been clearer or more precise. But the word "resolved" has a distinct connotation of finality that a settlement does not necessarily convey—at least not to anyone with significant experience in civil litigation.

7. I met with Ms. Foster only once more after that settlement, on June 14, 20__, which was for the sole purpose of having Ms. Foster initial and sign the release form sent by Fidelity.

Whether or not Wallace made mistakes in advising Ms. Foster, it seems clear that she can be a skilled lawyer. Look carefully at the two sentences in this paragraph of the affidavit. They could have each been given their own numbered paragraphs (indeed that might have been the more technically correct choice). But Wallace has a reason for connecting the two sentences and presenting them as one thought. Do you see why she did so?

8. After the release form was signed I sent it to the Clerk of the Court, and kept a copy for my files. Upon information and belief the dismissal with prejudice was formally entered on June 16, 20__.

9. Because I fully believed my representation of Ms. Foster to have been concluded, I considered my June 14th actions in providing the release to my former client and in mailing it to the court to be conducted in fulfillment of my ongoing obligations as an officer of the court.

Joya N. Wallace, Esq.

Sworn to and subscribed before me
on this 7th day of July, 20__.

NOTARY PUBLIC

R.C. § 2305.11

2305.11 Time limitations for bringing certain actions

Effective: March 14, 2017

(A) An action for libel, slander, malicious prosecution, or false imprisonment, an action for malpractice other than an action upon a medical, dental, optometric, or chiropractic claim, or an action upon a statute for a penalty or forfeiture shall be commenced within one year after the cause of action accrued, provided that an action by an employee for the payment of unpaid minimum wages, unpaid overtime compensation, or liquidated damages by reason of the non-payment of minimum wages or overtime compensation shall be commenced within two years after the cause of action accrued.

(B) A civil action for unlawful abortion pursuant to section 2919.12 of the Revised Code, a civil action authorized by division (H) of section 2317.56 of the Revised Code, a civil action pursuant to division (B) of section 2307.52 of the Revised Code for terminating or attempting to terminate a human pregnancy after viability in violation of division (A) of section 2919.17 of the Revised Code, and a civil action for terminating or attempting to terminate a human pregnancy of a pain-capable unborn child in violation of division (E) of section 2919.201 of the Revised Code shall be commenced within one year after the performance or inducement of the abortion or within one year after the attempt to perform or induce the abortion in violation of division (A) of section 2919.17 of the Revised Code or division (E) of section 2919.201 of the Revised Code.

(C) As used in this section, "medical claim," "dental claim," "optometric claim," and "chiropractic claim" have the same meanings as in section 2305.113 of the Revised Code.

Ann. Mod. Rules Prof. Cond. § 1.16

Annotated Model Rules of Professional Conduct, Eighth Edition | 2015

American Bar Association

Ellen J. Bennett, Elizabeth J. Cohen & Helen W. Gunnarsson, Center for Professional Responsibility

Copyright © 2015 by the American Bar Association

CLIENT-LAWYER RELATIONSHIP

Declining or Terminating Representation

(a) Except as stated in paragraph (c), a lawyer shall not represent a client or, where representation has commenced, shall withdraw from the representation of a client if:

(1) the representation will result in violation of the Rules of Professional Conduct or other law;

(2) the lawyer's physical or mental condition materially impairs the lawyer's ability to represent the client; or

(3) the lawyer is discharged.

(b) Except as stated in paragraph (c), a lawyer may withdraw from representing a client if:

(1) withdrawal can be accomplished without material adverse effect on the interests of the client;

(2) the client persists in a course of action involving the lawyer's services that the lawyer reasonably believes is criminal or fraudulent;

(3) the client has used the lawyer's services to perpetrate a crime or fraud;

(4) the client insists upon taking action that the lawyer considers repugnant or with which the lawyer has a fundamental disagreement;

(5) the client fails substantially to fulfill an obligation to the lawyer regarding the lawyer's services and has been given reasonable warning that the lawyer will withdraw unless the obligation is fulfilled;

(6) the representation will result in an unreasonable financial burden on the lawyer or has been rendered unreasonably difficult by the client; or

(7) other good cause for withdrawal exists.

(c) A lawyer must comply with applicable law requiring notice to or permission of a tribunal when terminating a representation. When ordered to do so by a tribunal, a lawyer shall continue representation notwithstanding good cause for terminating the representation.

(d) Upon termination of representation, a lawyer shall take steps to the extent reasonably practicable to protect a client's interests, such as giving reasonable notice to the client, allowing time for employment of other counsel, surrendering papers and property to which the client is entitled and refunding any advance payment of fee or expense that has not been earned or incurred. The lawyer may retain papers relating to the client to the extent permitted by other law.

COMMENT

[1] A lawyer should not accept representation in a matter unless it can be performed competently, promptly, without improper conflict of interest and to completion. Ordinarily, a representation in a matter is completed when the agreed-upon assistance has been concluded. See Rules 1.2(c) and 6.5. See also Rule 1.3, Comment [4].

Mandatory Withdrawal

[2] A lawyer ordinarily must decline or withdraw from representation if the client demands that the lawyer engage in conduct that is illegal or violates the Rules of Professional Conduct or other law. The lawyer is not obliged to decline or withdraw simply because the client suggests such a course of conduct; a client may make such a suggestion in the hope that a lawyer will not be constrained by a professional obligation.

[3] When a lawyer has been appointed to represent a client, withdrawal ordinarily requires approval of the appointing authority. See also Rule 6.2. Similarly, court approval or notice to the court is often required by applicable law before a lawyer withdraws from pending litigation. Difficulty may be encountered if withdrawal is based on the client's demand that the

lawyer engage in unprofessional conduct. The court may request an explanation for the withdrawal, while the lawyer may be bound to keep confidential the facts that would constitute such an explanation. The lawyer's statement that professional considerations require termination of the representation ordinarily should be accepted as sufficient. Lawyers should be mindful of their obligations to both clients and the court under Rules 1.6 and 3.3.

Discharge

[4] A client has a right to discharge a lawyer at any time, with or without cause, subject to liability for payment for the lawyer's services. Where future dispute about the withdrawal may be anticipated, it may be advisable to prepare a written statement reciting the circumstances.

[5] Whether a client can discharge appointed counsel may depend on applicable law. A client seeking to do so should be given a full explanation of the consequences. These consequences may include a decision by the appointing authority that appointment of successor counsel is unjustified, thus requiring self-representation by the client.

[6] If the client has severely diminished capacity, the client may lack the legal capacity to discharge the lawyer, and in any event the discharge may be seriously adverse to the client's interests. The lawyer should make special effort to help the client consider the consequences and may take reasonably necessary protective action as provided in Rule 1.14.

Optional Withdrawal

[7] A lawyer may withdraw from representation in some circumstances. The lawyer has the option to withdraw if it can be accomplished without material adverse effect on the client's interests. Withdrawal is also justified if the client persists in a course of action that the lawyer reasonably believes is criminal or fraudulent, for a lawyer is not required to be associated with such conduct even if the lawyer does not further it. Withdrawal is also permitted if the lawyer's services were misused in the past even if that would materially prejudice the client. The lawyer may also withdraw where the client insists on taking action that the lawyer considers repugnant or with which the lawyer has a fundamental disagreement.

[8] A lawyer may withdraw if the client refuses to abide by the terms of an agreement relating to the representation, such as an agreement concerning fees or court costs or an agreement limiting the objectives of the representation.

Assisting the Client upon Withdrawal

[9] Even if the lawyer has been unfairly discharged by the client, a lawyer must take all reasonable steps to mitigate the consequences to the client. The lawyer may retain papers as security for a fee only to the extent permitted by law. See Rule 1.15.

Definitional Cross-References

"Fraud" and "Fraudulent" *See* Rule 1.0(d)

"Reasonable" *See* Rule 1.0(h)

"Reasonably believes" *See* Rule 1.0(i)

"Tribunal" *See* Rule 1.0(m)

State Rules Comparison

http://ambar.org/MRPCStateCharts

<u>ANNOTATION</u>

OVERVIEW

Rule 1.16 addresses the circumstances under which a lawyer must or may decline or withdraw from a representation, and sets out the lawyer's obligations upon termination of the representation. A lawyer should not undertake representation unless it can be performed competently, promptly, and without conflict of interest. Cmt. [1]. Once a lawyer agrees to represent a client, the duties of competence (Rule 1.1) and diligence (Rule 1.3) imply an obligation to continue the representation through completion.

When withdrawing from the representation, the lawyer should take steps to protect the client's interests. If the matter is before a tribunal, the lawyer must comply with applicable legal procedures and must continue the representation if the tribunal so orders. Even after the representation ceases the lawyer retains certain obligations, including the duty to return documents and unearned fees, as well as the duties of confidentiality and loyalty. *See generally* Rule 1.9 (Duties to Former Clients).

[* * * *Annotations on Paragraphs (a)-(c) omitted*]

Paragraph (d): Duties upon Termination of Representation

DUTY TO PROTECT CLIENT'S INTEREST

Paragraph (d) provides that upon termination of representation a lawyer must take reasonable steps to protect the client's interest, such as giving reasonable notice, allowing time for employment of other counsel, surrendering papers and property to which the client is entitled, and refunding any advance payments of unearned fees or unincurred expenses. *See, e.g., In re Mitchell*, 727 A.2d 308 (D.C. 1999) (lawyer failed to advise client that firm filed for bankruptcy and client's retainer--deposited in firm's general expense account-- became property of bankruptcy estate); *In re Soderberg*, 316 P.3d 762 (Kan. 2014) (lawyer withdrew without correcting deficiencies in qualified domestic relations order she prepared at end of divorce proceedings); *In re Disciplinary Action against Samborski*, 644 N.W.2d 402 (Minn. 2002) (lawyer failed to take any action to protect clients' interests after termination); *In re Quintana*, 29 P.3d 527 (N.M. 2001) (suspension from practice of law involuntarily terminates representation; it does not extinguish lawyer's responsibility to protect client interests); *Hawkins v. Comm'n for Lawyer Discipline*, 988 S.W.2d 927 (Tex. App. 1999) (appointed counsel defied court order to continue representation of criminal defendant and failed to protect client's interest in process); *In re Disciplinary Proceedings against Baehr*, 639 N.W.2d 708 (Wis. 2002) (while serving disciplinary suspension, lawyer failed to forward clients' court-issued notices or respond to calls); *cf.* N.C. Ethics Op. 2007–8 (2007) (usually "the act of withdrawal is a professional obligation of the lawyer, for the benefit of the lawyer" and so cost must be borne by lawyer). *See generally* Meegan B. Nelson, *When Clients Become "Ex-Clients": The Duties Owed After Discharge*, 26 J. Legal Prof. 233 (2001–2002).

• Reasonable Notice

A lawyer must give a client reasonable notice before withdrawing from the representation. *See, e.g., In re Trickey*, 46 P.3d 554 (Kan. 2002) (failure to notify client in time to secure other counsel); *Att'y Grievance Comm'n v. Pinno*, 85 A.3d 159 (Md. 2014) (abandonment of clients without notice and failure to return unearned fees); *In re Coleman*, 295 S.W.3d 857 (Mo. 2009) (failure to notify client of motions to withdraw from three cases); *Cleveland Metro. Bar Ass'n v. Fonda*, 7 N.E.3d 1164 (Ohio 2014) (failure to advise client of intent to withdraw notwithstanding client's clear belief lawyer would continue representation); *State ex rel. Okla. Bar Ass'n v. Wagener*, 48 P.3d 771 (Okla. 2002) (failure to notify client of withdrawal from case or provide client with information enabling him to protect his interests); *In re Conduct of Paulson*, 216 P.3d 859 (Or. 2009) (failure to inform client of disciplinary suspension until few days before scheduled trial); *Eureste v. Comm'n for Lawyer Discipline*, 76 S.W.3d 184 (Tex. App. 2002) (failure to notify client of plan to withdraw or that office being closed); Ariz. Ethics Op. 01–08 (2001) (lawyer who lost communication with client may withdraw, but must give client written notice of withdrawal and mail notice to "all known addresses as well as all addresses which may be discovered by the lawyer through the exercise of reasonable diligence"); Va. Ethics Op. 1817 (2005) (criminal defense lawyer whose error caused dismissal of appeal must, before attempting to withdraw, inform client of error and conflict it creates and offer to help client pursue other relief); *see also In re Burton*, 442 B.R. 421 (Bankr. W.D.N.C. 2009) (bankruptcy lawyer's retainer agreement included improper provision allowing lawyer to withdraw without notice if periodic fees not paid).

* * *

This section of the Model Rules of Professional Conduct is supposed to address the termination of lawyer-client relationships. Does it tell you very much about what actually needs to happen for that relationship to be concluded? If not, why not? And what does your answer reveal about the nature of these rules, and about what authority a court will look to for the *Foster* case?

failure to notify/inform

121 Ohio App.3d 221
Court of Appeals of Ohio,
Eighth District, Cuyahoga County.
WOZNIAK, Appellant,

v.

TONIDANDEL et al., Appellees.*

Nos. 70110, 70633.

|

Decided June 9, 1997.

Attorneys and Law Firms

John J. Mueller, Cincinnati, for appellant.

Mark O'Neill, Cleveland, for appellees.

Opinion

KARPINSKI, Judge.

Plaintiff-appellant, Thomas J. Wozniak, appeals from the judgment of the trial court in favor of defendant-appellee, Ronald Tonidandel. Plaintiff brought a legal malpractice claim against defendant as a result of defendant's representation of plaintiff in the litigation surrounding the administration of the estate of plaintiff's mother. The trial court granted defendant's motion for summary judgment because plaintiff had filed his complaint outside the applicable statute of limitations for a legal malpractice claim. On appeal, plaintiff argues that the trial court erred by (1) using the wrong date to determine the termination of the attorney-client relationship, (2) denying plaintiff's motion to compel discovery, and (3) denying plaintiff's motion for relief from judgment. For the reasons that follow, we find no merit to plaintiff's arguments and affirm the judgment of the court below.

Plaintiff was sued by his brother, who alleged that plaintiff had misappropriated assets from their mother's estate. After a trial, the jury found that both brothers were guilty of embezzlement and concealment. Plaintiff appealed and the court of appeals affirmed the judgment. *Wozniak v. Wozniak* (1993), 90 Ohio App.3d 400, 629 N.E.2d 500.

Prior to the probate trial, plaintiff fired his previous attorney and hired defendant, who was referred to plaintiff by another attorney. They first met on July 29, 1992, one week before the case was scheduled to go to trial. On July 30, 1992, defendant sent plaintiff a letter confirming that plaintiff had hired him. The letter stated as follows:

"In accordance with our discussions, we are writing to confirm our understanding. You wish to retain this office to be your counsel and represent you in the trial of the pending suit by your brother against you in the Probate Court of Summit County."

Plaintiff signed and returned this letter. Defendant states in his affidavit that "[m]y engagement was to serve as counsel during the trial. I did not agree to represent Tom Wozniak for anything following the trial. The engagement letter of July 30, 1992 and the amendment of August 2, 1992 speak expressly in terms of the trial of the action."

Trial was postponed until November 4, 1992. After eight days of trial, the jury rendered its verdict on November 16, 1992. In his affidavit, defendant further states that after the verdict was announced, "I told Tom Wozniak in the courtroom that my firm's engagement was over. We had agreed to represent him in the trial. The trial was behind us. I told him that I would do no further work." Thereafter, on November 24, 1992, defendant sent a letter to plaintiff which stated as follows:

"As you know, this office's engagement was to represent you at the recently concluded jury trial in the above case.

"This will confirm our discussion following the trial that we are not responsible for any post-trial procedures which you might desire, such as a motion for new trial, motion for judgment notwithstanding the verdict, notice of appeal or any other possible procedures, and we do not intend to do any such procedures.

"For your information, the deadline for filing motions for new trial and/or judgment notwithstanding the verdict is fourteen days after entry of judgment.

> **Professionalism side note:** this quotation of the retainer agreement suggests the case may turn on the specifics of the lawyer's promises in the retainer agreement with the client. We do not have a copy of any retainer our client signed with Wallace. Seeing this in the case law, a proactive attorney should probably request a copy of any retainer agreement in a Request for Documents sent to defendant Wallace as part of discovery in this case.
>
> Meanwhile, the question for you analytically is how this decision may be analogized or distinguished when compared to the facts in our case.

As you know, the deadline for filing a notice of appeal is thirty days after entry of judgment.

"In accordance with your telephone discussion with Debbie Kackley, we are advising plaintiff's counsel that we are not authorized to approve the judgment. You can check the court's docket to see when the judgment is entered."

On December 14, 1992, plaintiff, acting *pro se,* filed a motion for judgment notwithstanding the verdict and a motion for a new trial. These motions were denied by the probate court.

Subsequent to these motions, defendant filed a motion to withdraw as counsel. On December 21, 1992, the trial court journalized the order granting defendant's motion to withdraw.

Thereafter, on December 3, 1993, plaintiff filed the instant legal malpractice case against defendant. After defendant filed his motion for summary judgment on June 1, 1994, plaintiff voluntarily dismissed the case on June 30, 1994. Plaintiff refiled the complaint on June 28, 1995. Again, on September 8, 1995, defendant moved for summary judgment, arguing that the claim was barred by the statute of limitations and that plaintiff did not present any expert testimony to support his claim. The trial court granted defendant's motion and stated that plaintiff failed to bring the action within the one-year statute of limitations for legal malpractice claims. Plaintiff timely appeals and raises three assignments of error.

I. The first assignment of error has four issues:

Issue 1. "Whether the failure of the trial court, in malpractice actions, to point to an affirmative act by either the attorney or client that signals the end of the relationship, clear [sic] and unambiguously, precludes granting summary judgment on grounds of the statute of limitations in malpractice actions?

Issue 2. "Whether the trial court's grant of summary judgment was error due to the existence of several genuine issues of material facts as to whether or not the action was time barred?

Issue 3. "Whether the trial court's grant of summary judgment was error as a matter of law where local rule requires permission of trial court to withdraw?

Issue 4. "Whether the trial court's granting of summary judgment was barred by the doctrine of equitable estoppel, where the defendant advised the plaintiff that permission of the court was required to withdraw?"

In this assignment, plaintiff argues that the trial court erred in granting summary judgment for defendant on statute of limitations grounds. We disagree.

The standard for summary judgment is as follows:

"Before summary judgment may be granted, it must be determined that (1) no genuine issue as to any material fact remains to be litigated, (2) the moving party is entitled to judgment as a matter of law, and (3) it appears from the evidence that reasonable minds can come to but one conclusion, and viewing such evidence most strongly in favor of the nonmoving party, that conclusion is adverse to the party against whom the motion for summary judgment is made. *Temple v. Wean United, Inc.* (1977), 50 Ohio St.2d 317, 327, 4 O.O.3d 466, 472, 364 N.E.2d 267, 274." *Mootispaw v. Eckstein* (1996), 76 Ohio St.3d 383, 385, 667 N.E.2d 1197, 1199.

Under R.C. 2305.11(A), a legal malpractice claim must be brought within one year from the time the cause of action accrues. The Ohio Supreme Court summarized the law governing the commencement of the statute of limitations in the syllabus of *Zimmie v. Calfee, Halter & Griswold* (1989), 43 Ohio St.3d 54, 538 N.E.2d 398:

"Under 2305.11(A), an action for legal malpractice accrues and the statute of limitations begins to run when there is a cognizable event whereby the client discovers or should have discovered that his injury was related to his attorney's act or non-act and the client is put on notice of a need to pursue his possible remedies against the attorney or when the attorney-client relationship for that particular transaction or undertaking terminates, whichever occurs later."

"In other words, the statute of limitations does not begin to run until the later of the following two events, viz.: (1) the termination of the attorney-client relationship, or (2) the occurrence of a 'cognizable event.'" *In re America* (Feb. 8, 1996), Cuyahoga App. Nos. 66808 and 66947, unreported, 1996 WL 50815, at 6.

Cognizable Event

[1] [2] A "cognizable event" is an event sufficient to alert a reasonable person that in the course of legal representation his attorney committed an improper act. *Spencer v. McGill* (1993), 87 Ohio App.3d 267, 622

N.E.2d 7. A cognizable event can occur when the client learns of an adverse decision during litigation. See, generally, *McDade v. Spencer* (1991), 75 Ohio App.3d 639, 600 N.E.2d 371 (cognizable event when plaintiff was cited for contempt for failing to comply with a settlement agreement); *Cutcher v. Chapman* (1991), 72 Ohio App.3d 265, 594 N.E.2d 640 (cognizable event when trial granted summary judgment on statute of limitations grounds); *Lowe v. Cassidy* (Nov. 3, 1994), Franklin App. No. 94APE06–784, unreported, 1994 WL 612376 (cognizable event when jury returned an adverse jury verdict).

[3] In the case at bar, the probate jury returned an adverse verdict on November 16, 1992. Plaintiff's claim of malpractice centers on defendant's representation during the probate trial. When the jury returned a finding that plaintiff had concealed and embezzled assets from his mother's estate, plaintiff was on sufficient notice that his attorney had allegedly committed an improper act.

Termination of Attorney–Client Relationship

[4] [5] For purposes of the statute of limitations, an attorney-client relationship is consensual in nature and the actions of either party that dissolve the essential mutual confidence between attorney and client can signal the termination of the relationship. *Brown v. Johnstone* (1982), 5 Ohio App.3d 165, 5 OBR 347, 450 N.E.2d 693. A letter from an attorney to a client can terminate the attorney-client relationship. *Chapman v. Basinger* (1991), 71 Ohio App.3d 5, 592 N.E.2d 908; *Hickle v. Malone* (1996), 110 Ohio App.3d 703, 675 N.E.2d 48; *Hobbs v. Enz* (June 28, 1996), Franklin App. No. 96APE02—135, unreported, 1996 WL 362042.

[6] In the case at bar, the attorney-client relationship was terminated on November 16, 1992 when, after the jury verdict, defendant told plaintiff that his firm's engagement was over. The fact that plaintiff understood that their relationship terminated on this date is reflected by his own affidavit, which states as follows:

"After the jury portion of the trial was concluded, the defendant approached me in the lunch area of the court house and advised me that his firm "was not going to handel [*sic*] the appeal." I acknowledged this statement, as this was my understanding of the agreement. He then advised me that he knew of a client of his who had hired one attorney for negotiations, one for trial and one for appeal portion of a case."

Thus, plaintiff understood that the attorney-client relationship, which had existed for trial only, had been terminated by defendant after the return of the jury verdict. This termination was confirmed in the November 24, 1992 letter, in which defendant unambiguously states that his firm will not be responsible for any post-trial or appellate matters and advises plaintiff of the time frame if plaintiff wanted to file any post-trial motions or an appeal. This letter unequivocally communicated to plaintiff that any further action in the case would occur without defendant as his attorney. It is reasonable to infer that plaintiff understood from this letter that the relationship was over because he subsequently filed his own *pro se* motion for judgment notwithstanding the verdict and new trial.

Plaintiff's argument that defendant's representation lasted until the court granted his motion to withdraw is meritless. This court recently rejected this very argument and held that in a statute of limitations context the conduct of an attorney can terminate an attorney-client relationship prior to the filing of the notice of withdrawal. *Erickson v. Misny* (May 9, 1996), Cuyahoga App. No. 69213, unreported, 1996 WL 239883, at 6.

Accordingly, because the filing of plaintiff's complaint (December 3, 1993) was more than one year after the claim for legal malpractice accrued (November 16, 1992), the trial court did not err in granting summary judgment for defendant based on the statute of limitations.

"II. Whether trial court abused its discretion in not granting plaintiff–appellant's motion to compel discovery?"

[7] [8] In this assignment, plaintiff argues that the trial court abused its discretion by denying his request to review his legal file, which was in the possession of defendant. A trial court's decision to deny a discovery request is reviewed under an abuse of discretion standard. *State ex rel. Daggett v. Gessaman* (1973), 34 Ohio St.2d 55, 63 O.O.2d 88, 295 N.E.2d 659. Defendant correctly points out that courts have recognized a common-law lien that allows an attorney to retain a client's file until the client has paid the attorney's fee. *Foor v. Huntington Natl. Bank* (1986), 27 Ohio App.3d 76, 27 OBR 95, 499 N.E.2d 1297. Accordingly, because plaintiff had not paid his legal bill, the trial court did not abuse its discretion in denying his discovery request.

"III. Whether the trial court abused its discretion in denying appellant's motion to vacate judgment under Civil Rule 60(B) 1–5, fraudulent concealment of a cause of action, when the defendants, while in possession of knowledge of their malpractice, failed to advise plaintiff and actively concealed this knowledge from the plaintiff."

[9] [10] [11] In order to prevail on a motion brought under Civ.R. 60(B), the movant must demonstrate the following: (1) movant has a meritorious defense or claim to present if relief is granted, (2) movant is entitled to relief under one of the grounds stated in Civ.R. 60(B) (1) through (5), and (3) the motion is made within a reasonable time, and, where the grounds of relief are Civ.R. 60(B)(1), (2) or (3), not more than one year after the judgment, order, or proceeding was entered or taken. *GTE Automatic Elec., Inc. v. ARC Industries, Inc.* (1976), 47 Ohio St.2d 146, 1 O.O.3d 86, 351 N.E.2d 113, paragraph two of the syllabus. A motion for relief from judgment will be overruled if these three elements are not satisfied. *Rose Chevrolet, Inc. v. Adams* (1988), 36 Ohio St.3d 17, 520 N.E.2d 564. A trial court's decision to deny a Civ.R. 60(B) motion is reviewed under an abuse of discretion standard. *Adomeit v. Baltimore* (1974), 39 Ohio App.2d 97, 68 O.O.2d 251, 316 N.E.2d 469. Finally, a party may not use a Civ.R. 60(B) motion as a substitute for appeal. *Doe v. Trumbull Cty. Children Serv. Bd.* (1986), 28 Ohio St.3d 128, 28 OBR 225, 502 N.E.2d 605.

[12] In the case at bar, the trial court did not abuse its discretion in denying plaintiff's motion for relief from judgment. As stated above, in order to obtain relief, movant must allege sufficient grounds for relief. Plaintiff filed his motion to obtain relief from the order of the trial court granting summary judgment in favor of defendant. Plaintiff seems to argue that defendant committed various fraudulent acts regarding the probate court trial. Any fraud that would be grounds for relief of the probate court case would have to be raised in that forum. Any alleged fraudulent acts by defendant that may be potential grounds for relief in that case are not relevant to the case at bar. Because plaintiff has not alleged any mistake or fraud that warrants relief from the trial court's grant of summary judgment in the case at bar, this assignment is, accordingly, overruled.

Judgment affirmed.

JAMES D. SWEENEY, P.J., and MATIA, J., concur.

162 Ohio App.3d 689
Court of Appeals of Ohio,
Eleventh District, Trumbull County.

BUSACCA, Admr., et al., Appellants,

v.

MAGUIRE & SCHNEIDER, LLP, et al., Appellees.

No. 2004-T-0032.

|

Decided Aug. 12, 2005.

Attorneys and Law Firms

J. Thomas Henretta, Akron, for appellants.

John T. McLandrich and Frank H. Scialdone, Cleveland, for appellees.

Opinion

ROBERT A. NADER, Judge.

In this accelerated calendar case, appellants, Sara Busacca, administrator of the estate of Frederick Hahn, and Mary Jane Hahn appeal the judgment entered by the Trumbull County Court of Common Pleas. The trial court entered summary judgment in favor of appellees, Maguire & Schneider, LLP, f.k.a. Maguire, Schneider, Zapka, & Leuchtag; Emery J. Leuchtag; and Dennis P. Zapka.

{ ¶ 2} Mary Jane Hahn was married to Fred Hahn. She believed a doctor had committed medical malpractice in the treatment of Fred Hahn. She hired attorneys Dennis Tackett and Emery Leuchtag from Tackett, Zapka & Leuchtag to represent her in pursuing a medical malpractice action against the doctor on behalf of her husband. While the action was pending, Fred Hahn died. Sara Busacca, Fred and Mary Jane Hahn's daughter, was appointed administrator of Fred Hahn's estate. Thereafter, the medical malpractice action was refiled, with Sara Busacca named plaintiff in her capacity as administrator of the estate.

{ ¶ 3} The medical malpractice action was dismissed without prejudice on September 10, 1997. It was not refiled.

{ ¶ 4} In 1999, appellants became concerned about the status of the case. They called Tackett and discussed the matter with him. In response, on August 9, 1999, Tackett sent a letter to Mary Jane Hahn. Therein, he informed her that the law firm of Tackett, Zapka & Leuchtag had dissolved in January 1997. He told her that Zapka and Leuchtag had possession of the medical malpractice file. In addition, he stated that the medical malpractice action had been dismissed on September 10, 1997, and according to the Ohio Rules of Civil Procedure, it could have been refiled within one year of that date. Also, he mentioned that Sara Busacca informed him that the dismissal of the case occurred without appellants' knowledge.

{ ¶ 5} On December 9, 1999, Sara Busacca sent a letter to Zapka and Leuchtag. The letter claimed that her phone calls to the attorneys had not been returned. In addition, the letter stated it was a demand for a status report on the medical malpractice case.

{ ¶ 6} On October 16, 2000, appellants sent another letter to Zapka and Leuchtag. In this letter, appellants state that the attorneys had not responded to their previous letter from December 1999. In addition, the letter states, "Since my mother, Mary Jane Hahn, has not received any status report from you, or any return calls, I am advising you that my mother and I are hiring another attorney." This letter mentions numerous phone calls and letters to the attorneys from appellants that have gone unanswered. Then, it instructs the attorneys to call Sara Busacca directly at any of three telephone numbers. The letter concludes with the statement, "My mother, Mary Jane Hahn, and I demand that you immediately provide us with a status report regarding the above referenced cases."

{ ¶ 7} On February 21, 2001, appellants sent a final letter to Zapka and Leuchtag. This letter references the December 1999 and October 2000 letters and asserts that appellants received no response to them. The letter contains the same statement as the October 2000 letter: "I am advising you that my mother and I are hiring another attorney." Further, the letter demands that the attorneys return the entire file relating to the medical malpractice case. Lastly, the letter states that the information is needed "immediately and certainly prior to our March 27, 2001 meeting with our new attorney."

{ ¶ 8} On November 13, 2001, appellants filed the instant action for legal malpractice against appellees. Appellees filed a motion for summary judgment.

{ ¶ 9} The trial court issued a judgment entry, on January 24, 2003, entering summary judgment in favor of appellees. In its judgment entry, the trial court noted appellants did not file a response to the motion for summary judgment. However, a response had been filed earlier that day. Appellants appealed this judgment.

{¶ 10} On June 2, 2003, appellants, pursuant to Civ.R. 60, filed a motion with the trial court for relief from judgment. In addition, appellants filed a motion with this court requesting that the case be remanded to the trial court to rule on their Civ.R. 60 motion. On June 4, 2003, this court granted their motion.

{¶ 11} On June 6, 2003, the trial court granted appellants' Civ.R. 60 motion for a new trial. In response, appellants requested a dismissal of the pending appeal. This court then dismissed the case on June 23, 2003.

{¶ 12} The trial court issued another judgment entry on March 8, 2004. Therein, the trial court indicated that it had considered appellants' response to appellees' motion for summary judgment. The court again entered summary judgment in favor of appellees. Appellants timely appealed this judgment, resulting in the instant appeal.

{¶ 13} At oral argument, an issue arose as to whether this court had jurisdiction to hear this appeal. The parties were permitted to file supplemental briefs. After considering the supplemental briefs of the parties and upon review of the record, we see that the trial court ruled on appellants' Civ.R. 60 motion when the matter was remanded to the jurisdiction of the trial court. When the case was returned to the jurisdiction of this court, the matter was dismissed upon appellants' request. The dismissal was made without ruling on the merits of the case.

{¶ 14} The matter was back in the trial court's jurisdiction when the trial court entered summary judgment on March 8, 2004. This court has jurisdiction to hear the merits of the instant appeal resulting from the March 8, 2004 judgment entry. We will now address the merits of this case.

{¶ 15} Appellants raise the following assignment of error:

{¶ 16} "The trial court erred to the prejudice of plaintiffs-appellants by granting Defendants' motion for summary judgment."

{¶ 17} Pursuant to Civ.R. 56(C), summary judgment is appropriate when there is no genuine issue of material fact and the moving party is entitled to judgment as a matter of law. *Dresher v. Burt* (1996), 75 Ohio St.3d 280, 293, 662 N.E.2d 264. In addition, it must

appear from the evidence and stipulations that reasonable minds can come to only one conclusion, which is adverse to the nonmoving party. Civ.R. 56(C). The standard of review for the granting of a motion for summary judgment is de novo. *Grafton v. Ohio Edison Co.* (1996), 77 Ohio St.3d 102, 105, 671 N.E.2d 241.

{¶ 18} In *Dresher v. Burt,* the Supreme Court of Ohio set forth a burden-shifting procedure on a summary-judgment determination. Initially, the moving party must point to evidentiary materials to show that there are no genuine issues of material fact and that it is entitled to judgment as a matter of law. *Burt,* 75 Ohio St.3d at 293, 662 N.E.2d 264. If the moving party meets this burden, a reciprocal burden is placed on the nonmoving party to show that there is a genuine issue of fact for trial. Id.

{¶ 19} "R.C. 2305.11(A) provides that a party must bring a claim for legal malpractice within one year after the cause of action accrued." *Biddle v. Maguire & Schneider, LLP,* 11th Dist. No. 2003-T-0041, 2003-Ohio-7200, at ¶ 17. In interpreting this statute, the Supreme Court of Ohio has held:

{¶ 20} "Under R.C. 2305.11(A), an action for legal malpractice accrues and the statute of limitations begins to run when there is a cognizable event whereby the client discovers or should have discovered that his injury was related to his attorney's act or non-act and the client is put on notice of a need to pursue his possible remedies against the attorney or when the attorney-client relationship for that particular transaction or undertaking terminates, whichever occurs later." *Zimmie v. Calfee, Halter & Griswold* (1989), 43 Ohio St.3d 54, 538 N.E.2d 398, syllabus.

{¶ 21} In addition, the Supreme Court of Ohio has also held:

{¶ 22} "For the purposes of determining the accrual date of R.C. 2305.11(A) in a legal malpractice action, the trial court must explore the particular facts of the action and make the following determinations: when the injured party became aware, or should have become aware, of the extent and seriousness of his or her alleged legal problem; whether the injured party was aware, or should have been aware, that the damage or injury alleged was related to a specific legal transaction or undertaking previously rendered him or her; and whether such damage or injury would put a reasonable person on notice of the need for further inquiry as to the cause of such damage or injury." *Omni-Food*

& Fashion, Inc. v. Smith (1988), 38 Ohio St.3d 385, 528 N.E.2d 941, paragraph two of the syllabus.

{ ¶ 23} In the case sub judice, the trial court did not indicate in its judgment entry whether it found appellants' claims were barred by the statute of limitations because the attorney-client relationship ended or due to the existence of a cognizable event. In addition, the trial court did not indicate a specific date of accrual for purposes of R.C. 2305.11(A).

{ ¶ 24} We conclude that there is a genuine issue of material fact as to when the attorney-client relationship terminated. Since there is a genuine issue of material fact on this issue, summary judgment was inappropriate, and we are remanding this matter to the trial court. Whether or not a cognizable event occurred has not been raised. The issue of when the attorney-client relationship terminated is determinative of this appeal.

[1] { ¶ 25} The remainder of this analysis will focus on when the attorney-client relationship is terminated. "The issue of when the attorney-client relationship terminated is a question of fact." *Trickett v. Krugliak, Wilkins, Griffiths & Dougherty Co., L.P.A.* (Oct. 26, 2001), 11th Dist. No. 2000-P-0105, 2001 WL 1301557, at *3, citing *Omni-Food & Fashion, Inc. v. Smith* (1988), 38 Ohio St.3d 385, 388, 528 N.E.2d 941.

[2] { ¶ 26} Obviously, an attorney-client relationship can terminate based on an "affirmative act" of either the attorney or the client. Id. at *3. An example of this termination would be a formal letter specifically indicating that the representation has terminated. Id.

[3] { ¶ 27} Leuchtag, in his affidavit, states that the attorney-client relationship terminated on September 10, 1997, when he filed the dismissal in the underlying action. He states that he called Mary Jane Hahn and informed her that the case was being dismissed, and he had no intention of refiling it. He indicates that he had no further contact with appellants after September 10, 1997. However, Mary Jane Hahn, in her affidavit, expressly denies that Leuchtag informed her that the case was being dismissed and that he did not intend to refile it. Since there are competing affidavits on this point, there is a genuine issue of material fact as to whether Attorney Leuchtag called Mary Jane Hahn and terminated the relationship.

{ ¶ 28} Appellants claim that the February 21, 2001 letter officially ended the attorney-client relationship.

Appellees counter that the October 2000 letter ended the relationship, because it said that appellants were hiring another attorney. If the October 2000 letter terminated the relationship, appellants' legal malpractice action, filed in November 2001, would be barred by the statute of limitations.

{ ¶ 29} It is undisputed that, as of the February 2001 letter, the attorney-client relationship had terminated. Therein, appellants state that they are hiring another attorney, demand that the file be returned, and reference a meeting with their new attorney.

[4] { ¶ 30} We will now address whether the relationship could be determined to have concluded as of the October 2000 letter.

{ ¶ 31} There are two reasonable interpretations of the October 2000 letter. The first, advanced by appellees, is that appellants' statement advising them that they were hiring a new attorney was an affirmative act that terminated the attorney-client relationship. However, the statement could also be viewed as a threat: if the additional requests of the letter are not complied with, another attorney will be hired. After the statement about another attorney, appellants demand to discuss the matter and receive a status report. Thus, they were asking the attorneys to perform additional work. In addition, if the October 2000 letter and the February 2001 letter were both presented to a trier of fact, in comparing the two, a trier of fact could reasonably conclude that the additional language in the February 2001 letter requesting the return of the file and referencing the "new attorney" suggests that the October 2000 letter was merely a threat, as it did not contain these statements.

{ ¶ 32} There is a genuine issue of material fact regarding whether the October 2000 letter terminated the attorney-client relationship.

[5] { ¶ 33} In *Trickett,* this court held that, in certain circumstances, the attorney-client relationship may terminate on its own. *Trickett,* 11th Dist. No. 2000-P-0105, 2001 WL 1301557, at *3. Termination may occur when the underlying action has concluded or when the attorney has exhausted all remedies in the case and had declined to provide additional legal services on related issues. Id.

[6] { ¶ 34} For the following reasons, there are genuine issues of material fact as to whether the attorney-client relationship terminated "on its own." In this matter,

Sara Busacca's testimony clearly indicated that she did not believe that the case had concluded. Rather, her testimony and actions, including the October 2000 letter, represent her belief that appellees were still working on the legal malpractice action. The underlying matter in the *Trickett* case was a zoning appeal that progressed to this court. The appellant had exhausted his administrative remedies, and settlement negotiations were unsuccessful. Thus, this court held that there was nothing left for the attorneys to do. Id. However, in the case at bar, appellees voluntarily dismissed and never refiled the underlying lawsuit, apparently without notice to appellants, who believed refiling was still possible after being informed of appellees' action. Accordingly, this matter is distinguishable from this court's holding in *Trickett*.

{ ¶ 35} Appellees argue that appellants knew the attorney-client relationship terminated when the one-year statute of limitations expired for the underlying lawsuit. We disagree. Appellants as lay persons cannot be presumed to know the significance of a legal action being barred by a statute of limitations without being advised of the pending occurrence and its consequences by their attorney. Thus, there was a genuine issue of material fact as to when the attorney-client relationship terminated.

{ ¶ 36} The trial court erred in entering summary judgment in favor of appellees.

{ ¶ 37} Appellants' assignment of error has merit.

{ ¶ 38} The judgment of the trial court is reversed, and this matter is remanded to the trial court for further proceedings consistent with this opinion.

Judgment reversed and cause remanded.

DONALD R. FORD, P.J., concurs.

DIANE V. GRENDELL, J., concurs separately.

ROBERT A. NADER, J., retired, sitting by assignment.

DIANE V. GRENDELL, Judge, concurring.

{ ¶ 39} I agree with the majority that genuine issues of material fact exist as to whether Leuchtag called Mary Jane Hahn and terminated the attorney-client relationship in September 1997 and whether the October 2000 letter from appellants to Zapka and Leuchtag terminated the attorney-client relationship. I write separately to emphasize that the August 1999 letter from Tackett to appellants fails, as a matter of law, to adequately notify appellants that the attorney-client relationship had terminated.

{ ¶ 40} Although a client may terminate the attorney-client relationship at any time, "an attorney is not free to withdraw from the relationship absent notice to his client." *Columbus Credit Co. v. Evans* (1992), 82 Ohio App.3d 798, 804, 613 N.E.2d 671; *Mobberly v. Hendricks* (1994), 98 Ohio App.3d 839, 843, 649 N.E.2d 1247. Disciplinary Rule 2-110(A)(2) provides that "a lawyer shall not withdraw from employment until the lawyer has taken reasonable steps to avoid foreseeable prejudice to the rights of his or her client, including giving due notice to his or her client, allowing time for employment of other counsel, [and] delivering to the client all papers and property to which the client is entitled." See, also, Ethical Consideration 2–31 ("a lawyer should protect the welfare of his client by giving due notice of his withdrawal").

{ ¶ 41} While there may be a few limited circumstances in which the attorney-client relationship may terminate on its own, see, e.g. *Trickett v. Krugliak, Wilkins, Griffiths & Dougherty Co., L.P.A.,* (Oct. 26, 2001), 11th Dist. No. 2000-P-0105, 2001 WL 1301557, this case is *not* one of them.

{ ¶ 42} The August 1999 letter from Tackett to Mary Jane Hahn informed Hahn that the law partnership of Tackett, Zapka & Leuchtag had dissolved in January 1997; that Zapka and Leuchtag had taken possession of the medical malpractice case file; that Zapka and Leuchtag had filed a voluntary dismissal without prejudice of the lawsuit on September 10, 1997; and that "[a]ccording to the Ohio Rules of Civil Procedure, your lawsuit could have been re-filed against Dr. Sudheendra, within one (1) year after the original Dismissal was filed."

{ ¶ 43} Tackett's cryptic statement that "the lawsuit could have been refiled within one (1) year after the original Dismissal" is not adequate, as a matter of law, to inform laypersons that their lawsuit has been permanently barred by the running of the statute of limitations. Attorney Tackett's letter does not mention or explain the statute of limitations and does not suggest

The points in this paragraph seem important and potentially helpful to your case. But they were raised in a concurrence rather than signed onto by a majority of the court. How will that affect the way you use this opinion?

at all whether the case had been refiled or the implications of failing to refile the suit within one year of the voluntary, original dismissal. While an attorney could be expected to grasp the significance of Tackett's words, appellants could not be expected to do so.

{ ¶ 44} Furthermore, an attorney cannot benefit from his benign neglect or active avoidance of a client. By not responding to appellants' telephone calls and correspondence, appellees continued to foster the impression, if not the fact, that appellees had a professional relationship with appellants. Appellees could have and should have notified appellants that they had dismissed the lawsuit and no longer represented appellants with regards to that matter. An attorney cannot string a client along for a year after committing malpractice to avoid being held liable for such professional misconduct by the passing of the statute of limitations.

{ ¶ 45} As this court has stated previously, "By actively concealing the existence of their misconduct through deception and avoidance, an attorney cannot toll the running of the statute of limitations. To hold differently would 'potentially encourage[ ] an unscrupulous attorney to conceal his or her malpractice until that time when the statute of limitations has run its course.' " *Biddle v. Maguire & Schneider, LLP,* 11th Dist. No. 2003-T-0041, 2003-Ohio-7200, at ¶ 26, quoting *Omni-Food & Fashion, Inc. v. Smith* (1988), 38 Ohio St.3d 385, 387, 528 N.E.2d 941.

109 Ohio St.3d 141
Supreme Court of Ohio.

SMITH, Appellee,

v.

CONLEY, Appellant.

No. 2005–0247.

|

Submitted Nov. 29, 2005.

|

Decided May 10, 2006.

Attorneys and Law Firms

Clayton B. Smith, pro se.

Reminger & Reminger Co., L.P.A., Clifford C. Masch, W. Bradford Longbrake, and Holly M. Wilson, Cleveland, for appellant.

Gallagher Sharp and Timothy J. Fitzgerald, Cleveland, urging reversal for amicus curiae, Ohio Association of Civil Trial Attorneys.

Opinion

MOYER, C.J.

{ ¶ 1} The sole issue presented in this appeal is whether the termination of the attorney-client relationship for purposes of R.C. 2305.11 (time limitation on bringing a legal-malpractice claim) is dependent upon the filing of a motion to withdraw pursuant to a local rule of court.

I

{ ¶ 2} Appellant, attorney Craig Conley, represented appellee, Clayton Smith, in a criminal trial. At the conclusion of that trial, on August 21, 2002, Smith was found guilty of one count of passing bad checks in violation of R.C. 2913.11. Smith's sentencing hearing was scheduled for September 26, 2002. In the interim, Smith allegedly discovered exculpatory evidence and asked Conley to request a new trial. Conley disputed the value of the evidence and that the evidence was "newly discovered," as contemplated by Crim.R. 33. This dispute culminated with two letters from Conley to Smith, dated August 26, 2002, and August 28, 2002, memorializing an August 26 telephone conversation between the two, purporting to terminate the attorney-client relationship. Without the assistance of counsel, Smith filed a pro se motion for a new trial on September 3, 2002. On September 6, 2002, Conley filed a motion to withdraw

as counsel. It is not clear from the record, but Smith alleges in his brief that the trial court did not rule on Conley's motion to withdraw until April 11, 2005.

{ ¶ 3} Smith filed a complaint against Conley on September 5, 2003, alleging that Conley's legal malpractice had resulted in Smith's conviction. Conley filed a motion for summary judgment, arguing that the complaint had not been filed within the one-year limitations period set forth in R.C. 2305.11. The trial court found that for the purposes of R.C. 2305.11, Smith's cause of action had accrued no later than September 3, 2002 (when Smith filed his pro se motion for a new trial) and that Smith's complaint was untimely. Upon Smith's appeal, the court of appeals reversed the trial court's judgment, holding that the statute of limitations did not begin to run until September 6, 2002, when Conley filed his motion to withdraw. We accepted Conley's discretionary appeal.

II

[1] { ¶ 4} R.C. 2305.11(A) is the statute of limitations for the filing of legal-malpractice claims: "[A]n action for * * * malpractice * * * shall be commenced within one year after the cause of action accrued * * *." "Under R.C. 2305.11(A), an action for legal malpractice accrues and the statute of limitations begins to run when there is a cognizable event whereby the client discovers or should have discovered that his injury was related to his attorney's act or non-act and the client is put on notice of a need to pursue his possible remedies against the attorney or when the attorney-client relationship for that particular transaction or undertaking terminates, whichever occurs later." *Zimmie v. Calfee, Halter & Griswold* (1989), 43 Ohio St.3d 54, 538 N.E.2d 398, syllabus, citing *Omni–Food & Fashion, Inc. v. Smith* (1988), 38 Ohio St.3d 385, 528 N.E.2d 941. *Zimmie* and *Omni–Food* require two factual determinations: (1) When should the client have known that he or she may have an injury caused by his or her attorney? and (2) When did the attorney-client relationship terminate? The latter of these two dates is the date that starts the running of the statute of limitations. *Zimmie*, syllabus; *Omni–Food*, paragraph one of the syllabus.

[2] [3] { ¶ 5} In his complaint, Smith avers that Conley committed legal malpractice when he failed to request a directed verdict and when he failed to offer for admission into evidence transcripts of tape-recorded conversations between Smith and the police, which Smith alleges clearly exonerate him. Trial strategy and the presentation of evidence are usually in the sole discre-

tion of the trial attorney. *State v. Williams*, 99 Ohio St.3d 493, 2003-Ohio-4396, 794 N.E.2d 27, ¶ 127 ("Decisions about what evidence to present and which witnesses to call * * * are committed to counsel's professional judgment"). Therefore, the admission or lack of admission of evidence by itself would not put the criminal defendant on notice of potential malpractice. However, since Smith's complaint is that Conley's malpractice resulted in a conviction, the date of the conviction is the date that Smith should have known that he had an injury caused by Conley. "Because [plaintiff's] allegations of negligence pertained to actions taken by [his attorney] during the pendency of the criminal case, we conclude he should have discovered these alleged errors, at the latest, when he was convicted of the [criminal] charge * * *." *Collins v. Morgan* (Nov. 16, 1995), Cuyahoga App. No. 68680, 1995 WL 680923. We conclude that the cognizable event that should have put Smith on notice that his attorney may have committed malpractice was his August 21, 2002 conviction. Having determined the date that corresponds to the first prong of the *Zimmie* test, i.e., when Smith should have known he had an injury caused by Conley, we consider the second prong, i.e., when the attorney-client relationship ended.

III

[4] [5] { ¶ 6} The attorney-client relationship is a relationship based on trust. "The overriding consideration in the attorney-client relationship is trust and confidence between the client and his or her attorney." *Fox & Assoc. Co., L.P.A. v. Purdon* (1989), 44 Ohio St.3d 69, 71, 541 N.E.2d 448. While, in general, clients may dismiss their attorneys at any time, the withdrawal of an attorney from representation is covered at least in part by the Code of Professional Responsibility. DR 2–110 lists circumstances under which an attorney must or may withdraw from representation. DR 2–110(A)(2) instructs attorneys not to withdraw without first guarding the client's welfare and allowing time for the client to employ other counsel. DR 2–110(A)(1) requires an attorney to request permission from the appropriate tribunal to withdraw as counsel when required by the rules of the tribunal. Smith argues that because the local rules of the Stark County Court of Common Pleas require an attorney to move to withdraw, the date a motion to withdraw is filed is the date of termination of the attorney-client relationship.

{ ¶ 7} Loc.R. 17.05(D) of the Stark County Court of Common Pleas states, "An attorney * * * shall not be permitted to withdraw except in open court in the pres-

ence of the defendant and upon written entry approved and filed NOT LESS THAN thirty (30) days before the date assigned for trial." (Emphasis sic.) Smith argues, and the court of appeals held, that this rule requires counsel to file a motion in the trial court before counsel may terminate an attorney-client relationship for purposes of R.C. 2305.11. Smith avers that the rule is intended to protect his Sixth Amendment right to counsel. We do not agree.

{ ¶ 8} Many trial courts have adopted local rules regarding attorney withdrawal. Loc.R. 10 of the Cuyahoga County Common Pleas Court requires written notice to withdraw from both civil and criminal cases, but does not specify a time limit for filing the motion. Loc.R. 18 of the Franklin County Court of Common Pleas requires that a motion to withdraw be filed at least 20 days before trial and also does not differentiate between civil and criminal proceedings. Loc.R. 10(D) of the Hamilton County Court of Common Pleas requires an attorney in a civil case to file a written motion to withdraw and directs the judge to hear the motion within ten days. And attorneys in criminal cases must file a motion to withdraw and must show good cause. Loc.R. 1.31(I)(B) of the Montgomery County Court of Common Pleas does not impose a time requirement but requires attorneys wishing to withdraw in criminal cases to appear in open court in the presence of the defendant. Loc.R. 7.20 of the Summit County Court of Common Pleas allows withdrawal for good cause upon written motion.

[6] [7] { ¶ 9} The differences between the local court rules, coupled with the other Stark County rules, cause us to conclude that when determining legal duties created by R.C. 2305.11, these local rules are administrative in nature—designed to facilitate case management. Local rules of court are promulgated by and applied by local courts for the convenience of the local bench and bar. They do not implicate constitutional rights. The purpose of Stark County Loc.R. 17.05(D) is to require the attorney to advise the court that the attorney-client relationship has ended. We reaffirm our statement in *Omni–Food* that the date of termination of the attorney-client relationship is a question of fact and is to be determined by considering the actions of the parties. Id., 38 Ohio St.3d at 388, 528 N.E.2d 941. For purposes of R.C. 2305.11, the termination of an attorney-client relationship is not controlled by local rules of court.

{ ¶ 10} In the instant case, Conley clearly informed Smith no later than August 28, 2002, that he no longer could represent him and would not file further actions on his behalf. The efficient administration of justice would not be served if the various local rules of court regarding attorney withdrawal determined the date of termination of the attorney-client relationship.

IV

{¶ 11} Our holding today is limited to the application of R.C. 2305.11 and should not be applied to diminish adherence to local rules of court in other circumstances.

[8] {¶ 12} We have held that local rules of court provide sufficient notice to a party regarding a summary-judgment hearing and deadlines for supporting filings. *Hooten v. Safe Auto Ins. Co.*, 100 Ohio St.3d 8, 2003-Ohio-4829, 795 N.E.2d 648, ¶ 33. However, we also noted that relying on local rules requires individual analysis. Id. at ¶ 31. The date of termination of an attorney-client relationship for R.C. 2305.11 purposes is a fact-specific determination to be made according to the rules set forth by statute and by case law. The determination is not dependent on local rules of court. Attorneys are required to follow local rules and must file the appropriate motion with a court to withdraw from representation, but the date of termination of the attorney-client relationship for purposes of R.C. 2305.11 is determined by the actions of the parties.

{¶ 13} The judgment of the court of appeals is reversed, and the cause is remanded to the trial court for a determination of the termination date.

Judgment reversed and cause remanded.

RESNICK, PFEIFER, O'CONNOR, O'DONNELL and LANZINGER, JJ., concur.

LUNDBERG STRATTON, J., dissents.

LUNDBERG STRATTON, J., dissenting.

{¶ 14} I respectfully dissent. I do not agree that Stark County Court of Common Pleas Loc.R. 17.05(D) is merely "administrative in nature" or that an attorney-client relationship can be considered terminated when the attorney has not complied with the rule's express requirements for withdrawal from representation. In circumstances in which a local court rule dictates how and when an attorney may withdraw from a case, the client should be entitled to rely on continued representation if those conditions have not been met. I believe that the local rule establishes a bright line that clearly advises all parties when an attorney-client

relationship has been terminated and eliminates the need for further factual inquiry into the actions of the parties.

{¶ 15} The majority considers the local court rule to be merely "administrative in nature—designed to facilitate case management." This, in effect, trivializes the significance of local rules. Local rules are a valid exercise of a court's rule-making power. *Vorisek v. N. Randall* (1980), 64 Ohio St.2d 62, 63, 18 O.O.3d 296, 413 N.E.2d 793. A judge has discretion to order sanctions, including dismissal, for a party's violation of a local rule. Id. at 65, 18 O.O.3d 296, 413 N.E.2d 793, (dismissing an appeal for failure to file a civil-appeal statement in compliance with local rule). See, also, *Eddie v. Veterinary Sys., Inc.* (Feb. 25, 1994), Trumbull App. No. 93–T–4886, 1994 WL 110911 (affirming dismissal for failure to comply with local rules to perfect appeal of arbitration award); *Richardson Bros., Inc. v. Dave's Towing Serv.* (1983), 14 Ohio App.3d 1, 14 OBR 3, 469 N.E.2d 850 (affirming trial court's dismissal for failure to file affidavit pursuant to local rule to perfect appeal); *Meyers v. First Natl. Bank of Cincinnati* (1981), 3 Ohio App.3d 209, 3 OBR 238, 444 N.E.2d 412 (refusing to set aside dismissal granted when opposing party did not file memorandum contra motion to dismiss pursuant to municipal court rule). It is inconsistent to allow sanctions, even dismissal, for some rule violations while disregarding other rule infractions, concluding that the rule is merely "administrative in nature."

{¶ 16} If an attorney is concerned about establishing the date of the termination of the attorney-client relationship, that attorney should be diligent about filing and pursuing the final judicial order authorizing withdrawal as counsel of record.

{¶ 17} In addition, I believe that this opinion will create difficulty and confusion for trial court judges. If the termination of an attorney-client relationship is no longer dictated by the applicable local court rule, then the judge may be faced with the situation in which an attorney remains counsel of record in a case, yet the attorney-client relationship is considered terminated for malpractice purposes. Should a court sanction counsel for failing to appear for a hearing when the attorney has not withdrawn from the case pursuant to local court rule, but the attorney-client relationship is otherwise considered terminated? Does today's majority opinion permit the attorney to raise as a defense in a disciplinary proceeding that he or she terminated the attorney-client relationship even though there was no compliance with a local court rule? (See *Cuyahoga Cty. Bar Assn. v. Ballou,* 109 Ohio St.3d 152, 2006–Ohio-2037, 846 N.E.2d 519, in which an attorney was disciplined for failing to attend an eviction hearing after he had informed the client and opposing counsel that he would not represent the client unless payment was made).

{¶ 18} In addition, how will a client know whether his or her counsel will appear in court when the attorney has not withdrawn in accordance with local court rules? The client can easily access the text of the local rule, yet may have no understanding that, under today's decision, counsel can terminate the attorney-client relationship in contradiction of a local rule.

{¶ 19} I believe that when a local rule of court mandates the terms and conditions for attorney withdrawal, those terms and conditions must be satisfied before the relationship can be considered terminated. Adhering to local rules regarding termination of the relationship provides unequivocal notice to judges, attorneys, and clients of that termination. Therefore, I respectfully dissent.

765 F.Supp.2d 1006
United States District Court,
N.D. Ohio,
Western Division.

Paul A. WALTERS, et al., Plaintiffs,

v.

George R. ROYER, Defendant.

Case No. 3:10 CV 1526.

|

Feb. 24, 2011.

Attorneys and Law Firms

Harold M. Steinberg, C. William Bair, Fan Zhang, Wagoner & Steinberg, Holland, OH, for Plaintiffs.

Jason D. Winter, Holly M. Wilson, Reminger & Reminger, Cleveland, OH, for Defendant.

MEMORANDUM OPINION AND ORDER

JACK ZOUHARY, District Judge.

INTRODUCTION

Before the Court is Defendant George Royer's ("Royer") Motion for Summary Judgment, alleging Plaintiff Paul Walters' ("Walters") malpractice claim is time-barred as a matter of law (Doc. No. 6). Walters' Complaint (Doc. No. 1) alleges Royer, an Ohio-licensed attorney at law, is liable to Walters for legal malpractice in connection with Royer's failure to timely prosecute several patent applications for Walters. Royer argues Walters' claim is not timely under Ohio's one-year statute of limitations (Doc. No. 4). This Court has diversity jurisdiction pursuant to 28 U.S.C. § 1332.

STATEMENT OF FACTS AND BACKGROUND

On May 6, 2009, Walters filed a grievance against Royer with the Toledo Bar Association pertaining to three patent applications that Royer had failed to timely prosecute, despite Royer telling Walters that the applications had been properly filed (Doc. No. 4, Ex. 1). Walters stated in his grievance that he was seeking disciplinary action and referral to a malpractice attorney.

Walters received a response from the Toledo Bar Association, dated June 19, 2009, stating that his claim against Royer was being investigated (Doc. No. 11, Ex. 1). The letter also indicated that Royer had been sent a copy, but Royer denies ever receiving the letter (Doc. No. 13).

On June 26, 2009, Royer faxed Walters a letter regarding one of the projects referenced in Walters' grievance, a patent for a "gas tank indicator" (Doc. No. 11, Ex. 8). In the letter, Royer advised that an amendment for the patent application had to be filed by July 20, 2009 or the application would be abandoned. Royer also advised that the amendment would take several hours to complete, but that he would not charge Walters for the time and would pay for any extension fees as he had done before. Royer concluded: "If you do not want me to complete the amendment, please advise. Otherwise, I have always intended and will complete the response."

On July 10, 2009, Royer sent Walters a proposed amendment for the gas tank indicator patent application (Doc. No. 11, Ex. 11). In the fax transmittal form, Royer informed Walters that he could elect to use the attached amendment, or he could hire another attorney to complete a response, but that any response must be filed by July 26, 2009 to maintain the pending status of the application. Royer repeated that he had no intention to bill Walters for the amendment.

On July 15, 2009, Walters sent Royer a letter demanding that he "cease any efforts to file this patent" (Doc. No. 11, Ex. 15). Walters stated that he had employed Royer eight years earlier to file the patent, and charged that Royer had allowed the patent to lapse without filing the appropriate documents despite Walters repeatedly contacting him over the years. Walters explained that it was now too late, as the whole marketplace for the gas tank indicator had changed from a "growing, thriving market" to a "dying" one since Royer was first employed to obtain the patent in 2001. Walters further stated that he could not justify startup costs that could easily exceed $100,000 for a rapidly dying market.

Royer acknowledged receipt of the July 15 letter, and would comply with Walters' request (Doc. No. 11, Ex. 17). Royer further stated that there was no lapse in the patent application, provided the amendment was filed by July 26, and that the amendment was ready to be sent to the Patent Office, at no charge, if Walters approved.

On July 23, 2009, Walters sent letters to officials at the Patent and Trademark Office ("PTO") informing them that Royer no longer represented him on any filings, and requesting that the office refrain from sharing any information with Royer (Doc. No. 11, Ex. 19, 21, 22 & 34).

On July 9, 2010, Walters filed an action before this Court, asserting legal malpractice by Royer (Doc. No. 1). Royer filed a Motion for Judgment on the Pleadings, claiming the action was time-barred (Doc. No. 6). The motion was converted to a Motion for Summary Judgment under Federal Civil Rule 56 per the Case Management Conference Order (Doc. No. 10).

STANDARD

Pursuant to Federal Civil Rule 56(c), summary judgment is appropriate where there is "no genuine issue as to any material fact" and "the moving party is entitled to judgment as a matter of law." *Id.* When considering a motion for summary judgment, the court must draw all inferences from the record in the light most favorable to the non-moving party. *Matsushita Elec. Indus. Co. v. Zenith Radio Corp.,* 475 U.S. 574, 587, 106 S.Ct. 1348, 89 L.Ed.2d 538 (1986). The court is not permitted to weigh the evidence or determine the truth of any matter in dispute; rather, the court determines only whether the case contains sufficient evidence from which a jury could reasonably find for the non-moving party. *Anderson v. Liberty Lobby, Inc.,* 477 U.S. 242, 248–49, 106 S.Ct. 2505, 91 L.Ed.2d 202 (1986).

ANALYSIS

The statute governing the time limit for legal malpractice actions in Ohio requires that the action be commenced within one year after the cause of action accrues. O.R.C. § 2305.11(A). The Ohio Supreme Court has stated:

> [A]n action for legal malpractice accrues and the statute of limitations begins to run when there is a cognizable event whereby the client discovers or should have discovered that his injury was related to his attorney's act or non-act and the client is put on notice of a need to pursue his possible remedies against the attorney or when the attorney-client relationship for that particular transaction or undertaking terminates, whichever occurs later.

Zimmie v. Calfee, Halter & Griswold, 43 Ohio St.3d 54, 58, 538 N.E.2d 398 (1989).

[1] The rule in *Zimmie* establishes that the statute of limitations begins to run on the later of two dates: (1) when Walters discovered Royer's alleged malpractice in failing to prosecute the patents, or (2) when the attorney-client relationship between Walters and Royer terminated.

Discovery of Alleged Malpractice

There is no argument that Walters discovered Royer's alleged malpractice on May 6, 2009, as evidenced by Walters' grievance to the Toledo Bar Association (Doc. No. 4, Ex. 1). The grievance form and the accompanying letter written by Walters explicitly indicate that: (1) Walters had a conversation with the PTO on May 6, 2009; (2) Walters learned from the conversation with the PTO that the patents had not been properly prosecuted by Royer; and (3) Walters requested disciplinary action and assistance in finding a malpractice attorney.

Walters' Grievance

[2] Walters argues that the attorney-client relationship with Royer was terminated, in writing, on July 15, 2009 (Doc. No. 1, ¶ 20). Therefore, Walters asserts his Complaint was timely filed on July 9, 2010—within one year of the termination of the attorney-client relationship. Royer argues the attorney-client relationship was effectively terminated by the filing of the grievance on May 6, 2009, and therefore the complaint is time-barred. When an attorney-client relationship has terminated is a question of fact. *Omni–Food & Fashion, Inc. v. Smith,* 38 Ohio St.3d 385, 388, 528 N.E.2d 941 (1988).

Arguing that the attorney-client relationship terminated when the grievance was filed, Royer relies on *Brown v. Johnstone,* 5 Ohio App.3d 165, 450 N.E.2d 693 (Ohio Ct.App.1982), where the Ohio court of appeals stated that "conduct which dissolves the essential mutual confidence between attorney and client signals the termination of the professional relationship." *Id.* at 166, 450 N.E.2d 693. The court further explained that "[i]nitiating grievance proceedings before the local bar association evidences a client's loss of confidence in his attorney such as to indicate a termination of the professional relationship." *Id.*

The court of appeals later clarified *Brown,* stating that "the termination of the attorney-client relationship depends, not on a subjective loss of confidence on the part of the client, but on conduct, an affirmative act by either the attorney or the client that signals the end of the relationship. For a trial court to grant summary judgment on this basis, such an act must be clear and unambiguous, so that reasonable minds can come to but one conclusion from it." *Mastran v. Marks,* 1990 WL 34845, at *4 (Ohio Ct.App.1990).

The Court could interpret the filing of the grievance as an affirmative act that signaled the end of the attorney-client relationship, as the Court did in *Brown.* However, *Brown* is factually distinguishable. First, the court in *Brown* noted that Brown had no contact with his lawyer after Brown contacted the bar association.

Here, there is evidence that Royer remained in contact with Walters regarding the patent application after the grievance was filed and offered to continue working on the application, unpaid.

The court in *Brown* explained that Brown was advised by the local bar association that Johnstone was being reprimanded as a result of the grievance and that Brown should discuss the matter with another attorney. *Brown,* 5 Ohio App.3d at 167, 450 N.E.2d 693. Here, Walters did not receive any such advice from the bar association that would advise him that the professional relationship with Royer had been, or should be, terminated.

Furthermore, while the filing of the grievance in this case could be seen as an act signaling the end of the professional relationship, the act is not so clear and unambiguous that reasonable minds could not differ on its significance. The form that Walters filled out to initiate the grievance specifically asked if Royer had withdrawn or been dismissed, to which Walters responded "no" (Doc. No. 4, Ex. 1). Further, Walters testified that until July 23, 2010, he still considered Royer to be his attorney for two other patents Royer had worked on, and that the July 15, 2009 letter only instructed Royer to cease pursuing the gas tank indicator patent (Doc. No. 11, Ex. 2, at 13–14). Walters further testified that his purpose in filing the grievance was to get more information to determine whether or not Royer had acted inappropriately in handling the patents and whether malpractice had actually occurred (Doc. No. 11, Ex. 2, at 2–3). A reasonable trier of fact could come to the conclusion that the filing of the grievance was not a clear and unambiguous affirmative act that ended the attorney-client relationship.

In *Dzambasow v. Abakumov,* 2005 WL 3475792 (Ohio Ct.App.2005), the court of appeals distinguished *Brown,* holding that whether or not the filing of a bar grievance terminates the attorney-client relationship is a question of fact. Determining that factual issue, the court looked to the totality of the circumstances surrounding the case. The court also stated, referencing the dissent in *Brown,* that one who is untrained in the law may reasonably believe that the function of filing a grievance was simply to enlist the bar association's help in resolving the issue they were having with their attorney.

Royer argues that the filing of the grievance signaled a lack of trust and confidence on the part of Walters such that the attorney-client relationship was severed. However, this lack of trust and confidence alone does not necessarily end the relationship. Another Ohio appel-

late court, in *R.E. Holland Excavating, Inc. v. Martin, et al.,* 162 Ohio App.3d 471, 833 N.E.2d 1273 (Ohio Ct. App.2005), distinguished *Brown,* holding that "a lack of trust and confidence in counsel may, but will not necessarily always, lead to the termination of the attorney-client relationship; in any event, that lack of trust and confidence does not constitute the termination of the relationship." *Id.* at 475–76, 833 N.E.2d 1273. The court in *R.E. Holland* further held that because the litigation in which the defendant-attorney represented Holland was not quite over, a reasonable mind could find that he still represented Holland. *Id.* Here, Walters believed Royer still represented him in matters relating to other patents (Doc. No 12–1, at 74). The fact that patent applications were still pending and required additional work could lead a trier of fact to believe that Walters did not intend the attorney-client relationship to end when he filed the grievance.

Walters' Termination Letter

[3] Walters also argues that under the doctrine of "continuous representation", the statute of limitations did not begin to run until Plaintiffs took action to terminate the professional relationship in either the July 15, 2009 letter to Royer or the July 23, 2009 letters to the PTO officials. "Continuous representation" tolls the one-year statute of limitations for legal malpractice actions during the period of the attorney-client relationship. *Vail v. Townsend,* 29 Ohio App.3d 261, 504 N.E.2d 1183 (Ohio Ct.App.1985). The doctrine allows the attorney the opportunity to correct any errors that may lead to malpractice rather than requiring the client to immediately file a claim for any errors their attorney may commit in order to preserve their rights. *Id.* at 263, 504 N.E.2d 1183.

That is what appears to have happened here—Royer attempted to correct his mistakes after the grievance was filed but before he received the July letter from Walters. While Royer denies having received a copy of the grievance letter from the Toledo Bar Association,[1] the timing of Royer's contact with Walters about resuming work on the patent is suspect. While nearly four months had passed since Royer and Walters' last discussion about the patent application, Royer's June—July offers to continue working, unpaid, on the gas tank indicator patent began a mere one week after the grievance letter was allegedly sent to Royer. Without addressing the merits of the parties' contentions regarding receipt of the grievance letter, this Court believes a question of fact exists on whether Royer received the grievance letter and whether the continuous representation doctrine would apply. If the continuous representation doctrine applies, because the Complaint was filed July 9, 2010, the action would be timely with respect to either of the July 2009 letters sent by Walters.

1   The parties argue about the receipt and authentication of the Toledo Bar Association letter. Regardless of whether Royer knew of the grievance when he performed the legal services, there still remains a question of material fact as to whether the filing of the grievance ended the attorney-client relationship.

In the end, this Court is presented with a factual dispute between Walters and Royer as to which of two events terminated the relationship between them: the filing of the grievance or the sending of the July 2009 letters. A jury could reasonably conclude that either of the two events terminated the parties' attorney-client relation-ship. *Thayer v. Fuller & Henry, Ltd.*, 503 F.Supp.2d 887, 892 (N.D.Ohio 2007). While Walters was unsatisfied with Royer, a jury could find that Walters had decided to continue an "imperfect relationship" with Royer despite his loss of confidence in him, or that Walters had considered giving Royer a chance to correct his mistakes. *Id.* at 893. Alternatively, a jury could find that the grievance ended the relationship. Accordingly, summary judgment at this stage is not proper.

CONCLUSION

There is a genuine issue of material fact as to when the attorney-client relationship concluded. Royer's Motion for Summary Judgment is denied.

IT IS SO ORDERED.

Understand the Problem

Though affidavits are crafted in the voice of the affiant (that is, the person who is signing it), they are usually written by lawyers.[2] The attorney's official objective in crafting an affidavit is to accurately record information from a party or witness in a series of numbered points, each of which the affiant affirms under oath. But as all with all lawyering tasks, strategy considerations always lurk. Lawyers can draft affidavits thoughtfully to help construct favorable yet truthful narratives to further their overall goals.

As is the case with most legal documents, there are some standard organizational patterns to affidavits that you should be aware of.[3]

An affidavit prepared amid litigation is usually headed by the case's caption. It then explicitly states that the information contained within it is attested and sworn to by the affiant. Usually then, the first point or two introduces the affiant and lays out his or her basis for knowing the information contained in the document.

A well-crafted affidavit will generally go about laying out the affiant's story in a logical and orderly fashion. This is done through a series of short numbered sentences (or occasionally, very short paragraphs), each of which makes a specific individual point. Information within the affiant's own personal experience is stated directly, usually in the first person. Information that the affiant has good reason to know, but cannot be said to have personally observed, is usually offered "upon [the affiant's] information and belief." That phrasing indicates the affiant is willing to swear under oath that the information is true to the best of his or her actual knowledge, but may have come by that knowledge somewhat indirectly.

At the conclusion of the affidavit's substantive narrative will be the affiant's signature, which has been witnessed by a notary public whose seal should be affixed. It is that attestation that takes the individual allegations and turns them into testamentary evidence.

Extract Material Facts

Consider your purpose and the facts at your disposal

Based on the record developed so far in your case, there are really only two sources of facts to rely on for this early-stage motion.[4]

In addition to whatever information you can use out of the defendant's sworn affidavit, you will have at your disposal your own client's statements from her interview with your supervisor. The client's statements are currently unsworn (and privileged) communications with counsel. They become usable as evidence in support of your motion when the client signs an affidavit attesting to the relevant facts and the affidavit is entered into the record. This is why your supervisor sees the affidavit you have been asked to draft as so key to the case.

---

2. Affidavits occasionally come from the attorneys themselves if they happen to be the ones who most directly possess knowledge of specific relevant facts (meaning, not legal arguments or second-hand information). Since licensed attorneys are officers of the court, they may in some circumstances be permitted to submit their factual information without the additional step of swearing an oath and having it notarized. In many jurisdictions such personally-certified statements are referred to as "Affirmations" rather than "Affidavits." Regardless of nomenclature, if the statements are signed and submitted under penalty of perjury they will carry the same weight.

3. Not that keen attorneys always adhere to convention. Sometimes there are genuine advantages to be gained from the unexpected. But good lawyers should always be aware of common norms and customs, and then actively choose whether to follow or deviate from them to their clients' greatest advantage.

4. A more extensive factual record will likely be developed as the case progresses through discovery, but of course it will only get to that stage if it survives defendant's present motion to dismiss.

Evaluate your factual evidence in light of the law

Your boss has asked you to draft the client's affidavit and then to prepare a short summary explaining your reasons for crafting it the way you did. Put simply, Kaliman wants to see what story you put together, and to understand the legal analysis that led you to put it together that way. There is no requirement that you do the work in that order, however. And in fact, you really shouldn't. You will want to know first what the law would require to win the present motion and what facts would support that. Then if an interpretation of events could in some way support that narrative, you will need to build it. Whether you draft that cover memo before writing the affidavit or not, you need to have a pretty good sense of what it will say before you are *ready* to start constructing the affidavit.

So as with almost all legal reasoning tasks, your work in this assignment is going to require you to move back and forth between law and fact. What does your client believe happened? When does the attorney-client relationship need to have been terminated in this case in order to survive the motion to dismiss? What does the law tell you about when and how the attorney-client relationship between Foster and Wallace may have been severed? Is there more than one plausible possibility? Does one or more of those possibilities comport with the client's experience? If so, then that, or those, should be the narrative thread in your affidavit. (Side note: what if it couldn't? If there were absolutely no possible way for an honest reading of the facts to support your client's positions you would probably have to concede. But such unambiguously bad facts are unusual—and lawyers are usually loath to believe that much of anything is so definitively one-sided.)

> It might be helpful in this process to create your own resource summarizing facts taken from the interview log and pairing each fact with important legal concepts drawn from the rules and cases. That way you can see how the rules and facts interact.
>
> This sort of self-crafted guide also helps you double-check your work. Any rules that have no facts attached might need further consideration in light of the case before you. And any facts that end up not paired with legal concepts might be immaterial (but they might not, so look again carefully!).

As always, the facts your client has given you inevitably shape the way you read and understand the law. And the law will in turn affect how you shape your client's story, so long as it is within the bounds of truth as far as you are aware.

Use Legal Authority

The cases make it clear under Ohio law the rule about when the statute of limitations for legal malpractice begins to run is when there is some "cognizable event" whereby the client would or could have known of malpractice, *or* when the lawyer-client relationship is terminated. It is worth unpacking this a bit to make certain you understand it.

It might be tempting to argue that in Ms. Foster's case the "cognizable event" occurred when she learned of the difficulty of proving suicide in single-car crashes. Thus through her own research became aware that her attorney's advice to forego most of the triple-indemnity on her husband's life insurance policy was (arguably) unwise. But courts generally shy away from rules that would trigger statutes of limitations based purely on one party's subjective awareness. Do you see why? An important principle of statutes of limitations is offering certainty and definiteness for all parties. This purpose suggests that it makes most sense for these rules to be triggered by objectively knowable events, which any party could be aware of or find out about.[5]

Perhaps the argument about the cause of action accruing only when Foster discovered that there might not be enough evidence to prove suicide in her husband's case would be worth making.

---

5. Like most general rules there are exceptions here, of course. In some instances jurisdictions have developed rules tolling the commencement of limitations statutes at the point until, for example, a victim's suppressed memories of traumatic events surface. But such rules are rare and not without controversy. In general, courts prefer objectively-determinable periods for statutes of limitations.

Counsel should acknowledge, however, that such an argument might be hard to win, because many courts would instead conclude that the "cognizable event" here was the settlement itself. In contrast to the case in which a lawsuit was dismissed in court without the client ever being notified, here there is absolutely no question Foster was aware the case was being negotiated and settled. She was actually present, and she signed the settlement memorandum. True, she may have entered the agreement erroneously believing her case was weaker than it was. But most courts would focus on the fact that with sufficient research she *could* have been aware of the strength of her evidence, however, which would suffice legally no matter what she in fact knew at the time.

This is why the Foster case is likely to be more successful if it is positioned as hinging on when Wallace terminated the lawyer-client relationship. Ms. Wallace suggests that the case was legally concluded when the settlement agreement was signed, and everything occurring afterward was simply implementation paperwork. What can you find in the cases to support your contention that the case did not end until some later point?

In your cover memo, you should explain to your boss what legal authority there is to support a later termination date. And then your affidavit should marshal the facts at your disposal to convey a narrative of the facts most consistent with that interpretation.

Frame Legal Issues Strategically

There are several possible termination points that are arguable in this case, and which could support your legal claim that the malpractice case is not time-barred. You might contend the relationship concluded when the lawyer completed her last act in handling the case, which seems to have been mailing the signed settlement papers to the court on June 14th. Instead, you could argue that the relationship was not severed until the lawsuit was deemed formally closed by the court several days later. Or you might offer both theories in the alternative. Your legal and strategic reasoning for deciding among these possibilities should be spelled out in your cover memo, and your affidavit should aim to seamlessly characterize the facts in harmony with that legal theory.

By the way: you will probably see in reviewing the Ohio case law that in many instances the exact point of terminating the attorney-client relationship depends on factual context, and is therefore often a question for the trier of fact to decide. That probably gives your side an upper hand in this motion to dismiss as a matter of law. But it by no means guarantees success.

Understand and Craft Legal Documents

Look closely at how opposing counsel constructed her affidavit

Ms. Wallace's brief affidavit is pretty typical. It is organized conventionally: it starts with a statement that its assertions are made under oath, it next explains who the affiant is and how she is connected to the captioned case, and then finally it sets out the individual facts in sequentially enumerated paragraphs. If you had never seen an affidavit before, this would be a perfectly reasonable model of how they are usually put together.

Do not be content with just using Wallace's affidavit as an example of *form*, though. It is also an example of lawyerly narrative shaping, and not a bad one.

Consider the story Wallace tells and how she tells it in paragraphs 2–5. Essentially she says "I had a client, I filed a lawsuit for her, I helped settle the case, and that's all there is to it." Move along folks — nothing more to see here. The construction tries to make Wallace's interpretation of the facts seem indisputable. Even the ease and brevity of the document are designed to give an impression that there is a very simple question for the court to resolve, presumably in her favor.

Moreover, every numbered statement is crafted in such a way that Wallace could legitimately believe that she was asserting the truth as she knew it. But do you see that in the second half of the affidavit there are interpretations of fact that subtly serve as arguments, or at least might be deemed argument-ish? These paragraphs contain both statements of observable fact and explanations of Wallace's subjective reasons for doing what she states she did ["Since I fully believed my representation of Ms. Foster to have been concluded... (para. 9)]. Because both the events and their significance might be relevant information for the court, and both are within Ms. Wallace's knowledge, it is not improper for them to be included in a sworn affidavit. But it certainly pushes at the boundaries to frame information in the way Ms. Wallace wants the judge to view it.·

A careful reader might also observe that each of the narrative paragraphs in points 2–5 consists of a single sentence, yet in the more argumentative paragraphs 6–9 there either two sentences (or in the case of paragraph 7, a compound sentence containing several clauses). Why would that be? Probably because interposing the two thoughts in the same numbered paragraph implies a stronger causal relationship between them than if they had been separated—all without having to explicitly argue that the connection exists. For example, the second sentence in paragraph 6 is plainly intended to modify the first. Yet it also has the effect of somewhat burying the "she came to my office again" thought within an overall "I told her the case was done" assertion. Those sentences could have each been individual numbered paragraphs, but if they had been, the reader's perception might be ever-so-slightly different. Similarly, the dependent clause characterizing the purpose of the June 14th meeting in paragraph 7 gives Wallace a way to insist that this was merely a post-representation formality, rather than a client meeting to fully conclude the case. Again, without quite explicitly making that argument.

This is not to say that Wallace was right in all of her choices. Different lawyers could agree or disagree with her tactics, and some might believe that she had crossed the line from factual attestation into advocacy. These kinds of judgments are genuinely debatable. But you can only join into this professional debate (which hopefully you find invigorating) if you can surface and analyze the decisions that the lawyers are making.

Writing in your client's voice

Writing affidavits can be challenging for lawyers because in crafting them we are virtually creating dialogue for another person. What the affidavit states must be true, and to be maximally effective it must also *seem true* because of a sensation of authenticity. That means your affidavit draft should to some degree sound like it comes from the client.

Don't overdo that—everyone understands that affidavits are professionally crafted documents. There is an expectation that they should conform to ordinary phrasing and grammar conventions even if that does not precisely reflect the way your client speaks. Still, factual assertions will be most persuasive when they appear most genuine. Try to use wording and constructions consistent with your actual client's language as much as possible, while nonetheless remaining professional.

Transfer to a Law School Setting

We now switch gears and address related issues under the crime-fraud exception in a sample law school essay exam question.

Sample exam question

Essay – 40 minutes

Maya and Joseph Guirera divorced three years ago. They have joint legal custody of their two sons, now 11 and 8. The boys spend most of their time physically in Maya's home.

One day a few months ago both children seemed ill, so Maya took them to their pediatrician. The doctor determined both boys had a viral infection and in addition he noted that the younger child seemed to have contracted a bacterial bronchitis. The doctor prescribed antibiotics. Maya's feverish son fell asleep in the car on the way to the drug store, so she left him to sleep under the supervision of his older brother while she ran in to fill his prescription. The line at the pharmacy was longer than Maya expected and she was gone approximately 12–15 minutes. When she came out of the store she found a police officer talking with her elder son. The officer asked Maya whether she had left the two boys alone in the car. When she confirmed that she had done so "for just a minute," the officer placed her under arrest. Maya is now charged with two counts of child endangerment. She engaged attorney Marta Hoch to defend her against these criminal charges.

Joseph Guirera is not a party to Maya's criminal case, but has intervened to ask the court to remove Hoch as Maya's defense counsel. Since Hoch represented Joseph in their divorce, Joseph contends that Hoch remains *his* lawyer and is therefore ineligible to represent his ex-wife in the criminal matter. Ms. Hoch, on the other hand, insists that her representation of Joseph concluded when his divorce settlement was reached.

Ms. Hoch's law firm had done work for Joseph on several matters over the course of 10 years. She was the one who at Joseph's request drafted the prenuptial agreement Mr. and Ms. Guirera signed. Early in the marriage, she prepared wills and health proxies for both partners to sign. When Joseph sold his business she helped him place the proceeds into various trusts that she set up for him and his children. And when the couple decided to dissolve their union, she represented Joseph in the divorce proceeding from the initial legal separation through to the final mediated divorce settlement.

Joseph's position is that Ms. Hoch has been his exclusive attorney for family concerns for more than a decade, and that he reasonably believed she would continue to serve in that capacity when the need arose. Based on the current charges against Maya, he intends to seek sole custody of his sons and he states that he fully expected Ms. Hoch would continue representing him in this and all related family matters.

Ms. Hoch believes that her representation of Joseph concluded over three years ago when the divorce was finalized. She notes that she has no current retainer from Joseph, and that there is no documentation of an indefinite or continuous attorney-client relationship.

Has the attorney-client relationship between Ms. Hoch and Joseph Guirera been terminated? Explain why or why not.

Attacking the exam question

When you first read the problem does it strike you as unwise for Hoch to represent Ms. Guirera after working so long with her now ex-husband? Perhaps it should, but we can also understand circumstances in which that might happen: the criminal case really does not seem to have anything to do with the prior legal business, and particularly in less populated areas there may be a limited pool of lawyers for the client to retain. In any case, whether it was a good choice for the attorney to represent Guirera is only tangentially germane to whether she violated the rules of professional responsibility. So you might want to briefly note any concerns or recommendations you may have, but should focus on the analysis before the court: Mr. Guirera's motion to remove Hoch as counsel.

> This could be precisely the reason a professor would choose this kind of example. Your professor may want you to see that there may be a difference between legal and excellent decision-making by lawyers, and may hope that you will consider the distinction between the two.

Considering what we know about termination of attorney-client relationships it should seem to you that this question could go either way. Your job, then, will be to outline and assess the strongest arguments for each side.

We can infer from the fact pattern that there was no formal agreement to terminate Hoch's representation of Mr. Guirera (and of course, you should quickly note that this is one way to terminate the lawyer-client relationship, and explain why that option does not apply to your facts). What remains, then, is analyzing whether the conclusion of the divorce settlement was the kind of "cognizable event" that would end the representation. A good answer should consider this question in depth, and will probably examine the divorce proceeding context: Ending a specific lawsuit seems like a fairly logical stopping point for a lawyer's work. But on the other hand, divorce and custody disputes frequently raise new or ongoing issues over time that may need further resolution.

Sample answer with commentary

Below is an example of what might be a reasonably high-scoring student response. The sample has weaknesses, but reflects what a strong law student might be able to complete in the short time given for the problem.

Student Answer

When there is disagreement about the termination of an attorney-client relationship the courts will usually view this as a question of fact which has to be decided by a jury. Therefore it may not be possible to give a definite answer to this question.

Once it is created, an attorney-client relationship is presumed to continue until it is actively terminated. That happens either by agreement of the parties or by some "cognizable event." Finishing a legal case like a divorce could be exactly the kind of event that would lead a court to find the lawyer's representation of the client to be concluded. That seems to be what Hoch is arguing happened in this case, and it is her best argument for representing Maya now.

> This rule statement is correct, but it still seems a little incomplete and unclear. How could the student have made it better?

It would be helpful to know whether there was a written retainer agreement in Joseph's divorce case. If there was, we would want to know what it committed Hoch to do (in the fact pattern it says that there "is no current agreement" but that does not mean there had never been one). If there was a retainer it would probably have been for the divorce case, which might strengthen Hoch's argument that the relationship with Joseph was over when that case was done.

> The student does a nice job of reading the facts carefully, and also of imagining what could be true, and if it was, might alter the analysis. The points made in this paragraph aren't essential to reasoning through this problem, but most readers would believe they add to the analysis. That is the kind of thinking that can make a notable difference in how the essay is scored. One note of caution, however: some professors advise against speculation or referencing facts not given in the fact pattern. If those are your professor's instructions, follow them!

> The student is correct that case law suggests termination of the attorney-client relationship is a factual issue. However, she or he is almost certainly wrong that it would be left to a jury in this instance. There is no pending case centered on the lawyer-client matter (just a distinct criminal action where the issue has been raised by a third party). The exigencies of needing to clarify Maya's representation for the criminal proceeding would likely push the judge to rule on Joseph's motion right away, and to decide it as a matter of law. Therefore a jury hearing Maya's criminal case would probably never have Joseph's attorney-client question before it.

> An important point for law students taking exams, however, is that it would take some experience in practice to anticipate this. Most law professors try hard to ensure that students' comparative inexperience will not be held against them if they are doing their best to provide solid legal analysis based on what they have learned so far. Chances are good, then, that a professor would credit this response with at least getting the gist of distinguishing between factual and legal issues.

Joseph's strongest argument will be that he actually believed Hoch was still his attorney because she worked for him on a variety of things over a decade. Regularly working on whatever legal matters arose could suggest that she was his attorney on an ongoing basis and not just for those specific

There are some pretty good explanations in this paragraph. Reasons are given for most conclusions, which makes the analysis much more solid. As is almost always true, however, there is still room to beef up these explanations even more.

issues. Clients' subjective beliefs about their attorneys matter because the whole point of the attorney-client relationship is supposed to be to protect the client. A court might give a lot of weight to what Joseph thought. It might matter as well that Joseph now wants to change the custody arrangements from the divorce. The court could view that as part of representing him in the overall family law case, which would strengthen Joseph's arguments that his relationship with Hoch was ongoing.

There is room for a court to go either way on this issue, but most courts would probably lean toward protecting Joseph's expectation that Hoch would still be his lawyer and requiring Maya to find a different attorney for her criminal case.

Professional Role Project Checklist

Read your own drafts while looking carefully for each point raised below. If the points are included, please make sure that they are accurately presented and fully developed and explained. If they are not, consider whether and how your analysis can be made more complete.

Memo

1. Where does your cover memo state the rule for terminating existing attorney-client relationships?

2. What legal authority does the memo reference for that rule?

3. Where does the memo explain your theory about when that relationship concluded for Foster and Wallace, and what specific events triggered its ending?

4. Does the memo consider from whose perspective that legal termination point makes sense, and does it explain why? Does it explicitly analyze any counterarguments that might grow out of the other party's perspective?

5. Does the memo explain what factual narrative will best support your legal theory?

6. Where in the memo do you explain the tactical considerations that led you to craft the affidavit as you did?

Affidavit

7. Is everything in the affidavit entirely truthful from your client's perspective so far as you are aware?

8. Does your draft of the affidavit include only facts within your client's knowledge? If facts are inferred from indirect personal experience, are they offered "upon information and belief" rather than directly declared?

9. Does the affidavit avoid making legal arguments, yet ideally *suggest* conclusions to the legally educated reader?

10. Where does your affidavit draft state or indicate facts supporting the memo's conclusions about when the attorney-client relationship ended?

11. Does the affidavit depict the facts to minimize or preclude other possible interpretations that would not support your position? How?

12. Will your client have any qualms about signing this affidavit? Why or why not?

Both

13. Is the analysis clearly presented and will it be persuasive to readers?

14. Were the affidavit and cover memo proofread, with technical errors and awkwardness eliminated?